For my students at Indiana University of Pennsylvania

Marx Today

Selected Works and Recent Debates

Edited by

John F. Sitton

First published in 2010 by
PALGRAVE MACMILLAN®
in the United States – a division of St. Martin's Press LLC,
175 Fifth Avenue, New York, NY 10010.

Where this book is distributed in the UK, Europe and the rest of the world,
this is by Palgrave Macmillan, a division of Macmillan Publishers Limited,
registered in England, company number 785998, of Houndmills, Basingstoke,
Hampshire RG21 6XS.

Palgrave Macmillan is the global academic imprint of the above companies
and has companies and representatives throughout the world.

Palgrave® and Macmillan® are registered trademarks in the United States,
the United Kingdom, Europe and other countries.

ISBN: 978–0–230–10240–8   Hardcover
ISBN: 978–0–230–10241–5   Paperback

Library of Congress Cataloging-in-Publication Data

Marx, Karl, 1818–1883.
   Marx today : selected works and recent debates / edited by John F. Sitton.
       p. cm.
     ISBN: 978–0–230–10240–8 Hardcover
     ISBN: 978–0–230–10241–5 Paperback
   1. Marxian economics.   2. Capitalism.   I. Sitton, John F., 1952–   II. Title.
HB97.5.M33424 2010
335.4—dc22
                                                        2010018613

A catalogue record of the book is available from the British Library.

Design by MPS Limited, A Macmillan Company

First edition: December 2010

10 9 8 7 6 5 4 3 2 1

Printed in the United States of America.

CONTENTS

ACKNOWLEDGMENTS

I would like to thank the following for permission to reprint the included works:

1. Permission of International Publishers Company, Inc., New York, for the selections from *Marx-Engels Collected Works*: Frederick Engels, "Preface to the 1888 English Edition of the *Manifesto of the Communist Party*"; Karl Marx and Frederick Engels, *Manifesto of the Communist Party*; Frederick Engels, "Protection and Free Trade: Preface to the Pamphlet: Karl Marx, *Speech on the Question of Free Trade*"; Karl Marx, *Speech on the Question of Free Trade*; Karl Marx, "Preface to *A Contribution to the Critique of Political Economy*"; Karl Marx, "Marx to Engels in Manchester"; Karl Marx, *Value, Price and Profit*; Frederick Engels, "Introduction" to Karl Marx's *The Civil War in France*; Karl Marx, *The Civil War in France*; Karl Marx, *Critique of the Gotha Programme*.
2. Professor Terry Eagleton, for "Where Do Postmodernists Come From?"
3. *Monthly Review*, for John Bellamy Foster and Robert W. McChesney, "Monopoly-Finance Capital and the Paradox of Accumulation," and John Bellamy Foster, "Marx and the Environment."
4. South End Press, for Heidi Hartmann, "The Unhappy Marriage of Marxism and Feminism: Towards a More Progressive Union."
5. David Laibman, Editor of *Science & Society*, for John Brentlinger, "Revolutionizing Spirituality: Reflections on Marx and Religion."

Permission is very gratefully acknowledged.

I would also like to thank Dennis McDaniel, Helen Tangires, Andy Hazelton, and Mac Fiddner for reading and commenting on an earlier draft of the introduction, and Kyleen Ressler of the Department of Political Science at Indiana University of Pennsylvania and Emily Cantin of the Gumberg Library of Duquesne University for help in preparing the manuscript.

The cover art is an untitled work by Michael Lowe, a painter who lives and works in Seattle, Washington. I thank him for permission to use it here and for making the world a more beautiful and welcoming place.

INTRODUCTION

MARX'S SOCIAL THEORY BEARS THE BURDEN OF HISTORY. For a large part of the twentieth century, hundreds of millions of people lived under governments that claimed, rightly or wrongly, some inspiration from the ideas of Karl Marx. It is therefore exceedingly difficult to extricate Marx's own arguments from the long shadows of Lenin, Stalin, and Mao Zedong. Nevertheless, in this already chaotic twenty-first century, Marx, the most probing critic of capitalism as a way of organizing social life, is worth exploring.

Until quite recently, many might have thought it odd to dispute the virtues of capitalism. Beginning with the fall of the Berlin Wall, capitalism apparently drove all other contenders from the field. Even countries that still call themselves "communist," such as China and Vietnam, have vigorously embraced markets and profit-seeking enterprises. Defined by its promoters as private property and competitive markets, capitalism appears to simply be the most efficient way of organizing production. In contrast to a state-planned economy, under capitalism what is produced, in what quantities, and how distributed is determined by producers and consumers responding to prices. Given competition, individual producers have powerful incentives to reduce their costs of production, and therefore prices, to the lowest possible minimum. Waste of resources is discouraged because anyone who uses more raw materials than necessary or employs more workers or machines than necessary will find herself or himself at a competitive disadvantage. Profits depend on developing better technologies, finding ever more clever ways of combining people and machines, and on seeking out, even creating, new potential markets. In this way capitalism, without requiring of individuals anything more than pursuing their self-interest in a competitive situation, forces producers to do things that serve society's interests as a whole. It thus institutes the famous "invisible hand" of Adam Smith, where the "unintended consequences" of private self-seeking promotes the public good.

A further proclaimed advantage of capitalism is that it is essentially self-regulating, eliminating the need for a large and potentially threatening government. Investment for production is automatically redistributed according to where above average profits can be made. This steering of production and investment by profits in quick order restores the competitive equilibrium, ensuring that any possible monopoly profits will be short-lived. The consequence is that scarce resources in society—especially capital and labor—are guided toward their most productive uses. Needless to say, this makes government regulation not only unnecessary, but seriously disruptive to the self-sustaining system of markets.

As more and more societies orient their production to global markets, free trade extends these efficiencies to the entire world by encouraging specialization. The classical economist David Ricardo famously argued that even if a nation is superior to other nations in several kinds of production, it should still concentrate its production on the one thing at which it has the greatest superiority. To use his example, even if Portugal were superior to England in producing both wine and cloth, it should focus its energies on the one of these at which it has the greater "comparative advantage."[1] If all nations were to concentrate on the one thing they do best, the global production system as a whole would be more efficient. The consequence is that, as the saying goes, "everyone benefits from trade."

Finally, capitalism as a way of organizing social life is seen as morally defensible in that it advances a number of values besides efficient production. It institutionalizes freedom because no one is forced to work for a particular employer, at a particular line of work, or invest their resources a certain way. Further, everyone is legally equal in that they are all owners of some resource, even if only the ability to work, enshrining the natural right to property. Consequently, contracts are freely entered as individuals meet in the market exchanging their goods and services. Such an open, competitive system also encourages individuals to seek out new opportunities for advancement, promoting individuality itself. By institutionalizing freedom and equality, and by rewarding productivity, capitalism presents societies with their best chance for the happiness of the greatest number.

This powerful and attractive vision has now suffered a profound blow. In 2008, precipitously declining housing prices initiated an avalanche of devaluations of various kinds of other financial investments, paralyzing credit markets and causing global stock markets to eventually lose 40 percent of their value. Some of the leading financial institutions in the world collapsed and many others were at least technically insolvent, surviving on life support rapidly, even frantically, provided by governments.

In short order, unemployment in the largest capitalist country, the United States, doubled. With most pensions now based on individual investments in the stock market, workers who had pension benefits at all found their retirement funds drop in tandem with stock markets, losing from a quarter to half their value in a few short weeks. A leading investment company estimates that from 2008 through early 2009, global stocks lost $30 trillion in value and home values declined by $11 trillion.[2] For comparison, the entire Gross Domestic Product of the United States in a year is a little over $14 trillion.

A major consequence of these events has been serious challenges to the conventional wisdom of the economics profession, leading to sharp discussions within the profession itself. Paul Krugman, winner of the Nobel Prize in Economics in 2008, declared in a public lecture that macroeconomic theory of the past 30 years has been "spectacularly useless at best, and positively harmful at worst."[3] In Congressional testimony in October 2008, Alan Greenspan, former long-serving Chair of the Federal Reserve, focused on the extensive underestimation of risk by financial institutions, partly caused by two decades of "euphoria." He claimed that he was in "a state of shocked disbelief" at the failures by lending institutions and that the "whole intellectual edifice" of risk management had "collapsed."[4]

Given the present economic and intellectual rubble, it is time to give renewed attention to less orthodox analyses of the structure and dynamic of capitalist economies. Over a century ago, Karl Marx developed the most prominent and politically consequential of these analyses, explaining the historical distinctiveness of the capitalist economy and its most likely trajectory. Marx's theory continues to provide insights into the conflictual, even contradictory, dynamic of capitalism, the unstable nature of which is now being demonstrated every night on the evening news.

Marx developed his economic theory in its most detailed form in the three volumes of *Capital*. Because of its length and difficulty, *Capital* is little read. Therefore it is useful to outline that argument in this introduction, partly to provide context for the much briefer and more wide-ranging works of Marx that make up the bulk of the readings in the present anthology. However, the strongest caution is necessary at the outset: Only the broad contours of Marx's theory can be offered here. How to interpret key concepts of Marx's theory, especially "value," is incredibly contentious, therefore I will only pursue the main line of his argument. The brief bibliography at the end of this work will guide those who seek a more lengthy and nuanced exploration.

I. THE HISTORICAL ORIGINS OF CAPITALISM

Marx always insisted that customary portrayals of capitalism such as the one provided above are merely a report on the ways things "appear" to those involved in a market economy, insufficient to actually understand what is going on. "[A]ll science would be superfluous if the outward appearance and the essence of things directly coincided."[5] Comprehending the true dynamic of capitalism requires uncovering those relations that determine the surface movements. It requires going far beyond the common sense understandings of those mesmerized by the dance of competition.

Marx begins by confronting some confusions that obscure what is historically distinctive about capitalism. First of all, contrary to common belief, capitalism and the use of markets are not the same thing. Throughout history many societies have utilized markets. Exchanging one's surplus for another's surplus and retaining the larger part of production to directly satisfy one's own needs has been quite common in diverse societies. This is one of the reasons why its proponents contend that capitalism is "natural."[6]

However, the role and importance of markets in the overall life of a society differ. With an increasing division of labor, facilitated by the use of money, markets take on a qualitatively different role in organizing social life. Society's members no longer produce what they will directly consume and merely trade the surplus—as when they were independent "subsistence" farmers—but rather produce *for* exchange in order to make a living. A key feature of capitalism is this dependence of everyone on the exchange of commodities. In a society with an extensive division of labor, exchange is not only an aspect of production, it is the central feature of production.

But further, according to Marx capitalism is only fully established with the widespread use of wage-labor, when individuals, having no other way of supporting themselves, must sell their ability to work. "The historical conditions of its existence are by no means given with the mere circulation of money and commodities. It arises only when the owner of the means of production and subsistence finds the free worker available, on the market, as the seller of his own labor-power. And this one historical pre-condition comprises a world's history. Capital, therefore, announces from the outset a new epoch in the process of social production."[7] This complete generalization of the commodity form, including the labor market, creates a web of economic relations in which all individuals are ensnared, making everyone dependent on a dynamic that is beyond anyone's control.

As for being natural, Marx points out that "nature does not produce on the one hand owners of money or commodities, and on the other hand men possessing nothing but their own labor-power."[8] He casts aside "idyllic" accounts of "so-called primitive accumulation," such as that of John Locke, that this enormous inequality of resources was a consequence of gradual accumulation based on differing talents and hard work. These classes were created historically by the dissolution of serfdom, the destruction of guilds, the seizing of church properties, and the enclosure of the common lands in various places, stripping individuals of their livelihoods and forcing them into wage-labor. Primitive accumulation "is nothing else than the historical process of divorcing the producer from the means of production." Although merchant capital acquired through long-distance trade played a role, it would not have expanded very far without the forcible creation of a proletariat. "[T]his history, the history of their expropriation, is written in the annals of mankind in letters of blood and fire."[9]

II. THE HIDDEN DYNAMIC OF CAPITALISM

Capitalism is neither natural nor eternal. It is a specific way of organizing economic and social life that emerged at a particular time in history and after intense (and continuing) struggles. Having established the historical genesis of capitalism, Marx develops his own understanding of the "laws of motion" of this economic form. He begins by asking about the origin of the relative prices of goods that regulate exchange, why, say, a dress shirt costs about ten times as much as a gallon of milk. Most people believe that prices are determined by the supply and demand for goods, with demand established by what consumers are willing to pay to satisfy their idiosyncratic desires. But this renders the whole system of exchange relations entirely subjective and therefore inexplicable.[10] Marx objects that if this were so, when supply and demand balance each other they would not be able to explain why the price settles where it does. "If supply and demand balance one another, they cease to explain anything, do not affect market-values, and therefore leave us so much more in the dark about the reasons why the market-value is expressed in just this sum of money and no other."[11]

He therefore reformulates the issue this way: In a society of independent producers exchanging their products with one another, what makes one product, a shirt, comparable with another, milk, so that an exchange can occur in the first place? Marx argues that for commodities to be comparable they must have some common element that regulates the rate of exchange. Adopting a concept from classical economists such as Ricardo, Marx contends that it is the respective "value" of individual commodities that allows the concrete and independent labors of individuals in the social division of labor to be related to each other. Supply and demand merely cause the price of a particular commodity to "oscillate" around the commodity's inherent value. But this leaves the question of what constitutes the value of a commodity.

Locke famously stated in the *Second Treatise on Government* that "'tis labor indeed that puts the difference of value on every thing." (Section 40) Marx agrees. The "value" of a good is determined by its overall labor content, including the value embodied in the machines and raw materials transferred into the final product by the laborer. Specifically, this means how much "socially necessary labor-time" is required to produce a particular good. "Socially necessary labor-time" is the amount of labor that must be used in producing a thing, given typical conditions of production for that particular commodity. In sum, in a competitive economy, on average things exchange at their value, which is determined by how much socially necessary labor-time has been invested in them.

Marx's explorations were furthered by a puzzle that emerged from the classical economists. Since commodities tend to exchange at their value, each gets as much back in labor, embodied in the commodity, as her or his own commodity contains. But if this is so, then where does profit come from? The classical economists gave varied answers, but Marx's response established that capitalism, whatever its appearances to the contrary, is a society composed of distinct and antagonistic classes.

Marx pursues the issue by drawing on a distinction made by Aristotle in *The Politics*. Aristotle argued that things have two kinds of value, its value when it is used (for example, when shoes are worn), but also the value something has in that it can be exchanged for other things one needs. Marx develops a similar distinction in regard to the capacity for labor, the only thing that most people can sell. He distinguishes the *exchange*-value of labor from its *use*-value. The *exchange*-value of labor—what it will bring in the market—is determined the same way as that of all commodities, by the quantity of labor required to produce it. This means that the exchange-value of labor is determined by the socially necessary labor content of the goods required to sustain the laborer from day to day.[12] This capacity to work Marx now specifically calls "labor-power."[13] To put it simply, the value of labor-power is determined by the subsistence needs of the worker, with the usual oscillations around this value caused by temporary imbalances in supply and demand for workers.

Marx distinguishes the exchange-value of *labor-power* from the use-value of *labor* properly so-called. "Labor" is the application of the energy and creativity of human beings in transforming the natural world for human purposes. It is the activity that creates value.[14] Due to competition among workers for jobs, the exchange-value of labor-power is kept at subsistence. However, there is no such limitation on how much value labor can produce in *use*, that is, when applied in production. The application of labor in production can therefore generate more value than labor-power costs when it is purchased by an employer. This "surplus-value," produced by the fact that under competitive labor market conditions labor produces more value than it costs, is the great secret of capitalism.

The distinction between labor and labor-power allowed Marx to formulate a provocative historical perspective, that capitalism is a class society very much like slavery and feudalism before it. The surplus generated in these previous societies clearly came from the unpaid labor of slaves and serfs. Marx argues that the difference under capitalism is merely one of the "form" in which this surplus labor is extracted. "What distinguishes the various economic formations of society—the distinction between for example a society based on slave-labor and a society based on wage-labor—is the form in which this surplus labor is in each case extorted from the immediate producer, the worker."[15]

Unlike slavery and feudalism, in capitalism the origin of the surplus is hidden by the fact that the society is based on exchange, especially the commodification of the ability to work. Capitalism is a society in which most people, the "proletariat," do not own property from which they can independently derive a living. (This is specifically what Marx means by "property," as opposed to mere "possessions.") Therefore, they must seek employment from those, the "bourgeoisie," who do own "means of production": fields, factories, ships, business offices, et cetera. Like the serf working his own fields three days a week and working the lord's fields the other three days of the week without pay, Marx argues that the working day is in effect divided into two parts. The first part of the day the worker adds value equal to the cost of his or her labor-power, his or her wages. The second part of the day, however, the worker continues to add value to the product, value that is uncompensated. The surplus-value produced in the actual application of labor accrues to the employer of labor, the owner of the means of production who has hired the worker. Since the worker is paid by the day, the participants in the labor contract are unaware of this. "All his [a slave's] labor appears as unpaid labor. In wage-labor, on the contrary, even surplus labor, or unpaid labor, appears as paid."[16] The worker is only concerned with wages, that is, the exchange-value of her or his labor-power. The employer believes the surplus comes from his or her ingenuity in combining various factors of production and from his or her prowess in the market. Therefore the exploitation of labor, and the fact that capitalism is *also* a class society based on unpaid labor, are both hidden from the parties involved.

This exploitation is relatively easy to disguise in that, unlike in slave society and serfdom, direct domination in extracting surplus labor is not required. Workers in capitalist society do not own independent means of production, that is, they cannot supply their own needs. Therefore, for exploitation to take place, all that is necessary is that a class of owners of means of production exists on the one side and a class of people who own nothing but their ability to labor, and therefore must hire themselves out to the owners, exists on the other side. All can still nominally appear as free equals exchanging what each owns at the proper value.

Marx makes it clear that the worker is not actually "cheated" in selling his labor-power. The exchange-value of labor-power, the labor embodied in the consumption basket, is fully paid. "If, therefore, the amount of value advanced in wages is not merely found again in the product, but augmented by a surplus-value, this is not because the seller has been defrauded, for he has really received the value of his commodity; it is due solely to the fact that this commodity has been used up by the buyer."[17] That the commodity labor-power can create more value when it is used than it costs to buy "is a piece of good luck for the buyer, but by no means an injustice towards the seller." On the other hand, Marx argues, once the capitalist process is going, before long the capitalist is paying for labor-power with funds that came from previous (unpaid) surplus labor, therefore "there is only an apparent exchange."[18]

The dominance of the capitalist class over production allows them to take advantage of more "free gifts" than merely the difference between the use-value and exchange-value of labor-power. By their monopoly of the means of production, they profit from a number of things they did not create. For example, the productivity of capital is tremendously enhanced by the general advance of natural science, which is actually a consequence of broad social and cultural developments. Marx adds that even the "accumulated skill of the individual laborers" is a gift to the employing class.[19]

Above all, however, and central to Marx's understanding of capitalism, is that the owning class appropriates the benefits of large-scale social production, that is, the productive force that emerges from social cooperation itself. To use Marx's example, just as an army regiment is more powerful than individual soldiers fighting independently, so is cooperative labor a force more than the sum of its parts. "Not only do we have here an increase in the productive power of the individual, by means of co-operation, but the creation of a new productive power, which is intrinsically a collective one."[20] This productive force emerges with the development of large-scale production and the ever more detailed division of labor in society. As Marx states it in the *Manifesto*, no previous generation could imagine the productive power "that slumbered in the lap of social labor."

Since the power of socialized labor was *promoted* by the development of capitalism, it appears as if this productivity is *inherent* in capital itself. It is actually another "free gift" that capital appropriates because of its ownership of the means of production. "The socially productive power of labor develops as a free gift to capital whenever the workers are placed under certain conditions, and it is capital which places them under these conditions. Because this power costs capital nothing, while on the other hand it is not developed by the worker until his labor belongs to capital, it appears as a power which capital possesses by its nature—a productive power inherent in capital."[21] Marx's argument is that, although capital definitely serves a historically progressive role by encouraging this development, the power of socialized labor is separable from private ownership of the means of production and, second, another example of a class appropriating, simply because of its *class* position, wealth that is actually generated by *society* as a whole.[22]

The consequence of this structure of capitalist production is the relentless expansion of capital. Labor in use produces more value than it costs as a commodity, an effect multiplied by the productivity inherent in cooperative labor itself. The development of technology and the expansion of world trade further increase the extraction of surplus-value by cheapening inputs.[23] Importantly, the value of this accumulating capital can only be transferred to new commodities if it is employed. Therefore, to maintain the embodied value of existing capital, it must be deployed on an ever-increasing scale, resulting in even more capital. Not for nothing does Marx exclaim, "Accumulate, accumulate! That is Moses and the prophets!"[24]

Marx argues that the scale of production and the attempts to preserve the value of existing investments create two major problems for the capitalist mode of production. First, the increased use of machines relative to living labor tends to reduce the rate of profit in the system as a whole. Marx contends that only living labor creates new value, while machines and raw materials merely pass on their pre-existing, embodied value. In Howard and King's phrase, means of production are *physically* productive but do not create *value*.[25]

If surplus-value can only be extracted from living labor, as the percentage of machines in production increases, the base for exploitation becomes *relatively* smaller. The existing value embodied in machines becomes a larger portion of the investment as a whole relative to the new value produced by the employed workers. Profit, however, is calculated as the return on the total investment, including machines. Therefore this "increasing organic composition of capital" tends to lower the *rate* of surplus or profit achieved on the total capital advanced. With the more extensive use of technology, the overall rate of profit in the economy tends to decline.

Many classical economists before Marx proposed that the rate of profit would fall as capitalism matured, but they generally believed it would do so because of the declining productivity of inputs to the productive process, such as the cultivation of increasingly marginal farmland.[26] In contrast, Marx argues that the rate of profit tends to fall because of *increasing* productivity of capital through greater employment of machinery. "The progressive tendency of the general rate of profit to fall is, therefore, just *an expression peculiar to the capitalist mode of production* of the progressive development of the social productivity of labor."[27] Marx insisted that this was only a tendency, one that could be retarded by reactions of producers. But these reactions would be very disruptive, especially the forcible devaluation of some of the existing means of production. This improves the situation by reducing the value invested in machines relative to the new value generated by labor, restoring the rate of profit on the total investment, but with chaotic consequences. "The periodical depreciation of existing capital—one of the means immanent in capitalist production to check the fall of the rate of profit and hasten accumulation of capital-value through formation of new capital . . . is therefore accompanied by sudden stoppages and crises in the production process."[28]

The second problem is that the powerful drive to expand production disconnects production from immediate demand. "With the development of capitalist production, the scale of production is determined less and less by the direct demand for the product and more and more by the amount of capital available."[29] This presents the problem for capitalists of how to "realize," in the market, the value that has already been generated within the process of production. "The conditions of direct exploitation, and those of realizing it, are not identical."[30] Marx argues that the realization of surplus-value has a number of preconditions. "Although the excess value of a commodity over its cost-price is shaped in the immediate process of production, it is realized only in the process of circulation . . . since in reality, under competition, in the actual market, it depends on market conditions whether or not and to what extent this surplus is realized." Marx even acknowledges that realization of the surplus-value actually requires certain skills on the part of the seller, that is, it "depends as much on the sharpness of his business wits as on the direct exploitation of labor."[31] This contributes to the illusion that profits originate in market operations rather than from the prior appropriation of surplus labor in production.

The "realization" problem actually has two aspects. On the one side is the overproduction of capital, which, since capital always exists as "many capitals," stimulates the "furious combat" of competition as capital seeks profitable investment opportunities.[32] On the other side, capitalism generates insufficient demand for goods because of the constraints on the exchange-value of labor-power. In a competitive labor market, the wage-laborer's pay tends to be limited by the general law of the exchange of commodities under capitalism: things exchange at their respective labor content.

In *Capital* Marx spends much of the time explaining how the structure of capitalist production inherently generates overproduction. But he also repeatedly acknowledges in *Capital* that insufficient consumption is indeed a barrier to the realization of the surplus. "The ultimate reason for all real crises always remains the poverty and restricted consumption of the masses as opposed to the drive of capitalist production to develop the productive forces as though only the absolute consuming power of society constituted their limit."[33] "Social demand" is limited by the existing class relations, including the "ratio of total surplus-value to wages" and the specific distribution of surplus-value in "profit, interest, ground-rent, taxes, etc."[34]

However, Marx rejects the possibility of avoiding crises by sustaining sufficient demand through wage increases. "It is sheer tautology to say that crises are caused by the scarcity of effective consumption, or of effective consumers. . . . But if one were to attempt to give this tautology the semblance of a profounder justification by saying that the working-class receives too small a portion of its own product and the evil would be remedied as soon as it receives a larger share of it and its wages increase in consequence," this would just prepare the way for other serious disruptions so that the increased prosperity would prove only "momentary."[35] Marx's argument appears to rest on a kind of "automatic recoil" (to borrow John Dryzek's phrase) of capital investment if wage increases reduce the extraction of surplus-value. "[A] reaction sets in: a smaller part of revenue is capitalized, accumulation slows down, and the rising movement of wages comes up against an obstacle. The rise of wages is therefore confined within limits that not only leave intact the foundations of the capitalist system, but also secure its reproduction on an increasing scale."[36] That is, there are insuperable structural barriers to a rise of wages that would secure sufficient demand.

The upshot of these various difficulties is that capitalism is a crisis-ridden mode of production. A general crisis regularly ensues in which the depreciation of existing capital causes "reproduction" to be "halted and thrown into confusion by a general drop in prices." "The chain of payment obligations due at specific dates is broken in a hundred places. The confusion is augmented by the attendant collapse of the credit system, which develops simultaneously with capital, and leads to violent and acute crises, to sudden and forcible depreciations, to the actual stagnation and disruption of the process of reproduction, and thus to a real falling off in reproduction."[37] This depreciation in the value of existing capital, plus a lowering of wages due to unemployment, restore profitability, but only to lay the basis for the "same vicious circle . . . under expanded conditions of production, with an expanded market and increased productive forces."[38] To continue functioning, capitalism must periodically eliminate excess capital via crisis. This means that capitalism is not only prone to economic crisis, leading to periodic depressions, but its inherent problems are only resolved even temporarily *through* crisis. James O'Connor, among others, has correctly emphasized that capitalism is not only crisis-prone, it is "crisis-*dependent*" for its historical functioning.[39]

Again, capitalist production is ever more constrained not because it becomes less productive—Marx says over and over that it is increasingly productive. However, the productivity of capitalism is shackled by the value form that governs a capitalist economy. This is demonstrated by the limited consumption of the masses, increasing inequality of wealth, and periodic depressions that forcibly *devalue* means of production, bankrupting employers and throwing workers out of work. "The means—unconditional development of the productive forces of society—comes continually into conflict with the limited purpose, the self-expansion of the existing capital.

The capitalist mode of production is, for this reason, a historical means of developing the material forces of production and creating an appropriate world-market and is, at the same time, a continual conflict between this its historical task and its own corresponding relations of social production."[40] Capitalism will not collapse on its own, but it becomes increasingly unreliable as a way of organizing social life.

One might retort that even if capitalism does run into severe difficulties, the right of property must still be respected or something important will be lost. Marx responds that contemporary capitalist ownership is purposely conflated with "notions of law and property inherited from a pre-capitalist world," which have less and less to do with the mainsprings of production.[41] Capitalist production is actually private appropriation of *social* production. Capitalists appropriate the fruits of *social* labor, deriving from their class mastery of surplus labor, the productiveness of an extensive social division of labor, and the benefits of scientific achievements. In the course of industry becoming concentrated, they also appropriate by *expropriating* small farmers, trades people, and small capitalist owners who cannot compete. This type of appropriation is obscured by precapitalist notions of property, as if individuals still owned their own farms and workshops and produced independently. The illusion is further sustained by the labor contract, where "owners" freely meet as equals and exchange what they own.

Capitalist owners may nevertheless protest that they are being rewarded for the important work of organization and superintendence of production. Marx admits that directing the labor process is productive labor and necessary for any "combined social process."[42] However, he also points to the separation of ownership and management in large enterprises, showing that the two functions are hardly identical and that managers could simply be hired for moderate pay. This is demonstrated in stock companies and occasional worker-owned factories where paid managers are substituted for the actual owners. This proves that the capitalist *as owner* is "superfluous" for production. "With the development of co-operation on the part of the laborers, and of stock enterprises on the part of the bourgeoisie, even the last pretext for the confusion of profit of enterprise and wages of management was removed, and profit appeared also in practice as it undeniably appeared in theory, as mere surplus-value, a value for which no equivalent was paid, as realized unpaid labor."[43] In fact, stock companies can be seen as "the abolition of capital as private property within the framework of capitalist production itself," pointing toward a different possible future.[44]

III. THE POLITICAL TRAJECTORY OF CAPITALISM

Marx anticipated that because of their experience with economic crises, the majority will eventually come to understand that the structure of property relations itself (capitalist "relations of production") stands in the way of production that will satisfy people's needs. Capitalism is again like previous class societies in this respect. The binding of serfs to the land under feudal relations of production restricted the further development of productive capacity ("forces of production"), which could only advance on the basis of free labor. For this reason, feudalism was replaced by the capitalist property form, and so now must the capitalist property form also be replaced for further progress. With the forces of production "fettered" by the existing relations of production, we enter a period of revolution. "This result of the ultimate development of capitalist production is a necessary transitional phase towards the reconversion of capital into the property of producers, although no longer as the private property of the individual producers, but rather as the property of associated producers, as outright social property."[45] What Marx says of landlords could easily be extended to private property in general: "From the standpoint of a higher economic form of society, private ownership of the globe by single individuals will appear quite as absurd as private ownership of one man by another."[46] Capitalism will prove to be as transitory a historical epoch as slavery or feudalism before it.

The tensions between the use of existing productive forces and the property form within which they are developed, and the various difficulties obstructing the smooth reproduction of capitalist economic relations, are features of the capitalist mode of production that operate regardless of the will and consciousness of the individuals involved. They are properties of the system itself and are therefore the objective side of historical development. Marx certainly emphasizes this objective aspect in many places, leading to the recurring use of the word "inevitable" in his writings. However, although these objective aspects exist, Marx also characterizes history as a "history of class struggles," suggesting the importance of human agency and organization for the ultimate trajectory of history. In fact, many have noted that Marx appears to have not one theory of history but two. On the one hand, he states a more objective theory of the clash of the forces of production with the relations of production, forcing the replacement of an existing property form with one more conducive to the use and development of the productive forces. On the other hand, Marx clearly has a second theory of history that views historical outcomes as a consequence of the struggle of classes against each other. Bringing these two theories of history into communication with each other has spawned many intriguing discussions but to a considerable degree remains an unresolved tension in Marxian theory as a whole.

That said, there does seem to be a large consensus of Marxian thinkers that, as G. A. Cohen puts it, "[t]here is no economically legislated final breakdown."[47] At some point human beings must decide their future. This was never better stated than by Leon Trotsky. "There is no crisis that can be, by itself, fatal to capitalism. The oscillations of the business cycle only create a situation in which it will be easier, or more difficult, for the proletariat to overthrow capitalism. The transition from a bourgeois society to a socialist society presupposes the activity of living people who are makers of their own history. They do not make history by accident, or according to their caprice, but under the influence of objectively determined causes. However, their actions—their initiative, audacity, devotion, and likewise their stupidity and cowardice—are necessary links in the chain of historical development."[48] In considering this issue, Erik Olin Wright and Andrew Levine convincingly argue that the economic difficulties of capitalism could simply result in stagnation unless an agency emerges capable of pushing beyond capitalism. Unless "class capacities" are developed, capacities to pursue class goals against capitalist social relations, the historical supersession of capitalism is doubtful.[49]

Despite occasional setbacks, Marx himself was actually quite confident that such a revolutionary agent was developing. Capitalism makes revolution likely by depriving the vast majority of productive property and concentrating ownership of the means of production in a few hands. The dynamic of capitalism tends toward simplification of class relationships. The landed nobility either become agricultural capitalists or are impoverished, falling into the proletariat, and independent farmers become agricultural proletarians. Further, there is a tendency for all intermediate strata, small capitalists, and artisans to be proletarianized as concentration of capital proceeds.[50]

Marx expected that class *structure* would in a relatively unproblematic way generate class-based *actors*. This is why Marx can repeatedly state that "the emancipation of the working classes must be conquered by the working classes themselves."[51] The role of communists is confined to clarifying the social situation and the necessary goals of the proletariat, hastening political developments by revealing the structural sources of the problems of the working class. (This does not mean that Marx and Engels were mere commentators. As August H. Nimtz has demonstrated at length, they were extraordinarily active in nineteenth-century working class politics.)[52] Marx's theory is itself a contribution to the emergence of the consciousness of the proletariat that its class interest is in irreconcilable conflict with the bourgeois property form and with the bourgeoisie. Above all, communists keep in the forefront the main revolutionary protagonist, the proletariat.

According to the "Critique of the Gotha Programme," with the revolution there will then be two phases in the development of communism. When the proletariat takes power, they must reorient production toward the direct satisfaction of needs by public control of production. This is only the first phase because bourgeois concepts of "justice" will persist, that is, individual contributions at work will continue to be the principle of distribution of goods until greater abundance is achieved. Also, the class struggle must still be fought domestically and national defense be sustained against capitalist nations bent on restoring a universal capitalist order.

Marx did not shy away from acknowledging the role of force in history. As seen above, in writing about the transition from feudalism to capitalism, he emphasized the importance of naked coercion, concluding that "[f]orce is the midwife of every old society which is pregnant with a new one. It is itself an economic power."[53] Marx made clear that this necessity will occur again in the transition from capitalism to communism. Criticizing the anarchist Mikhail Bakunin, Marx insisted that "so long as the other classes, especially the capitalist class, still exists [*sic*], so long as the proletariat struggles with it (for when it attains government power its enemies and the old organization of society have not yet vanished), it must employ *forcible* means, hence governmental means."[54]

Specifically, Marx argues that in this transition, political power of the workers must take the form of the "revolutionary dictatorship of the proletariat." This ominous phrase requires explanation. Marx first used the term *against* the idea of a dictatorship of an elite group of revolutionaries acting on *behalf* of the working class, the alternative idea of August Blanqui, a prominent revolutionary in 1830s and 1840s France.[55]

Unfortunately, Marx never further clarified what would be the form of the proletariat organized as the ruling class. But an important later remark by Engels does shed some additional light. "Of late, the German philistine has once more been filled with wholesome terror at the words: Dictatorship of the Proletariat. Well and good, gentlemen, do you want to know what this dictatorship looks like? Look at the Paris Commune. That was the Dictatorship of the Proletariat."[56]

The Paris Commune of 1871 was a revolutionary government established in the wake of the French defeat in the Franco-Prussian War. In the *Manifesto,* the seizure of political power only results in turning the existing state apparatus to new purposes. In contrast, Marx and Engels argued in later prefaces to the *Manifesto* that the Paris Commune of 1871 had taught an important lesson. The "existing state" could not simply be seized but must be "smashed" so that political power was now under immediate popular control. For the transformation of society to proceed, and, we might add, to ensure that the proletariat will continue to be in charge of its own emancipation, the transitional state must be structured so that the force concentrated in the state can become directly responsive to society. Some of the structural changes instituted by the Commune were immediate recall of officials, popular election of judges, a citizens' militia rather than an army, and worker's wages for all public officials.

Marx expected that these developments would culminate in the higher stage of communism, organized around the famous principle of "from each according to his abilities, to each according to his needs." Individuality will flower as people are given the means to pursue their own ideas of the good life. Fulfilling its historical role, the growth of socialized production under capitalism will have laid the foundations for "a higher form of society, a society in which the full and free development of every individual forms the ruling principle."[57] With the abolition of class society, "the prehistory of human society" is ended and its true history can begin.[58]

IV. PROBLEMS WITH MARX'S THEORY

THE THEORY OF VALUE

A number of perplexities emerge from the above overview of Marx's account of capitalist society, difficulties that must be confronted if Marxian theory is to contribute to the politics of the twenty-first century. These have been matters of debate for decades, so I claim no originality in briefly raising them here. First and foremost is Marx's argument that "value," determined by labor, regulates capitalist production. As mentioned earlier, the usefulness of the concept "value" in Marxian economic theory is hotly contested, even by those who are sympathetic to Marxism. One problem is that it requires treating skilled labor as ultimately reducible to unskilled labor so that the labor content of a commodity, and therefore its value, can be specified. If instead, as Jon Elster puts it, labor is "genuinely and irreducibly heterogeneous . . . it prevents the labor theory of value from even getting off the ground, since the basic concepts cannot be defined."[59] Even if this reduction is accomplished, one then must face the "transformation problem," that is, how the labor values of commodities are transformed into the prices that appear in the day-to-day operations of capitalism. If one cannot meaningfully convert labor values into prices, it is hard to apply Marx's economic analysis to the dynamics of markets governed by prices.[60] It follows that if Marx's concept of value is uncertain, then so is the central thesis of his economic theory: that capitalist production is governed and constrained by the values of capital and commodities.[61]

Marx employed the theory of value to comprehend how the specific labors of separate individuals become commensurate with each other such that they are exchanged in a regularized way. It is value that makes exchanges systematic and lawful rather than a series of accidents and *ad hoc* adjustments of supply to the unpredictable depth of desire that constitutes demand. Value is therefore not a "thing" but rather an attempt to characterize the rules governing the *relation* between individual producers exchanging their wares. In this way, the theory of value aspires to uncover the basis for the very coherence of a capitalist economy.[62]

However, even if the other difficulties could be resolved, there are legitimate doubts as to whether the law of value would actually apply to contemporary capitalism. Following the classical economists, and giving them their best argument, Marx assumed a fully competitive exchange society with many potential producers of any good. As indicated by the phrase "socially necessary labor-time," value relations are enforced by competitive pressures. David Harvey notes that a "movement away from the 'authority' of competition" is "a movement away from the regulatory power of the law of value."[63] Therefore the frequent insistence on the "monopoly" character of contemporary capitalism, a situation in which large firms are to some extent relieved of pricing pressures, necessarily reduces the relevance of the concept of "value."

It is instructive that several prominent Marxian analyses do not employ the labor theory of value. In the works of Baran and Sweezy, Foster and Magdoff, and Robert Brenner, the word "value" sometimes occurs but is not used in any theoretical way. Although Harvey wrote an extraordinarily detailed and sophisticated analysis of Marx's concept of value, *The Limits to Capital*, the theory of value plays no role in his recent critical analysis of global capitalism, *The New Imperialism*.[64] Instead, the above authors focus on the generation of a "surplus" of capital (Baran and Sweezy, Foster and Magdoff), "over-capacity and over-production" (Brenner), or "overaccumulation" (Harvey). As we will explore later, these works are helping to develop a robust critical theory of capitalism that does not rely on the labor theory of value.

This does not mean that the theory of value, this line of "investigation" as Engels called it, should simply be abandoned.[65] However, its usefulness for analyzing contemporary capitalism still awaits demonstration.

THE PROLETARIAT

A second key difficulty of Marx's overall theory is the relative eclipse of working-class identity in contemporary capitalism. Marx believed that the development of capitalist social relations necessarily means the growth of the proletariat, eventually becoming the "vast majority" facing a minority of exploitative capitalist owners. This absolutely crucial expectation is now very hard to defend. As Adam Przeworski has argued well, the facts are that the clearly defined "proletariat" simply did *not* grow to become the vast majority. As more and more individuals were separated from farms, skilled trades, and other independent ways of supporting themselves, they did not become "proletarians" except in the broad sense of wageworkers. For example, petty bourgeois hardware store owners who lose to larger competitors do not necessarily become proletarians. They can become mid-level managers at Walmart or Home Depot. They are still wageworkers, but this concept is too coarsely grained to capture the lived experiences of workers. Working lives differ dramatically in terms of control over one's working conditions, flexibility in performing one's job, or simply in social status. Defining the proletariat in the face of myriad occupations and diverse managerial strata has become an extraordinary theoretical burden.[66]

The issue is even more complex when one looks at the working classes in the world at large. "Proletarianization" in any straightforward sense has not occurred, nor is it likely to. Immanuel Wallerstein has argued that throughout the globe, besides wage-work and subsistence agriculture, "household income has been assembled from petty commodity production, rents, transfer payments, and gifts."[67] Even in the United States, individuals often combine wage-labor with small-scale trading, sales of crafts, and direct services for others. These various ways of sustaining a household show no sign of diminishing over time.

Intensifying the problem, the interest structure of the non-owning class has become increasingly complex. In regard to developed countries, the investing of workers' pension funds in the stock market creates confusion as to the class interest of workers as a whole. The stock market often rewards companies that lay off workers by raising the value of their stock. If their retirement funds are invested in these companies, some workers actually have a material interest in firms laying off workers in other companies.[68] Another of many possible examples, there is a general conflict of interest between the solid jobs lost to cheaper overseas manufacturers and the lower prices enjoyed by American workers as consumers. And of course there have always been conflicts of interest among the working classes of different countries. Contemporary discussion among workers in the United States about the impact of Mexican immigrants on wages almost perfectly echoes nineteenth-century discussion in England regarding the Irish, including the frequent bigotry. In a dark mood, Engels himself noted this kind of conflict as it extends to foreign policy (1882): "You ask me what the English workers think about colonial policy. Well, exactly the same as they think about politics in general: the same as the bourgeois think. There is no workers' party here . . . and the workers are cheerfully consuming their share of England's monopoly of the world market and the colonies."[69] Moral exhortation will not make these objective conflicts of interest go away.

Finally, in all countries the "life chances" of individuals, to use Max Weber's phrase, are clearly affected by nonclass criteria of gender, race, ethnicity, religion, and sexual orientation, providing a material basis for the growth of "identity politics." In times of economic and political uncertainty, utilizing collective identity to gain a competitive edge over other groups or even to monopolize resources may make considerable sense.[70] As the economic and cultural ground shifts beneath people's feet, it is reasonable to expect defensive reassertions of identity in gender, religion, ethnicity or race (real or imagined), and language.[71] The standard expectation has been that modernity reduces the importance of "ascriptive" identities, those into which one is born. Instead, the economic turbulence that defines contemporary capitalism may end up reinforcing them. Joseph Schumpeter argued that a major virtue of capitalism is that it produces a "perennial gale of creative destruction." It should be unsurprising when people seek the shelter of religion, gender, and blood.[72]

IMMISERATION

Besides value theory and what "proletarian" means today, a third problem with Marx's analysis of capitalism is the ambiguity regarding the increasing "misery" of the workforce. Although the *Manifesto* strongly suggests that workers will be further impoverished as capitalism develops, in well-known later passages it is clear that Marx is not referring to a "bare physical minimum," except perhaps for those completely marginalized in society. In several places he does note that, due to fluctuations in the labor market, wages may temporarily sink toward a physiological minimum. "[T]here is no animal with the same talent for 'Irishing' himself."[73] But this is clearly considered a temporary phenomenon like all fluctuations of commodities around their labor value, in this case "subsistence" of the laborer.

The problem results from the fact that in various places in *Capital*, Marx expands the notion of "subsistence" in ways that undercut the idea of increasing misery. First, Marx argues that subsistence of a laborer includes being able to support children, "in order that this race of peculiar commodity-owners may perpetuate its presence on the market." Second, Marx is clear that "the number and extent of his so-called necessary requirements, as also the manner in which they are satisfied, are themselves products of history, and depend therefore to a great extent on the level of civilization attained by a country; in particular they depend on the conditions in which, and consequently on the habits and expectations with which, the class of free workers has been formed. In contrast, therefore, with the case of other commodities, the determination of the value of labor-power contains a historical and moral element."[74] Although historically and culturally formed, these are experienced as real needs, and in one place Marx even refers to them as "second nature."[75]

Marx has interesting company in arguing that the meaning of what is necessary for a basic living should be historically and culturally defined. Adam Smith made precisely the same point in *The Wealth of Nations*. "By necessaries I understand, not only the commodities which are indispensably necessary for the support of life, but whatever the custom of the country renders it indecent for creditable people, even of the lowest order, to be without. A linen shirt, for example, is, strictly speaking, not a necessary of life. The Greeks and Romans lived, I suppose, very comfortably, although they had no linen. But in the present times, through the greater part of Europe, a creditable day-laborer would be ashamed to appear in public without a linen shirt, the want of which would be supposed to denote that disgraceful degree of poverty, which, it is presumed, no body [*sic*] can well fall into without extreme bad conduct. Custom, in the same manner, has rendered leather shoes a necessary of life in England. The poorest creditable person of either sex would be ashamed to appear in public without them." Smith goes on to say that "rules of decency" differ in other countries: in Scotland barefoot women are acceptable and in France it is not considered bad form for either gender to be barefoot or in wooden shoes in public.[76]

Be that as it may, the redefinition of subsistence must alter our understanding of the "immiseration" of the working class. Marx shifts the focus to growing inequality between the classes and to the brutalizing conditions of labor markets and factory work, made even worse because they are increasingly historically unnecessary. "[A]ll means for the development of production undergo a dialectical inversion so that they become means of domination and exploitation of the producers. . . . It follows therefore that in proportion as capital accumulates, the situation of the worker, *be his payment high or low*, must grow worse. . . . Accumulation of wealth at one pole is, therefore, at the same time accumulation of misery, the torment of labor, slavery, ignorance, brutalization and moral degradation at the opposite pole, i.e. on the side of the class that produces its own product as capital."[77]

This different understanding of immiseration is reinforced by Marx's argument, stated in several places, that "it is possible, given increasing productivity of labor, for the price of labor-power to fall constantly and for this fall to be accompanied by a constant growth in the mass of the worker's means of subsistence."[78] As productivity increases, labor unions can try to use their bargaining power to tap some of the productivity gains. As the Marxian economist Ernest Mandel put it, "by preventing the capitalists from lowering the value of labor-power, trade unions can at least prevent all the results of increased productivity of labor from automatically accruing to the former: in other words they can achieve an increase in real wages, through the inclusion in the value of labor-power (in its moral-historical element) of the counter-value of new mass-produced commodities satisfying newly acquired needs."[79] Marx explicitly agrees with this position, arguing that unions can improve the bargaining position of workers in regard to their labor contract and that the importance of trade unions "can scarcely be overestimated."[80] "Real wages," that is, purchasing power, can therefore increase due to increasing productivity. But, Marx cautions, never "in proportion to the productivity of labor."[81] Although the worker's "necessities" can grow, so will inequality with the owning class.

Given this, the immiseration of the working class has come to mean the following: Capitalism is properly described as crisis-ridden, periodic depressions that impoverish enormous numbers cannot be avoided, the threat of depression means a condition of continual uncertainty for workers and their families, and a significant proportion of the population will always be permanently marginalized. Workers are condemned to the "dark Satanic mills" described by William Blake, to increasing inequality with the capitalist class, and to an alienated and alienating form of production in general. However, on the other hand, workers *may*, depending on organization, be able to expand the prevailing notion of "subsistence" and thereby improve their position compared to previous generations.

But if this is true, then even *within* the premises of the labor theory of value the working class has more political options than Marx seems to recognize. Prezeworski argues that, given the possibility of improving their living standards, even a radicalized and unified working class would not necessarily choose socialist revolution. There will always be transition costs of any move toward socialism: rational capitalists fearing expropriation will stop investing and even try to move their resources to more congenial climes, producing an immediate disaster for a nation's economy. A rational working class would have to weigh their chances of improvement under existing conditions against the arduous and disruptive task of building socialism, even if the latter would be in their interest in the long run. To employ the usual phrase, a "class compromise" is possible, even likely.[82]

There are of course limits to the bargaining capacity of the working class. If their demands threaten profitability, and if there are other places to invest, capital will flow away from areas with high living standards. The "automatic recoil" of capital cannot be eluded. Also, the bargaining power of workers depends on the freedom to organize trade unions and political groups; therefore it expands or contracts with how democratic a country is.

Nevertheless, under democratic conditions the material interest grounds for revolution are, although hardly eliminated, certainly reduced in force. It is true that workers may well continue to aspire to transcend capitalism on other grounds, especially in the name of freedom.[83] Marx's language of "emancipation" is no mere literary flourish. He believed that human beings are indeed oppressed by this alienated network of economic forces, forces that sweep aside human concerns with the indifference of a hurricane. Marginal improvement of material conditions does not alter this debased situation, as Marx memorably put it, any more than better food and clothing abolishes the condition of slavery.[84] However, contrary to Marx, under at least a democratic capitalism, workers may well choose the devil they know.

THE STATE IN CAPITALIST SOCIETY

This conclusion is reinforced by another consideration of Marx's argument. Marx's analysis of the capitalist mode of production is guided by the notion that capitalism is simply a new, more subtle way for a class to appropriate the labor of others, in this respect similar to the previous slave and feudal modes of production. This parallel is very thought-provoking for analyzing the origins and distribution of wealth in capitalist society. However, Marx also notes an important difference in the situations of the serf and the proletarian: the serf retains control of the means of production. The extraction of unpaid labor from the serf therefore requires direct domination. "[I]n all forms in which the direct laborer remains the 'possessor' of the means of production and labor conditions necessary for the production of his own means of subsistence, the property relationship must simultaneously appear as a direct relation of lordship and servitude, so that the direct producer is not free."[85] Unlike with serfs, the very propertylessness of the worker forces her or him to sell labor-power to the capitalist. Direct coercion is therefore unnecessary. The condition of wage-labor itself is sufficient for the capitalist class to appropriate the surplus. "The silent compulsion of economic relations sets the seal on the domination of the capitalist over the worker. Direct extra-economic force is still of course used, but only in exceptional cases."[86]

This difference between serfdom and wage-labor actually has extremely important political consequences for capitalism as a whole. Marx argues that since the pressure on workers is exerted by their situation, by "invisible threads" rather than outright coercion, with capitalism the *political* sphere is separated from the *economic* sphere. This is the *differentia specifica* of the capitalist mode of production. The separation of the economic and the political results in, to use the usual term, the "relative autonomy of the state" in capitalist society.[87] Marx mentions this but does not seem to fully appreciate its implications.

As suggested by Marx and Engels themselves in various places, the autonomy of the political actually allows the state to affect economic developments as a more or less independent actor. For example, Marx states that "[t]he specific economic form, in which unpaid surplus-labor is pumped out of direct producers, determines the relationship of rulers and ruled, as it grows directly out of production itself and, in turn, reacts upon it as a determining element."[88] Further, in a series of letters in 1890, Engels repeatedly makes the point that various factors enter into the historical process and that production is only the "*ultimately* determining factor." "It is the interaction of two unequal forces: on the one hand, the economic movement, on the other, the new political power, which strives for as much independence as possible, and which, having once been set up, is endowed with a movement of its own. On the whole, the economic movement prevails, but it has also to endure reactions from the political movement which it itself set up and endowed with relative independence."[89] Although Marx and Engels would resist the conclusion, the thrust of these comments is that the separation of the political and the economic creates the possibility of trying to actively manage capitalist production. This is of course the case today, through monetary policy, trade policy, fiscal policy, and innumerable specific interventions. It also seems to be the lesson of the Ten Hours Bill of 1847, discussed at length by Marx in the first volume of *Capital*, which limited the working day in England.

The autonomy of the political therefore creates the possibility, under democratic conditions, of smoothing the harsher edges of markets. This autonomy is only relative because state action is indeed constrained in various ways. Government's tax revenues are skimmed off the top of economic activity, which is determined by the level of investment. Under capitalism, investment is largely controlled by private organizations and individuals. Unwelcome government policies will be met by a "capital strike," that is a lowered level of investment, leading to reduced government revenues and therefore reduced social spending. This "privileged position of business" creates a kind of veto over unwelcome policies and the necessity of maintaining a "good business climate."[90] Even progressive leaders, once in power, must acknowledge this dynamic if they are to have the revenues to provide social programs and infrastructure improvements. Still, the autonomy of the political makes reform a possibility and, again, socialist revolution less compelling. Under democratic conditions, it is simply not true that workers have nothing to lose but their chains.

There is another aspect of the difference between wage-labor and serfdom or slavery that, from the perspective of the individual worker, may reduce the plausibility of Marx's portrayal of capitalism as another version of class society. Unlike slavery and serfdom, under capitalism workers appear as independent owners of their individual labor-power, the sale of which is governed by a labor contract. Since the wage-laborer *must* sell his or her labor to someone in the class of employers, Marx often states that this "freedom" is an illusion. "The Roman slave was held by chains; the wage-laborer is bound to his owner by invisible threads. The appearance of independence is maintained by a constant change in the person of the individual employer, and by the legal fiction of a contract."[91] But Marx himself admits that this "appearance" of individual freedom is reinforced by the fact that the worker, unlike the slave, is also an autonomous consumer. "It is the worker himself who converts the money into whatever use-values he desires; it is he who buys commodities as he wishes and, as the *owner of money*, as the buyer of goods, he stands in precisely the same relationship to the sellers of goods as any other buyer. Of course, the conditions of his existence—and the limited amount of money he can earn—compel him to make his purchases from a fairly restricted selection of goods. But some variation is possible as we can see from the fact that newspapers, for example, form part of the essential purchases of the urban English worker. He can save or hoard a little. Or else he can squander his money on drink. But even so he acts as a free agent; he must pay his own way; he is responsible to himself for the way he spends his wages."[92] Given this reality, Marx did not anticipate how class identity could be effaced by the status of consumer. The status of independent—although severely constrained—owner of the commodity labor-power, and of owner of money who can spend it as he or she pleases, makes it easy to see how in people's minds *class* differences come to be considered as merely differences in *income*.

This "appearance" of freedom is bolstered in an additional way. As Marx acknowledges, although class situation greatly reduces the range, there are some differences in individual wages depending on skill. For a worker, there is therefore "an incentive to develop his own labor-power" so as to increase his or her wages. "[T]here is scope for variation (within narrow limits) to allow for the worker's *individuality*, so that partly as between *different* trades, partly in the *same* one, we find that wages vary depending on the diligence, skill or strength of the worker, and to some extent on his actual personal achievement. Thus the size of his wage packet appears to vary in keeping with the results of his own work and its individual quality. . . . Certain though it be that the mass of work must be performed by more or less unskilled labor, so that the vast majority of wages are determined by the *value of simple labor-power*, it nevertheless remains open to individuals to raise themselves to higher spheres by exhibiting a particular talent or energy."[93] Marx is not explicit, but, combined with the possibility of changing one's employer, this opens up the prospect of some, although small, measure of social mobility. Marx is correct that this does not abolish the essential nature of wage-labor as oppression. However, Marx greatly underappreciated the effects that even these limited opportunities have on an individual's perception of life under capitalism and the sense of belonging to a class.

The possibility of advancing one's economic situation by developing one's individual talents or simply through greater "diligence" encourages many members of the working class to believe that one can "make it" through hard work. It is no surprise that many people believe that an individual's prospects are not determined by class structure but by individual virtues or the lack thereof. These facts of working class existence, raised by Marx himself, make the class analysis of capitalism, whatever its broader theoretical cogency, less convincing to great numbers.

In the *Manifesto*, Marx asks, "Does it require deep intuition to comprehend that man's ideas, views and conceptions, in one word, man's consciousness, changes with every change in the conditions of his material existence, in his social relations and in his social life?"[94] What Marx failed to understand is that freedom to choose employers, the equal autonomy of consumers, the limited but real possibilities for individual and generational advancement, and the limited but real political possibilities of democratically managing the economy *are* the lived experiences of individuals under capitalism.[95] These shape how people today perceive their lives and how they perceive the legitimacy of the existing order. For the Marxian tradition to find a larger audience, it must be able to connect its broad theory of capitalism as a class-structured society with the actual experiences of individuals in capitalist society, rather than dismissing those freedoms as illusory. Workers do not experience them as illusory, and this makes it plausible for them to blame their economic situation on themselves, rather than on a class structure.

MORAL ARGUMENT

Finally, the above weaknesses of Marx's analysis are exacerbated by his unrelenting disdain for explicit moral argument. In many places—the *Manifesto*, the "1859 Preface," the "Critique of the Gotha Programme"—Marx suggests that since moral evaluations arise within a specific society, they can have no application beyond that society. "Right can never be higher than the economic structure of society and its cultural development which this determines."[96] Moral criticism of capitalist society is therefore beside the point.

Although Marx may have had philosophical objections to moral critique, there is another reason he was reluctant to engage in it. There is always a danger that critical social theory will descend into mere moralizing, ineffectually lobbing moral demands at an indifferent reality. Marx feared that opposition to capitalism would become precisely that, displacing analysis of the real, objective grounds of struggle for an alternative society. Marx bitterly criticized "superwise Doctors of Philosophy who want to give socialism a 'superior, idealistic' orientation, that is to say, to replace its materialistic basis (which demands serious, objective study from anyone who tries to use it) by modern mythology with its goddesses of Justice, Liberty, Equality, and Fraternity."[97] This is the stimulus for Marx's criticism of utopian socialism in the *Manifesto* and for his more historically grounded approach to the construction of socialism.

Nevertheless, for a number of reasons Marx's marginalization of moral critique was a very serious error. Human beings have a powerful urge to make sense of the world. The world must be comprehensible and an aspect of this is that it be *morally* comprehensible. Even members of the dominant classes feel this urge. As Max Weber put it, "The fortunate is seldom satisfied with the fact of being fortunate. Beyond this, he needs to know that he has a *right* to his good fortune."[98] The perceived legitimacy of an order is crucial to its continuance. We truly do not live by bread alone, and this presents opportunities for contesting capitalism.[99]

Another reason for the importance of moral critique is that claims of rights and justice have played a powerful role in the history of the workers movement. Marx himself once acknowledged this in a stray comment in *The German Ideology*. "[I]n reality the proletarians arrive at this unity only through a long process of development in which the appeal to their right also plays a part. Incidentally, this appeal to their right is only a means of making them take shape as 'they,' as a revolutionary, united mass."[100] The importance of such claims might help explain Marx's own frequent description of capitalism as "robbery," "theft," "vampire-like," and even the term "exploitation" itself.[101]

Finally, even if moral ideas *are* grounded in existing society, this does not mean that these ideas have no application beyond that society. Moral argument, like all arguments, has a logic of its own. Argument on any topic, to be understandable to others, requires clear concepts, logical consistency, and principled conclusions. This internal logic means that moral conceptions cannot be reduced to mere expressions of a particular social structure. Social conditions do of course provide the occasion for the development of ideas. But the logic of ideas cannot be reduced to occasions. Ideas, including moral ideas, thereby achieve some autonomy in social life. Like the political, autonomous moral argument can independently affect the trajectory of history. Engels was correct in stating that "although the material mode of existence is the *primum agens* this does not prevent the ideological spheres from reacting upon it and influencing it in their turn."[102] For all these reasons, moral argument is crucial to making the case for alternatives to capitalism.

V. MARXISM AND CONTEMPORARY CAPITALISM

Since the collapse of communism twenty years ago, capitalism has actually suffered many severe problems: the debt crisis in Asian countries and elsewhere in the 1990s; the stagnation of the second largest economy in the world, Japan, throughout the 1990s; the pricking of the "dotcom" bubble in 2001–2002; and the virtual collapse of global credit markets in 2008. Each resulted in the destruction of large amounts of paper wealth, rocketing unemployment, intense budgetary problems for governments, and shocked disbelief on the part of experts. In the face of what the *Financial Times* in early 2009 called "the deepest, broadest and most dangerous financial crisis since the 1930s," the anomalies are starting to look more like the rule.[103]

There are a number of ways in which Marxian analysis can help us fathom these depths. As mentioned, many recent Marxian arguments focus on the generation of a surplus that cannot be absorbed, leading to serious difficulties. It is possible that this position, somewhat paradoxically, could be integrated with Marx's argument that the rate of profit tends to decline in capitalism. We must be precise: Marx says the *rate* of profit tends to decline. However, the "absolute *mass*" of surplus-value can nonetheless increase. The rate of profit declines because the surplus appropriated from labor is an ever-smaller fraction of the total value, that is including machines, mobilized in creating a product. As Harvey summarizes, "Marx is at pains to emphasize that a falling *rate* of profit is accompanied by an increasing *mass* of profit, by which he means that crises tend to result not from absolute declines in the production of surplus value but because the mass of surplus value produced cannot keep pace with the expansion of the amount of capital looking to capture it."[104] Given this, Harvey argues that "[s]urplus absorption is, then, the central problem. Crises of devaluation result when the capacity for that absorption breaks down."[105]

Foster and Magdoff (and Foster and McChesney, included below) argue similarly that the surplus incessantly produced by capitalism cannot find productive outlets, leading to overaccumulation and stagnation in the "real" economy. They focus our attention especially on the recent accumulation of money capital. "The total cash available to corporations, just 'sitting in the till,' at the end of 2005 was, according to *Barron's*, a record $2 trillion."[106] Stagnation caused these holders of money capital to seek other profitable investments, especially in various aspects of finance, such as the multiple exotic financial instruments that have been much discussed. The consequence was that finance became a primary source of profits in the economy, accounting for 40 percent of all profits in the United States in 2005, compared to only 15 percent in the 1960s.[107] Even non-financial enterprises such as Deere and Company, Target, and General Motors derived a large percentage of their profits from their finance arms.

The explosion of investment in the financial sector, usually designated as FIRE (finance, insurance, real estate), led to outright speculation. Speculation feeds on itself in that strong demand for houses or other investment instruments bids up the price of the asset, justifying further speculation on those assets since their value is rising. This was accompanied by the massive extension of credit and mobilization of debt, facilitated by the Federal Reserve's policy of maintaining low interest rates to stimulate investment. Taking on debt multiplies even marginal returns on speculative investments, so some financial institutions ended up "leveraged" at a ratio of 30 to 1, that is, a little over $3 in collateral could be used to finance a $100 investment.

Not only were banks involved but so were other financial institutions such as insurance companies and hedge funds, often called the "shadow banking sector" because they are largely unregulated.[108]

Although his remarks are fragmentary, in Volume III of *Capital* Marx had something useful to contribute to this discussion as well. In analyzing the rise of credit, Marx pointed out that "[a]ll this paper actually represents nothing more than accumulated claims, or legal titles, to future production whose money or capital value represents either no capital at all, as in the case of state debts, or is regulated independently of the value of real capital which it represents."[109] Credit is a claim on future production that may not take place. Although it is not exactly "fictitious capital," "the capital-value of such paper is nevertheless wholly illusory."

The phrase "fictitious capital" frequently crops up in recent Marxian discussion and, although the idea again needs elaboration, is particularly resonant today. Just how fleeting "paper" or "financial claims to wealth" can be has now become painfully obvious to the entire world, from the late financial firm Lehman Brothers to the middle-aged worker reluctantly putting off plans for retirement.

As suggested above, the relative autonomy of the state creates the possibility of, to some degree, directing the economy. In response to the present crisis, governments in many major capitalist countries, especially the United States and Great Britain, have intervened in a massive way to try to manage a more orderly devaluation of capital. Citing the financial information company Bloomberg, Foster and McChesney report that "by early 2009, over $12 trillion in capital infusions, debt support, and other financial commitments to corporations were provided in the bailout by the U.S. Government alone."[110] The problem is that this intervention seriously challenges any traditional justifications of capitalism, such as those discussed at the beginning of this introduction, that are built on the premise that capitalism is potentially self-regulating. Questions over whether and how government intervention can be legitimized are already provoking significant, and likely enduring, political conflict.

There is a final way in which Marx's insights about capitalism are supported by more recent analyses. One of the major ideological props of the existing order is the deeply ingrained belief that wealth is individually created and therefore should be privately owned. As discussed earlier, Marx argued at length to the contrary, that wealth is actually collectively created in developed capitalism and therefore the idea of individual ownership is a historical anachronism, perhaps appropriate to societies of self-subsistent farmers but no longer. As part of this argument, Marx showed the various ways in which, by virtue of their ownership of the means of production, the bourgeoisie benefit from things they did not create. Various "free gifts" come to the owners of the means of production, which greatly contribute to their wealth, including, Marx noted, the broad growth of scientific knowledge. "[T]o the degree that large industry develops, the creation of real wealth comes to depend less on labor time and on the amount of labor employed than on the power of the agencies set in motion during labor time, whose 'powerful effectiveness' is itself in turn out of all proportion to the direct labor time spent on their production, but depends rather on the general state of science and on the progress of technology, or the application of this science to production."[111]

This argument has been recently reinforced by studies presented by Gar Alperowitz and Lew Daly. They contend that much of economic growth is actually a consequence of the general progress of knowledge, *not* from present contributions of either capital *or* labor. "In general, most economists now agree that a very large share of economic growth over much of the last century—one leading expert suggests roughly 80 percent—was created not by the labor and capital inputs of workers and employers, but by technological progress broadly understood."[112] Further, contrary to heroic myth-making, technological and scientific "breakthroughs" such as the telephone or the double helix structure of DNA were actually the consequence of steady progress in a particular field, leading to a point where "the next so-called 'breakthrough' becomes all but inevitable." In fact, Alperowitz and Daly marshal evidence to support that many breakthroughs would have happened even if the individuals later celebrated for the innovation—Alexander Graham Bell, Crick and Watson—had not even participated.[113] Finally, the infrastructure built by previous generations, such as the electricity grid from which Bill Gates has derived so much money, is the inherited wealth of all Americans. Paid for by earlier taxpayers, this collective inheritance greatly contributes to the creation of wealth in our own day. "All this comes to us today as a 'free lunch,' the generous gift of the past."[114]

Alperowitz and Daly squarely face the distributional consequences of this argument. "[S]ince the wealth we today enjoy is largely a gift of the past, and since no one individual contributes more than a minor amount compared to the gift of the past, therefore society as a whole (after due consideration of all other issues of policy and incentive) has a primary moral claim to that (very large) portion of wealth that the inherited knowledge it has contributed now creates."[115] This echoes Marx's insistence that wealth is a collective creation—now conceived inter-generationally— and firmly supports his conclusion that individualized notions of wealth creation should be relegated to the "dustbin of history."

VI. CONCLUSION

Engels once complained that "[t]he materialist conception of history has a lot of dangerous friends nowadays, who use it as an excuse for *not* studying history."[116] Marx and Engels repeatedly cautioned that historical materialism is not a framework that can simply be forced on various social and historical circumstances. The same general social basis can lead to different configurations depending on "empirically given circumstances" that cannot be deduced from a general theory. Although "the economic movement is finally bound to assert itself," history is a consequence of the interaction of many factors that must always be empirically analyzed in their specific situations. Engels admitted, "Marx and I are ourselves partly to blame for the fact that the younger people sometimes lay more stress on the economic side than is due to it. We had to emphasize the main principle vis-à-vis our adversaries, who denied it, and we had not always the time, the place or the opportunity to give their due to the other factors involved in the interaction."[117]

Marx's analysis of capitalism will always be abstract. The dynamic he describes will continue to be refracted in differing ways through the ethnic, religious, cultural, racial, gender, and political structures of individual societies.[118] However, uncovering the extent of the economic reasons for social and political developments is an essential task. Many of the most important aspects of human affairs do have a material grounding. Not all aspects to be sure, and to seek "economic causes" in all social phenomena would be, as Engels said, "pedantic."[119] But the Marxian tradition provides a framework to uncover whatever material causes there may be. Any explanation of social and political conflict must include an analysis of the social classes that crystallize around property relations and the economic relationships that humans create in reproducing their societies. For this, the Marxian approach continues to be indispensable.

Marx famously stated in *The Eighteenth Brumaire of Louis Bonaparte* that "[m]en make their own history, but they do not do it just as they please; they do not make it under circumstances chosen by themselves, but under circumstances directly encountered, given and transmitted from the past."[120] Present circumstances appear to be these. Classes do exist in that a small group controls investment, thereby controlling employment and the tax revenues that can be utilized by governments for social programs. However, class structure does not produce coherent class actors. The latter are forged through political organizations, by events, and by the plausibility of ideas to great numbers. Further, historically capitalism has exceeded Marxist expectations in providing use-values. However, given the recurring crises to which capitalism is prone, Marx's argument is also important that under the capitalist mode of production use-values are only produced if they also produce value, and this requirement will continue to constrain production to satisfy people's needs. Marx anticipated that at some point in human development this will simply become absurd. Nevertheless, we can no longer confidently state with Marx that the existing order is pregnant with a new one.

Defenders of capitalism have long argued that capitalism is a natural order and therefore the final stage of human affairs. Marx once characterized this view as, "Thus there has been history, but there is no longer any."[121] Even the neoconservative Irving Kristol rejected this argument, saying, "There is nothing more natural about capitalist civilization than about many others that have had, or will have, their day."[122] Capitalism is a constructed system, which among other things is demonstrated by the furious attempts of its proponents to institute free trade agreements, support capital-friendly governments, and extend intellectual property laws. Capitalism must be embodied in policies and political regimes that actively encourage its spread.

This is its primary weakness, as fragile lives are caught in a devastating storm of impersonal economic forces. Besides economic instability, increasing numbers find that the restructuring of societies for a capitalist world order also means an assault on the meaningfulness of their lives. From the earliest days of capitalism, this criticism has been voiced. A prominent example is the early nineteenth-century conservative Thomas Carlyle, part of the "Young England" movement criticized as "feudal socialists" in the *Manifesto*. Carlyle lamented the erosion of traditional relationships by the spread of market relations and longed for the days before "*Cash Payment*" had "grown to be the universal sole nexus of man to man."[123] Today it is likely that the striking rise of fundamentalism in many parts of the world is at least partly a reaction to the attack on traditional communities that has always been necessary to capitalism. It is unsurprising that in the missives of Osama bin Laden, calls for all peoples to "submit to Allah" are interwoven with repudiation of capitalism.[124]

Along with this "loss of meaning," there are other ominous rumblings. As mentioned, attempts to manage the capitalist economy—unlike a "naturally" functioning system—require actively justifying various policies, increasing the burden of legitimacy on the system as a whole.[125] Second, in a global economic system, there are limits on the extent to which capitalism can be politically managed by nation-states. Finally, more and more people are becoming convinced that industrial society as we have known it may well be ecologically unsustainable. Under a capitalist economy, what it is individually rational to do, or even what it is rational for individual countries—like China—to do, can be collectively disastrous.

Multiple forces of opposition are gathering in the world today. Some are trying to protect their jobs, their culture, the environment, or their families. Others are simply asserting human dignity in the face of crushing circumstance. Overthrow by a self-conscious proletariat has never been the only possibility. Capitalism may well rattle itself apart as more and more people conclude that the promise of economic productivity cannot substitute for lives that make sense. Whatever their motives, they will be determined that economies exist to serve people, not people to serve economies.

NOTES

1. *The Principles of Political Economy and Taxation* (New York: Everyman's Library, 1973 [original 1817]), p. 82 and p. 175.
2. "The Long Climb: A Special Report on the World Economy," *The Economist*, October 3, 2009, p. 4. The investment company making the estimate was Goldman Sachs.
3. Quoted in *The Economist*, July 18, 2009, p. 65.
4. Testimony of Dr. Alan Greenspan, Committee of Government Oversight and Reform, October 23, 2008.
5. *Capital: A Critique of Political Economy* Volume III (New York: International Publishers, 1967), p. 817. Unless otherwise noted, in all quotes emphases are in the original.
6. For example, Adam Smith speaks of the natural "propensity to truck, barter, and exchange one thing for another." *An Inquiry into the Nature and Causes of the Wealth of Nations: Representative Selections* (Indianapolis: Bobbs-Merrill Company, 1961), p. 13.
7. *Capital: A Critique of Political Economy* Volume I (New York: Vintage Books, 1977), p. 274. "Only where wage-labor is its basis does commodity production impose itself upon society as a whole": p. 733.
8. *Capital* Volume I, p. 273.
9. *Capital* Volume I, pp. 873–875. "In actual history, it is a notorious fact that conquest, enslavement, robbery, murder, in short, force play the greatest part." David Harvey argues very convincingly that this "primitive accumulation," which he calls "accumulation by dispossession," continues today: *The New Imperialism* (New York: Oxford University Press, 2003), p. 144 and all of Chapter Four.
10. Alfred Marshall argued that demand (the "desire to have it") and cost of production both determine the value of a commodity, the former with more weight in the short run and the latter with more weight in the long run. *Principles of Economics* (Amherst, NY: Prometheus Books, 1997 [original 1890 and 1920]), pp. 164–165. Contemporary economists typically call consumer preferences "exogenous," that is, something merely "given" from the outside and allowing little further explanation.
11. *Capital* Volume III, p. 189; cf. *Capital* Volume I, p. 678.

12. *Capital* Volume I, p. 274 and p. 293. See also M. C. Howard and J. E. King, *The Political Economy of Marx* Second Edition (New York: Longman, 1985), p. 93.

13. *Capital* Volume I, pp. 270–271. Aristotle, *The Politics*, Book 1, Chapter IX, Section 2. Marx's reference to Aristotle on the dual value of things is in *Capital* Volume I, p. 179.

14. *Capital* Volume I, pp. 296–301. Labor therefore has no value, which is only a property of a commodity. The phrase "value" or "price" of labor is "just as irrational as a yellow logarithm." *Capital* Volume III, p. 818.

15. *Capital* Volume I, p. 325.

16. *Capital* Volume I, p. 680.

17. *Capital* Volume I, p. 731.

18. *Capital* Volume I, p. 301 and p. 729.

19. *Capital: A Critique of Political Economy* Volume II (New York: International Publishers, 1967), p. 356; *Capital* Volume I, p. 647 and p. 1024. For related comments on "free gifts" to capital, see *Capital* Volume III, p. 643 and p. 645.

20. *Capital* Volume I, p. 443.

21. *Capital* Volume I, p. 451.

22. *Capital* Volume I, p. 481 and p. 1052. Also, *Capital* Volume II, p. 356.

23. *Capital* Volume III, pp. 80–81, pp. 107–108, and p. 237.

24. *Capital* Volume I, p. 742.

25. Howard and King, *The Political Economy of Marx*, p. 51. *Capital* Volume III, p. 149.

26. Howard and King, op. cit., p. 79.

27. *Capital* Volume III, p. 213.

28. *Capital* Volume III, p. 249. Other things that retard the fall of the rate of profit are increasing productivity in regard to consumption goods, reducing the value of the consumption basket and the value of labor-power and thereby increasing surplus-value, and cheaper inputs from abroad: Ibid., pp. 236–239.

    Marx's value theory quickly leads into technical discussions that can have no place here. A superb overview is Howard and King, op. cit. A more detailed and masterful attempt to clarify and defend the theory of value is David Harvey, *The Limits to Capital* (London: Verso, 2006). Other disputes over value theory, even its very relevance for economic analysis, are presented in the contending articles in Ian Steedman et al., *The Value Controversy* (London: Verso, 1981), and in a vigorous debate in *Historical Materialism* 4 (Summer 1999) over Robert Brenner's article "Uneven Development and the Long Downturn: The Advanced Capitalist Economies from Boom to Stagnation, 1950–1998," *New Left Review* Number 229 (May/June 1998), pp. 1–265 (entire issue). Finally, one can find innovative arguments on the topic in almost any issue of the long-standing Marxist journal *Science & Society*.

29. *Capital* Volume II, p. 144; *Capital* Volume I, pp. 1037–1038.

30. *Capital* Volume III, p. 244.

31. *Capital* Volume III, p. 43. See also ibid., pp. 138–139, p. 639, and p. 827.

32. For the phrase "many capitals," *Grundrisse: Foundations of the Critique of Political Economy* (New York: Vintage Books, 1973), p. 414. On "furious combat," *Capital* Volume I, p. 582. Marx's analysis of the internal dynamic of capitalist production causes him to reconsider the actual role of competition in capitalism. Most economists would insist that competition is the mainspring of capitalism. In contrast, Marx argues that focusing on competition can be very misleading. "The vulgar economist does practically no more than translate the singular concepts of the capitalists, who are in the thrall of competition, into a seemingly more theoretical and generalized language,

and attempt to substantiate the justice of these conceptions." *Capital* Volume III, p. 231. Marx does acknowledge that it is "the thirst for profits on the one hand, and competition on the other, which compels the cheapest possible production of commodities." *Capital* Volume III, p. 86. He even refers to "competition on the world-market" as "the basis and the vital element of capitalist production." *Capital* Volume III, p. 110. However, for Marx these "horizontal" relations among capitalists are secondary to the "vertical" relation of capital as a whole to labor as a whole. For Marx, competition does not create the laws of capitalist production. The overall structure of social production, especially the exploitative relation between labor and capital, does that. "Competition generally, this essential locomotive force of the bourgeois economy, does not establish its laws, but is rather their executor." *Grundrisse*, p. 552. As Marx says, in competition, "everything appears reversed." *Capital* Volume III, p. 209.

The phrases "vertical" and "horizontal" were used by Brenner, "Uneven Development and the Long Downturn," p. 23. Brenner emphasizes the importance of the horizontal relations, that is, capitalist competition.

33. *Capital* Volume III, p. 484. See also ibid., p. 244. It is limited by "antagonistic conditions of distribution, which reduce the consumption of the bulk of society to a minimum varying within more or less narrow limits." Again, ibid., p 256, Marx refers to the "limited dimensions of consumption under capitalism." Finally, in a note by Marx inserted by Engels as a footnote in *Capital* Volume II, Marx states the insufficiency of demand by workers in very strong terms: p. 316 footnote.

34. *Capital* Volume III, p. 181.

35. *Capital* Volume II, pp. 410–411.

36. *Capital* Volume I, p. 771. See John S. Dryzek, *Democracy in Capitalist Times: Ideals, Limits, and Struggles* (New York: Oxford University Press, 1996), p. 27 and passim.

37. Both, *Capital* Volume III, p. 254.

38. *Capital* Volume III, p. 255.

39. James O'Connor, "Capitalism, Nature, Socialism: A Theoretical Introduction," *Capitalism, Nature, Socialism* Number One (Fall 1988), p. 20. My emphasis.

40. *Capital* Volume III, p. 250.

41. *Capital* Volume I, p. 931. "[T]he capitalist himself in *his own mind* is pleased to confuse his mode of property and appropriation, which is based on the expropriation of the immediate producer in its origins, and on the acquisition of the labor of others in its further progress, with its opposite: with a mode of production that presupposes that the *immediate producer privately owns his own conditions of production.*" Ibid., p. 1083.

42. *Capital* Volume III, p. 383. Also, *Capital* Volume I, p. 299 and p. 1048.

43. *Capital* Volume III, pp. 388–389.

44. *Capital* Volume III, p. 436. Marx later says that the development of the credit and banking system for capitalist finance "does away with the private character of capital and thus contains in itself, but only in itself, the abolition of capital itself." Ibid., p. 607.

45. *Capital* Volume III, p. 437.

46. *Capital* Volume III, p. 776.

47. G. A. Cohen, *Karl Marx's Theory of History: A Defense* (Princeton, NJ: Princeton University Press, 1978), pp. 203–204. The prominent Marxist economist Ernest Mandel concurs: "Introduction" to *Capital* Volume I, p. 83.

48. Quoted in Alex Callinicos, "Capitalism, Competition and Profits: A Critique of Robert Brenner's Theory of Crisis," *Historical Materialism* 4 (Summer 1999), pp. 28–29. For the original: Leon Trotsky, "Whither France," Part I (March 28, 1935), on the Website www.marxists.org.

49. See the discussion in Sitton, Chapter One: "The Proletariat and Historical Progress," *Recent Marxian Theory: Class Formation and Social Conflict in Contemporary Capitalism* (Albany, NY: State University of New York Press, 1996).

50. When analyzing the dynamic of contemporary political situations, Marx was more nuanced, indicating multiple strata in existing countries: the peasantry, urban petty bourgeois (shopkeepers, independent skilled craftsmen, small manufacturers), multiple fractions of the bourgeoisie (financial, industrial, merchant, agricultural), and the "lumpenproletariat" (the completely marginalized, including the criminal element).

51. "Documents of the First International: Provisional Rules," in *The First International and After*, ed. David Fernbach. (New York: Random House, 1974), p. 82.

52. August H. Nimtz, Jr., *Marx and Engels: Their Contribution to the Democratic Breakthrough* (Albany, NY: State University of New York Press, 2000).

53. *Capital* Volume I, p. 916.

54. "Conspectus of Bakunin's *Statism and Anarchy*," in *The First International and After*, ed. David Fernbach, p. 333. The passage continues: "It is itself still a class and the economic conditions from which the class struggle and the existence of classes derive have still not disappeared and must forcibly be either removed out of the way or transformed, this transformation process being forcibly hastened."

55. See "Critique of the Gotha Programme," below. Blanqui actually coined the term "dictatorship of the proletariat" but he meant by it an elite of conspirators who would overthrow the state that sustained capitalism: David Fernbach, "Introduction" to *The Revolutions of 1848*, ed. Fernbach (New York: Random House, 1973), p. 24. For an overview of the various uses of what was a common phrase among revolutionaries in Marx's day, see Hal Draper, *The "Dictatorship of the Proletariat" from Marx to Lenin* (New York: Monthly Review Press, 1987). I believe that the idea probably originates in the ancient Roman office of "dictator." In times of grave crisis, the Roman Senate would choose a dictator, serving a six-month or less term, with full powers to manage the crisis.

56. See Engels's introduction to *The Civil War in France*, below. In my brief preface to this piece, I mention that Engels's statement was allegedly occasioned by a remark of Marx at a banquet.

57. *Capital* Volume I, p. 739.

58. See "Preface" to Karl Marx's *A Contribution to the Critique of Political Economy* (New York: International Publishers, 1970) below.

59. Jon Elster, *Making Sense of Marx* (London: Cambridge University Press, 1985), p. 131. For a more optimistic but still critical appraisal of the issue, see Howard and King, op. cit., pp. 123–126. Marx actually agrees that the reduction of skilled labor to simple labor is an "abstraction," but one that is nevertheless accomplished in the capitalist process itself, necessary for relating the concrete labors of individuals to each other. "This reduction appears to be an abstraction, but it is an abstraction which is made every day in the social process of production." In *A Contribution to the Critique of Political Economy*, p. 30. In *Capital* Volume I, he adds that it is "established by a social process that goes on behind the backs of the producers": p. 135. It is therefore what Jürgen Habermas calls a "real abstraction."

60. A large part of the third volume of *Capital* is devoted to analyzing what causes the divergence of prices from labor values. A general cause is that individual capitals have a differing organic composition, that is, differing ratios of technology, living labor, and surplus-value. Since competition over investment opportunities tends to equalize profit rates throughout the capitalist economy regardless of the above differing compositions, embodied "value" and "prices of production" diverge. Focusing on

individual firms rather than the economy as a whole makes this difficult to perceive. Marx argued that capitalists are actually like shareholders in society's production, being rewarded according to their relative investments in capital, and dividing up the fruits of collective labor. See *Capital* Volume III, pp. 157–158 and p. 209. Also see in their entirety Chapter IX, "Formation of a General Rate of Profit (Average Rate of Profit) and Transformation of the Values of Commodities into Prices of Production," pp. 154–172; and, Chapter X, "Equalization of the General Rate of Profit Through Competition. Market-Prices and Market-Values. Surplus-Profit." pp. 173–199.

61. John Roemer further objects that the "exploitability" of labor is actually not unique, that any commodity can be shown to produce more value than it costs. "Labor power, however, is not the only productive factor that possesses the property of exploitability. . . . One can adopt any good as the value numeraire and prove a Generalized Commodity Exploitation Theorem, which states that profits exist if and only if each produced commodity possesses the property of exploitability when it is taken as the numeraire for calculating embodied value." *Free to Lose: An Introduction to Marxist Economic Philosophy* (Cambridge, MA: Harvard University Press, 1988), p. 53.

62. As David Harvey states, "value is a social relation and this is always immaterial but objective." *The Limits to Capital*, p. xx.

63. *The Limits to Capital*, p. 141.

64. Paul A. Baran and Paul M. Sweezy, *Monopoly Capital: An Essay on the American Economic and Social Order* (New York: Monthly Review Press, 1966); John Bellamy Foster and Fred Magdoff, *The Great Financial Crisis: Causes and Consequences* (New York: Monthly Review Press, 2009); Robert Brenner, "Uneven Development and the Long Downturn"; and David Harvey, *The New Imperialism*.

65. Engels complained of commentators on *Capital*, that their arguments "rest upon the false assumption that Marx wishes to define where he only investigates": "Preface" to *Capital* Volume III, p. 13.

66. Przeworski, "Proletariat into a Class: The Process of Class Formation from Karl Kautsky's *The Class Struggle* to Recent Controversies," *Politics and Society* Volume 7, Number 4 (1977), pp. 343–401. Hal Draper argues that Marx never predicted that the middle strata would be proletarianized, only that their social and political importance would decline. Although the argument seems rather labored, see Draper's discussion in "Special Note F: The Alleged Theory of the Disappearance of the Middle Classes," *Karl Marx's Theory of Revolution*, Volume II, *The Politics of Social Classes* (New York: Monthly Review Press, 1978), pp. 613–627.

67. *Unthinking Social Science: The Limits of Nineteenth-Century Paradigms* (Cambridge: Polity Press, 1991), p. 164.

68. Wally Seccombe, "Contradictions of Shareholder Capitalism: Downsizing Jobs, Enlisting Savings, Destabilizing Families," *Socialist Review 1999* (London: Merlin Press, 1999), pp. 92–94.

69. *Marx-Engels Selected Correspondence* (Moscow: Progress Publishers, 1975), pp. 330–331.

70. Russell Hardin, *One for All: The Logic of Group Conflict* (Princeton, NJ: Princeton University Press, 1995), pp. 58–59.

71. See France Fox Piven, "Globalizing Capitalism and the Rise of Identity Politics," in *Socialist Review 1995* (London: Merlin Press, 1995), pp. 102–116. There are, of course, many reasons for the weakening of working class identity. The decline of trade unions leaves the field to other identifications by default, and the defeat of explicitly anti-capitalist movements in the twentieth century no doubt encouraged social movements to seek a different organizing principle. Claus Offe has argued that

a weakening of class identity is also caused by public policies that aggregate groups on the basis of gender, ethnicity, age, or region rather than class, dividing groups who may actually share a class position. Finally, in several works, Adam Przeworski has detailed the importance of the political strategy of social democratic parties themselves—to create mass-based parties with broad parliamentary appeal—for the weakening of class identity. Claus Offe, "Political Authority and Class Structures—An Analysis of Late Capitalist Societies," *International Journal of Sociology* Spring 1972, pp. 73–108. Adam Przeworski, *Capitalism and Social Democracy* (Cambridge: Cambridge University Press, 1985), pp. 24–28.

72. Joseph Schumpeter, *Capitalism, Socialism, and Democracy* 3rd ed. (New York: Harper and Row, 1942), p. 84. On the importance of ascriptive identities even within capitalism, see Claus Offe, *Disorganized Capitalism: Contemporary Transformations of Work and Politics* (Cambridge, MA: MIT Press, 1985), pp. 10–51, especially pp. 35–39.

73. *Capital* Volume I, p. 1068. Of the completely marginalized, Marx refers to "the demoralized, the ragged, and those unable to work, chiefly people who succumb to their incapacity for adaptation, an incapacity which results from the division of labor." Ibid., p. 797. Also Mandel, op. cit., pp. 66–73.

74. Both, *Capital* Volume I, p. 275. In "Value, Price and Profit" in defining subsistence, Marx refers to the importance of the "traditional mode of life," below.

75. *Capital* Volume III, p. 859: "The actual value of his labor-power deviates from this physical minimum; it differs according to climate and level of social development; it depends not merely upon the physical, but also upon the historically developed social needs, which become second nature." Marx believed that the variability of what is considered "subsistence" does not weaken the concept of the value of labor-power because at any particular time "subsistence" can be taken to be a fixed quantity.

76. Adam Smith, *An Inquiry into the Nature and Causes of the Wealth of Nations* (New York: Modern Library, 1994), pp. 938–939.

77. *Capital* Volume I, p. 799. My emphasis.

78. *Capital* Volume I, p. 659.

79. "Introduction to Appendix," *Capital* Volume I, p. 947.

80. *Capital* Volume I, p. 1069.

81. *Capital* Volume I, p. 753.

82. Przeworski, *Capitalism and Social Democracy*; Elster, op. cit., p. 292. This is even more likely, given doubts about the "reserve industrial army" being able to hold down wage increases: Howard and King, op. cit., pp. 197–199.

83. Howard and King, among many others, are quite right to emphasize that Marx's overriding goal was to expand freedom: op. cit., pp. 16–18.

84. *Capital* Volume I, p. 769.

85. *Capital* Volume III, p. 790.

86. *Capital* Volume I, p. 899.

87. Engels says "relative independence": *Marx-Engels Selected Correspondence*, p. 399. For "invisible threads": *Capital* Volume I, p. 719.

88. *Capital* Volume III, p. 791.

89. *Marx-Engels Selected Correspondence*, p. 399; "*ultimately* determining factor," p. 394.

90. Charles E. Lindblom, *Politics and Markets: The World's Political-Economic Systems* (New York: Basic Books, 1977), pp. 170–188.

91. *Capital* Volume I, p. 719. This is one of the things that Marx was referring to when he sarcastically remarked that the market is "a very Eden of the innate rights of man." Ibid., p. 280.

92. *Capital* Volume I, p. 1033.
93. *Capital* Volume I, p. 1032.
94. *Manifesto*, below. Again, in "Preface": "It is not the consciousness of men that deter-
    mines their existence, but their social existence that determines their consciousness."
    Below.
95. On the possibility of generational advance, see *Capital* Volume I, p. 1034.
96. "Critique of the Gotha Programme," below.
97. *Selected Correspondence*, p. 290. In a letter to Engels, Marx explains the appearance of
    moral terms in the "Preamble to the Provisional Rules of the International Working
    Men's Association" that Marx wrote: "I was obliged to insert two phrases about 'duty'
    and 'right' into the Preamble to the Rules, and also about 'truth, morality and justice,'
    but these are placed in such a way that they can do no harm." Ibid., p. 139.
98. Max Weber, "The Social Psychology of the World Religions," in *From Max Weber:
    Essays in Sociology*, ed. H. H. Gerth and C. Wright Mills (New York: Oxford
    University Press, 1958), p. 271. Thomas Carlyle put it this way: "It is not what a man
    outwardly has or wants that constitutes the happiness or misery of him. Nakedness,
    hunger, distress of all kinds, death itself have been cheerfully suffered, when the
    heart was right. It is the feeling of *injustice* that is insupportable to all men." *Critical
    and Miscellaneous Essays in Five Volumes*, Volume IV (New York: AMS Press, 1969
    [1839]), pp. 144–145.
99. One issue on which capitalism is vulnerable is what "freedom" means. Although
    it is true that the freedoms of capitalism are not illusory, there are other equally
    important dimensions of freedom that need to be formulated. For example, Amartya
    Sen, winner of the Nobel Prize in Economics, defines freedom as "capabilities" that
    allow one "to choose a life one has reason to value." Sen defends markets and tradi-
    tional democratic liberties but insists that we must think about freedom in a more
    comprehensive way. If we do so, we will recognize that "[d]espite unprecedented
    increases in overall opulence, the contemporary world denies elementary freedoms
    to vast numbers—perhaps even the majority—of people." *Development As Freedom*
    (New York: Anchor Books, 1999), pp. 3–4 and p. 74. The argument that capital-
    ism maximizes individual freedom can be challenged in another way. G. A. Cohen
    argued that private property restricts *my* freedom to set up a tent in your backyard
    because I have no other place to live: *History, Labour, and Freedom: Themes from
    Marx* (Oxford: Clarendon Press, 1988), pp. 293–294. Cohen traces the argument to
    Jeremy Bentham.
100. *Marx-Engels Collected Works* Volume 5 (New York: International Publishers, 1976),
    p. 323.
101. Maurice Dobb argued that for Marx "exploitation" is merely a technical term that
    has no moral implications. The use of this term enabled Marx to explain a theoretical
    problem: How can *surplus*-value be generated in a circumstance where, due to
    competition, commodities generally trade at their values? Dobb insisted on this
    interpretation in order to distinguish Marx's position from a mere updating of John
    Locke, that one has a natural right to the fruits of one's labor and to be deprived of
    these is injustice. "Introduction" to Marx's *A Contribution to the Critique of Political
    Economy*, p. 12. See also Howard and King, op. cit., p. 52 and p. 168. Others work-
    ing in the Marxian tradition, although accepting the validity of moral critique, argue
    that appropriation of the surplus production on the basis of ownership is unjust
    only if the prior distribution of property was unjust. They thereby shift the moral
    issue from what happens in production to the defensibility of the initial distribution
    of property. See John Roemer, "Should Marxists Be Interested in Exploitation?" in

Analytical Marxism, ed. Roemer (Cambridge: Cambridge University Press, 1986), pp. 277–278; and G. A. Cohen, *History, Labour, and Freedom*, pp. 234–235. Cohen argues that the failure of Marxists to understand the importance of moral claims is a consequence of "ill-conceived philosophical commitments": p. 298. Finally, a full exploration of the concept of exploitation would have to consider Marx's argument that the peasantry is also "exploited" by landlords, usurers, and the like.

102. *Selected Correspondence*, p. 393; also pp. 394–395. Engels mentions something similar in regard to legal argument: "In a modern state, law must not only correspond to the general economic condition and be its expression, but must also be an *internally coherent* expression which does not, owing to internal conflicts, contradict itself. And in order to achieve this, the faithful reflection of economic conditions suffers increasingly." Ibid., p. 399.

103. Martin Wolf, "Seeds of Its Own Destruction," FT.com (online version of the *Financial Times*), March 8, 2009: www.ft.com.

104. Harvey, *The Limits to Capital*, p. 197. Marx, *Capital* Volume 3, p. 216.

105. Harvey, ibid., p. xxiv. In another place, Harvey argues explicitly that the present crisis of overaccumulation can be elaborated from the tendency of the rate of profit to fall. "The central point of this argument concerned a chronic tendency within capitalism, theoretically derived out of a reformulation of Marx's theory of the tendency for the profit rate to fall, to produce crises of overaccumulation. Such crises are typically registered as surpluses of capital (in commodity, money, or productive capacity forms) and surpluses of labour power side by side, without there apparently being any means to bring them together profitably to accomplish socially useful tasks." Harvey, *The New Imperialism*, pp. 87–88. Oddly, however, Harvey argues in his 2006 Introduction to *The Limits to Capital* that "[c]rises arise when the ever-increasing quantities of surplus value that capitalists produce cannot profitably be absorbed. The operative word here is 'profitably' (and I should make clear that this has nothing directly to do with the supposed law of falling profits)." P. xxiii.

106. Foster and Magdoff, *The Great Financial Crisis*, p. 37.

107. *The Great Financial Crisis*, p. 54.

108. Paul Krugman and many others use this term: Paul Krugman, *The Return of Depression Economics and the Crisis of 2008* (New York: W. W. Norton and Company, 2009), p. 160.

109. *Capital* Volume III, p. 468. For the following, p. 466.

110. John Bellamy Foster and Robert W. McChesney, "Monopoly-Finance Capital and the Paradox of Accumulation," *Monthly Review* Volume 61, Number 5 (October 2009), p. 17. See below.

111. Marx continues: "In this transformation, it is neither the direct human labor he himself performs, nor the time during which he works, but rather the appropriation of his own general productive power, his understanding of nature and his mastery over it by virtue of his presence as a social body—it is, in a word, the development of the social individual which appears as the great foundation-stone of production and of wealth. The *theft of alien labor time, on which the present wealth is based*, appears a miserable foundation in face of this new one, created by large-scale industry itself. As soon as labor in the direct form has ceased to be the great well-spring of wealth, labor time ceases and must cease to be its measure, and hence exchange-value [must cease to be the measure] of use-value." *Grundrisse*, pp. 704–705. Brackets and emphases in the original.

112. *Unjust Deserts: How the Rich Are Taking Our Common Inheritance* (New York: The New Press, 2008), p. 6. Along these lines, the political theorist Robert Dahl, quoted

by Alperowitz and Daly, once asked the pointed question: "Who has made a larger contribution to the operation of General Electric—its chief executives or Albert Einstein or Michael Faraday or Isaac Newton?" Ibid., p. 126. Among many others, Alperowitz and Daly draw on the work and comments of Robert Solow and Herbert Simon, both winners of the Nobel Prize in Economics, and the comments of Warren Buffet.

113. *Unjust Deserts*, p. 9 and pp. 59–63.

114. *Unjust Deserts*, p. 151.

115. *Unjust Deserts*, p. 127.

116. *Selected Correspondence*, p. 393. In the same place, he remarks that "our conception of history is above all a guide to study."

117. *Selected Correspondence*, p. 396.

118. A superb work on this topic is Amy Chua, *World on Fire: How Exporting Free Market Democracy Breeds Ethnic Hatred and Global Instability* (New York: Anchor Books, 2004).

119. *Selected Correspondence*, p. 400.

120. *The Eighteenth Brumaire of Louis Bonaparte* (New York: International Publishers, 1963, p. 15.

121. *The Poverty of Philosophy* (New York: International Publishers, 1963), p. 121.

122. Irving Kristol, *Two Cheers for Capitalism* (New York: Basic Books, 1978), p. 257.

123. Thomas Carlyle, "Chartism," in *Critical and Miscellaneous Essays,* p. 162. In *Condition of the English Working-Class in 1844* (Stanford: Stanford University Press, 1958) Engels quoted frequently from Carlyle, e.g., p. 312. More recently, John Gray, former adviser to Prime Minister Margaret Thatcher, warned about the transformation of market economies into market *societies*, that is, the colonization of all social relations especially caused by the "market fundamentalism" that the United States in particular has foisted on an increasingly reluctant world: *False Dawn: The Delusions of Global Capitalism* (New York: The New Press, 1998). Also, over the last thirty years, American conservatives such as Daniel Bell, Irving Kristol, and others have pointed out the effects of unrestrained market relations on traditional institutions. Daniel Bell, *The Cultural Contradictions of Capitalism* Twentieth Anniversary Edition (New York: Basic Books, 1996); Irving Kristol, *Two Cheers for Capitalism*; ed. Mark Gerson, *The Essential Neoconservative Reader* (New York: Addison-Wesley Company, Inc.,1996).

124. In the September 2007 statement, he recommends that Westerners "should liberate yourselves from the deception, shackles and attrition of the capitalist system." "Transcript of Osama Bin Laden Tape September 2007," www.mideastweb.org/log/archives.

125. Jürgen Habermas has powerfully made the case that contemporary capitalism suffers from intensified legitimation requirements: *Legitimation Crisis* (Boston: Beacon Press, 1975). He also argues at length that it suffers from a "loss of meaning." See John F. Sitton, *Habermas and Contemporary Society* (New York: Palgrave Macmillan, 2003).

Part I

CHAPTER 1

MANIFESTO OF THE COMMUNIST PARTY

TRANSLATED INTO INNUMERABLE LANGUAGES, Isaiah Berlin called the *Manifesto* "a great revolutionary hymn." "No other modern political movement or cause can claim to have produced anything comparable with it in eloquence and power."[1] The work was written for the League of Communists in late 1847 and published in London (in German) in early 1848. The League was an association of German exiles in London, Brussels, and Paris forged in order to promote political change in Germany. Marx and Engels were a part of its Brussels branch.

We must make a few comments on the title and other language of the *Manifesto*. First, as Engels notes in the 1888 Preface to an English edition included here, the label "communist" was only adopted because the word "socialist" was already taken. At the time the *Manifesto* was composed, "socialists" especially referred to various promoters of utopian schemes, ideal communities that would come about through moral and intellectual persuasion. The specific label chosen by Marx and Engels was therefore governed by the need to distinguish their own approach from alternative perspectives in their day. Today the word "socialist" would serve as well to describe their position, indeed perhaps better because of the twentieth-century experience with so-called communist governments.

Second, the word "party" in the title does not refer to the specific organization the League of Communists. In the nineteenth century in both German (Partei) and English, "party" largely meant "movement" or "tendency" rather than a discrete political organization.[2] The "communist party" therefore means the broad movement of revolutionary workers, regardless of the organizational forms this movement takes.

There are other phrases that may be confusing to a modern reader. "Middle class" does not mean what it does today, rather in middle nineteenth-century England it refers to the capitalist owners, the bourgeoisie. In Europe the aristocracy was the upper class, with the bourgeoisie a social and political step below them. Later, in the nineteenth century, Marx and Engels sometimes use "middle class" closer to its more recent meaning, that of small owners, tradespeople, et cetera. However, they never use the term to refer to the working class.

The infamous phrase "the idiocy of rural life," often interpreted as a slur against the peasantry, is in sore need of clarification. Confusion on this has badly misled people regarding Marx's views on the role of the peasantry in the revolutionary transformation of society. The term "idiocy" employed here most decidedly does not mean stupidity. Instead, the original German phrase "dem Idiotismus des Landslebens" refers to the isolation of rural life, a situation that reduces the ability of the peasantry to pursue its political interests autonomously. The common opinion that Marx and Engels generally derided the peasantry and their importance for revolution has been completely dismantled by August Nimtz.[3]

Finally, the famous closing phrase—"Working Men of All Countries, Unite!"— was the motto of the League of Communists. The phrase appears on the first issue of their organ the *Communist Review* in 1847.[4] A variation also appears on Marx's tombstone in Highgate Cemetery in London.

As Engels's preface, quoting from the earlier 1872 preface, states, the *Manifesto* of 1848 would need alteration in at least two important respects. First, the transitional measures mentioned in the *Manifesto* were purely a product of the time and therefore quickly became out-of-date. As transitional measures, they would need continual revision as the movement proceeded. Second, and more importantly, the original *Manifesto* suggests that the existing state machinery could be seized and simply turned to new, communist purposes. As argued in various prefaces after the Paris Commune of 1871, this is mistaken. The Paris Commune convinced Marx and Engels that the capitalist state could not be taken over but must be "smashed" and replaced by a participatory form of government. This new form would subordinate armed force and decision-making to the working class and only through it could the working class take control of its own destiny.

NOTES

1. Isaiah Berlin, *Karl Marx: His Life and Environment* (New York: Oxford University Press, 1959), p. 150.

2. David Fernbach, introduction to *The Revolutions of 1848* (New York: Random House, 1973), p. 28 footnote; August H. Nimtz, Jr., *Marx and Engels: Their Contribution to the Democratic Breakthrough* (Albany, NY: State University of New York Press, 2000), p. 59; Hal Draper, *Karl Marx's Theory of Revolution*, Volume II, *The Politics of Social Classes* (New York: Monthly Review Press, 1978), p. 212 footnote. See also Marx's letter to Ferdinand Freiligrath, February 29, 1860: "The League . . . was simply an episode in the history of a party that is everywhere springing up naturally out of the soil of modern society." In *Marx-Engels Collected Works*, Volume 41 (New York: International Publishers), p. 82.

3. Nimtz, *Marx and Engels*, p. x, p. 51, and passim. Draper clarifies the terminology here in an interesting footnote: "The Greeks had a word for the kind of social mentality that Engels was describing in his travel sketches: the privatized person, withdrawn from public concerns, *apolitical* in the original sense of isolation from the sociopolitical community of the larger whole. The word was *idiotes*," *Karl Marx's Theory of Revolution*, pp. 344–345. We can add that the Greek root refers to something one has that separates one from others, like the English words idiom and idiosyncrasy.

4. David Caute, *The Left in Europe since 1789* (New York: McGraw-Hill Book Company, 1966), p. 205. See also Nimtz, p. 46.

PREFACE TO THE 1888 ENGLISH EDITION OF THE *MANIFESTO OF THE COMMUNIST PARTY*

FREDERICK ENGELS

THE "MANIFESTO" WAS PUBLISHED AS THE PLATFORM OF THE "COMMUNIST LEAGUE," a working-men's association, first exclusively German, later on international, and, under the political conditions of the Continent before 1848, unavoidably a secret society. At a Congress of the League, held in London in November, 1847, Marx and Engels were commissioned to prepare for publication a complete theoretical and practical party programme. Drawn up in German, in January, 1848, the manuscript was sent to the printer in London a few weeks before the French revolution of February 24th. A French translation was brought out in Paris, shortly before the insurrection of June, 1848. The first English translation, by Miss Helen Macfarlane, appeared in George Julian Harney's "Red Republican," London, 1850. A Danish and a Polish edition had also been published.

The defeat of the Parisian insurrection of June, 1848,—the first great battle between Proletariat and Bourgeoisie—drove again into the background, for a time, the social and political aspirations of the European working-class. Thenceforth, the struggle for supremacy was again, as it had been before the revolution of February, solely between different sections of the propertied class; the working class was reduced to a fight for political elbow-room, and to the position of extreme wing of the Middle-class Radicals. Wherever independent proletarian movements continued to show signs of life, they were ruthlessly hunted down. Thus the Prussian police hunted out the Central Board of the Communist League, then located in Cologne. The members were arrested, and, after eighteen months' imprisonment, they were tried in October, 1852. This celebrated "Cologne Communist trial" lasted from October 4th till November 12th; seven of the prisoners were sentenced to terms of imprisonment in a fortress, varying from three to six years. Immediately after the sentence, the League was formally dissolved by the remaining members. As to the "Manifesto," it seemed thenceforth to be doomed to oblivion.

When the European working-class had recovered sufficient strength for another attack on the ruling classes, the International Working Men's Association sprang up. But this association, formed with the express aim of welding into one body the whole militant proletariat of Europe and America, could not at once proclaim the principles laid down in the "Manifesto." The International was bound to have a programme broad enough to be acceptable to the English Trades' Unions, to the followers of Proudhon in France, Belgium, Italy, and Spain, and to the Lassalleans in Germany. Marx, who drew up this programme to the satisfaction of all parties, entirely trusted to the intellectual development of the working-class, which was sure to result from combined action and mutual discussion. The very events and vicissitudes of the struggle against Capital, the defeats even more than the victories, could not help bringing home to men's minds the insufficiency of their various favourite nostrums, and preparing the way for a more complete insight into the true conditions of working-class emancipation. And Marx was right. The International, on its breaking up in 1874, left the workers quite different men from what it had found them in 1864. Proudhonism in France, Lassalleanism in Germany were dying out, and even the Conservative English Trades' Unions, though most of them had long since severed their connexion with the International, were gradually advancing towards that point at which, last year at Swansea, their President could say in their name "Continental Socialism has lost its terrors for us." In fact: the principles of the "Manifesto" had made considerable headway among the working men of all countries.

The *Manifesto* itself thus came to the front again. The German text had been, since 1850, reprinted several times in Switzerland, England and America. In 1872, it was translated into English in New York, where the translation was published in *Woodhull and Claflin's Weekly*. From this English version, a French one was made in "Le Socialiste" of New York. Since then at least two more English translations, more or less mutilated, have been brought out in America, and one of them has been reprinted in England. The first Russian translation, made by Bakounine, was published at Herzen's "Kolokol" office in Geneva, about 1863; a second one, by the heroic Vera Zasulitch, also in Geneva, 1882. A new Danish edition is to be found in "Socialdemokratisk Bibliothek," Copenhagen, 1885; a fresh French translation in "Le Socialiste," Paris, 1886. From this latter a Spanish version was prepared and published in Madrid, 1886. The German reprints are not to be counted, there have been twelve altogether at the least. An Armenian translation, which was to be published in Constantinople some months ago, did not see the light, I am told, because the publisher was afraid of bringing out a book with the name of Marx on it, while the translator declined to call it his own production. Of further translations into other languages I have heard, but have not seen them. Thus the history of the Manifesto reflects, to a great extent, the history of the modern working-class movement; at present it is undoubtedly the most wide-spread, the most international production of all Socialist Literature, the common platform acknowledged by millions of working men from Siberia to California.

Yet, when it was written, we could not have called it a *Socialist* Manifesto. By Socialists, in 1847, were understood, on the one hand, the adherents of the various Utopian systems: Owenites in England, Fourierists in France, both of them already reduced to the position of mere sects, and gradually dying out; on the other hand, the most multifarious social quacks, who, by all manners of tinkering, professed to redress, without any danger to capital and profit, all sorts of social grievances in both cases men outside the working class movement, and looking rather to the "educated" classes for support. Whatever portion of the working class had become convinced of the insufficiency of mere political revolutions, and had proclaimed the necessity of a total social change, that portion, then, called itself Communist. It was a crude, rough-hewn, purely instinctive sort of Communism; still, it touched the cardinal point and was powerful enough amongst the working class to produce the Utopian Communism, in France, of Cabet, and in Germany, of Weitling. Thus, Socialism was, in 1847, a middle-class movement, Communism a working class movement. Socialism was, on the Continent at least, "respectable"; Communism was the very opposite. And as our notion, from the very beginning, was that "the emancipation of the working class must be the act of the working class itself," there could be no doubt as to which of the two names we must take. Moreover, we have, ever since, been far from repudiating it.

The "Manifesto" being our joint production, I consider myself bound to state that the fundamental proposition which forms its nucleus, belongs to Marx. That proposition is: that in every historical epoch, the prevailing mode of economic production and exchange, and the social organisation necessarily following from it, form the basis upon which is built up, and from which alone can be explained, the political and intellectual history of that epoch; that consequently the whole history of mankind (since the dissolution of primitive tribal society, holding land in common ownership) has been a history of class struggles, contests between exploiting and exploited, ruling and oppressed classes; that the history of these class struggles form a series of evolution in which, nowadays, a stage has been reached where the exploited and oppressed class—the proletariat—cannot attain its emancipation from the sway of the exploiting and ruling class—the bourgeoisie—without, at the same time, and once and for all emancipating society at large from all exploitation, oppression, class-distinctions and class-struggles.

This proposition which, in my opinion, is destined to do for history what Darwin's theory has done for biology, we, both of us, had been gradually approaching for some years before 1845. How far I had independently progressed towards it, is best shown by my "Condition of the Working Class in England." But when I again met Marx at Brussels, in spring, 1845, he had it ready worked out, and put it before me, in terms almost as clear as those in which I have stated it here.

From our joint preface to the German edition of 1872, I quote the following: —

> However much the state of things may have altered during the last 25 years, the general principles laid down in this Manifesto are, on the whole, as correct to-day as ever. Here and there some detail might be improved. The practical application of the principles will depend, as the manifesto itself states, everywhere and at all times, on the historical conditions for the time being existing, and, for that reason, no special stress is laid on the revolutionary measures proposed at the end of Section II. That passage would, in many respects, be very differently worded to-day. In view of the gigantic strides of Modern Industry since 1848, and of the accompanying improved and extended organisation of the working-class, in view of the practical experience gained, first in the

February revolution, and then, still more, in the Paris Commune, where the proletariat for the first time held political power for two whole months, this programme has in some details become antiquated. One thing especially was proved by the Commune, viz., that 'the working-class cannot simply lay hold of the ready-made State machinery, and wield it for its own purposes.' (See "The Civil War in France; Address of the General Council of the International Working-men's Association," London, Truelove, 1871, p. 15, where this point is further developed.) Further, it is self-evident, that the criticism of socialist literature is deficient in relation to the present time, because it comes down only to 1847; also, that the remarks on the relation of the Communists to the various opposition-parties (Section IV.), although in principle still correct, yet in practice are antiquated, because the political situation has been entirely changed, and the progress of history has swept from off the earth the greater portion of the political parties there enumerated.

But then, the Manifesto has become a historical document which we have no longer any right to alter.

The present translation is by Mr. Samuel Moore, the translator of the greater portion of Marx's *Capital.* We have revised it in common, and I have added a few notes explanatory of historical allusions.

London, 30th January, 1888
Frederick Engels

First published in K. Marx and F. Engels, *Manifesto of the Communist Party,* London, 1888.

MANIFESTO OF THE COMMUNIST PARTY

KARL MARX AND FREDERICK ENGELS

A SPECTRE IS HAUNTING EUROPE—THE SPECTRE OF COMMUNISM. All the Powers of old Europe have entered into a holy alliance to exorcise this spectre: Pope and Czar, Metternich and Guizot, French Radicals and German police-spies.

Where is the party in opposition that has not been decried as Communistic by its opponents in power? Where the Opposition that has not hurled back the branding reproach of Communism, against the more advanced opposition parties, as well as against its reactionary adversaries?

Two things result from this fact:

I. Communism is already acknowledged by all European Powers to be itself a Power.
II. It is high time that Communists should openly, in the face of the whole world, publish their views, their aims, their tendencies, and meet this nursery tale of the Spectre of Communism with a Manifesto of the party itself.

To this end, Communists of various nationalities have assembled in London, and sketched the following Manifesto, to be published in the English, French, German, Italian, Flemish and Danish languages.

I. BOURGEOIS AND PROLETARIANS

The history of all hitherto existing society is the history of class struggles.

Freeman and slave, patrician and plebeian, lord and serf, guild-master and jour-neyman, in a word, oppressor and oppressed, stood in constant opposition to one another, carried on an uninterrupted, now hidden, now open fight, a fight that each time ended, either in a revolutionary re-constitution of society at large, or in the common ruin of the contending classes.

In the earlier epochs of history, we find almost everywhere a complicated arrange-ment of society into various orders, a manifold gradation of social rank. In ancient Rome we have patricians, knights, plebeians, slaves; in the Middle Ages, feudal lords, vassals, guild-masters, journeymen, apprentices, serfs; in almost all of these classes, again, subordinate gradations.

The modern bourgeois society that has sprouted from the ruins of feudal society has not done away with class antagonisms. It has but established new classes, new conditions of oppression, new forms of struggle in place of the old ones.

Our epoch, the epoch of the bourgeoisie, possesses, however, this distinctive feature: it has simplified the class antagonisms. Society as a whole is more and more splitting up into two great hostile camps, into two great classes directly facing each other: Bourgeoisie and Proletariat.

From the serfs of the Middle Ages sprang the chartered burghers of the earliest towns. From these burgesses the first elements of the bourgeoisie were developed.

The discovery of America, the rounding of the Cape, opened up fresh ground for the rising bourgeoisie. The East-Indian and Chinese markets, the colonisation of America, trade with the colonies, the increase in the means of exchange and in commodities generally, gave to commerce, to navigation, to industry, an impulse never before known, and thereby, to the revolutionary element in the tottering feudal society, a rapid development.

The feudal system of industry, under which industrial production was monopolised by closed guilds, now no longer sufficed for the growing wants of the new markets. The manufacturing system took its place. The guild-masters were pushed on one side by the manufacturing middle class; division of labour between the different corporate guilds vanished in the face of division of labour in each single workshop.

Meantime the markets kept ever growing, the demand ever rising. Even manufacture no longer sufficed. Thereupon, steam and machinery revolutionised industrial production. The place of manufacture was taken by the giant, Modern Industry, the place of the industrial middle class, by industrial millionaires, the leaders of whole industrial armies, the modern bourgeois.

Modern industry has established the world market, for which the discovery of America paved the way. This market has given an immense development to commerce, to navigation, to communication by land. This development has, in its turn, reacted on the extension of industry; and in proportion as industry, commerce, navigation, railways extended, in the same proportion the bourgeoisie developed, increased its capital, and pushed into the background every class handed down from the Middle Ages.

We see, therefore, how the modern bourgeoisie is itself the product of a long course of development, of a series of revolutions in the modes of production and of exchange.

Each step in the development of the bourgeoisie was accompanied by a corresponding political advance of that class. An oppressed class under the sway of the feudal nobility, an armed and self-governing association in the medieval commune; here independent urban republic (as in Italy and Germany), there taxable "third estate" of the monarchy (as in France), afterwards, in the period of manufacture proper, serving either the semi-feudal or the absolute monarchy as a counterpoise against the nobility, and, in fact, cornerstone of the great monarchies in general, the bourgeoisie has at last, since the establishment of Modern Industry and of the world market, conquered for itself, in the modern representative State, exclusive political sway. The executive of the modern State is but a committee for managing the common affairs of the whole bourgeoisie.

The bourgeoisie, historically, has played a most revolutionary part.

The bourgeoisie, wherever it has got the upper hand, has put an end to all feudal, patriarchal, idyllic relations. It has pitilessly torn asunder the motley feudal ties that bound man to his "natural superiors," and has left remaining no other nexus between man and man than naked self-interest, than callous "cash payment." It has drowned the most heavenly ecstasies of religious fervour, of chivalrous enthusiasm, of philistine sentimentalism, in the icy water of egotistical calculation. It has resolved personal worth into exchange value, and in place of the numberless indefeasible chartered freedoms, has set up that single, unconscionable freedom—Free Trade. In one word, for exploitation, veiled by religious and political illusions, it has substituted naked, shameless, direct, brutal exploitation.

The bourgeoisie has stripped of its halo every occupation hitherto honoured and looked up to with reverent awe. It has converted the physician, the lawyer, the priest, the poet, the man of science, into its paid wage-labourers.

The bourgeoisie has torn away from the family its sentimental veil, and has reduced the family relation to a mere money relation.

The bourgeoisie has disclosed how it came to pass that the brutal display of vigour in the Middle Ages, which Reactionists so much admire, found its fitting complement in the most slothful indolence. It has been the first to show what man's activity can bring about. It has accomplished wonders far surpassing Egyptian pyramids, Roman aqueducts, and Gothic cathedrals; it has conducted expeditions that put in the shade all former Exoduses of nations and crusades.

The bourgeoisie cannot exist without constantly revolutionising the instruments of production, and thereby the relations of production, and with them the whole relations of society. Conservation of the old modes of production in unaltered form, was, on the contrary, the first condition of existence for all earlier industrial classes. Constant revolutionising of production, uninterrupted disturbance of all social conditions, everlasting uncertainty and agitation distinguish the bourgeois epoch from all earlier ones. All fixed, fast-frozen relations, with their train of ancient and venerable prejudices and opinions, are swept away, all new-formed ones become antiquated before they can ossify. All that is solid melts into air, all that is holy is profaned, and man is at last compelled to face with sober senses, his real conditions of life, and his relations with his kind.

The need of a constantly expanding market for its products chases the bourgeoisie over the whole surface of the globe. It must nestle everywhere, settle everywhere, establish connexions everywhere.

The bourgeoisie has through its exploitation of the world market given a cosmopolitan character to production and consumption in every country. To the great chagrin of Reactionists, it has drawn from under the feet of industry the national ground on which it stood. All old-established national industries have been destroyed or are daily being destroyed. They are dislodged by new industries, whose introduction becomes a life and death question for all civilised nations, by industries that no longer work up indigenous raw material, but raw material drawn from the remotest zones; industries whose products are consumed, not only at home, but in every quarter of the globe. In place of the old wants, satisfied by the productions of the country, we find new wants, requiring for their satisfaction the products of distant lands and climes. In place of the old local and national seclusion and self-sufficiency, we have intercourse in every direction, universal inter-dependence of nations. And as in material, so also in intellectual production. The intellectual creations of individual nations become common property. National one-sidedness and narrow-mindedness become more and more impossible, and from the numerous national and local literatures, there arises a world literature.

The bourgeoisie, by the rapid improvement of all instruments of production, by the immensely facilitated means of communication, draws all, even the most barbarian, nations into civilisation. The cheap prices of its commodities are the heavy artillery with which it batters down all Chinese walls, with which it forces the barbarians' intensely obstinate hatred of foreigners to capitulate. It compels all nations, on pain of extinction, to adopt the bourgeois mode of production; it compels them to introduce what it calls civilisation into their midst, *i.e.*, to become bourgeois themselves. In one word, it creates a world after its own image.

The bourgeoisie has subjected the country to the rule of the towns. It has created enormous cities, has greatly increased the urban population as compared with the rural, and has thus rescued a considerable part of the population from the idiocy of rural life. Just as it has made the country dependent on the towns, so it has made barbarian and semi-barbarian countries dependent on the civilised ones, nations of peasants on nations of bourgeois, the East on the West.

The bourgeoisie keeps more and more doing away with the scattered state of the population, of the means of production, and of property. It has agglomerated population, centralised means of production, and has concentrated property in a few hands. The necessary consequence of this was political centralisation. Independent, or but loosely connected, provinces with separate interests, laws, governments and systems of taxation became lumped together into one nation, with one government, one code of laws, one national class-interest, one frontier and one customs-tariff.

The bourgeoisie, during its rule of scarce one hundred years, has created more massive and more colossal productive forces than have all preceding generations together. Subjection of Nature's forces to man, machinery, application of chemistry to industry and agriculture, steam-navigation, railways, electric telegraphs, clearing of whole continents for cultivation, canalisation of rivers, whole populations conjured out of the ground—what earlier century had even a presentiment that such productive forces slumbered in the lap of social labour?

We see then: the means of production and of exchange, on whose foundation the bourgeoisie built itself up, were generated in feudal society. At a certain stage in the development of these means of production and of exchange, the conditions under which feudal society produced and exchanged, the feudal organisation of agriculture and manufacturing industry, in one word, the feudal relations of property became no longer compatible with the already developed productive forces; they became so many fetters. They had to be burst asunder; they were burst asunder.

Into their place stepped free competition, accompanied by a social and political constitution adapted to it, and by the economical and political sway of the bourgeois class.

A similar movement is going on before our own eyes. Modern bourgeois society with its relations of production, of exchange and of property, a society that has conjured up such gigantic means of production and of exchange, is like the sorcerer, who is no longer able to control the powers of the nether world whom he has called up by his spells. For many a decade past the history of industry and commerce is but the history of the revolt of modern productive forces against modern conditions of production, against the property relations that are the conditions for the existence of the bourgeoisie and of its rule. It is enough to mention the commercial crises that by their periodical return put on its trial, each time more threateningly, the existence of the entire bourgeois society. In these crises a great part not only of the existing products, but also of the previously created productive forces, are periodically destroyed. In these crises there breaks out an epidemic that, in all earlier epochs, would have seemed an absurdity—the epidemic of over-production. Society suddenly finds itself put back into a state of momentary barbarism; it appears as if a famine, a universal war of devastation had cut off the supply of every means of subsistence; industry and commerce seem to be destroyed; and why? Because there is too much civilisation, too much means of subsistence, too much industry, too much commerce. The productive forces at the disposal of society no longer tend to further the development of the conditions of bourgeois property; on the contrary, they have become too powerful for these conditions, by which they are fettered, and so soon as they overcome these fetters, they bring disorder into the whole of bourgeois society, endanger the existence of bourgeois property. The conditions of bourgeois society are too narrow to comprise the wealth created by them. And how does the bourgeoisie get over these crises? On the one hand by enforced destruction of a mass of productive forces; on the other, by the conquest of new markets, and by the more thorough exploitation of the old ones. That is to say, by paving the way for more extensive and more destructive crises, and by diminishing the means whereby crises are prevented.

The weapons with which the bourgeoisie felled feudalism to the ground are now turned against the bourgeoisie itself.

But not only has the bourgeoisie forged the weapons that bring death to itself; it has also called into existence the men who are to wield those weapons—the modern working class—the proletarians.

In proportion as the bourgeoisie, *i.e.,* capital, is developed, in the same proportion is the proletariat, the modern working class, developed—a class of labourers, who live only so long as they find work, and who find work only so long as their labour increases capital. These labourers, who must sell themselves piecemeal, are a commodity, like every other article of commerce, and are consequently exposed to all the vicissitudes of competition, to all the fluctuations of the market.

Owing to the extensive use of machinery and to division of labour, the work of the proletarians has lost all individual character, and, consequently, all charm for the workman. He becomes an appendage of the machine, and it is only the most simple, most monotonous, and most easily acquired knack, that is required of him. Hence, the cost of production of a workman is restricted, almost entirely, to the means of subsistence that he requires for his maintenance, and for the propagation of his race. But the price of a commodity, and therefore also of labour, is equal to its cost of production. In proportion, therefore, as the repulsiveness of the work increases, the wage decreases. Nay more, in proportion as the use of machinery and division of labour increases, in the same proportion the burden of toil also increases, whether by prolongation of the working hours, by increase of the work exacted in a given time or by increased speed of the machinery, etc.

Modern industry has converted the little workshop of the patriarchal master into the great factory of the industrial capitalist. Masses of labourers, crowded into the factory, are organised like soldiers. As privates of the industrial army they are placed under the command of a perfect hierarchy of officers and sergeants. Not only are they slaves of the bourgeois class, and of the bourgeois State; they are daily and hourly enslaved by the machine, by the overlooker, and, above all, by the individual bourgeois manufacturer himself. The more openly this despotism proclaims gain to be its end and aim, the more petty, the more hateful and the more embittering it is.

The less the skill and exertion of strength implied in manual labour, in other words, the more modern industry becomes developed, the more is the labour of men superseded by that of women. Differences of age and sex have no longer any distinctive social validity for the working class. All are instruments of labour, more or less expensive to use, according to their age and sex.

No sooner is the exploitation of the labourer by the manufacturer, so far, at an end, and he receives his wages in cash, than he is set upon by the other portions of the bourgeoisie, the landlord, the shopkeeper, the pawnbroker, etc.

The lower strata of the middle class—the small tradespeople, shopkeepers, and retired tradesmen generally, the handicraftsmen and peasants—all these sink gradually into the proletariat, partly because their diminutive capital does not suffice for the scale on which Modern Industry is carried on, and is swamped in the competition with the large capitalists, partly because their specialised skill is rendered worthless by new methods of production. Thus the proletariat is recruited from all classes of the population.

The proletariat goes through various stages of development. With its birth begins its struggle with the bourgeoisie. At first the contest is carried on by individual labourers, then by the workpeople of a factory, then by the operatives of one trade, in one locality, against the individual bourgeois who directly exploits them. They direct their attacks not against the bourgeois conditions of production, but against the instruments of production themselves; they destroy imported wares that compete with their labour, they smash to pieces machinery, they set factories ablaze, they seek to restore by force the vanished status of the workman of the Middle Ages.

At this stage the labourers still form an incoherent mass scattered over the whole country, and broken up by their mutual competition. If anywhere they unite to form more compact bodies, this is not yet the consequence of their own active union, but of the union of the bourgeoisie, which class, in order to attain its own political ends, is compelled to set the whole proletariat in motion, and is moreover yet, for a time, able to do so. At this stage, therefore, the proletarians do not fight their enemies, but the enemies of their enemies, the remnants of absolute monarchy, the landowners, the non-industrial bourgeois, the petty bourgeoisie. Thus the whole historical movement is concentrated in the hands of the bourgeoisie; every victory so obtained is a victory for the bourgeoisie.

But with the development of industry the proletariat not only increases in number; it becomes concentrated in greater masses, its strength grows, and it feels that strength more. The various interests and conditions of life within the ranks of the proletariat are more and more equalised, in proportion as machinery obliterates all distinctions of labour, and nearly everywhere reduces wages to the same low level. The growing competition among the bourgeois, and the resulting commercial crises, make the wages of the workers ever more fluctuating. The unceasing improvement of machinery, ever more rapidly developing, makes their livelihood more and more precarious; the collisions between individual workmen and individual bourgeois take more and more the character of collisions between two classes. Thereupon the workers begin to form combinations (Trades' Unions) against the bourgeois; they club together in order to keep up the rate of wages; they found permanent associations in order to make provision beforehand for these occasional revolts. Here and there the contest breaks out into riots.

Now and then the workers are victorious, but only for a time. The real fruit of their battles lies, not in the immediate result, but in the ever-expanding union of the workers. This union is helped on by the improved means of communication that are created by modern industry and that place the workers of different localities in contact with one another. It was just this contact that was needed to centralise the numerous local struggles, all of the same character, into one national struggle between classes. But every class struggle is a political struggle. And that union, to attain which the burghers of the Middle Ages, with their miserable highways, required centuries, the modern proletarians, thanks to railways, achieve in a few years.

This organisation of the proletarians into a class, and consequently into a political party, is continually being upset again by the competition between the workers themselves. But it ever rises up again, stronger, firmer, mightier. It compels legislative recognition of particular interests of the workers, by taking advantage of the divisions among the bourgeoisie itself. Thus the ten-hours' bill in England was carried.

Altogether collisions between the classes of the old society further, in many ways, the course of development of the proletariat. The bourgeoisie finds itself involved in a constant battle. At first with the aristocracy; later on, with those portions of the bourgeoisie itself, whose interests have become antagonistic to the progress of industry; at all times, with the bourgeoisie of foreign countries. In all these battles it sees itself compelled to appeal to the proletariat, to ask for its help, and thus, to drag it into the political arena. The bourgeoisie itself, therefore, supplies the proletariat with its own elements of political and general education, in other words, it furnishes the proletariat with weapons for fighting the bourgeoisie.

Further, as we have already seen, entire sections of the ruling classes are, by the advance of industry, precipitated into the proletariat, or are at least threatened in their conditions of existence. These also supply the proletariat with fresh elements of enlightenment and progress.

Finally, in times when the class struggle nears the decisive hour, the process of dissolution going on within the ruling class, in fact within the whole range of old society, assumes such a violent, glaring character, that a small section of the ruling class cuts itself adrift, and joins the revolutionary class, the class that holds the future in its hands. Just as, therefore, at an earlier period, a section of the nobility went over to the bourgeoisie, so now a portion of the bourgeoisie goes over to the proletariat, and in particular, a portion of the bourgeois ideologists, who have raised themselves to the level of comprehending theoretically the historical movement as a whole.

Of all the classes that stand face to face with the bourgeoisie today, the proletariat alone is a really revolutionary class. The other classes decay and finally disappear in the face of Modern Industry; the proletariat is its special and essential product.

The lower middle class, the small manufacturer, the shopkeeper, the artisan, the peasant, all these fight against the bourgeoisie, to save from extinction their existence as fractions of the middle class. They are therefore not revolutionary, but conservative. Nay more, they are reactionary, for they try to roll back the wheel of history. If by chance they are revolutionary, they are so only in view of their impending transfer into the proletariat, they thus defend not their present, but their future interests, they desert their own standpoint to place themselves at that of the proletariat.

The "dangerous class," the social scum, that passively rotting mass thrown off by the lowest layers of old society may, here and there, be swept into the movement by a proletarian revolution; its conditions of life, however, prepare it far more for the part of a bribed tool of reactionary intrigue.

In the conditions of the proletariat, those of old society at large are already virtually swamped. The proletarian is without property; his relation to his wife and children has no longer anything in common with the bourgeois family relations; modern industrial labour, modern subjection to capital, the same in England as in France, in America as in Germany, has stripped him of every trace of national character. Law, morality, religion, are to him so many bourgeois prejudices, behind which lurk in ambush just as many bourgeois interests.

All the preceding classes that got the upper hand, sought to fortify their already acquired status by subjecting society at large to their conditions of appropriation. The proletarians cannot become masters of the productive forces of society, except by abolishing their own previous mode of appropriation, and thereby also every other previous mode of appropriation. They have nothing of their own to secure and to fortify; their mission is to destroy all previous securities for, and insurances of, individual property.

All previous historical movements were movements of minorities, or in the interest of minorities. The proletarian movement is the self-conscious, independent movement of the immense majority, in the interest of the immense majority. The proletariat, the lowest stratum of our present society, cannot stir, cannot raise itself up, without the whole superincumbent strata of official society being sprung into the air.

Though not in substance, yet in form, the struggle of the proletariat with the bourgeoisie is at first a national struggle. The proletariat of each country must, of course, first of all settle matters with its own bourgeoisie.

In depicting the most general phases of the development of the proletariat, we traced the more or less veiled civil war, raging within existing society, up to the point where that war breaks out into open revolution, and where the violent overthrow of the bourgeoisie lays the foundation for the sway of the proletariat.

Hitherto, every form of society has been based, as we have already seen, on the antagonism of oppressing and oppressed classes. But in order to oppress a class, certain conditions must be assured to it under which it can, at least, continue its slavish existence. The serf, in the period of serfdom, raised himself to membership in the commune, just as the petty bourgeois, under the yoke of feudal absolutism, managed to develop into a bourgeois. The modern labourer, on the contrary, instead of rising with the progress of industry, sinks deeper and deeper below the conditions of existence of his own class. He becomes a pauper, and pauperism develops more rapidly than population and wealth. And here it becomes evident, that the bourgeoisie is unfit any longer to be the ruling class in society, and to impose its conditions of existence upon society as an over-riding law. It is unfit to rule because it is incompetent to assure an existence to its slave within his slavery, because it cannot help letting him sink into such a state, that it has to feed him, instead of being fed by him. Society can no longer live under this bourgeoisie, in other words, its existence is no longer compatible with society.

The essential condition for the existence, and for the sway of the bourgeois class, is the formation and augmentation of capital; the condition for capital is wage-labour. Wage-labour rests exclusively on competition between the labourers. The advance of industry, whose involuntary promoter is the bourgeoisie, replaces the isolation of the labourers, due to competition, by their revolutionary combination, due to association. The development of Modern Industry, therefore, cuts from under its feet the very foundation on which the bourgeoisie produces and appropriates products. What the bourgeoisie, therefore, produces, above all, is its own grave-diggers. Its fall and the victory of the proletariat are equally inevitable.

II. PROLETARIANS AND COMMUNISTS

In what relation do the Communists stand to the proletarians as a whole?

The Communists do not form a separate party opposed to other working-class parties.

They have no interests separate and apart from those of the proletariat as a whole.

They do not set up any sectarian principles of their own, by which to shape and mould the proletarian movement.

The Communists are distinguished from the other working-class parties by this only: (1) In the national struggles of the proletarians of the different countries, they point out and bring to the front the common interests of the entire proletariat, independently of all nationality. (2) In the various stages of development which the struggle of the working class against the bourgeoisie has to pass through, they always and everywhere represent the interests of the movement as a whole.

The Communists, therefore, are on the one hand, practically, the most advanced and resolute section of the working-class parties of every country, that section which pushes forward all others; on the other hand, theoretically, they have over the great mass of the proletariat the advantage of clearly understanding the line of march, the conditions, and the ultimate general results of the proletarian movement.

The immediate aim of the Communists is the same as that of all the other proletarian parties: formation of the proletariat into a class, overthrow of the bourgeois supremacy, conquest of political power by the proletariat.

The theoretical conclusions of the Communists are in no way based on ideas or principles that have been invented, or discovered by this or that would-be universal reformer.

They merely express, in general terms, actual relations springing from an existing class struggle, from a historical movement going on under our very eyes. The abolition of existing property relations is not at all a distinctive feature of Communism.

All property relations in the past have continually been subject to historical change consequent upon the change in historical conditions.

The French Revolution, for example, abolished feudal property in favour of bourgeois property.

The distinguishing feature of Communism is not the abolition of property generally, but the abolition of bourgeois property. But modern bourgeois private property is the final and most complete expression of the system of producing and appropriating products, that is based on class antagonisms, on the exploitation of the many by the few.

In this sense, the theory of the Communists may be summed up in the single sentence: Abolition of private property.

We Communists have been reproached with the desire of abolishing the right of personally acquiring property as the fruit of a man's own labour, which property is alleged to be the groundwork of all personal freedom, activity and independence.

Hard-won, self-acquired, self-earned property! Do you mean the property of the petty artisan and of the small peasant, a form of property that preceded the bourgeois form? There is no need to abolish that; the development of industry has to a great extent already destroyed it, and is still destroying it daily.

Or do you mean modern bourgeois private property?

But does wage-labour create any property for the labourer? Not a bit. It creates capital, *i.e.,* that kind of property which exploits wage-labour, and which cannot increase except upon condition of begetting a new supply of wage-labour for fresh exploitation. Property, in its present form, is based on the antagonism of capital and wage-labour. Let us examine both sides of this antagonism.

To be a capitalist is to have not only a purely personal, but a social *status* in production. Capital is a collective product, and only by the united action of many members, nay, in the last resort, only by the united action of all members of society, can it be set in motion.

Capital is, therefore, not a personal, it is a social power.

When, therefore, capital is converted into common property, into the property of all members of society, personal property is not thereby transformed into social property. It is only the social character of the property that is changed. It loses its class character.

Let us now take wage-labour.

The average price of wage-labour is the minimum wage, *i.e.,* that quantum of the means of subsistence, which is absolutely requisite to keep the labourer in bare existence as a labourer. What, therefore, the wage-labourer appropriates by means of his labour, merely suffices to prolong and reproduce a bare existence. We by no means intend to abolish this personal appropriation of the products of labour, an appropriation that is made for the maintenance and reproduction of human life, and that leaves no surplus wherewith to command the labour of others. All that we want to do away with is the miserable character of this appropriation, under which the labourer lives merely to increase capital, and is allowed to live only in so far as the interest of the ruling class requires it.

In bourgeois society, living labour is but a means to increase accumulated labour. In Communist society, accumulated labour is but a means to widen, to enrich, to promote the existence of the labourer.

In bourgeois society, therefore, the past dominates the present; in Communist society, the present dominates the past. In bourgeois society capital is independent and has individuality, while the living person is dependent and has no individuality. And the abolition of this state of things is called by the bourgeois abolition of individuality and freedom! And rightly so. The abolition of bourgeois individuality, bourgeois independence, and bourgeois freedom is undoubtedly aimed at.

By freedom is meant, under the present bourgeois conditions of production, free trade, free selling and buying.

But if selling and buying disappears, free selling and buying disappears also. This talk about free selling and buying, and all the other "brave words" of our bourgeoisie about freedom in general, have a meaning, if any, only in contrast with restricted selling and buying, with the fettered traders of the Middle Ages, but have no meaning when opposed to the Communistic abolition of buying and selling, of the bourgeois conditions of production, and of the bourgeoisie itself.

You are horrified at our intending to do away with private property. But in your existing society, private property is already done away with for nine-tenths of the population; its existence for the few is solely due to its non-existence in the hands of those nine-tenths. You reproach us, therefore, with intending to do away with a form of property, the necessary condition for whose existence is the non-existence of any property for the immense majority of society.

In one word, you reproach us with intending to do away with your property. Precisely so; that is just what we intend.

From the moment when labour can no longer be converted into capital, money, or rent, into a social power capable of being monopolised, *i.e.,* from the moment when individual property can no longer be transformed into bourgeois property, into capital, from that moment, you say, individuality vanishes.

You must, therefore, confess that by "individual" you mean no other person than the bourgeois, than the middle-class owner of property. This person must, indeed, be swept out of the way, and made impossible.

Communism deprives no man of the power to appropriate the products of society; all that it does is to deprive him of the power to subjugate the labour of others by means of such appropriation.

It has been objected that upon the abolition of private property all work will cease, and universal laziness will overtake us.

According to this, bourgeois society ought long ago to have gone to the dogs through sheer idleness; for those of its members who work, acquire nothing, and those who acquire anything, do not work. The whole of this objection is but another expression of the tautology: that there can no longer be any wage-labour when there is no longer any capital.

All objections urged against the Communistic mode of producing and appropriating material products, have, in the same way, been urged against the Communistic modes of producing and appropriating intellectual products. Just as, to the bourgeois, the disappearance of class property is the disappearance of production itself, so the disappearance of class culture is to him identical with the disappearance of all culture.

That culture, the loss of which he laments, is, for the enormous majority, a mere training to act as a machine.

But don't wrangle with us so long as you apply, to our intended abolition of bourgeois property, the standard of your bourgeois notions of freedom, culture, law, &c. Your very ideas are but the outgrowth of the conditions of your bourgeois production and bourgeois property, just as your jurisprudence is but the will of your class made into a law for all, a will, whose essential character and direction are determined by the economical conditions of existence of your class.

The selfish misconception that induces you to transform into eternal laws of nature and of reason, the social forms springing from your present mode of production and form of property—historical relations that rise and disappear in the progress of production—this misconception you share with every ruling class that has preceded you. What you see clearly in the case of ancient property, what you admit in the case of feudal property, you are of course forbidden to admit in the case of your own bourgeois form of property.

Abolition of the family! Even the most radical flare up at this infamous proposal of the Communists.

On what foundation is the present family, the bourgeois family, based? On capital, on private gain. In its completely developed form this family exists only among the bourgeoisie. But this state of things finds its complement in the practical absence of the family among the proletarians, and in public prostitution.

The bourgeois family will vanish as a matter of course when its complement vanishes, and both will vanish with the vanishing of capital.

Do you charge us with wanting to stop the exploitation of children by their parents? To this crime we plead guilty.

But, you will say, we destroy the most hallowed of relations, when we replace home education by social.

And your education! Is not that also social, and determined by the social conditions under which you educate, by the intervention, direct or indirect, of society, by means of schools, &c.? The Communists have not invented the intervention of society in education; they do but seek to alter the character of that intervention, and to rescue education from the influence of the ruling class.

The bourgeois clap-trap about the family and education, about the hallowed co-relation of parent and child, becomes all the more disgusting, the more, by the action of Modern Industry, all family ties among the proletarians are torn asunder, and their children transformed into simple articles of commerce and instruments of labour.

But you Communists would introduce community of women, screams the whole bourgeoisie in chorus.

The bourgeois sees in his wife a mere instrument of production. He hears that the instruments of production are to be exploited in common, and, naturally, can come to no other conclusion than that the lot of being common to all will likewise fall to the women.

He has not even a suspicion that the real point aimed at is to do away with the status of women as mere instruments of production.

For the rest, nothing is more ridiculous than the virtuous indignation of our bourgeois at the community of women which, they pretend, is to be openly and officially established by the Communists. The Communists have no need to introduce community of women; it has existed almost from time immemorial.

Our bourgeois, not content with having the wives and daughters of their proletarians at their disposal, not to speak of common prostitutes, take the greatest pleasure in seducing each other's wives.

Bourgeois marriage is in reality a system of wives in common and thus, at the most, what the Communists might possibly be reproached with, is that they desire to introduce, in substitution for a hypocritically concealed, an openly legalised community of women. For the rest, it is self-evident that the abolition of the present system of production must bring with it the abolition of the community of women springing from that system, *i.e.,* of prostitution both public and private.

The Communists are further reproached with desiring to abolish countries and nationality.

The working men have no country. We cannot take from them what they have not got. Since the proletariat must first of all acquire political supremacy, must rise to be the leading class of the nation, must constitute itself *the* nation, it is so far, itself national, though not in the bourgeois sense of the word.

National differences and antagonisms between peoples are daily more and more vanishing, owing to the development of the bourgeoisie, to freedom of commerce, to the world market, to uniformity in the mode of production and in the conditions of life corresponding thereto.

The supremacy of the proletariat will cause them to vanish still faster. United action, of the leading civilised countries at least, is one of the first conditions for the emancipation of the proletariat.

In proportion as the exploitation of one individual by another is put an end to, the exploitation of one nation by another will also be put an end to. In proportion as the antagonism between classes within the nation vanishes, the hostility of one nation to another will come to an end.

The charges against Communism made from a religious, a philosophical, and, generally, from an ideological standpoint, are not deserving of serious examination.

Does it require deep intuition to comprehend that man's ideas, views and conceptions, in one word, man's consciousness, changes with every change in the conditions of his material existence, in his social relations and in his social life?

What else does the history of ideas prove, than that intellectual production changes its character in proportion as material production is changed? The ruling ideas of each age have ever been the ideas of its ruling class.

When people speak of ideas that revolutionise society, they do but express the fact, that within the old society, the elements of a new one have been created, and that the dissolution of the old ideas keeps even pace with the dissolution of the old conditions of existence.

When the ancient world was in its last throes, the ancient religions were overcome by Christianity. When Christian ideas succumbed in the 18th century to rationalist ideas, feudal society fought its death battle with the then revolutionary bourgeoisie.

The ideas of religious liberty and freedom of conscience merely gave expression to the sway of free competition within the domain of knowledge.

"Undoubtedly," it will be said, "religious, moral, philosophical and juridical ideas have been modified in the course of historical development. But religion, morality, philosophy, political science, and law, constantly survived this change.

"There are, besides, eternal truths, such as Freedom, Justice, etc., that are common to all states of society. But Communism abolishes eternal truths, it abolishes all religion and all morality, instead of constituting them on a new basis; it therefore acts in contradiction to all past historical experience."

What does this accusation reduce itself to? The history of all past society has consisted in the development of class antagonisms, antagonisms that assumed different forms at different epochs.

But whatever form they may have taken, one fact is common to all past ages, *viz.,* the exploitation of one part of society by the other. No wonder, then, that the social consciousness of past ages, despite all the multiplicity and variety it displays, moves within certain common forms, or general ideas, which cannot completely vanish except with the total disappearance of class antagonisms.

The Communist revolution is the most radical rupture with traditional property relations; no wonder that its development involves the most radical rupture with traditional ideas.

But let us have done with the bourgeois objections to Communism.

We have seen above, that the first step in the revolution by the working class is to raise the proletariat to the position of ruling class, to win the battle of democracy.

The proletariat will use its political supremacy to wrest, by degrees, all capital from the bourgeoisie, to centralise all instruments of production in the hands of the State, *i.e.,* of the proletariat organised as the ruling class; and to increase the total of productive forces as rapidly as possible.

Of course, in the beginning, this cannot be effected except by means of despotic inroads on the rights of property, and on the conditions of bourgeois production; by means of measures, therefore, which appear economically insufficient and untenable, but which, in the course of the movement, outstrip themselves, necessitate further inroads upon the old social order, and are unavoidable as a means of entirely revolutionising the mode of production.

These measures will of course be different in different countries.

Nevertheless in the most advanced countries, the following will be pretty generally applicable:

1. Abolition of property in land and application of all rents of land to public purposes.
2. A heavy progressive or graduated income tax.
3. Abolition of all right of inheritance.
4. Confiscation of the property of all emigrants and rebels.
5. Centralisation of credit in the hands of the State, by means of a national bank with State capital and an exclusive monopoly.
6. Centralisation of the means of communication and transport in the hands of the State.

7. Extension of factories and instruments of production owned by the State; the bringing into cultivation of waste-lands, and the improvement of the soil generally in accordance with a common plan.
8. Equal liability of all to labour. Establishment of industrial armies, especially for agriculture.
9. Combination of agriculture with manufacturing industries; gradual abolition of the distinction between town and country, by a more equable distribution of the population over the country.
10. Free education for all children in public schools. Abolition of children's factory labour in its present form. Combination of education with industrial production, &c., &c.

When, in the course of development, class distinctions have disappeared, and all production has been concentrated in the hands of a vast association of the whole nation, the public power will lose its political character. Political power, properly so called, is merely the organised power of one class for oppressing another. If the proletariat during its contest with the bourgeoisie is compelled, by the force of circumstances, to organise itself as a class, if, by means of a revolution, it makes itself the ruling class, and, as such, sweeps away by force the old conditions of production, then it will, along with these conditions, have swept away the conditions for the existence of class antagonisms and of classes generally, and will thereby have abolished its own supremacy as a class.

In place of the old bourgeois society, with its classes and class antagonisms, we shall have an association, in which the free development of each is the condition for the free development of all.

III. Socialist and Communist Literature

1. Reactionary Socialism

a. Feudal Socialism
Owing to their historical position, it became the vocation of the aristocracies of France and England to write pamphlets against modern bourgeois society. In the French revolution of July 1830, and in the English reform agitation, these aristocracies again succumbed to the hateful upstart. Thenceforth, a serious political contest was altogether out of question. A literary battle alone remained possible. But even in the domain of literature the old cries of the restoration period had become impossible.

In order to arouse sympathy, the aristocracy were obliged to lose sight, apparently, of their own interests, and to formulate their indictment against the bourgeoisie in the interest of the exploited working class alone. Thus the aristocracy took their revenge by singing lampoons on their new master, and whispering in his ears sinister prophecies of coming catastrophe.

In this way arose feudal Socialism; half lamentation, half lampoon; half echo of the past, half menace of the future; at times, by its bitter, witty and incisive criticism, striking the bourgeoisie to the very heart's core; but always ludicrous in its effect, through total incapacity to comprehend the march of modern history.

The aristocracy, in order to rally the people to them, waved the proletarian alms-bag in front for a banner. But the people, so often as it joined them, saw on their hindquarters the old feudal coats of arms, and deserted with loud and irreverent laughter.

One section of the French Legitimists and "Young England" exhibited this spectacle.

In pointing out that their mode of exploitation was different to that of the bourgeoisie, the feudalists forget that they exploited under circumstances and conditions that were quite different, and that are now antiquated. In showing that, under their rule, the modern proletariat never existed, they forget that the modern bourgeoisie is the necessary offspring of their own form of society.

For the rest, so little do they conceal the reactionary character of their criticism that their chief accusation against the bourgeoisie amounts to this, that under the bourgeois *régime* a class is being developed, which is destined to cut up root and branch the old order of society.

What they upbraid the bourgeoisie with is not so much that it creates a proletariat, as that it creates a *revolutionary* proletariat.

In political practice, therefore, they join in all coercive measures against the working class; and in ordinary life, despite their high-falutin phrases, they stoop to pick up the golden apples dropped from the tree of industry, and to barter truth, love, and honour for traffic in wool, beetroot-sugar, and potato spirits.

As the parson has ever gone hand in hand with the landlord, so has Clerical Socialism with Feudal Socialism.

Nothing is easier than to give Christian asceticism a Socialist tinge. Has not Christianity declaimed against private property, against marriage, against the State? Has it not preached in the place of these, charity and poverty, celibacy and mortification of the flesh, monastic life and Mother Church? Christian Socialism is but the holy water with which the priest consecrates the heart-burnings of the aristocrat.

b. Petty-Bourgeois Socialism

The feudal aristocracy was not the only class that was ruined by the bourgeoisie, not the only class whose conditions of existence pined and perished in the atmosphere of modern bourgeois society. The medieval burgesses and the small peasant proprietors were the precursors of the modern bourgeoisie. In those countries which are but little developed, industrially and commercially, these two classes still vegetate side by side with the rising bourgeoisie.

In countries where modern civilisation has become fully developed, a new class of petty bourgeois has been formed, fluctuating between proletariat and bourgeoisie and ever renewing itself as a supplementary part of bourgeois society. The individual members of this class, however, are being constantly hurled down into the proletariat by the action of competition, and, as modern industry develops, they even see the moment approaching when they will completely disappear as an independent section of modern society, to be replaced, in manufactures, agriculture and commerce, by overlookers, bailiffs and shopmen.

In countries like France, where the peasants constitute far more than half of the population, it was natural that writers who sided with the proletariat against the bourgeoisie, should use, in their criticism of the bourgeois *régime,* the standard of the peasant and petty bourgeois, and from the standpoint of these intermediate classes should take up the cudgels for the working class. Thus arose petty-bourgeois Socialism. Sismondi was the head of this school, not only in France but also in England.

This school of Socialism dissected with great acuteness the contradictions in the conditions of modern production. It laid bare the hypocritical apologies of economists. It proved, incontrovertibly, the disastrous effects of machinery and division of labour; the concentration of capital and land in a few hands; over-production and crises; it pointed out the inevitable ruin of the petty bourgeois and peasant, the misery of the proletariat, the anarchy in production, the crying inequalities in the distribution of wealth, the industrial war of extermination between nations, the dissolution of old moral bonds, of the old family relations, of the old nationalities.

In its positive aims, however, this form of Socialism aspires either to restoring the old means of production and of exchange, and with them the old property relations, and the old society, or to cramping the modern means of production and of exchange, within the framework of the old property relations that have been, and were bound to be, exploded by those means. In either case, it is both reactionary and Utopian.

Its last words are: corporate guilds for manufacture; patriarchal relations in agriculture.

Ultimately, when stubborn historical facts had dispersed all intoxicating effects of self-deception, this form of Socialism ended in a miserable fit of the blues.

c. German, or "True," Socialism

The Socialist and Communist literature of France, a literature that originated under the pressure of a bourgeoisie in power, and that was the expression of the struggle against this power, was introduced into Germany at a time when the bourgeoisie, in that country, had just begun its contest with feudal absolutism.

German philosophers, would-be philosophers, and *beaux esprits*, eagerly seized on this literature, only forgetting, that when these writings immigrated from France into Germany, French social conditions had not immigrated along with them. In contact with German social conditions, this French literature lost all its immediate practical significance, and assumed a purely literary aspect. Thus, to the German philosophers of the Eighteenth Century, the demands of the first French Revolution were nothing more than the demands of "Practical Reason" in general, and the utterance of the will of the revolutionary French bourgeoisie signified in their eyes the laws of pure Will, of Will as it was bound to be, of true human Will generally.

The work of the German *literati* consisted solely in bringing the new French ideas into harmony with their ancient philosophical conscience, or rather, in annexing the French ideas without deserting their own philosophic point of view.

This annexation took place in the same way in which a foreign language is appropriated, namely, by translation.

It is well known how the monks wrote silly lives of Catholic Saints *over* the manuscripts on which the classical works of ancient heathendom had been written. The German *literati* reversed this process with the profane French literature. They wrote their philosophical nonsense beneath the French original. For instance, beneath the French criticism of the economic functions of money, they wrote "Alienation of Humanity," and beneath the French criticism of the bourgeois State they wrote, "Dethronement of the Category of the General," and so forth.

The introduction of these philosophical phrases at the back of the French historical criticisms they dubbed "Philosophy of Action," "True Socialism," "German Science of Socialism," "Philosophical Foundation of Socialism," and so on.

The French Socialist and Communist literature was thus completely emasculated. And, since it ceased in the hands of the German to express the struggle of one class with the other, he felt conscious of having overcome "French one-sidedness" and of representing, not true requirements, but the requirements of Truth; not the interests of the proletariat, but the interests of Human Nature, of Man in general, who belongs to no class, has no reality, who exists only in the misty realm of philosophical fantasy.

This German Socialism, which took its schoolboy task so seriously and solemnly, and extolled its poor stock-in-trade in such mountebank fashion, meanwhile gradually lost its pedantic innocence.

The fight of the German, and, especially, of the Prussian bourgeoisie, against feudal aristocracy and absolute monarchy, in other words, the liberal movement, became more earnest.

By this, the long wished-for opportunity was offered to "True" Socialism of confronting the political movement with the Socialist demands, of hurling the traditional anathemas against liberalism, against representative government, against bourgeois competition, bourgeois freedom of the press, bourgeois legislation, bourgeois liberty and equality, and of preaching to the masses that they had nothing to gain, and everything to lose, by this bourgeois movement. German Socialism forgot, in the nick of time, that the French criticism, whose silly echo it was, presupposed the existence of modern bourgeois society, with its corresponding economic conditions of existence, and the political constitution adapted thereto, the very things whose attainment was the object of the pending struggle in Germany.

To the absolute governments, with their following of parsons, professors, country squires and officials, it served as a welcome scarecrow against the threatening bourgeoisie.

It was a sweet finish after the bitter pills of floggings and bullets with which these same governments, just at that time, dosed the German working-class risings.

While this "True" Socialism thus served the governments as a weapon for fighting the German bourgeoisie, it, at the same time, directly represented a reactionary interest, the interest of the German Philistines. In Germany the *petty-bourgeois* class, a relic of the sixteenth century, and since then constantly cropping up again under various forms, is the real social basis of the existing state of things.

To preserve this class is to preserve the existing state of things in Germany. The industrial and political supremacy of the bourgeoisie threatens it with certain destruction; on the one hand, from the concentration of capital; on the other, from the rise of a revolutionary proletariat. "True" Socialism appeared to kill these two birds with one stone. It spread like an epidemic.

The robe of speculative cobwebs, embroidered with flowers of rhetoric, steeped in the dew of sickly sentiment, this transcendental robe in which the German Socialists wrapped their sorry "eternal truths," all skin and bone, served to wonderfully increase the sale of their goods amongst such a public.

And on its part, German Socialism recognised, more and more, its own calling as the bombastic representative of the petty-bourgeois Philistine.

It proclaimed the German nation to be the model nation, and the German petty Philistine to be the typical man. To every villainous meanness of this model man it gave a hidden, higher, Socialistic interpretation, the exact contrary of its real character. It went to the extreme length of directly opposing the "brutally destructive" tendency of Communism, and of proclaiming its supreme and impartial contempt of all class struggles. With very few exceptions, all the so-called Socialist and Communist publications that now (1847) circulate in Germany belong to the domain of this foul and enervating literature.

2. CONSERVATIVE, OR BOURGEOIS, SOCIALISM

A part of the bourgeoisie is desirous of redressing social grievances, in order to secure the continued existence of bourgeois society.

To this section belong economists, philanthropists, humanitarians, improvers of the condition of the working class, organisers of charity, members of societies for the prevention of cruelty to animals, temperance fanatics, hole-and-corner reformers of every imaginable kind. This form of Socialism has, moreover, been worked out into complete systems.

We may cite Proudhon's *Philosophie de la Misére* as an example of this form.

The Socialistic bourgeois want all the advantages of modern social conditions without the struggles and dangers necessarily resulting therefrom. They desire the existing state of society minus its revolutionary and disintegrating elements. They wish for a bourgeoisie without a proletariat. The bourgeoisie naturally conceives the world in which it is supreme to be the best; and bourgeois Socialism develops this comfortable conception into various more or less complete systems. In requiring the proletariat to carry out such a system, and thereby to march straightway into the social New Jerusalem, it but requires in reality, that the proletariat should remain within the bounds of existing society, but should cast away all its hateful ideas concerning the bourgeoisie.

A second and more practical, but less systematic, form of this Socialism sought to depreciate every revolutionary movement in the eyes of the working class, by showing that no mere political reform, but only a change in the material conditions of existence, in economical relations, could be of any advantage to them. By changes in the material conditions of existence, this form of Socialism, however, by no means understands abolition of the bourgeois relations of production, an abolition that can be effected only by a revolution, but administrative reforms, based on the continued existence of these relations; reforms, therefore, that in no respect affect the relations between capital and labour, but, at the best, lessen the cost, and simplify the administrative work, of bourgeois government.

Bourgeois Socialism attains adequate expression, when, and only when, it becomes a mere figure of speech.

Free trade: for the benefit of the working class. Protective duties: for the benefit of the working class. Prison Reform: for the benefit of the working class. This is the last word and the only seriously meant word of bourgeois Socialism.

It is summed up in the phrase: the bourgeois is a bourgeois—for the benefit of the working class.

3. CRITICAL-UTOPIAN SOCIALISM AND COMMUNISM

We do not here refer to that literature which, in every great modern revolution, has always given voice to the demands of the proletariat, such as the writings of Babeuf and others.

The first direct attempts of the proletariat to attain its own ends, made in times of universal excitement, when feudal society was being overthrown, these attempts necessarily failed, owing to the then undeveloped state of the proletariat, as well as to the absence of the economic conditions for its emancipation, conditions that had yet to be produced, and could be produced by the impending bourgeois epoch alone. The revolutionary literature that accompanied these first movements of the proletariat had necessarily a reactionary character. It inculcated universal asceticism and social levelling in its crudest form.

The Socialist and Communist systems properly so called, those of Saint-Simon, Fourier, Owen and others, spring into existence in the early undeveloped period, described above, of the struggle between proletariat and bourgeoisie (see Section I. Bourgeois and Proletarians).

The founders of these systems see, indeed, the class antagonisms, as well as the action of the decomposing elements in the prevailing form of society. But the proletariat, as yet in its infancy, offers to them the spectacle of a class without any historical initiative or any independent political movement.

Since the development of class antagonism keeps even pace with the development of industry, the economic situation, as they find it, does not as yet offer to them the material conditions for the emancipation of the proletariat. They therefore search after a new social science, after new social laws, that are to create these conditions.

Historical action is to yield to their personal inventive action, historically created conditions of emancipation to fantastic ones, and the gradual, spontaneous class organisation of the proletariat to an organisation of society specially contrived by these inventors. Future history resolves itself, in their eyes, into the propaganda and the practical carrying out of their social plans.

In the formation of their plans they are conscious of caring chiefly for the interests of the working class, as being the most suffering class. Only from the point of view of being the most suffering class does the proletariat exist for them.

The undeveloped state of the class struggle, as well as their own surroundings, causes Socialists of this kind to consider themselves far superior to all class antagonisms. They want to improve the condition of every member of society, even that of the most favoured. Hence, they habitually appeal to society at large, without distinction of class; nay, by preference, to the ruling class. For how can people, when once they understand their system, fail to see in it the best possible plan of the best possible state of society?

Hence, they reject all political, and especially all revolutionary, action; they wish to attain their ends by peaceful means, and endeavour, by small experiments, necessarily doomed to failure, and by the force of example, to pave the way for the new social Gospel.

Such fantastic pictures of future society, painted at a time when the proletariat is still in a very undeveloped state and has but a fantastic conception of its own position, correspond with the first instinctive yearnings of that class for a general reconstruction of society.

But these Socialist and Communist publications contain also a critical element. They attack every principle of existing society. Hence they are full of the most valuable materials for the enlightenment of the working class. The practical measures proposed in them—such as the abolition of the distinction between town and country, of the family, of the carrying on of industries for the account of private individuals, and of the wage system, the proclamation of social harmony, the conversion of the functions of the State into a mere superintendence of production, all these proposals point solely to the disappearance of class antagonisms which were, at that time, only just cropping up, and which, in these publications, are recognised in their earliest indistinct and undefined forms only. These proposals, therefore, are of a purely Utopian character.

The significance of Critical-Utopian Socialism and Communism bears an inverse relation to historical development. In proportion as the modern class struggle develops and takes definite shape, this fantastic standing apart from the contest, these fantastic attacks on it, lose all practical value and all theoretical justification. Therefore, although the originators of these systems were, in many respects, revolutionary, their disciples have, in every case, formed mere reactionary sects. They hold fast by the original views of their masters, in opposition to the progressive historical development of the proletariat. They, therefore, endeavour, and that consistently, to deaden the class struggle and to reconcile the class antagonisms. They still dream of experimental realisation of their social Utopias, of founding isolated "phalanstéres," of establishing "Home Colonies," of setting up a "Little Icaria"—duodecimo editions of the New Jerusalem—and to realise all these castles in the air, they are compelled to appeal to the feelings and purses of the bourgeois. By degrees they sink into the category of the reactionary [or] conservative Socialists depicted above, differing from these only by more systematic pedantry, and by their fanatical and superstitious belief in the miraculous effects of their social science.

They, therefore, violently oppose all political action on the part of the working class; such action, according to them, can only result from blind unbelief in the new Gospel.

The Owenites in England, and the Fourierists in France, respectively oppose the Chartists and the *Réformistes.*

IV. POSITION OF THE COMMUNISTS IN RELATION TO THE VARIOUS EXISTING OPPOSITION PARTIES

Section II has made clear the relations of the Communists to the existing working-class parties, such as the Chartists in England and the Agrarian Reformers in America.

The Communists fight for the attainment of the immediate aims, for the enforcement of the momentary interests of the working class; but in the movement of the present, they also represent and take care of the future of that movement. In France the Communists ally themselves with the Social-Democrats, against the conservative and radical bourgeoisie, reserving, however, the right to take up a critical position in regard to phrases and illusions traditionally handed down from the great Revolution.

In Switzerland they support the Radicals, without losing sight of the fact that this party consists of antagonistic elements, partly of Democratic Socialists, in the French sense, partly of radical bourgeois.

In Poland they support the party that insists on an agrarian revolution as the prime condition for national emancipation, that party which fomented the insurrection of Cracow in 1846.

In Germany they fight with the bourgeoisie whenever it acts in a revolutionary way, against the absolute monarchy, the feudal squirearchy, and the petty bourgeoisie.

But they never cease, for a single instant, to instil into the working class the clearest possible recognition of the hostile antagonism between bourgeoisie and proletariat, in order that the German workers may straightway use, as so many weapons against the bourgeoisie, the social and political conditions that the bourgeoisie must necessarily introduce along with its supremacy, and in order that, after the fall of the reactionary classes in Germany, the fight against the bourgeoisie itself may immediately begin.

The Communists turn their attention chiefly to Germany, because that country is on the eve of a bourgeois revolution that is bound to be carried out under more advanced conditions of European civilisation, and with a much more developed proletariat, than that of England was in the seventeenth, and of France in the eighteenth century, and because the bourgeois revolution in Germany will be but the prelude to an immediately following proletarian revolution.

In short, the Communists everywhere support every revolutionary movement against the existing social and political order of things.

In all these movements they bring to the front, as the leading question in each, the property question, no matter what its degree of development at the time.

Finally, they labour everywhere for the union and agreement of the democratic parties of all countries.

The Communists disdain to conceal their views and aims. They openly declare that their ends can be attained only by the forcible overthrow of all existing social conditions. Let the ruling classes tremble at a Communistic revolution. The proletarians have nothing to lose but their chains. They have a world to win.

WORKING MEN OF ALL COUNTRIES, UNITE!

Written in December 1847–January 1848.
First published as a separate edition in London in February 1848.
Printed according to the text of the English edition of 1888, checked with the German editions of 1848, 1872, 1883, and 1890.

CHAPTER 2

"SPEECH ON FREE TRADE," WITH ENGELS'S PREFACE OF 1888

THE OCCASION OF MARX'S SPEECH IN BRUSSELS WAS THE EFFORT to overturn the "Corn Laws," a restrictive tariff on imports of various grains into England, including wheat, barley, and "maize." With the conclusion of the Napoleonic wars in 1815, the price of agricultural goods plummeted. To protect themselves, landlords pushed through the bitterly contested Corn Laws, which were in effect from 1815 until 1846.[1] The Corn Laws protected British landlords from competition from agriculture abroad. Manufacturers wanted their elimination on general free trade grounds but also because cheaper grains meant cheaper foodstuffs, allowing them to reduce wages. The Corn Laws were abolished in 1846, but the arguments over free trade continued and still do.

The discussion of Marx and Engels is very illuminating in the context of debates over free trade today. Included is not only Marx's original lecture from early 1848 but also Engels's introduction for an English edition for an American audience, published forty years later. Engels's preface is as long as the original and is of interest for a number of reasons. In his overview of developments in the nineteenth century, Engels gives sound arguments for when protectionism is useful to a country for building its manufacturing base, as he and Marx both put it, for "manufacturing manufacturers." However, Engels also points out that protecting certain industries that provide inputs for other industries can adversely affect the competitiveness of the latter, especially when many companies have developed to the point that they must become exporters of their products. Although fierce battles among interest groups continue, Engels argues that at a certain stage, a country will nonetheless find itself "drifting slowly though not majestically in the direction of Free Trade."[2]

Marx's own essay is distinguished by bringing out the three-way class interests involved in his own day: manufacturers, landlords, and workers. Although a proponent of free trade, he skewers the double-talk of the manufacturers, who justify the policy by claiming that it is in the interest of the working class, an interest manufacturers fiercely resist in other areas. Marx focuses his argument on the effects of free trade driving down the cost of necessaries, which, given competition for jobs, presents manufacturers with a pretext for driving down wages.

Marx and Engels are both clear that the debate over free trade is entirely confined within the existing capitalist relations of production. They support free trade on the very narrow but important grounds that free trade does hasten the development of the productive forces. Free trade therefore builds the foundation for a different organization of society, one free of the periodic and devastating convulsions that are inescapably a part of the dynamic of capitalism.

NOTES

1. E. J. Hobsbawm, *Industry and Empire* (London: Penguin Books, 1968), pp. 99–100. The British use the word "corn" as a general term to refer to various grains and "maize" for what Americans call corn. In the original French of Marx's speech, the corn laws are called "lois céréales."
2. Below. An excellent overview of the history of debates about free trade is Douglas A. Irwin, *Against the Tide: An Intellectual History of Free Trade* (Princeton, NJ: Princeton University Press, 1996).

Protection and Free Trade Preface to the Pamphlet: Karl Marx, Speech on the Question of Free Trade

[Frederick Engels]

Towards the end of 1847, a Free Trade Congress was held at Brussels. It was a strategic move in the Free Trade campaign then carried on by the English manufacturers. Victorious at home, by the repeal of the Corn Laws in 1846, they now invaded the continent in order to demand, in return for the free admission of continental corn into England, the free admission of English manufactured goods to the continental markets. At this Congress, Marx inscribed himself on the list of speakers; but, as might have been expected, things were so managed that before his turn came on, the Congress was closed. Thus, what Marx had to say on the Free Trade question, he was compelled to say before the Democratic Association of Brussels, an international body of which he was one of the vice-presidents.

The question of Free Trade or Protection being at present on the order of the day in America, it has been thought useful to publish an English translation of Marx' speech, to which I have been asked to write an introductory preface.

"The system of protection," says Marx, "was an artificial means of manufacturing manufacturers, of expropriating independent laborers, of capitalizing the national means of production and subsistence, and of forcibly abbreviating the transition from the medieval to the modern mode of production." Such was protection at its origin in the seventeenth century; such it remained well into the nineteenth century. It was then held to be the normal policy of every civilized state in Western Europe. The only exceptions were the smaller states of Germany and Switzerland—not from dislike of the system, but from the impossibility of applying it to such small territories.

It was under the fostering wing of protection that the system of modern industry—production by steam-moved machinery—was hatched and developed in England during the last third of the eighteenth century. And, as if tariff-protection was not sufficient, the wars against the French Revolution helped to secure to

England the monopoly of the new industrial methods. For more than twenty years English men-of-war cut off the industrial rivals of England from their respective colonial markets, while they forcibly opened these markets to English commerce. The secession of the South American colonies from the rule of their European mother-countries, the conquest by England of all French and Dutch colonies worth having, the progressive subjugation of India, turned the people of all these immense territories into customers for English goods. England thus supplemented the protection she practised at home, by the Free Trade she forced upon her possible customers abroad; and, thanks to this happy mixture of both systems, at the end of the wars, in 1815, she found herself, with regard to all important branches of industry, in possession of the virtual monopoly of the trade of the world.

This monopoly was further extended and strengthened during the ensuing years of peace. The start which England had obtained during the war, was increased from year to year; she seemed to distance more and more all her possible rivals. The exports of manufactured goods in ever growing quantities became indeed a question of life and death to that country. And there seemed but two obstacles in the way: the prohibitive or protective legislation of other countries, and the taxes upon the import of raw materials and articles of food in England.

Then the Free Trade doctrines of classical political economy—of the French physiocrats and their English successors, Adam Smith and Ricardo—became popular in the land of John Bull. Protection at home was needless to manufacturers who beat all their foreign rivals, and whose very existence was staked on the expansion of their exports. Protection at home was of advantage to none but the producers of articles of food and other raw materials, to the agricultural interest, which, under then existing circumstances in England, meant the receivers of rent, the landed aristocracy. And this kind of protection was hurtful to the manufacturers. By taxing raw materials it raised the price of the articles manufactured from them; by taxing food, it raised the price of labor; in both ways, it placed the British manufacturer at a disadvantage as compared with his foreign competitor. And, as all other countries sent to England chiefly agricultural products, and drew from England chiefly manufactured goods, repeal of the English protective duties on corn and raw materials generally, was at the same time an appeal to foreign countries, to do away with, or at least, to reduce, in return, the import duties levied by them on English manufactures.

After a long and violent struggle, the English industrial capitalists, already in reality the leading class of the nation, that class whose interests were then the chief national interests, were victorious. The landed aristocracy had to give in. The duties on corn and other raw materials were repealed. Free Trade became the watchword of the day. To convert all other countries to the gospel of Free Trade, and thus to create a world in which England was the great manufacturing centre, with all other countries for its dependent agricultural districts, that was the next task before the English manufacturers and their mouthpieces, the political economists.

That was the time of the Brussels Congress, the time when Marx prepared the speech in question. While recognizing that protection may still, under certain circumstances, for instance in the Germany of 1847, be of advantage to the manufacturing capitalists; while proving that Free Trade was not the panacea for all the evils under which the working class suffered, and might even aggravate them; he pronounces, ultimately and on principle, in favor of Free Trade. To him, Free Trade is the normal condition of modern capitalistic production. Only under Free Trade can the immense productive powers of steam, of electricity, of machinery, be fully developed; and the quicker the pace of this development, the sooner and the more fully will be realized its inevitable results: society splits up into two classes, capitalists here, wage-laborers there; hereditary wealth on one side, hereditary poverty on the other; supply outstripping demand, the markets being unable to absorb the ever growing mass of the productions of industry; an ever recurring cycle of prosperity, glut, crisis, panic, chronic depression and gradual revival of trade, the harbinger not of permanent improvement but of renewed overproduction and crisis; in short, productive forces expanding to such a degree that they rebel, as against unbearable fetters, against the social institutions under which they are put in motion; the only possible solution: a social revolution, freeing the social productive forces from the fetters of an anti-quated social order, and the actual producers, the great mass of the people, from wage-slavery. And because Free Trade is the natural, the normal atmosphere for this historical evolution, the economic medium in which the conditions for the inevitable social revolution will be the soonest created,—for this reason, and for this alone, did Marx declare in favor of Free Trade.

Anyhow, the years immediately following the victory of Free Trade in England seemed to verify the most extravagant expectations of prosperity founded upon that event. British commerce rose to a fabulous amount; the industrial monopoly of England on the market of the world seemed more firmly established than ever; new iron works, new textile factories arose by wholesale; new branches of industry grew up on every side. There was, indeed, a severe crisis in 1857, but that was overcome, and the onward movement in trade and manufactures soon was in full swing again, until in 1866 a fresh panic occurred, a panic, this time, which seems to mark a new departure in the economic history of the world.

The unparalleled expansion of British manufactures and commerce between 1848 and 1866 was no doubt due, to a great extent, to the removal of the protective duties on food and raw materials. But not entirely. Other important changes took place simultaneously and helped it on. The above years comprise the discovery and working of the Californian and Australian gold fields which increased so immensely the circulating medium of the world; they mark the final victory of steam over all other means of transport; on the ocean, steamers now superseded sailing vessels; on land, in all civilized countries, the railroad took the first place, the macadamized road the second; transport now became four times quicker and four times cheaper. No wonder that under such favorable circumstances British manufactures worked by steam should extend their sway at the expense of foreign domestic industries based upon manual labor. But were the other countries to sit still and to submit in humility to this change, which degraded them to be mere agricultural appendages of England, the "workshop of the world"?

The foreign countries did nothing of the kind. France, for nearly two hundred years, had screened her manufactures behind a perfect Chinese wall of protection and prohibition, and had attained in all articles of luxury and of taste a supremacy which England did not even pretend to dispute. Switzerland, under perfect Free Trade, possessed relatively important manufactures which English competition could not touch. Germany, with a tariff far more liberal than that of any other large continental country, was developing its manufactures at a rate relatively more rapid than even England. And America was, by the civil war of 1861, all at once thrown upon her own resources, had to find means how to meet a sudden demand for manufactured goods of all sorts, and could only do so by creating manufactures of her own at home. The war demand ceased with the war; but the new manufactures were there, and had to meet British competition. And the war had ripened, in America, the insight that a nation of thirty-five millions, doubling its numbers in forty years at most, with such immense resources, and surrounded by neighbors that must be for years to come chiefly agriculturalists, that such a nation had the "manifest destiny" to be independent of foreign manufactures for its chief articles of consumption, and to be so in time of peace as well as in time of war. And then America turned protectionist.

It may now be fifteen years ago, I travelled in a railway carriage with an intelligent Glasgow merchant, interested, probably, in the iron trade. Talking about America, he treated me to the old Free Trade lucubrations: "Was it not inconceivable that a nation of sharp business men like the Americans should pay tribute to indigenous iron masters and manufacturers, when they could buy the same, if not a better article, ever so much cheaper in this country?" And then he gave me examples as to how much the Americans taxed themselves in order to enrich a few greedy iron masters. "Well," I replied, "I think there is another side to the question. You know that in coal, water-power, iron and other ores, cheap food, home-grown cotton and other raw materials, America has resources and advantages unequalled by any European country; and that these resources cannot be fully developed except by America becoming a manufacturing country. You will admit, too, that nowadays a great nation like the Americans cannot exist on agriculture alone; that that would be tantamount to a condemnation to permanent barbarism and inferiority; no great nation can live, in our age, without manufactures of her own. Well, then, if America must become a manufacturing country, and if she has every chance of not only succeeding, but even outstripping her rivals, there are two ways open to her: either to carry on, for let us say fifty years, under Free Trade an extremely expensive competitive war against English manufactures that have got nearly a hundred years' start; or else to shut out, by protective duties, English manufactures, for say twenty-five years, with the almost absolute certainty that at the end of the twenty-five years she will be able to hold her own in the open market of the world. Which of the two will be the cheapest and the shortest? That is the question. If you want to go from Glasgow to London, you can take the parliamentary train at a penny a mile and travel at the rate of twelve miles an hour. But you do not; your time is too valuable, you take the express, pay twopence a mile and do forty miles an hour. Very well, the Americans prefer to pay express fare and to go express speed." My Scotch Free Trader had not a word in reply.

Protection, being a means of artificially manufacturing manufacturers, may, therefore, appear useful not only to an incompletely developed capitalist class still struggling with feudalism; it may also give a lift to the rising capitalist class of a country which, like America, has never known feudalism, but which has arrived at that stage of development where the passage from agriculture to manufactures becomes a necessity. America, placed in that situation, decided in favor of protection. Since that decision was carried out, the five and twenty years of which I spoke to my fellow-traveller have about passed, and, if I was not wrong, protection ought to have done its task for America, and ought to be now becoming a nuisance.

That has been my opinion for some time. Nearly two years ago, I said to a protectionist American: "I am convinced that if America goes in for Free Trade she will in ten years have beaten England in the market of the world."

Protection is at best an endless screw, and you never know when you have done with it. By protecting one industry, you directly or indirectly hurt all others, and have therefore to protect them too. By so doing you again damage the industry that you first protected, and have to compensate it; but this compensation reacts, as before, on all other trades, and entitles them to redress, and so on *in infinitum*. America, in this respect, offers us a striking example of the best way to kill an important industry by protection. In 1856, the total imports and exports by sea of the United States amounted to $641,604,850, of this amount, 75.2 per cent. were carried in American, and only 24.8 per cent. in foreign vessels. British ocean-steamers were already then encroaching upon American sailing vessels; yet, in 1860, of a total sea-going trade of $762,288,550, American vessels still carried 66.5 per cent. The civil war came on, and protection to American ship-building; and the latter plan was so successful that it has nearly completely driven the American flag from the high seas. In 1887 the total sea-going trade of the United States amounted to $1,408,502,979, but of this total only 13.8 per cent. were carried in American, and 86.2 per cent. in foreign bottoms. The goods carried by American ships amounted, in 1856, to $482,268,274; in 1860 to $507,247,757. In 1887 they had sunk to $194,356,746. Forty years ago, the American flag was the most dangerous rival of the British flag, and bade fair to outstrip it on the ocean; now it is nowhere. Protection to ship-building has killed both shipping and ship-building.

Another point. Improvements in the methods of production nowadays follow each other so rapidly, and change the character of entire branches of industry so suddenly and so completely, that what may have been yesterday a fairly balanced protective tariff is no longer so to-day. Let us take another example from the Report of the Secretary of the Treasury for 1887:

> Improvement in recent years in the machinery employed in combing wool has so changed the character of what are commercially known as worsted cloths that the latter have largely superseded woollen cloths for use as men's wearing apparel. This change . . . has operated to the serious injury of our domestic manufacturers of these (worsted) goods, because the duty on the wool which they must use is the same as that upon wool used in making woollen cloths, while the rates of duty imposed upon the latter when valued at not exceeding 80 cents per pound are 35 cents per pound and 35 per cent. ad valorem, whereas the duty on worsted cloths valued at not exceeding 80 cents ranges from 10 to 24 cents per pound and 35 per cent. ad valorem. In some cases the duty on the wool used in making worsted cloths *exceeds the duty imposed on the finished article.*

Thus what was protection to home industry yesterday, turns out to-day to be a premium to the foreign importer; and well may the Secretary of the Treasury say:

"There is much reason to believe that the manufacture of worsted cloths must soon cease in this country unless the tariff law in this regard is amended" (p. XIX).

But to amend it, you will have to fight the manufacturers of woollen cloths who profit by this state of things; you will have to open a regular campaign to bring the majority of both Houses of Congress, and eventually the public opinion of the country, round to your views, and the question is, Will that pay?

But the worst of protection is, that when you once have got it you cannot easily get rid of it. Difficult as is the process of adjustment of an equitable tariff, the return to Free Trade is immensely more difficult. The circumstances which permitted England to accomplish the change in a few years, will not occur again. And even there the struggle dated from 1823 (Huskisson), commenced to be successful in 1842 (Peel's tariff), and was continued for several years after the repeal of the Corn Laws. Thus protection to the silk manufacture (the only one which had still to fear foreign competition) was prolonged for a series of years and then granted in another, positively infamous form; while the other textile industries were subjected to the Factory Act, which limited the hours of labor of women, young persons and children, the silk trade was favored with considerable exceptions to the general rule, enabling them to work younger children, and to work the children and young persons longer hours, than the other textile trades. The monopoly that the hypocritical Free Traders repealed with regard to the foreign competitors, that monopoly they created anew at the expense of the health and lives of English children.

But no country will again be able to pass from Protection to Free Trade at a time when all, or nearly all branches of its manufactures can defy foreign competition in the open market. The necessity of the change will come long before such a happy state may be even hoped for. That necessity will make itself evident in different trades at different times; and from the conflicting interests of these trades, the most edifying squabbles, lobby intrigues, and parliamentary conspiracies will arise. The machinist, engineer, and ship-builder may find that the protection granted to the iron master raises the price of his goods so much that his export trade is thereby, and thereby alone, prevented; the cotton-cloth manufacturer might see his way to driving English cloth out of the Chinese and Indian markets, but for the high price he has to pay for the yarn, on account of protection to spinners; and so forth. The moment a branch of national industry has completely conquered the home market, that moment exportation becomes a necessity to it. Under capitalistic conditions, an industry either expands or wanes. A trade cannot remain stationary; stoppage of expansion is incipient ruin; the progress of mechanical and chemical invention, by constantly superseding human labor, and ever more rapidly increasing and concentrating capital, creates in every stagnant industry a glut both of workers and of capital, a glut which finds no vent everywhere, because the same process is taking place in all other industries. Thus the passage from a home to an export trade becomes a question of life and death for the industries concerned; but they are met by the established rights, the vested interests of others who as yet find protection either safer or more profitable than Free Trade. Then ensues a long and obstinate fight between Free Traders and Protectionists; a fight where, on both sides, the leadership soon passes out of the hands of the people directly interested into those of professional politicians, the wire-pullers of the traditional political parties, whose interest is, not a settlement of the question, but its being kept open forever; and the result of an immense loss of time, energy, and money is a series of compromises, favoring now one, now the other side, and drifting slowly though not majestically in the direction of Free Trade—unless Protection manages, in the meantime, to make itself utterly insupportable to the nation, which is just now likely to be the case in America.

There is, however, another kind of protection, the worst of all, and that is exhibited in Germany. Germany, too, began to feel, soon after 1815, the necessity of a quicker development of her manufactures. But the first condition of that was the creation of a home market by the removal of the innumerable customs lines and varieties of fiscal legislation formed by the small German states, in other words, the formation of a German Customs Union or Zollverein. That could only be done on the basis of a liberal tariff, calculated rather to raise a common revenue than to protect home production. On no other condition could the small states have been induced to join. Thus the new German tariff, though slightly protective to some trades, was, at the time of its introduction, a model of Free Trade legislation; and it remained so, although, ever since 1830, the majority of German manufacturers kept clamoring for protection. Yet, under this extremely liberal tariff, and in spite of German domestic industries based on hand-labor being mercilessly crushed out by the competition of English factories worked by steam, the transition from manual labor to machinery was gradually accomplished in Germany too, and is now nearly complete; the transformation of Germany from an agricultural to a manufacturing country went on at the same pace, and was, since 1866, assisted by favorable political events: the establishment of a strong central government, and federal legislature, ensuring uniformity in the laws regulating trade, as well as in currency, weights and measures, and, finally, the flood of the French milliards. Thus, about 1874, German trade on the market of the world ranked next to that of Great Britain, and Germany employed more steam power in manufactures and locomotion than any European Continental country. The proof has thus been furnished that even nowadays, in spite of the enormous start that English industry has got, a large country can work its way up to successful competition, in the open market, with England.

Then, all at once, a change of front was made: Germany turned protectionist, at a moment when more than ever Free Trade seemed a necessity for her. The change was no doubt absurd; but it may be explained. While Germany had been a corn-exporting country, the whole agricultural interest, not less than the whole shipping trade, had been ardent Free Traders. But in 1874, instead of exporting, Germany required large supplies of corn from abroad. About that time, America began to flood Europe with enormous supplies of cheap corn; wherever they went, they brought down the money revenue yielded by the land, and consequently its rent; and from that moment, the agricultural interest, all over Europe, began to clamor for protection. At the same time, manufacturers in Germany were suffering from the effect of the reckless overtrading brought on by the influx of the French milliards, while England, whose trade, ever since the crisis of 1866, had been in a state of chronic depression, inundated all accessible markets with goods unsalable at home and offered abroad at ruinously low prices. Thus it happened that German manufacturers, though depending, above all, upon export, began to see in protection a means of securing to themselves the exclusive supply of the home market. And the government, entirely in the hands of the landed aristocracy and squirearchy, was only too glad to profit by this circumstance, in order to benefit the receivers of the rent of land, by offering protective duties to both landlords and manufacturers. In 1878, a highly protective tariff was enacted both for agricultural products and for manufactured goods.

The consequence was that henceforth the exportation of German manufactures was carried on at the direct cost of the home consumers. Wherever possible, "rings" or "trusts" were formed to regulate the export trade and even production itself. The German iron trade is in the hands of a few large firms, mostly joint stock companies, who, betwixt them, can produce about four times as much iron as the average consumption of the country can absorb. To avoid unnecessary competition with one another, these firms have formed a trust which divides amongst them all foreign contracts, and determines in each case the firm that is to make the real tender. This "trust," some years ago, had even come to an agreement with the English iron masters, but this no longer subsists. Similarly, the Westphalian coal mines (producing about thirty million tons annually) had formed a trust to regulate production, tenders for contracts, and prices. And, altogether, any German manufacturer will tell you that the only thing the protective duties do for him is to enable him to recoup himself in the home market for the ruinous prices he has to take abroad. And this is not all. This absurd system of protection to manufacturers is nothing but the sop thrown to industrial capitalists to induce them to support a still more outrageous monopoly given to the landed interest. Not only is all agricultural produce subjected to heavy import duties which are increased from year to year, but certain rural industries, carried on on large estates for account of the proprietor, are positively endowed out of the public purse. The beet-root sugar manufacture is not only protected, but receives enormous sums in the shape of export premiums. One who ought to know is of opinion that if the exported sugar was all thrown into the sea, the manufacturer would still clear a profit out of the government premium. Similarly, the potato-spirit distilleries receive, in consequence of recent legislation, a present, out of the pockets of the public, of about nine million dollars a year. And as almost every large land-owner in Northeastern Germany is either a beet-root sugar manufacturer or a potato-spirit distiller, or both, no wonder the world is literally deluged with their productions.

This policy, ruinous under any circumstances, is doubly so in a country whose manufactures keep up their standing in neutral markets chiefly through the cheapness of labor. Wages in Germany, kept near starvation point at the best of times, through redundancy of population (which increases rapidly, in spite of emigration), must rise in consequence of the rise in all necessaries caused by protection; the German manufacturer will, then, no longer be able, as he too often is now, to make up for a ruinous price of his articles by a deduction from the normal wages of his hands, and will be driven out of the market. Protection, in Germany, is killing the goose that lays the golden eggs.

France, too, suffers from the consequences of protection. The system, in that country, has become, by its two centuries of undisputed sway, almost part and parcel of the life of the nation. Nevertheless, it is more and more becoming an obstacle. Constant changes in the methods of manufacture are the order of the day; but protection bars the road. Silk velvets have their backs nowadays made of fine cotton thread; the French manufacturer has either to pay protection price for that, or to submit to such interminable official chicanery as fully makes up for the difference between that price and the government drawback on exportation; and so the velvet trade goes from Lyons to Crefeld, where the protection price for fine cotton thread is considerably lower. French exports, as said before, consist chiefly of articles of luxury, where French taste cannot, as yet, be beaten; but the chief consumers, all over the world, of such articles are our modern upstart capitalists who have no education and no taste, and who are suited quite as well by cheap and clumsy German or English imitations, and often have these foisted upon them for the real French article at more than fancy prices. The market for those specialties which cannot be made out of France is constantly getting narrower, French exports of manufactures are barely kept up, and must soon decline; by what new articles can France replace those whose export is dying out? If anything can help here, it is a bold measure of Free Trade, taking the French manufacturer out of his accustomed hothouse atmosphere and placing him once more in the open air of competition with foreign rivals. Indeed, French general trade would have long since begun shrinking, were it not for the slight and vacillating step in the direction of Free Trade made by the Cobden treaty of 1860, but that has well-nigh exhausted itself and a stronger dose of the same tonic is wanted.

It is hardly worth while to speak of Russia. There, the protective tariff—the duties having to be paid in gold, instead of in the depreciated paper currency of the country—serves above all things to supply the pauper government with the hard cash indispensable for transactions with foreign creditors; on the very day on which that tariff fulfils its protective mission by totally excluding foreign goods, on that day the Russian government is bankrupt. And yet that same government amuses its subjects by dangling before their eyes the prospect of making Russia, by means of this tariff, an entirely self-supplying country, requiring from the foreigner neither food, nor raw material, nor manufactured articles, nor works of art. The people who believe in this vision of a Russian Empire, secluded and isolated from the rest of the world, are on a level with the patriotic Prussian lieutenant who went into a shop and asked for a globe, not a terrestrial or a celestial one, but a globe of Prussia.

To return to America. There are plenty of symptoms that Protection has done all it could for the United States, and that the sooner it receives notice to quit, the better for all parties. One of these symptoms is the formation of "rings" and "trusts" within the protected industries for the more thorough exploitation of the monopoly granted to them. Now, "rings" and "trusts" are truly American institutions, and, where they exploit natural advantages, they are generally, though grumblingly, submitted to. The transformation of the Pennsylvanian oil supply into a monopoly by the Standard Oil Company is a proceeding entirely in keeping with the rules of capitalist production. But if the sugar-refiners attempt to transform the protection granted them, by the nation, against foreign competition, into a monopoly against the home consumer, that is to say against the same nation that granted the protection, that is quite a different thing. Yet the large sugar-refiners have formed a "trust" which aims at nothing else. And the sugar trust is not the only one of its kind. Now, the formation of such trusts in protected industries is the surest sign that protection has done its work, and is changing its character; that it protects the manufacturer no longer against the foreign importer, but against the home consumer; that it has manufactured, at least in the special branch concerned, quite enough, if not too many manufacturers; that the money it puts into the purse of these manufacturers is money thrown away, exactly as in Germany.

In America, as elsewhere, Protection is bolstered up by the argument that Free Trade will only benefit England. The best proof to the contrary is that in England not only the agriculturists and landlords but even the manufacturers are turning protectionists. In the home of the "Manchester school" of Free Traders, on Nov. 1, 1886, the Manchester chamber of commerce discussed a resolution

"that, having waited in vain forty years for other nations to follow the Free Trade example of England, the chamber thinks the time has arrived to reconsider that position."

The resolution was indeed rejected, but by 22 votes against 21! And that happened in the centre of the cotton manufacture, i.e., the only branch of English manufacture whose superiority in the open market seems still undisputed! But, then, even in that special branch inventive genius has passed from England to America. The latest improvements in machinery for spinning and weaving cotton have come, almost all, from America, and Manchester has to adopt them. In industrial inventions of all kinds, America has distinctly taken the lead, while Germany runs England very close for second place. The consciousness is gaining ground in England that that country's industrial monopoly is irretrievably lost, that she is still relatively losing ground, while her rivals are making progress, and that she is drifting into a position where she will have to be content with being one manufacturing nation among many, instead of, as she once dreamt, "the workshop of the world." It is to stave off this impending fate that Protection, scarcely disguised under the veil of "fair trade" and retaliatory tariffs, is now invoked with such fervor by the sons of the very men who, forty years ago, knew no salvation but in Free Trade. And when English manufacturers begin to find that Free Trade is ruining them, and ask the government to protect them against their foreign competitors, then, surely, the moment has come for these competitors to retaliate by throwing overboard a protective system henceforth useless, to fight the fading industrial monopoly of England with its own weapon, Free Trade.

But, as I said before, you may easily introduce Protection, but you cannot get rid of it again so easily. The legislature, by adopting the protective plan, has created vast interests, for which it is responsible. And not every one of these interests—the various branches of industry—is equally ready, at a given moment, to face open competition. Some will be lagging behind, while others have no longer need of protective nursing. This difference of position will give rise to the usual lobby-plotting, and is in itself a sure guarantee that the protected industries, if Free Trade is resolved upon, will be let down very easy indeed, as was the silk manufacture in England after 1846. That is unavoidable under present circumstances, and will have to be submitted to by the Free Trade party so long as the change is resolved upon in principle.

The question of Free Trade or Protection moves entirely within the bounds of the present system of capitalist production, and has, therefore, no direct interest for us Socialists who want to do away with that system. Indirectly, however, it interests us, inasmuch as we must desire the present system of production to develop and expand as freely and as quickly as possible; because along with it will develop also those economic phenomena which are its necessary consequences, and which must destroy the whole system: misery of the great mass of the people, in consequence of overproduction; this overproduction engendering either periodical gluts and revulsions, accompanied by panic, or else a chronic stagnation of trade; division of society into a small class of large capitalists, and a large one of practically hereditary wage-slaves, proletarians, who, while their numbers increase constantly, are at the same time constantly being superseded by new labor-saving machinery; in short, society brought to a deadlock, out of which there is no escaping but by a complete remodelling of the economic structure which forms its basis. From this point of view, forty years ago, Marx pronounced, in principle, in favor of Free Trade as the more progressive plan, and, therefore, the plan which would soonest bring capitalist society to that deadlock. But if Marx declared in favor of Free Trade on that ground, is that not a reason for every supporter of the present order of society to declare against Free Trade? If Free Trade is stated to be revolutionary, must not all good citizens vote for Protection as a conservative plan?

If a country nowadays accept Free Trade, it will certainly not do so to please the Socialists. It will do so because Free Trade has become a necessity for the industrial capitalists. But if it should reject Free Trade, and stick to Protection, in order to cheat the Socialists out of the expected social catastrophe, that will not hurt the prospects of Socialism in the least. Protection is a plan for artificially manufacturing manufacturers, and therefore also a plan for artificially manufacturing wage-laborers. You cannot breed the one without breeding the other. The wage-laborer everywhere follows in the footsteps of the manufacturer; he is like the "gloomy care" of Horace, that sits behind the rider, and that he cannot shake off wherever he go. You cannot escape fate; in other words you cannot escape the necessary consequences of your own actions. A system of production based upon the exploitation of wage-labor, in which wealth increases in proportion to the number of laborers employed and exploited, such a system is bound to increase the class of wage-laborers, that is to say, the class which is fated one day to destroy the system itself. In the meantime, there is no help for it: you must go on developing the capitalist system, you must accelerate the production, accumulation, and centralization of capitalist wealth, and, along with it, the production of a revolutionary class of laborers. Whether you try the Protectionist or the Free Trade plan will make no difference in the end, and hardly any in the length of the respite left to you until the day when that end will come. For long before that day will protection have become an unbearable shackle to any country aspiring, with a chance of success, to hold its own in the world market.

Written in April and early May 1888.
First published in *Die Neue Zeit*, No. 7, July 1888 and also in the pamphlet K. Marx, *Free Trade*, Boston, 1888.

Speech on the Question of Free Trade Delivered to the Democratic Association of Brussels at Its Public Meeting of January 9, 1848

Karl Marx

Gentlemen,—The Repeal of the Corn Laws in England is the greatest triumph of Free Trade in the nineteenth century. In every country where manufacturers discuss Free Trade, they have in mind chiefly Free Trade in corn or raw material generally. To burden foreign corn with protective duties is infamous, it is to speculate on the hunger of the people.

Cheap food, high wages, for this alone the English Free Traders have spent millions, and their enthusiasm has already infected their Continental brethren. And, generally speaking, all those who advocate Free Trade do so in the interests of the working class.

But, strange to say, the people for whom cheap food is to be procured at all costs are very ungrateful. Cheap food is as ill reputed in England as is cheap government in France. The people see in these self-sacrificing gentlemen, in Bowring, Bright & Co., their worst enemies and the most shameless hypocrites.

Everyone knows that in England the struggle between Liberals and Democrats takes the name of the struggle between Free Traders and Chartists. Let us see how the English Free Traders have proved to the people the good intentions that animate them. This is what they said to the factory hands,—

"The duty on corn is a tax upon wages; this tax you pay to the landlords, those medieval aristocrats; if your position is a wretched one, it is so only on account of the high price of the most indispensable articles of food."

The workers in turn asked of the manufacturers,—

"How is it that in the course of the last thirty years, while our commerce and manufacture has immensely increased, our wages have fallen far more rapidly, in proportion, than the price of corn has gone up?

"The tax which you say we pay the landlords is about three pence a week per worker. And yet the wages of the hand-loom weaver fell, between 1815 and 1843, from 28s. per week to 5s., and the wages of the power-loom weaver, between 1823 and 1843, from 20s. per week to 8s.

"And during the whole of the time that portion of the tax which you say we pay the landlord has never exceeded three pence. And, then, in the year 1834, when bread was very cheap and business lively, what did you tell us? You said, 'If you are poor, it is only because you have too many children, and your marriages are more productive than your labor!'

These are the very words you spoke to us, and you set about making new Poor Laws, and building workhouses, those bastilles of the proletariat."

To this the manufacturers replied,—

"You are right, worthy laborers: it is not the price of corn alone, but competition of the hands among themselves as well, which determines wages.

"But just bear in mind the circumstance that our soil consists of rocks and sand-banks only. You surely do not imagine that corn can be grown in flower-pots! If, instead of wasting our labor and capital upon a thoroughly sterile soil, we were to give up agriculture, and devote ourselves exclusively to commerce and manufacture, all Europe would abandon its factories, and England would form one huge factory town, with the whole of the rest of Europe for its agricultural districts."

While thus haranguing his own workingmen, the manufacturer is interrogated by the small tradesmen, who exclaim,—

"If we repeal the Corn Laws, we shall indeed ruin agriculture; but, for all that, we shall not compel other nations to give up their own factories, and buy our goods. What will the consequences be? I lose my customers in the country, and the home market is destroyed."

The manufacturer turns his back upon the workingmen and replies to the shopkeeper,—

"As to that, you leave it to us! Once rid of the duty on corn, we shall import cheaper corn from abroad. Then we shall reduce wages at the very time when they are rising in the countries where we get our corn. Thus in addition to the advantages which we already enjoy we shall have lower wages, and, with all these advantages, we shall easily force the Continent to buy of us."

But now the farmers and agricultural laborers join in the discussion.

"And what, pray, is to become of us? Are we to help in passing a sentence of death upon agriculture, when we get our living by it? Are we to let the soil be torn from beneath our feet?"

For all answer the Anti-Corn Law League contented itself with offering prizes for the three best essays upon the wholesome influence of the Repeal of the Corn Laws on English agriculture.

These prizes were carried off by Messrs Hope, Morse, and Greg, whose essays were distributed broadcast throughout the agricultural districts. One of the prize essayists devotes himself to proving that neither the tenant farmer nor the agricultural laborer would lose by the repeal of the Corn Laws, and that the landlord alone would lose.

"The English tenant farmer," he exclaims, "need not fear repeal, because no other country can produce such good corn so cheaply as England. Thus, even if the price of corn fell, it would not hurt you, because this fall would only affect rent, which would go down, while the profit of capital and the wages of labor remain stationary."

The second prize essayist, Mr. Morse, maintains, on the contrary, that the price of corn will rise in consequence of repeal. He is at infinite pains to prove that protective duties have never been able to secure a remunerative price for corn.

In support of his assertion he quotes the fact that, whenever foreign corn has been imported, the price of corn in England has gone up considerably, and that when little corn has been imported the price has fallen extremely. This prize-winner forgets that the importation was not the cause of the high price, but that the high price was the cause of the importation. In direct contradiction of his colleague he asserts that every rise in the price of corn is profitable to both the tenant farmer and laborer, but does not benefit the landlord.

The third prize essayist, Mr. Greg, who is a large manufacturer and whose work is addressed to the large tenant farmers, could not afford to echo such silly stuff. His language is more scientific.

He admits that the Corn Laws can increase rent only by increasing the price of corn, and that they can raise the price of corn only by inducing the investment of capital upon land of inferior quality, and this is explained quite simply.

In proportion as population increases, it inevitably follows, if foreign corn cannot be imported, that less fruitful soil must be placed under cultivation. This involves more expense and the product of this soil is consequently dearer. There being a demand for all the corn thus produced, it will all be sold. The price for all of it will of necessity be determined by the price of the product of the inferior soil. The difference between this price and the cost of production upon soil of better quality constitutes the rent paid for the use of the better soil.

If, therefore, in consequence of the repeal of the Corn Laws, the price of corn falls, and if, as a matter of course, rent falls along with it, it is because inferior soil will no longer be cultivated. Thus the reduction of rent must inevitably ruin a part of the tenant farmers.

These remarks were necessary in order to make Mr. Greg's language comprehensible.

"The small farmers," he says, "who cannot support themselves by agriculture must take refuge in manufacture. As to the large tenant farmers, they cannot fail to profit by the arrangement: either the landlord will be obliged to sell them their land very cheap, or leases will be made out for long periods. This will enable tenant farmers to invest more capital in their farms, to use agricultural machinery on a larger scale, and to save manual labor, which will, moreover, be cheaper, on account of the general fall in wages, the immediate consequence of the repeal of the Corn Laws."

Dr. Bowring conferred upon all these arguments the consecration of religion, by exclaiming at a public meeting, "Jesus Christ is Free Trade, and Free Trade is Jesus Christ."

It will be evident that all this cant was not calculated to make cheap bread tasteful to workingmen.

Besides, how should the workingmen understand the sudden philanthropy of the manufacturers, the very men still busy fighting against the Ten-Hours Bill, which was to reduce the working day of the mill hands from twelve hours to ten?

To give you an idea of the philanthropy of these manufacturers, I would remind you of the factory regulations in force in all their mills.

Every manufacturer has for his own private use a regular penal code by means of which fines are inflicted for every voluntary or involuntary offence. For instance, the hand pays so much when he has the misfortune to sit down on a chair, or whisper, or speak, or laugh; if he is a few moments late; if any part of a machine breaks, or if he turns out work of an inferior quality, etc. The fines are always greater than the damage really done by the workman. And to give the workingman every opportunity for incurring fines the factory clock is set forward, and he is given bad material to make into good stuff. An overseer unskilful in multiplying infractions of rules is soon discharged.

You see, gentlemen, this private legislation is enacted for the especial purpose of creating such infractions, and infractions are manufactured for the purpose of making money. Thus the manufacturer uses every means of reducing the nominal wage, and even profiting by accidents over which the workers have no control.

And these manufacturers are the same philanthropists who have tried to persuade the workers that they were capable of going to immense expense for the sole and express purpose of improving the condition of these same workingmen! On the one hand they nibble at the workers' wages in the pettiest way, by means of factory legislation, and, on the other, they are prepared to make the greatest sacrifices to raise those wages by means of the Anti-Corn Law League.

They build great palaces, at immense expense, in which the League takes up its official residence. They send an army of missionaries to all corners of England to preach the gospel of Free Trade; they print and distribute gratis thousands of pamphlets to enlighten the workingman upon his own interests. They spend enormous sums to buy over the press to their side. They organize a vast administrative system for the conduct of the Free Trade movement, and bestow all the wealth of their eloquence upon public meetings. It was at one of these meetings that a workingman cried out,—

"If the landlords were to sell our bones, you manufacturers would be the first to buy them, and to put them through the mill and make flour of them."

The English workingmen have appreciated to the fullest extent the significance of the struggle between the lords of the land and of capital. They know very well that the price of bread was to be reduced in order to reduce wages, and that the profit of capital would rise by as much as rent fell.

Ricardo, the apostle of the English Free Traders, the leading economist of our century, entirely agrees with the workers upon this point.

In his celebrated work upon Political Economy he says:

"If instead of growing our own corn . . . we discover a new market from which we can supply ourselves . . . at a cheaper price, wages will fall and profits rise. The fall in the price of agricultural produce reduces the wages, not only of the laborer employed in cultivating the soil, but also of all those employed in commerce or manufacture" [t. I, pp. 178–79; Eng. ed., p. 137].

And do not believe, gentlemen, that it is a matter of indifference to the working-man whether he receives only four francs on account of corn being cheaper, when he had been receiving five francs before.

Have not his wages always fallen in comparison with profit? And is it not clear that his social position has grown worse as compared with that of the capitalist? Beside which he loses actually. So long as the price of corn was higher and wages were also higher, a small saving in the consumption of bread sufficed to procure him other enjoyments. But as soon as bread is cheap, and wages are therefore low, he can save almost nothing on bread, for the purchase of other articles.

The English workingmen have shown the English Free Traders that they are not the dupes of their illusions or of their lies; and if, in spite of this, the workers have made common cause with the manufacturers against the landlords, it is for the purpose of destroying the last remnant of feudalism, that henceforth they may have only one enemy to deal with. The workers have not miscalculated, for the land-lords, in order to revenge themselves upon the manufacturers, have made common cause with the workers to carry the Ten-Hours Bill, which the latter had been vainly demanding for thirty years, and which was passed immediately after the repeal of the Corn Laws.

When Dr. Bowring, at the Congress of Economists, drew from his pocket a long list to show how many head of cattle, how much ham, bacon, poultry, etc., is imported into England, to be consumed—as he asserted—by the workers, he forgot to state that at the same time the workers of Manchester and other factory towns were thrown out of work by the beginning of the crisis.

As a matter of principle in Political Economy, the figures of a single year must never be taken as the basis for formulating general laws. We must always take the average of from six to seven years, a period during which modern industry passes through the successive phases of prosperity, overproduction, crisis, thus completing the inevitable cycle.

Doubtless, if the price of all commodities falls,—and this is the necessary consequence of Free Trade—I can buy far more for a franc than before. And the workingman's franc is as good as any other man's. Therefore, Free Trade must be advantageous to the workingman. There is only one little difficulty in this, namely that the workman, before he exchanges his franc for other commodities, has first exchanged his labor for the money of the capitalist. If in this exchange he always received the said franc while the price of all other commodities fell, he would always be the gainer by such a bargain. The difficulty does not lie in proving that, the price of all commodities falling, more commodities can be bought for the same sum of money.

Economists always take the price of labor at the moment of its exchange with other commodities, and altogether ignore the moment at which labor accomplishes its own exchange with capital. When it costs less to set in motion the machinery which produces commodities, then the things necessary for the maintenance of this machine, called workman, will also cost less. If all commodities are cheaper, labor, which is a commodity too, will also fall in price, and we shall see later that this commodity, labor, will fall far lower in proportion than all other commodities. If the workingman still pins his faith to the arguments of the economists, he will find, one fine morning, that the franc has dwindled in his pocket, and that he has only five sous left.

Thereupon the economists will tell you,—

"We admit that competition among the workers will certainly not be lessened under Free Trade, and will very soon bring wages into harmony with the low price of commodities. But, on the other hand, the low price of commodities will increase consumption, the larger consumption will increase production, which will in turn necessitate a larger demand for labor and this larger demand will be followed by a rise in wages."

The whole line of argument amounts to this: Free Trade increases productive forces. When manufactures keep advancing, when wealth, when the productive forces, when, in a word, productive capital increases, the demand for the labor, the price of labor, and consequently the rate of wages, rises also.

The most favorable condition for the workingman is the growth of capital. This must be admitted: when capital remains stationary, commerce and manufacture are not merely stationary but decline, and in this case the workman is the first victim. He goes to the wall before the capitalist. And in the case of the growth of capital, under the circumstances, which, as we have said, are the best for the workingman, what will be his lot? He will go to the wall just the same. The growth of capital implies the accumulation and the concentration of capital. This centralization involves a greater division of labor and a greater use of machinery. The greater division of labor destroys the especial skill of the laborer; and by putting in the place of this skilled work labor which any one can perform it increases competition among the workers.

This competition becomes more fierce as the division of labor enables a single man to do the work of three. Machinery accomplishes the same result on a much larger scale. The accumulation of productive capital forces the industrial capitalist to work with constantly increasing means of production, ruins the small manufacturer, and drives him into the proletariat. Then, the rate of interest falling in proportion as capital accumulates, the little *rentiers* and retired tradespeople, who can no longer live upon their small incomes, will be forced to look out for some business again and ultimately to swell the number of proletarians. Finally, the more productive capital grows, the more it is compelled to produce for a market whose requirements it does not know,—the more supply tries to force demand, and consequently crises increase in frequency and in intensity. But every crisis in turn hastens the concentration of capital, adds to the proletariat. Thus, as productive capital grows, competition among the workers grows too, and grows in a far greater proportion. The reward of labor is less for all, and the burden of labor is increased for some at least.

In 1829 there were, in Manchester, 1,088 cotton spinners employed in 36 factories. In 1841 there were but 448, and they tended 53,353 more spindles than the 1,088 spinners did in 1829. If manual labor had increased in the same proportion as productive force, the number of spinners ought to have risen to 1,848; improved machinery had, therefore, deprived 1,400 workers of employment.

We know beforehand the reply of the economists—the people thus thrown out of work will find other kinds of employment. Dr. Bowring did not fail to reproduce this argument at the Congress of Economists. But neither did he fail to refute himself. In 1835, Dr. Bowring made a speech in the House of Commons upon the

50,000 hand-loom weavers of London who have been starving without being able to find that new kind of employment which the Free Traders hold out to them in the distance. Let us hear the most striking portion of this speech of Mr. Bowring.

"The misery of the hand-loom weavers," he says, "is the inevitable fate of all kinds of labor which are easily acquired, and which may, at any moment, be replaced by less costly means. As in these cases competition amongst the work-people is very great, the slightest falling-off in demand brings on a crisis. The hand-loom weavers are, in a certain sense, placed on the borders of human existence. One step further, and that existence becomes impossible. The slightest shock is sufficient to throw them on to the road to ruin. By more and more superseding manual labor, the progress of mechanical science must bring on, during the period of transition, a deal of temporary suffering. National well-being cannot be bought except at the price of some individual evils. The advance of industry is achieved at the expense of those who lag behind, and of all discoveries that of the power-loom weighs most heavily upon the hand-loom weavers. In a great many articles formerly made by hand, the weaver has been placed *hors de combat*; but he is sure to be beaten in a good many more stuffs that are now made by hand."

Further on he says,—"I hold in my hand a correspondence of the governor-general with the East India Company. This correspondence is concerning the weavers of the Dacca district. The governor says in his letter,—A few years ago the East India Company received from six to eight million pieces of calico woven upon the looms of the country. The demand fell off gradually and was reduced to about a million pieces. At this moment it has almost entirely ceased. Moreover, in 1800 North America received from India nearly 800,000 pieces of cotton goods. In 1830 it did not take even 4,000. Finally, in 1800 a million of pieces were shipped for Portugal; in 1830 Portugal did not receive above 20,000.

"The reports on the distress of the Indian weavers are terrible. And what is the origin of that distress? The presence on the market of English manufactures, the production of the same article by means of the power-loom. A great number of the weavers died of starvation; the remainder has gone over to the other employment, and chiefly to field labor. Not to be able to change employment amounted to a sentence of death. And at this moment the Dacca district is crammed with English yarns and calicoes. The Dacca muslin, renowned all over the world for its beauty and firm texture, has also been eclipsed by the competition of English machinery. In the whole history of commerce, it would, perhaps, be difficult to find suffering equal to what these whole classes in India had to submit to" [W. Atkinson, pp. 36–38].

Mr. Bowring's speech is the more remarkable because the facts quoted by him are correct, and the phrases with which he seeks to palliate them are characterized by the hypocrisy common to all Free Trade discourses. He represents the workers as means of production which must be superseded by less expensive means of production, pretends to see in the labor of which he speaks a wholly exceptional kind of labor, and in the machine which has crushed out the weavers an equally exceptional kind of machine. He forgets that there is no kind of manual labor which may not any day share the fate of the hand-loom weavers.

"The constant aim and tendency of every improvement of mechanism is indeed to do entirely without the labor of men, or to reduce its price, by superseding the labor of the adult males by that of women and children, or the work of the skilled by that of the unskilled workman. In most of the throstle mills, spinning is now entirely done by girls of sixteen years and less. The introduction of the self-acting mule has caused the discharge of most of the (adult male) spinners, while the children and young persons have been kept on" [p. 34; Eng. ed., p. 23].

The above words of the most enthusiastic of Free Traders, Dr. Ure, are calculated to complete the confessions of Dr. Bowring. Mr. Bowring speaks of certain individual evils, and, at the same time, says that these individual evils destroy whole classes; he speaks of the temporary sufferings during a transition period, and does not deny that these temporary evils have implied for the majority the transition from life to death, and for the rest a transition from a better to a worse condition. When he asserts, farther on, that the sufferings of the working class are inseparable from the progress of industry, and are necessary to the prosperity of the nation, he simply says that the prosperity of the bourgeois class presupposes as necessary the suffering of the laboring class.

All the comfort which Mr. Bowring offers the workers who perish, and, indeed, the whole doctrine of compensation which the Free Traders propound, amounts to this—

You thousands of workers who are perishing, do not despair! You can die with an easy conscience. Your class will not perish. It will always be numerous enough for the capitalist class to decimate it without fear of annihilating it. Besides, how could capital be usefully applied if it did not take care to keep up its exploitable material, i.e., the workingmen, to be exploited over and over again?

But, then, why propound as a problem still to be solved the question: What influence will the adoption of the Free Trade have upon the condition of the working class? All the laws formulated by the political economists from Quesnay to Ricardo, have been based upon the hypothesis that the trammels which still interfere with commercial freedom have disappeared. These laws are confirmed in proportion as Free Trade is adopted. The first of these laws is that competition reduces the price of every commodity to the minimum cost of production. Thus the minimum of wages is the natural price of labor. And what is the minimum of wages? Just so much as is required for production of the articles absolutely necessary for the maintenance of the worker, for the continuation, by hook or by crook, of his own existence and that of his class.

But do not imagine that the worker receives *only* this minimum wage, and still less that he *always* receives it. No, according to this law, the working class will sometimes be more fortunate, will sometimes receive something above the minimum, but this surplus will merely make up for the deficit which they will have received below the minimum in times of industrial depression. That is to say that within a given time which recurs periodically, in other words, in the cycle which commerce and industry describe while passing through the successive phases of prosperity, overproduction, stagnation, and crisis, when reckoning all that the working class has had above and below mere necessaries, we shall see that, after all, they have received neither more nor less than the minimum; i.e., the working class will have maintained itself as a class after enduring any amount of misery and misfortune, and after leaving many corpses upon the industrial battle-field. But what of that? The class will still exist; nay, more, it will have increased.

But this is not all. The progress of industry creates less and less expensive means of subsistence. Thus spirits have taken the place of beer, cotton that of wool and linen, and potatoes that of bread.

Thus, as means are constantly being found for the maintenance of labor on cheaper and more wretched food, the minimum of wages is constantly sinking. If these wages began by letting the man work to live, they end by forcing him to live the life of a machine. His existence has no other value than that of a simple productive force, and the capitalist treats him accordingly. This law of the commodity labor, of the minimum of wages will be confirmed in proportion as the supposition of the economists, Free Trade, becomes an actual fact. Thus, of two things one: either we must reject all political economy based upon the assumption of Free Trade, or we must admit that under this same Free Trade the whole severity of the economic laws will fall upon the workers.

To sum up, what is Free Trade under the present conditions of society? Freedom of Capital. When you have torn down the few national barriers which still restrict the free development of capital, you will merely have given it complete freedom of action. So long as you let the relation of wages-labor to capital exist, no matter how favorable the conditions under which you accomplish the exchange of commodities, there will always be a class which exploits and a class which is exploited. It is really difficult to understand the presumption of the Free Traders who imagine that the more advantageous application of capital will abolish the antagonism between industrial capitalists and wage-workers. On the contrary. The only result will be that the antagonism of these two classes will stand out more clearly.

Let us assume for a moment that there are no more Corn Laws or national and municipal import duties; that in a word all the accidental circumstances which to-day the workingman may look upon as a cause of his miserable condition have vanished, and we shall have removed so many curtains that hide from his eyes his true enemy.

He will see that capital released from all trammels will make him no less a slave than capital trammelled by import duties.

Gentlemen! Do not be deluded by the abstract word Freedom— whose freedom? Not the freedom of one individual in relation to another, but freedom of Capital to crush the worker.

Why should you desire farther to sanction unlimited competition with this idea of freedom, when the idea of freedom itself is only the product of a social condition based upon Free Competition?

We have shown what sort of fraternity Free Trade begets between the different classes of one and the same nation. The fraternity which Free Trade would establish between the nations of the earth would not be more real, to call cosmopolitan exploitation universal brotherhood is an idea that could only be engendered in the brain of the bourgeoisie. Every one of the destructive phenomena to which unlimited competition gives rise within any one nation is reproduced in more gigantic proportions in the market of the world. We need not pause any longer upon Free Trade sophisms on this subject, which are worth just as much as the arguments of our prize essayists Messrs Hope, Morse, and Greg.

For instance, we are told that Free Trade would create an international division of labor, and thereby give to each country those branches of production most in harmony with its natural advantages.

You believe perhaps, gentlemen, that the production of coffee and sugar is the natural destiny of the West Indies.

Two centuries ago, nature, which does not trouble itself about commerce, had planted neither sugar-cane nor coffee trees there. And it may be that in less than half a century you will find there neither coffee nor sugar, for the East Indies, by means of cheaper production, have already successfully broken down this so-called natural destiny of the West Indies.

And the West Indies, with their natural wealth, are as heavy a burden for England as the weavers of Dacca, who also were destined from the beginning of time to weave by hand.

One other circumstance must not be forgotten, namely that, just as everything has become a monopoly, there are also nowadays some branches of industry which prevail over all others, and secure to the nations which especially foster them the command of the market of the world. Thus in the commerce of the world cotton alone has much greater commercial importance than all the other raw materials used in the manufacture of clothing. It is truly ridiculous for the Free Traders to refer to the few specialties in each branch of industry, throwing them into the balance against the product used in everyday consumption, and produced most cheaply in those countries in which manufacture is most highly developed.

If the Free Traders cannot understand how one nation can grow rich at the expense of another, we need not wonder, since these same gentlemen also refuse to understand how in the same country one class can enrich itself at the expense of another.

Do not imagine, gentlemen, that in criticising freedom of commerce we have the least intention of defending Protection.

One may be opposed to constitutionalism without being in favor of absolutism.

Moreover, the Protective system is nothing but a means of establishing manufacture upon a large scale in any given country, that is to say, of making it dependent upon the market of the world; and from the moment that dependence upon the market of the world is established, there is more or less dependence upon Free Trade too. Besides this, the Protective system helps to develop free competition within a nation. Hence we see that in countries where the bourgeoisie is beginning to make itself felt as a class, in Germany for example, it makes great efforts to obtain Protective duties. They serve the bourgeoisie as weapons against feudalism and absolute monarchy, as a means for the concentration of its own powers for the realization of Free Trade within the country.

But, generally speaking, the Protective system in these days is conservative, while the Free Trade system works destructively. It breaks up old nationalities and carries antagonism of proletariat and bourgeoisie to the uttermost point. In a word, the Free Trade system hastens the Social Revolution. In this revolutionary sense alone, gentlemen, I am in favor of Free Trade.

First published in French as a pamphlet at the beginning of February 1848 in Brussels.
Signed: *Karl Marx*

CHAPTER 3

"PREFACE" TO A CONTRIBUTION TO THE CRITIQUE OF POLITICAL ECONOMY

MARX'S FIRST SUSTAINED EXPLORATION OF POLITICAL ECONOMY was the *Critique*. It is not often read today because much of the material was treated more methodically eight years later in *Capital*. In fact, this brief preface is probably the most read part of the original, and for good reason. It is a compressed but often quoted overview of Marx's self-described intellectual journey and also of the materialist theory of history, or historical materialism. Herein Marx argues that the economy is the key to the anatomy of society, pointing to the ultimate level of explanation of the dynamic of social life. "The mode of production of material life conditions the general process of social, political, and intellectual life." Further, and very important because it is so often overlooked, Marx states that no economic system is surpassed until it has accomplished its historical work.

A Contribution to the Critique of Political Economy

Part One Preface

Karl Marx

I EXAMINE THE SYSTEM OF BOURGEOIS ECONOMY in the following order: *capital, landed property, wage-labour; the State, foreign trade, world market.* The economic conditions of existence of the three great classes into which modern bourgeois society is divided are analysed under the first three headings; the interconnection of the other three headings is self-evident. The first part of the first book, dealing with Capital, comprises the following chapters: (1) The commodity; (2) Money or simple circulation; (3) Capital in general. The present part consists of the first two chapters. The entire material lies before me in the form of monographs, which were written not for publication but for self-clarification at widely separated periods; their remoulding into an integrated whole according to the plan I have indicated will depend upon circumstances.

A general introduction, which I had drafted, is omitted, since on further consideration it seems to me confusing to anticipate results which still have to be substantiated, and the reader who really wishes to follow me will have to decide to advance from the particular to the general. A few brief remarks regarding the course of my study of political economy may, however, be appropriate here.

Although jurisprudence was my special study, I pursued it as a subject subordinated to philosophy and history. In the year 1842–43, as editor of the *Rheinische Zeitung,* I first found myself in the embarrassing position of having to discuss what is known as material interests. The deliberations of the Rhine Province Assembly in thefts of wood and the division of landed property; the official polemic started by Herr von Schaper, then Oberpräsident of the Rhine Province, against the *Rheinische Zeitung* about the condition of the Mosel peasantry, and finally the debates on free trade and protective tariffs caused me in the first instance to turn my attention to economic questions. On the other hand, at that time when good intentions "to push forward" often took the place of factual knowledge, an echo of French socialism and communism, slightly tinged by philosophy, was noticeable in the *Rheinische Zeitung*. I objected to this dilettantism, but at the same time frankly admitted in a controversy with the *Allgemeine Augsburger Zeitung* that my previous studies did not allow me to express any opinion on the content of the French theories. When the publishers of the *Rheinische Zeitung* conceived the illusion that by a more compliant policy on the part of the paper it might be possible to secure the abrogation of the death sentence passed upon it, I eagerly grasped the opportunity to withdraw from the public stage to my study.

The first work which I undertook to dispel the doubts assailing me was a critical re-examination of the Hegelian philosophy of law; the introduction to this work being published in the *Deutsch-Französische Jahrbücher* issued in Paris in 1844. My inquiry led me to the conclusion that neither legal relations nor political forms could be comprehended whether by themselves or on the basis of a so-called general development of the human mind, but that on the contrary they originate in the material conditions of life, the totality of which Hegel, following the example of English and French thinkers of the eighteenth century, embraces within the term "civil society"; that the anatomy of this civil society, however, has to be sought in political economy. The study of this, which I began in Paris, I continued in Brussels, where I moved owing to an expulsion order issued by M. Guizot. The general conclusion at which I arrived and which, once reached, became the guiding principle of my studies can be summarised as follows. In the social production of their existence, men inevitably enter into definite relations, which are independent of their will, namely relations of production appropriate to a given stage in the development of their material forces of production. The totality of these relations of production constitutes the economic structure of society, the real foundation, on which arises a legal and political super-structure and to which correspond definite forms of social consciousness. The mode of production of material life conditions the general process of social, political and intellectual life. It is not the consciousness of men that determines their existence, but their social existence that determines their consciousness. At a certain stage of development, the material productive forces of society come into conflict with the existing relations of production or—this merely expresses the same thing in legal terms—with the property relations within the framework of which they have operated hitherto. From forms of development of the productive forces these relations turn into their fetters. Then begins an era of social revolution. The changes in the economic foundation lead sooner or later to the transformation of the whole immense superstructure. In studying such transformations it is always necessary to distinguish between the material transformation of the economic conditions of production, which can be determined with the precision of natural science, and the legal, political, religious, artistic or philosophic—in short, ideological forms in which men become conscious of this conflict and fight it out. Just as one does not judge an individual by what he thinks about himself, so one cannot judge such a period of transformation by its consciousness, but, on the contrary, this consciousness must be explained from the contradictions of material life, from the conflict existing between the social forces of production and the relations of production. No social formation is ever destroyed before all the productive forces for which it is sufficient have been developed, and new superior relations of production never replace older ones before the material conditions for their existence have matured within the framework of the old society. Mankind thus inevitably sets itself only such tasks as it is able to solve, since closer examination will always show that the problem itself arises only when the material conditions for its solution are already present or at least in the course of formation. In broad outline, the Asiatic, ancient, feudal and modern bourgeois modes of production may be designated as epochs marking progress in the economic development of society. The bourgeois relations of production are the last antagonistic form of the social process of production—antagonistic not in the sense of individual antagonism but of an antagonism that emanates from the individuals' social conditions of existence—but the productive forces developing within bourgeois society create also the material conditions for a solution of this antagonism. The prehistory of human society accordingly closes with this social formation.

Frederick Engels, with whom I maintained a constant exchange of ideas by correspondence since the publication of his brilliant essay on the critique of economic categories (printed in the *Deutsch-Französische Jahrbücher*), arrived by another road (compare his *Condition of the Working-Class in England*) at the same result as I, and when in the spring of 1845 he too came to live in Brussels, we decided to set forth together our conception as opposed to the ideological one of German philosophy, in fact to settle accounts with our former philosophical conscience. The intention was carried out in the form of a critique of post-Hegelian philosophy. The manuscript, two large octavo volumes, had long ago reached the publishers in Westphalia when we were informed that owing to changed circumstances it could not be printed. We abandoned the manuscript to the gnawing criticism of the mice all the more willingly since we had achieved our main purpose—self-clarification. Of the scattered works in which at that time we presented one or another aspect of our views to the public, I shall mention only the *Manifesto of the Communist Party*, jointly written by Engels and myself, and a *Speech on the Question of Free Trade*, which I myself published. The salient points of our conception were first outlined in an academic, although polemical, form in my *Poverty of Philosophy* . . . , this book which was aimed at Proudhon appeared in 1847. The publication of an essay on *Wage-Labour* written in German in which I combined the lectures I had held on this subject at the German Workers' Society in Brussels, was interrupted by the February Revolution and my forcible removal from Belgium in consequence.

The publication of the *Neue Rheinische Zeitung* in 1848 and 1849 and subsequent events cut short my economic studies, which I could only resume in London in 1850. The enormous amount of material relating to the history of political economy assembled in the British Museum, the fact that London is a convenient vantage point for the observation of bourgeois society, and finally the new stage of development which this society seemed to have entered with the discovery of gold in California and Australia, induced me to start again from the very beginning and to work carefully through the new material. These studies led partly of their own accord to apparently quite remote subjects on which I had to spend a certain amount of time. But it was in particular the imperative necessity of earning my living which reduced the time at my disposal. My collaboration, continued now for eight years, with the

New York Tribune, the leading Anglo-American newspaper, necessitated an excessive fragmentation of my studies, for I wrote only exceptionally newspaper correspondence in the strict sense. Since a considerable part of my contributions consisted of articles dealing with important economic events in Britain and on the Continent, I was compelled to become conversant with practical details which, strictly speaking, lie outside the sphere of political economy.

This sketch of the course of my studies in the domain of political economy is intended merely to show that my views—no matter how they may be judged and how little they conform to the interested prejudices of the ruling classes—are the outcome of conscientious research carried on over many years. At the entrance to science, as at the entrance to hell, the demand must be made:

> *Qui si convien lasciare ogni sospetto*
> *Ogni viltá convien che qui sia morta.**
> *Karl Marx*

London, January 1859.

Written in November 1858–January 1859.
Printed in Berlin in 1859. Signed: *Karl Marx*

NOTE

*Dante, *La Divina commedia*, Inferno, Canto III.

> Here all misgiving must thy mind reject.
> Here cowardice must die and be no more.

(English translation by Laurence Binyon—Dante, *The Divine Comedy*, Inferno, Canto III, ll. 14–15, Viking Portable Library, 1969.)

VALUE, PRICE AND PROFIT

A PASSAGE FROM A LETTER INDICATES THE OCCASION OF THIS WORK, often used along with the equally well-known 1847 lecture, "Wage-Labor and Capital," as a popular introduction to Marx's economic theory. "Value, Price and Profit," the title by which this work is known, is a lecture in two parts Marx gave to the International Working Men's Association in 1865, of which Marx was the leading figure. As Marx states in the letter, he was criticizing arguments by another prominent member named John Weston. Weston's position, derived from the arguments of the influential socialist leader Ferdinand Lassalle, was that wage increases would simply raise the price of necessary goods, meaning that the real purchasing power of the workers would be unchanged. Therefore struggling for wage increases and, by extension, trade union activity in general, is futile. In refutation, Marx took this as an opportunity to present some of the arguments he had been developing in the manuscript for *Capital*, to clarify the thinking of the workers about their situation in capitalist production.

"Value, Price and Profit" superbly lays out some of the main themes of Marx's economic analysis: that value regulates the exchange of goods, the crucial distinction between "labor" and "labor-power," and even mentions the bloody process of "original accumulation" of capital, usually known as "primitive accumulation," the phrase from *Capital*. Classical economists had argued that commodities exchange at their embodied labor values. If this is true, then there is a question as to where profits come from. A typical view at the time was that profits, rent, and interest are additional costs that are added, rather arbitrarily, to the cost of production of a commodity. In contrast, and as discussed above in the general introduction, Marx explains that there is a difference between the cost of labor-power in the labor market and the value that labor adds in the production process. Profits, rent, and interest are actually all derived from the surplus value extracted by the exploitation of labor. This surplus is a variable quantity, depending on the costs of labor-power, the length of the working day, and the intensity or productivity of labor. How much surplus value is ultimately available is therefore not fixed but rather a consequence of struggles between labor and capital over the relative shares of wages versus profits. Therefore, rather than being bound to some absolute minimum fixed by the price (value of embodied labor) of necessaries, that is, subsistence, working class struggle can improve the conditions of the working class. A good illustration of that is the Ten Hours Bill (the "Factory Act" of 1847), which, over fierce resistance by manufacturers, limited the working day beginning in 1848.

It should be noted that this is in general a more optimistic view of the possibilities of workers than that expressed in the three volumes of *Capital*. Closer to *Capital*, Marx also argues here that the Ten Hours Bill demonstrated something of great importance to the working class: that in "merely economic action capital is the stronger side." Therefore, the working class must engage in political struggle, legislation, if they are to protect themselves even in some degree from the consequences of their labor-power having been turned into a commodity.

Marx also mentions two other things that bear on the problems raised in the general introduction. First, he reiterates that the value of labor-power itself is not determined solely by the bare minimum, but also depends on popular understandings of a "traditional standard of life." Second, on the utility of moral appeals within the context of capitalism, Marx states bluntly, "What you think just or equitable is out of the question. The question is: What is necessary and unavoidable with a given system of production?"

Marx to Engels in Manchester

[London,] 20 May 1865

Dear Fred,

I am working like a horse at the moment, as I must make use of the time when I am fit for work, and the carbuncles are still with me, though they only trouble me locally and do not disturb the brain-pan.

In between times, since one cannot always be writing, I am doing some Differential Calculus dx/dy. I have no patience to read anything else at all. Any other kind of reading always drives me back to my writing-desk.

Special meeting of the 'International' this evening. A good old codger, an old Owenist, *Weston* (carpenter), has put up the following two propositions that he is constantly defending in *The Bee-Hive*:

1. that a general rate in the rise of the rate of wages would be of no benefit to the workers;
2. that the Trades-Unions for that reason, etc., are *harmful.*

If these two propositions, in which *he* alone in our Society believes, were to be accepted, we should be in a terrible mess, both in respect of the Trades-Unions here and the infection of strikes now prevailing on the Continent.

He will be supported in the matter by a native Englishman—since non-members are also admitted to this meeting—who has written a pamphlet to the same effect. I am, of course, expected to produce a refutation. I ought therefore really to have worked out my *réplique* for this evening, but I thought it more important to get on with writing my book, and so I shall have to rely on improvisation.

I know in advance, of course, what the two main points will be:

1. that *wages* determine the value of commodities;
2. that if the capitalists pay 5s. today instead of 4, tomorrow they will sell their commodities for 5s. instead of 4 (being enabled to do so by the increased demand).

Trite though that is, and however little it penetrates the topmost surface of things, it is, nevertheless, not easy to explain to the ignorant all the competing economic questions involved. You can't compress a course of Political Economy into 1 hour. But we shall do our best. . . .

    Salut.

Your

K. M.

First published in *Der Briefwechsel zwischen F. Engels und K. Marx,* Bd. 3, Stuttgart, 1913.

CHAPTER 4

[VALUE, PRICE AND PROFIT]

KARL MARX

Citizens,

Before entering into the subject-matter, allow me to make a few preliminary remarks.

There reigns now on the Continent a real epidemic of strikes, and a general clamour for a rise of wages. The question will turn up at our Congress. You, as the head of the International Association, ought to have settled convictions upon this paramount question. For my own part, I considered it, therefore, my duty to enter fully into the matter, even at the peril of putting your patience to a severe test.

Another preliminary remark I have to make in regard to Citizen Weston. He has not only proposed to you, but has publicly defended, in the interest of the working class, as he thinks, opinions he knows to be most unpopular with the working class. Such an exhibition of moral courage all of us must highly honour. I hope that, despite the unvarnished style of my paper, at its conclusion he will find me agreeing with what appears to me the just idea lying at the bottom of his theses, which, however, in their present form, I cannot but consider theoretically false and practically dangerous.

I shall now at once proceed to the business before us.

. . .

The uncritical way in which he has treated his subject will become evident from one single remark. He pleads against a rise of wages or against high wages as the result of such a rise. Now, I ask him, What are high wages and what are low wages? Why constitute, for example, five shillings weekly low, and twenty shillings weekly high, wages? If five is low as compared with twenty, twenty is still lower as compared with two hundred. If a man was to lecture on the thermometer, and commenced by declaiming on high and low degrees, he would impart no knowledge whatever. He must first tell me how the freezing-point is found out, and how the boiling-point, and how these standard points are settled by natural laws, not by the fancy of the sellers or makers of thermometers. Now, in regard to wages and profits, Citizen Weston has not only failed to deduce such standard points from economical laws, but he has not even felt the necessity to look after them. He satisfied himself with the acceptance of the popular slang terms of low and high as something having a fixed meaning, although it is self-evident that wages can only be said to be high or low as compared with a standard by which to measure their magnitudes.

He will be unable to tell me why a certain amount of money is given for a certain amount of labour. If he should answer me, "This was settled by the law of supply and demand," I should ask him, in the first instance, by what law supply and demand are themselves regulated. And such an answer would at once put him out of court. The relations between the supply and demand of labour undergo perpetual change, and with them the market prices of labour. If the demand overshoots the supply wages rise; if the supply overshoots the demand wages sink, although it might in such circumstances be necessary to *test* the real state of demand and supply by a strike, for example, or any other method. But if you accept supply and demand as the law regulating wages, it would be as childish as useless to declaim against a rise of wages, because, according to the supreme law you appeal to, a periodical rise of wages is quite as necessary and legitimate as a periodical fall of wages. If you do *not* accept supply and demand as the law regulating wages, I again repeat the question, why a certain amount of money is given for a certain amount of labour?

But to consider matters more broadly: You would be altogether mistaken in fancying that the value of labour or any other commodity whatever is ultimately fixed by supply and demand. Supply and demand regulate nothing but the temporary *fluctuations* of market prices. They will explain to you why the market price of a commodity rises above or sinks below its *value,* but they can never account for that *value* itself. Suppose supply and demand to equilibrate, or, as the economists call it, to cover each other. Why, the very moment these opposite forces become equal they paralyse each other, and cease to work in the one or the other direction. At the moment when supply and demand equilibrate each other, and therefore cease to act, the *market price* of a commodity coincides with its *real value,* with the standard price round which its market prices oscillate. In inquiring into the nature of that *value,* we have, therefore, nothing at all to do with the temporary effects on market prices of supply and demand. The same holds true of wages and of the prices of all other commodities.

5) [WAGES AND PRICES]

Reduced to their simplest theoretical expression, all our friend's arguments resolve themselves into this one single dogma: *"The prices of commodities are determined or regulated by wages."*

I might appeal to practical observation to bear witness against this antiquated and exploded fallacy. I might tell you that the English factory operatives, miners, shipbuilders, and so forth, whose labour is relatively high-priced, undersell, by the cheapness of their produce, all other nations; while the English agricultural labourer, for example, whose labour is relatively low-priced, is undersold by almost every other nation, because of the dearness of his produce. By comparing article with article in the same country, and the commodities of different countries, I might show, apart from some exceptions more apparent than real, that on an average the high-priced labour produces the low-priced, and the low-priced labour produces the high-priced commodities. This, of course, would not prove that the high price of labour in the one, and its low price in the other instance, are the respective causes of those diametrically opposed effects, but at all events it would prove that the prices of commodities are not ruled by the prices of labour. However, it is quite superfluous for us to employ this empirical method.

It might, perhaps, be denied that Citizen Weston has put forward the dogma: *"The prices of commodities are determined or regulated by wages."* In point of fact, he has never formulated it. He said, on the contrary, that profit and rent form also constituent parts of the prices of commodities, because it is out of prices of commodities that not only the working man's wages, but also the capitalist's profits and the landlord's rents must be paid. But how, in his idea, are prices formed? First by wages. Then an additional percentage is joined to the price on behalf of the capitalist, and another additional percentage on behalf of the landlord. Suppose the wages of the labour employed in the production of a commodity to be ten. If the rate of profit was 100 per cent. to the wages advanced, the capitalist would add ten, and if the rate of rent was also 100 per cent. upon the wages, there would be added ten more, and the aggregate price of the commodity would amount to thirty. But such a determination of prices would be simply their determination by wages. If wages in the above case rose to twenty, the price of the commodity would rise to sixty, and so forth. Consequently all the superannuated writers on political economy, who propounded the dogma that wages regulate prices, have tried to prove it by treating profit and rent *as mere additional percentages upon wages.* None of them were, of course, able to reduce the limits of those percentages to any economic law. They seem, on the contrary, to think profits settled by tradition, custom, the will of the capitalist, or by some other equally arbitrary and inexplicable method. If they assert that they are settled by the competition between the capitalists, they say nothing. That competition is sure to equalise the different rates of profit in different trades, or reduce them to one average level, but it can never determine the level itself, or the general rate of profit.

What do we mean by saying that the prices of the commodities are determined by wages? Wages being but a name for the price of labour, we mean that the prices of commodities are regulated by the price of labour. As *"price"* is exchangeable value—and in speaking of value I speak always of exchangeable value—is exchangeable *value expressed in money,* the proposition comes to this, that "the *value of commodities is determined by the value of labour,"* or that "the *value of labour is the general measure of value."*

But how, then, is the *"value of labour"* itself determined? Here we come to a standstill. Of course, to a standstill if we try reasoning logically. Yet the propounders of that doctrine make short work of logical scruples. Take our friend Weston, for example. First he told us that wages regulate the price of commodities and that consequently when wages rise prices must rise. Then he turned round to show us that a rise of wages will be no good because the prices of commodities had risen, and because wages were indeed measured by the prices of the commodities upon which they are spent. Thus we begin by saying that the value of labour determines the value of commodities, and we wind up by saying that the value of commodities determines the value of labour. Thus we move to and fro in the most vicious circle, and arrive at no conclusion at all.

On the whole it is evident that by making the value of one commodity, say labour, corn, or any other commodity, the general measure and regulator of value, we only shift the difficulty, since we determine one value by another, which on its side wants to be determined.

The dogma that "wages determine the prices of commodities," expressed in its most abstract terms, comes to this, that "value is determined by value," and this tautology means that, in fact, we know nothing at all about value. Accepting this premise, all reasoning about the general laws of political economy turns into mere twaddle. It was, therefore, the great merit of Ricardo that in his work *On the Principles of Political Economy*, published in 1817, he fundamentally destroyed the old, popular, and worn-out fallacy that "wages determine prices," a fallacy which Adam Smith and his French predecessors had spurned in the really scientific parts of their researches, but which they reproduced in their more exoterical and vulgarising chapters.

6) [VALUE AND LABOUR]

Citizens, I have now arrived at a point where I must enter upon the real development of the question. I cannot promise to do this in a very satisfactory way, because to do so I should be obliged to go over the whole field of political economy. I can, as the French would say, but *effleurer la question,* touch upon the main points.

The first question we have to put is: What is the *value* of a commodity? How is it determined?

At first sight it would seem that the value of a commodity is a thing quite *relative,* and not to be settled without considering one commodity in its relations to all other commodities. In fact, in speaking of the value, the value in exchange of a commodity, we mean the proportional quantities in which it exchanges with all other commodities. But then arises the question: How are the proportions in which commodities exchange with each other regulated?

We know from experience that these proportions vary infinitely. Taking one single commodity, wheat, for instance, we shall find that a quarter of wheat exchanges in almost countless variations of proportion with different commodities. Yet, *its value remaining always the same,* whether expressed in silk, gold, or any other commodity, it must be something distinct from, and independent of, these *different rates of exchange* with different articles. It must be possible to express, in a very different form, these various equations with various commodities.

Besides, if I say a quarter of wheat exchanges with iron in a certain proportion, or the value of a quarter of wheat is expressed in a certain amount of iron, I say that the value of wheat and its equivalent in iron are equal *to some third thing,* which is neither wheat nor iron, because I suppose them to express the same magnitude in two different shapes. Either of them, the wheat or the iron, must, therefore, independently of the other, be reducible to this third thing which is their common measure.

To elucidate this point I shall recur to a very simple geometrical illustration. In comparing the areas of triangles of all possible forms and magnitudes, or comparing triangles with rectangles, or any other rectilinear figure, how do we proceed? We reduce the area of any triangle whatever to an expression quite different from its visible form. Having found from the nature of the triangle that its area is equal to half the product of its base by its height, we can then compare the different values of all sorts of triangles, and of all rectilinear figures whatever, because all of them may be dissolved into a certain number of triangles.

The same mode of procedure must obtain with the values of commodities. We must be able to reduce all of them to an expression common to all, distinguishing them only by the proportions in which they contain that identical measure.

As the *exchangeable values* of commodities are only *social functions* of those things, and have nothing at all to do with their *natural* qualities, we must first ask, What is the common *social substance* of all commodities? It is *Labour*. To produce a commodity a certain amount of labour must be bestowed upon it, or worked up in it. And I say not only *Labour*, but *social Labour*. A man who produces an article for his own immediate use, to consume it himself, creates a *product*, but not a *commodity*. As a self-sustaining producer he has nothing to do with society. But to produce a *commodity*, a man must not only produce an article satisfying some *social* want, but his labour itself must form part and parcel of the total sum of labour expended by society. It must be subordinate to the *Division of Labour within Society*. It is nothing without the other divisions of labour, and on its part is required to *integrate* them.

If we consider *commodities as values*, we consider them exclusively under the single aspect of *realised, fixed*, or, if you like, *crystallised social labour*. In this respect they can *differ* only by representing greater or smaller quantities of labour, as, for example, a greater amount of labour may be worked up in a silken handkerchief than in a brick. But how does one measure *quantities of labour*? By the *time the labour lasts*, in measuring the labour by the hour, the day, etc. Of course, to apply this measure, all sorts of labour are reduced to average or simple labour as their unit.

We arrive, therefore, at this conclusion. A commodity has *a value*, because it is a *crystallisation of social labour*. The *greatness* of its value, or its *relative* value, depends upon the greater or less amount of that social substance contained in it; that is to say, on the relative mass of labour necessary for its production. The *relative values of commodities* are, therefore, determined by the *respective quantities* or *amounts of labour, worked up, realised, fixed in them*. The *correlative* quantities of commodities which can be produced in the *same time of labour* are *equal*. Or the value of one commodity is to the value of another commodity as the quantity of labour fixed in the one is to the quantity of labour fixed in the other.

I suspect that many of you will ask, Does then, indeed, there exist such a vast, or any difference whatever, between determining the values of commodities by *wages*, and determining them by the *relative quantities of labour* necessary for their production? You must, however, be aware that the *reward* for labour, and *quantity* of labour, are quite disparate things. Suppose, for example, *equal quantities of labour* to be fixed in one quarter of wheat and one ounce of gold. I resort to the example because it was used by *Benjamin Franklin* in his first Essay published in 1729, and entitled, *A Modest Inquiry into the Nature and Necessity of a Paper Currency*, where he, one of the first, hit upon the true nature of value. Well. We suppose, then, that one quarter of wheat and one ounce of gold are *equal values* or *equivalents*, because they are *crystallisations of equal amounts of average labour*, of so many days' or so many weeks' labour respectively fixed in them. In thus determining the relative values of gold and corn, do we refer in any way whatever to the *wages* of the agricultural labourer and the miner? Not a bit. We leave it quite *indeterminate how* their day's or week's labour was paid, or even whether wages labour was employed at all. If it was, wages may have been very unequal. The labourer whose labour is realised in the quarter of wheat may receive two bushels only, and the labourer employed in mining may receive one-half of the ounce of gold. Or, supposing their wages to be equal, they may deviate in all possible proportions from the values of the commodities produced by them. They may amount to one-half, one-third, one-fourth, one-fifth, or any other proportional part of the one quarter of corn or the one ounce of gold. Their *wages* can, of course, not *exceed*, not be *more* than the values of the commodities they produced, but they can be *less* in every possible degree. Their *wages* will be *limited* by the *values* of the products, but the *values of their products* will not be limited by the wages. And above all, the values, the relative values of corn and gold, for example, will have been settled without any regard whatever to the value of the labour employed, that is to say, to *wages.* To determine the values of commodities by the *relative quantities of labour fixed in them,* is, therefore, a thing quite different from the tautological method of determining the values of commodities by the value of labour, or by *wages.* This point, however, will be further elucidated in the progress of our inquiry.

In calculating the exchangeable value of a commodity we must add to the quantity of labour *last* employed the quantity of labour *previously* worked up in the raw material of the commodity, and the labour bestowed on the implements, tools, machinery, and buildings, with which such labour is assisted. For example, the value of a certain amount of cotton-yarn is the crystallisation of the quantity of labour added to the cotton during the spinning process, the quantity of labour previously realised in the cotton itself, the quantity of labour realised in the coal, oil and other auxiliary substances used, the quantity of labour fixed in the steam engine, the spindles, the factory building, and so forth. Instruments of production properly so-called, such as tools, machinery, buildings, serve again and again for a longer or shorter period during repeated processes of production. If they were used up at once, like the raw material, their whole value would at once be transferred to the commodities they assist in producing. But as a spindle, for example, is but gradually used up, an average calculation is made, based upon the average time it lasts, and its average waste or wear and tear during a certain period, say a day. In this way we calculate how much of the value of the spindle is transferred to the yarn daily spun, and how much, therefore, of the total amount of labour realised in a pound of yarn, for example, is due to the quantity of labour previously realised in the spindle. For our present purpose it is not necessary to dwell any longer upon this point.

It might seem that if the value of a commodity is determined by the *quantity of labour bestowed upon its production,* the lazier a man, or the clumsier a man, the more valuable his commodity, because the greater the time of labour required for finishing the commodity. This, however, would be a sad mistake. You will recollect that I used the word "*Social* labour," and many points are involved in this qualification of "*Social.*" In saying that the value of a commodity is determined by the *quantity of labour* worked up or crystallised in it, we mean *the quantity of labour necessary* for its production in a given state of society, under certain social average conditions of production, with a given social average intensity, and average skill of the labour employed. When, in England, the power-loom came to compete with the hand-loom, only one half of the former time of labour was wanted to convert a given amount of yarn into a yard of cotton or cloth. The poor hand-loom weaver now worked seventeen or eighteen hours daily, instead of the nine or ten hours he had worked before. Still the product of twenty hours of his labour represented now only ten social hours of labour, or ten hours of labour socially necessary for the conversion of a certain amount of yarn into textile stuffs. His product of twenty hours had, therefore, no more value than his former product of ten hours.

If then the quantity of socially necessary labour realised in commodities regulates their exchangeable values, every increase in the quantity of labour wanted for the production of a commodity must augment its value, as every diminution must lower it.

If the respective quantities of labour necessary for the production of the respective commodities remained constant, their relative values also would be constant. But such is not the case. The quantity of labour necessary for the production of a commodity changes continuously with the changes in the productive powers of the labour employed. The greater the productive powers of labour, the more produce is finished in a given time of labour, and the smaller the productive powers of labour, the less produce is finished in the same time. If, for example, in the progress of population it should become necessary to cultivate less fertile soils, the same amount of produce would be only attainable by a greater amount of labour spent, and the value of agricultural produce would consequently rise. On the other hand, if with the modern means of production, a single spinner converts into yarn, during one working day, many thousand times the amount of cotton which he could have spun during the same time with the spinning wheel, it is evident that every single pound of cotton will absorb many thousand times less of spinning labour than it did before, and, consequently, the value added by spinning to every single pound of cotton will be a thousand times less than before. The value of yarn will sink accordingly.

Apart from the different natural energies and acquired working abilities of different peoples, the productive powers of labour must principally depend:

Firstly. Upon the *natural* conditions of labour, such as fertility of soil, mines, and so forth;

Secondly. Upon the progressive improvement of the *Social Powers of Labour,* such as are derived from production on a grand scale, concentration of capital and combination of labour, subdivision of labour, machinery, improved methods, appliance of chemical and other natural agencies, shortening of time and space by means of communication and transport, and every other contrivance by which science presses natural agencies into the service of labour, and by which the social or co-operative character of labour is developed. The greater the productive powers of labour, the less labour is bestowed upon a given amount of produce; hence the smaller the value of this produce. The smaller the productive powers of labour, the more labour is bestowed upon the same amount of produce; hence the greater its value. As a general law we may, therefore, set it down that:—

The values of commodities are directly as the times of labour employed in their production, and are inversely as the productive powers of the labour employed.

Having till now only spoken of *Value,* I shall add a few words about *Price,* which is a peculiar form assumed by value.

Price, taken by itself, is nothing but the *monetary expression of value.* The values of all commodities of this country, for example, are expressed in gold prices, while on the Continent they are mainly expressed in silver prices. The value of gold or silver, like that of all other commodities, is regulated by the quantity of labour necessary for getting them. You exchange a certain amount of your national products, in which a certain amount of your national labour is crystallised, for the produce of the gold and silver producing countries, in which a certain quantity of *their* labour is crystallised. It is in this way, in fact by barter, that you learn to express in gold and silver the values of all commodities, that is, the respective quantities of labour bestowed upon them. Looking somewhat closer into the *monetary expression of value,* or what comes to the same, the *conversion of value into price,* you will find that it is a process by which you give to the *values* of all commodities an *independent* and *homogeneous form,* or by which you express them as quantities of *equal* social labour. So far as it is but the monetary expression of value, price has been called *natural price* by Adam Smith, *"prix nécessaire"* by the French physiocrats.

What then is the relation between *value* and *market prices,* or between *natural prices* and *market prices?* You all know that the *market price* is the *same* for all commodities of the same kind, however the conditions of production may differ for the individual producers. The market price expresses only the *average amount of social labour* necessary, under the average conditions of production, to supply the market with a certain mass of a certain article. It is calculated upon the whole lot of a commodity of a certain description.

So far the *market price* of a commodity coincides with its *value.* On the other hand, the oscillations of market prices, rising now over, sinking now under the value or natural price, depend upon the fluctuations of supply and demand. The deviations of market prices from values are continual, but as *Adam Smith* says:

"The natural price . . . is [. . .] the central price, to which the prices of all commodities are continually gravitating. Different accidents may sometimes keep them suspended a good deal above it, and sometimes force them down even somewhat below it. But whatever may be the obstacles which hinder them from settling in this centre of repose and continuance, they are constantly tending towards it."

I cannot now sift this matter. It suffices to say that *if* supply and demand equilibrate each other, the market prices of commodities will correspond to their natural prices, that is to say, to their values, as determined by the respective quantities of labour required for their production. But supply and demand *must* constantly tend to equilibrate each other, although they do so only by compensating one fluctuation by another, a rise by a fall, and vice versa. If instead of considering only the daily fluctuations you analyse the movement of market prices for longer periods, as Mr. Tooke, for example, has done in his *History of Prices,* you will find that the fluctuations of market prices, their deviations from values, their ups and downs, paralyse and compensate each other; so that, apart from the effect of monopolies and some other modifications I must now pass by, all descriptions of commodities are, on the average, sold at their respective *values* or natural prices. The average periods during which the fluctuations of market prices compensate each other are different for different kinds of commodities, because with one kind it is easier to adapt supply to demand than with the other.

If then, speaking broadly, and embracing somewhat longer periods, all descriptions of commodities sell at their respective values, it is nonsense to suppose that profit, not in individual cases, but that the constant and usual profits of different trades, spring from *surcharging* the prices of commodities, or selling them at a price over and above their *value*. The absurdity of this notion becomes evident if it is generalised. What a man would constantly win as a seller he would as constantly lose as a purchaser. It would not do to say that there are men who are buyers without being sellers, or consumers without being producers. What these people pay to the producers, they must first get from them for nothing. If a man first takes your money and afterwards returns that money in buying your commodities, you will never enrich yourselves by selling your commodities too dear to that same man. This sort of transaction might diminish a loss, but would never help in realising a profit.

To explain, therefore, the *general nature of profits*, you must start from the theorem that, on an average, commodities are *sold at their real value*, and that *profits are derived from selling them at their values*, that is, in proportion to the quantity of labour realised in them. If you cannot explain profit upon this supposition, you cannot explain it at all. This seems paradox and contrary to everyday observation. It is also paradox that the earth moves round the sun, and that water consists of two highly inflammable gases. Scientific truth is always paradox, if judged by everyday experience, which catches only the delusive appearance of things.

7) LABOURING POWER

Having now, as far as it could be done in such a cursory manner, analysed the nature of *Value*, of the *Value of any commodity whatever*, we must turn our attention to the specific *Value of Labour*. And here, again, I must startle you by a seeming paradox. All of you feel sure that what they daily sell is their Labour; that, therefore, Labour has a Price, and that, the price of a commodity being only the monetary expression of its value, there must certainly exist such a thing as the *Value of Labour*. However, there exists no such thing as the *Value of Labour* in the common acceptance of the word. We have seen that the amount of necessary labour crystallised in a commodity constitutes its value. Now, applying this notion of value, how could we define, say, the value of a ten hours' working day? How much labour is contained in that day? Ten hours' labour. To say that the value of a ten hours' working day is equal to ten hours' labour, or the quantity of labour contained in it, would be a tautological and, moreover, a nonsensical expression. Of course, having once found out the true but hidden sense of the expression *"Value of Labour,"* we shall be able to interpret this irrational, and seemingly impossible application of value, in the same way that, having once made sure of the real movement of the celestial bodies, we shall be able to explain their apparent or merely phenomenal movements.

What the working man sells is not directly his *Labour*, but his *Labouring Power*, the temporary disposal of which he makes over to the capitalist. This is so much the case that I do not know whether by the English Laws, but certainly by some Continental Laws, the *maximum time* is fixed for which a man is allowed to sell his labouring power. If allowed to do so for any indefinite period whatever, slavery would be immediately restored. Such a sale, if it comprised his lifetime, for example, would make him at once the lifelong slave of his employer.

One of the oldest economists and most original philosophers of England—Thomas Hobbes—has already, in his *Leviathan,* instinctively hit upon this point overlooked by all his successors. He says:

"*The value or worth of a man* is, as in all other things, his *price*: that is, so much as would be given for the *Use of his Power.*"

Proceeding from this basis, we shall be able to determine the *Value of Labour* as that of all other commodities.

But before doing so, we might ask, how does this strange phenomenon arise, that we find on the market a set of buyers, possessed of land, machinery, raw material, and the means of subsistence, all of them, save land in its crude state, the *products of labour,* and on the other hand, a set of sellers who have nothing to sell except their labouring power, their working arms and brains? That the one set buys continually in order to make a profit and enrich themselves, while the other set continually sells in order to earn their livelihood? The inquiry into this question would be an inquiry into what the economists call "*Previous,* or *Original Accumulation,*" but which ought to be called *Original Expropriation.* We should find that this so-called *Original Accumulation* means nothing but a series of historical processes, resulting in a *Decomposition of the Original Union* existing between the Labouring Man and his Instruments of Labour. Such an inquiry, however, lies beyond the pale of my present subject. The *Separation* between the Man of Labour and the Instruments of Labour once established, such a state of things will maintain itself and reproduce itself upon a constantly increasing scale, until a new and fundamental revolution in the mode of production should again overturn it, and restore the original union in a new historical form.

What, then, is the *Value of Labouring Power?*

Like that of every other commodity, its value is determined by the quantity of labour necessary to produce it. The labouring power of a man exists only in his living individuality. A certain mass of necessaries must be consumed by a man to grow up and maintain his life. But the man, like the machine, will wear out, and must be replaced by another man. Beside the mass of necessaries required for *his own* maintenance, he wants another amount of necessaries to bring up a certain quota of children that are to replace him on the labour market and to perpetuate the race of labourers. Moreover, to develop his labouring power, and acquire a given skill, another amount of values must be spent. For our purpose it suffices to consider only *average* labour, the costs of whose education and development are vanishing magnitudes. Still I must seize upon this occasion to state that, as the costs of producing labouring powers of different quality differ, so must differ the values of the labouring powers employed in different trades. The cry for an *equality of wages* rests, therefore, upon a mistake, is an *insane* wish never to be fulfilled. It is an offspring of that false and superficial radicalism that accepts premises and tries to evade conclusions. Upon the basis of the wages system the value of labouring power is settled like that of every other commodity; and as different kinds of labouring power have different values, or require different quantities of labour for their production, they *must* fetch different prices in the labour market. To clamour for *equal or even equitable retribution* on the basis of the wages system is the same as to clamour for *freedom* on the basis of the slavery system. What you think just or equitable is out of the question. The question is: What is necessary and unavoidable with a given system of production?

After what has been said, it will be seen that the *value of labouring power* is determined by the *value of the necessaries* required to produce, develop, maintain, and perpetuate the labouring power.

8) PRODUCTION OF SURPLUS-VALUE

Now suppose that the average amount of the daily necessaries of a labouring man require *six hours of average labour* for their production. Suppose, moreover, six hours of average labour to be also realised in a quantity of gold equal to 3s. Then 3s. would be the *Price,* or the monetary expression of the *Daily Value* of that man's *Labouring Power.* If he worked daily six hours he would daily produce a value sufficient to buy the average amount of his daily necessaries, or to maintain himself as a labouring man.

But our man is a wages labourer. He must, therefore, sell his labouring power to a capitalist. If he sells it at 3s. daily, or 18s. weekly, he sells it at its value. Suppose him to be a spinner. If he works six hours daily he will add to the cotton a value of 3s. daily. This value, daily added by him, would be an exact equivalent for the wages, or the price of his labouring power, received daily. But in that case *no surplus-value* or *surplus-produce* whatever would go to the capitalist. Here, then, we come to the rub.

In buying the labouring power of the workman, and paying its value, the capitalist, like every other purchaser, has acquired the right to consume or use the commodity bought. You consume or use the labouring power of a man by making him work as you consume or use a machine by making it run. By paying the daily or weekly value of the labouring power of the workman, the capitalist has, therefore, acquired the right to use or make that labouring power work during the *whole day or week.* The working day or the working week has, of course, certain limits, but those we shall afterwards look more closely at.

For the present I want to turn your attention to one decisive point.

. . . The *value* of the labouring power is determined by the quantity of labour necessary to maintain or reproduce it, but the *use* of that labouring power is only limited by the active energies and physical strength of the labourer. The daily or weekly *value* of the labouring power is quite distinct from the daily or weekly *exercise* of that power, the same as the food a horse wants and the time it can carry the horseman are quite distinct. The quantity of labour by which the *value* of the workman's labouring power is limited forms by no means a limit to the quantity of labour which his labouring power is apt to perform. Take the example of our spinner. We have seen that, to daily reproduce his labouring power, he must daily reproduce a value of three shillings, which he will do by working six hours daily. But this does not disable him from working ten or twelve or more hours a day. But by paying the daily or weekly *value* of the spinner's labouring power, the capitalist has acquired the right of using that labouring power during the *whole day or week.* He will, therefore, make him work daily, say, *twelve* hours. *Over and above* the six hours required to replace his wages, or the value of his labouring power, he will, therefore, have to work *six other hours,* which I shall call hours of *surplus-labour,* which surplus labour will realise itself in a *surplus-value* and a *surplus-produce.* If our spinner, for example, by his daily labour of six hours, added three shillings' value to the cotton, a value forming an exact equivalent to his wages, he will, in twelve hours, add six shillings' worth to the cotton, and produce *a proportional surplus of yarn.* As he has sold his labouring power to the capitalist, the whole value or produce created by him belongs to the capitalist, the owner *pro tempore* of his labouring power. By advancing three shillings, the capitalist will, therefore, realise a value of six shillings, because, advancing a value in which six hours of labour are crystallised, he will receive in return a value in which twelve hours of labour are crystallised. By repeating this same process daily, the capitalist will daily advance three shillings and daily pocket six shillings, one-half of which will go to pay wages anew, and the other half of which will form *surplus-value,* for which the capitalist pays no equivalent. It is *this sort of exchange between capital and labour* upon which capitalistic production, or the wages system, is founded, and which must constantly result in reproducing the working man as a working man, and the capitalist as a capitalist.

The rate of surplus-value, all other circumstances remaining the same, will depend on the proportion between that part of the working day necessary to reproduce the value of the labouring power and the *surplus-time* or *surplus-labour* performed for the capitalist. It will, therefore, depend on the *ratio in which the working day is prolonged over and above that extent,* by working which the working man would only reproduce the value of his labouring power, or replace his wages.

9) VALUE OF LABOUR

We must now return to the expression, *"Value, or Price of Labour."*

We have seen that, in fact, it is only the value of the labouring power, measured by the values of commodities necessary for its maintenance. But since the workman receives his wages *after* his labour is performed, and knows, moreover, that what he actually gives to the capitalist is his labour, the value or price of his labouring power necessarily appears to him as the *price* or *value of his labour itself.* If the price of his labouring power is three shillings, in which six hours of labour are realised, and if he works twelve hours, he necessarily considers these three shillings as the value or price of twelve hours of labour, although these twelve hours of labour realise themselves in a value of six shillings. A double consequence flows from this.

Firstly. The value or price of the labouring power takes the semblance of the *price or value of labour itself,* although, strictly speaking, value and price of labour are senseless terms.

Secondly. Although one part only of the workman's daily labour is *paid,* while the other part is *unpaid,* and while that unpaid or surplus-labour constitutes exactly the fund out of which *surplus-value* or *profit* is formed, it seems as if the aggregate labour was paid labour.

This false appearance distinguishes *wages labour* from other *historical* forms of labour. On the basis of the wages system even the *unpaid* labour seems to be *paid* labour. With the *slave,* on the contrary, even that part of his labour which is paid appears to be unpaid. Of course, in order to work the slave must live, and one part of his working day goes to replace the value of his own maintenance. But since no bargain is struck between him and his master, and no acts of selling and buying are going on between the two parties, all his labour seems to be given away for nothing.

Take, on the other hand, the peasant serf, such as he, I might say, until yesterday existed in the whole East of Europe. This peasant worked, for example, three days for himself on his own field or the field allotted to him, and the three subsequent days he performed compulsory and gratuitous labour on the estate of his lord. Here, then, the paid and unpaid parts of labour were visibly separated, separated in time and space; and our Liberals overflowed with moral indignation at the preposterous notion of making a man work for nothing.

In point of fact, however, whether a man works three days of the week for himself on his own field and three days for nothing on the estate of his lord, or whether he works in the factory or the workshop six hours daily for himself and six for his employer, comes to the same, although in the latter case the paid and unpaid portions of labour are inseparably mixed up with each other, and the nature of the whole transaction is completely masked by the *intervention of a contract* and the *pay* received at the end of the week. The gratuitous labour appears to be voluntarily given in the one instance, and to be compulsory in the other. That makes all the difference.

In using the expression *"value of labour,"* I shall only use it as a popular slang term for *"value of labouring power."*

10) Profit is Made by Selling A Commodity at its Value

Suppose an average hour of labour to be realised in a value equal to sixpence, or twelve average hours of labour to be realised in six shillings. Suppose, further, the value of labour to be three shillings or the produce of six hours' labour. If, then, in the raw material, machinery, and so forth, used up in a commodity, twenty-four hours of average labour were realised, its value would amount to twelve shillings. If, moreover, the workman employed by the capitalist added twelve hours of labour to those means of production, these twelve hours would be realised in an additional value of six shillings. The *total value of the product* would, therefore, amount to thirty-six hours of realised labour, and be equal to eighteen shillings. But as the value of labour, or the wages paid to the workman, would be three shillings only, no equivalent would have been paid by the capitalist for the six hours of surplus-labour worked by the workman, and realised in the value of the commodity. By selling this commodity at its value for eighteen shillings, the capitalist would, therefore, realise a value of three shillings, for which he had paid no equivalent. These three shillings would constitute the surplus-value or profit pocketed by him. The capitalist would consequently realise the profit of three shillings, not by selling his commodity at a price *over and above* its value, but by selling it *at its real value.*

The value of a commodity is determined by the *total quantity of labour* contained in it. But part of that quantity of labour is realised in a value for which an equivalent has been paid in the form of wages; part of it is realised in a value for which *no* equivalent has been paid. Part of the labour contained in the commodity is *paid* labour; part is *unpaid* labour. By selling, therefore, the commodity *at its value,* that is, as the crystallisation of the *total quantity of labour* bestowed upon it, the capitalist must necessarily sell it at a profit. He sells not only what has cost him an equivalent, but he sells also what has cost him nothing, although it has cost his workman labour. The cost of the commodity to the capitalist and its real cost are different things.

I repeat, therefore, that normal and average profits are made by selling commodities not *above* but *at their real values.*

11) THE DIFFERENT PARTS INTO WHICH SURPLUS-VALUE IS DECOMPOSED

The *surplus-value,* or that part of the total value of the commodity in which the *surplus-labour* or *unpaid labour* of the working man is realised, I call *Profit.* The whole of that profit is not pocketed by the employing capitalist. The monopoly of land enables the landlord to take one part of that *surplus-value,* under the name of *rent,* whether the land is used for agriculture, buildings or railways, or for any other productive purpose. On the other hand, the very fact that the possession of the *means of labour* enables the employing capitalist to produce a *surplus-value,* or, what comes to the same, to *appropriate to himself a certain amount of unpaid labour,* enables the owner of the means of labour, which he lends wholly or partly to the employing capitalist—enables, in one word, the *money-lending capitalist* to claim for himself under the name of *interest* another part of that surplus-value, so that there remains to the employing capitalist *as such* only what is called *industrial* or *commercial* profit.

By what laws this division of the total amount of surplus-value amongst the three categories of people is regulated is a question quite foreign to our subject. This much, however, results from what has been stated.

Rent, Interest, and Industrial Profit are only *different names for different parts* of the *surplus-value* of the commodity, or the *unpaid labour enclosed in it,* and they are *equally derived from this source, and from this source alone.* They are not derived from *land* as such or from *capital* as such, but land and capital enable their owners to get their respective shares out of the surplus-value extracted by the employing capitalist from the labourer. For the labourer himself it is a matter of subordinate importance whether that surplus-value, the result of his surplus-labour, or unpaid labour, is altogether pocketed by the employing capitalist, or whether the latter is obliged to pay portions of it, under the name of rent and interest, away to third parties. Suppose the employing capitalist to use only his own capital and to be his own landlord, then the whole surplus-value would go into his pocket.

It is the employing capitalist who immediately extracts from the labourer this surplus-value, whatever part of it he may ultimately be able to keep for himself. Upon this relation, therefore, between the employing capitalist and the wages labourer the whole wages system and the whole present system of production hinge. Some of the citizens who took part in our debate were, therefore, wrong in trying to mince matters, and to treat this fundamental relation between the employing capitalist and the working man as a secondary question, although they were right in stating that, under given circumstances, a rise of prices might affect in very unequal degrees the employing capitalist, the landlord, the moneyed capitalist, and, if you please, the tax-gatherer.

Another consequence follows from what has been stated.

That part of the value of the commodity which represents only the value of the raw materials, the machinery, in one word, the value of the means of production used up, forms *no revenue* at all, but replaces *only capital.* But, apart from this, it is false that the other part of the value of the commodity *which forms revenue,* or may be spent in the form of wages, profits, rent, interest, is *constituted* by the value of wages, the value of rent, the value of profits, and so forth. We shall, in the first instance, discard wages, and only treat industrial profits, interest, and rent. We have just seen that the *surplus-value* contained in the commodity or that part of its value in which *unpaid labour* is realised, *dissolves* itself into different fractions, bearing three different names. But it would be quite the reverse of the truth to say that its value is *composed* of, or *formed* by, the *addition* of the *independent values of these three constituents.*

If one hour of labour realises itself in a value of sixpence, if the working day of the labourer comprises twelve hours, if half of this time is unpaid labour, that surplus-labour will add to the commodity a *surplus-value* of three shillings, that is, a value for which no equivalent has been paid. This surplus-value of three shillings constitutes the *whole fund* which the employing capitalist may divide, in whatever proportions, with the landlord and the money-lender. The value of these three shillings constitutes the limit of the value they have to divide amongst them. But it is not the employing capitalist who adds to the value of the commodity an arbitrary value for his profit, to which another value is added for the landlord and so forth, so that the addition of these arbitrarily fixed values would constitute the total value. You see, therefore, the fallacy of the popular notion, which confounds the *decomposition of a given value* into three parts, with the *formation* of that value by the addition of three *independent* values, thus converting the aggregate value, from which rent, profit, and interest are derived, into an arbitrary magnitude.

If the total profit realised by a capitalist be equal to £100, we call this sum, considered as *absolute* magnitude, the *amount of profit.* But if we calculate the ratio which those £100 bear to the capital advanced, we call this *relative* magnitude, the *rate of profit.* It is evident that this rate of profit may be expressed in a double way.

Suppose £100 to be the capital *advanced in wages.* If the surplus value created is also £100—and this would show us that half the working day of the labourer consists of *unpaid* labour—and if we measured this profit by the value of the capital advanced in wages, we should say that the *rate of profit* amounted to one hundred per cent., because the value advanced would be one hundred and the value realised would be two hundred.

If, on the other hand, we should not only consider the *capital advanced in wages,* but the *total capital* advanced, say for example £500, of which £400 represented the value of raw materials, machinery, and so forth, we should say that the *rate of profit* amounted only to twenty per cent., because the profit of one hundred would be but the fifth part of the *total* capital advanced.

The first mode of expressing the rate of profit is the only one which shows you the real ratio between paid and unpaid labour, the real degree of the *exploitation* (you must allow me this French word) *of labour.* The other mode of expression is that in common use, and is, indeed, appropriate for certain purposes. At all events, it is very useful for concealing the degree in which the capitalist extracts gratuitous labour from the workman.

In the remarks I have still to make I shall use the word *Profit* for the whole amount of the surplus-value extracted by the capitalist without any regard to the division of the surplus-value between different parties, and in using the words *Rate of Profit,* I shall always measure profits by the value of the capital advanced in wages.

12) GENERAL RELATION OF PROFITS, WAGES AND PRICES

Deduct from the value of a commodity the value replacing the value of the raw materials and other means of production used upon it, that is to say, deduct the value representing the *past* labour contained in it, and the remainder of its value will dissolve into the quantity of labour added by the working man *last* employed. If that working man works twelve hours daily, if twelve hours of average labour crystallise themselves in an amount of gold equal to six shillings, this additional value of six shillings is the *only* value his labour will have created. This given value, determined by the time of his labour, is the only fund from which both he and the capitalist have to draw their respective shares or dividends, the only value to be divided into wages and profits. It is evident that this value itself will not be altered by the variable proportions in which it may be divided amongst the two parties. There will also be nothing changed if in the place of one working man you put the whole working population, twelve million working days, for example, instead of one.

Since the capitalist and workman have only to divide this limited value, that is, the value measured by the total labour of the working man, the more the one gets the less will the other get, and vice versa. Whenever a quantity is given, one part of it will increase inversely as the other decreases. If the wages change, profits will change in an opposite direction. If wages fall, profits will rise; and if wages rise, profits will fall. If the working man, on our former supposition, gets three shillings, equal to one half of the value he has created, or if his whole working day consists half of paid, half of unpaid labour, the *rate of profit* will be 100 per cent., because the capitalist would also get three shillings. If the working man receives only two shillings, or works only one-third of the whole day for himself, the capitalist will get four shillings, and the rate of profit will be 200 per cent. If the working man receives four shillings, the capitalist will only receive two, and the rate of profit would sink to 50 per cent., but all these variations will not affect the value of the commodity. A general rise of wages would, therefore, result in a fall of the general rate of profit, but not affect values.

But although the values of commodities, which must ultimately regulate their market prices, are exclusively determined by the total quantities of labour fixed in them, and not by the division of that quantity into paid and unpaid labour, it by no means follows that the values of the single commodities, or lots of commodities, produced during twelve hours, for example, will remain constant. The *number* or mass of commodities produced in a given time of labour, or by a given quantity of labour, depends upon the *productive power* of the labour employed, and not upon its *extent* or length. With one degree of the productive power of spinning labour, for example, a working day of twelve hours may produce twelve pounds of yarn, with a lesser degree of productive power only two pounds. If then twelve hours' average labour were realised in the value of six shillings, in the one case the twelve pounds of yarn would cost six shillings, in the other case the two pounds of yarn would also cost six shillings. One pound of yarn would, therefore, cost sixpence in the one case, and three shillings in the other.

This difference of price would result from the difference in the productive powers of the labour employed. One hour of labour would be realised in one pound of yarn with the greater productive power, while with the smaller productive power, six hours of labour would be realised in one pound of yarn. The price of a pound of yarn would, in the one instance, be only sixpence, although wages were relatively high and the rate of profit low; it would be three shillings in the other instance, although wages were low and the rate of profit high. This would be so because the price of the pound of yarn is regulated by the *total amount of labour worked up* in it, and not by the *proportional division of that total amount into paid and unpaid labour*. The fact I have before mentioned that high-priced labour may produce cheap, and low-priced labour may produce dear commodities, loses, therefore, its paradoxical appearance. It is only the expression of the general law that the value of a commodity is regulated by the quantity of labour worked up in it, and that the quantity of labour worked up in it depends altogether upon the productive powers of the labour employed, and will, therefore, vary with every variation in the productivity of labour.

13) MAIN CASES OF ATTEMPTS AT RAISING WAGES OR RESISTING THEIR FALL

Let us now seriously consider the main cases in which a rise of wages is attempted or a reduction of wages resisted.

1. We have seen that the *value of the labouring power*, or in more popular parlance, the *value of labour*, is determined by the value of necessaries, or the quantity of labour required to produce them. If, then, in a given country the value of the daily average necessaries of the labourer represented six hours of labour expressed in three shillings, the labourer would have to work six hours daily to produce an equivalent for his daily maintenance. If the whole working day was twelve hours, the capitalist would pay him the value of his labour by paying him three shillings. Half the working day would be unpaid labour, and the rate of profit would amount to 100 per cent. But now suppose that, consequent upon a decrease of productivity, more labour should be wanted to produce, say, the same amount of agricultural produce, so that the price of the average daily necessaries should rise from three to four shillings. In that case the *value* of labour would rise by one-third, or 33 1/3 per cent. Eight hours of the working day would be required to produce an equivalent for the daily maintenance of the labourer, according to his old standard of living. The surplus-labour would therefore sink from six hours to four, and the rate of profit from 100 to 50 per cent. But in insisting upon a rise of wages, the labourer would only insist upon getting the *increased value of his labour*, like every other seller of a commodity, who, the costs of his commodities having increased, tries to get its increased value paid. If wages did not rise, or not sufficiently rise, to compensate for the increased values of necessaries, the *price* of labour would sink *below the value of labour*, and the labourer's standard of life would deteriorate.

But a change might also take place in an opposite direction. By virtue of the increased productivity of labour, the same amount of the average daily necessaries might sink from three to two shillings, or only four hours out of the working day, instead of six, be wanted to reproduce an equivalent for the value of the daily necessaries. The working man would now be able to buy with two shillings as many necessaries as he did before with three shillings. Indeed, the *value of labour* would have sunk, but that diminished value would command the same amount of commodities as before. Then profits would rise from three to four shillings, and, the rate of profit from 100 to 200 per cent. Although the labourer's absolute standard of life would have remained the same, his *relative* wages, and therewith his *relative social position*, as compared with that of the capitalist, would have been lowered. If the working man should resist that reduction of relative wages, he would only try to get some share in the increased productive powers of his own labour, and to maintain his former relative position in the social scale. Thus, after the abolition of the Corn Laws, and in flagrant violation of the most solemn pledges given during the anti-corn law agitation, the English factory lords generally reduced wages ten per cent. The resistance of the workmen was at first baffled, but, consequent upon circumstances I cannot now enter upon, the ten per cent. lost were afterwards regained.

2. The *values* of necessaries, and consequently the *value of labour*, might remain the same, but a change might occur in their *money prices*, consequent upon a previous *change* in the *value of money*.

By the discovery of more fertile mines and so forth, two ounces of gold might, for example, cost no more labour to produce than one ounce did before. The *value* of gold would then be depreciated by one half, or fifty per cent. As the *values* of all other commodities would then be expressed in twice their former *money prices*, so also the same with the *value of labour*. Twelve hours of labour, formerly expressed in six shillings, would now be expressed in twelve shillings. If the working man's wages should remain three shillings, instead of rising to six shillings, the *money price of his labour* would only be equal to *half the value of his labour*, and his standard of life would fearfully deteriorate. This would also happen in a greater or lesser degree if his wages should rise, but not proportionately to the fall in the value of gold. In such a case nothing would have been changed, either in the productive powers of labour, or in supply and demand, or in values. Nothing could have changed except the money *names* of those values. To say that in such a case the workman ought not to insist upon a proportionate rise of wages, is to say that he must be content to be paid with names, instead of with things. All past history proves that whenever such a depreciation of money occurs the capitalists are on the alert to seize this opportunity for defrauding the workman. A very large school of political economists assert that, consequent upon the new discoveries of gold lands, the better working of silver mines, and the cheaper supply of quicksilver, the value of precious metals has been again depreciated. This would explain the general and simultaneous attempts on the Continent at a rise of wages.

3. We have till now supposed that the *working day* has given limits. The working day, however, has, by itself, no constant limits. It is the constant tendency of capital to stretch it to its utmost physically possible length, because in the same degree surplus-labour, and consequently the profit resulting therefrom, will be increased. The more capital succeeds in prolonging the working day, the greater the amount of other people's labour it will appropriate. During the seventeenth and even the first two-thirds of the eighteenth century a ten hours' working day was the normal working day all over England. During the anti-Jacobin war, which was in fact a war waged by the British barons against the British working masses capital celebrated its

bacchanalia, and prolonged the working day from ten to twelve, fourteen, eighteen hours. *Malthus,* by no means a man whom you would suspect of a maudlin sentimentalism, declared in a pamphlet, published about 1815, that if this sort of things was to go on the life of the nation would be attacked at its very source. A few years before the general introduction of the newly-invented machinery, about 1765, a pamphlet appeared in England under the title, *An Essay on Trade.* The anonymous author, an avowed enemy of the working classes, declaims on the necessity of expanding the limits of the working day. Amongst other means to this end, he proposes *working houses,* which, he says, ought to be *"Houses of Terror."* And what is the length of the working day he prescribes for these *"Houses of Terror"*? *Twelve hours,* the very same time which in 1832 was declared by capitalists, political economists, and ministers to be not only the existing but the necessary time of labour for a child under twelve years.

By selling his labouring power, and he must do so under the present system, the working man makes over to the capitalist the consumption of that power, but within certain rational limits. He sells his labouring power in order to maintain it, apart from its natural wear and tear, but not to destroy it. In selling his labouring power at its daily or weekly value, it is understood that in one day or one week that labouring power shall not be submitted to two days' or two weeks' waste or wear and tear. Take a machine worth £1,000. If it is used up in ten years it will add to the value of the commodities in whose production it assists £100 yearly. If it be used up in five years it would add £200 yearly, or the value of its annual wear and tear is in inverse ratio to the quickness with which it is consumed. But this distinguishes the working man from the machine. Machinery does not wear out exactly in the same ratio in which it is used. Man, on the contrary, decays in a greater ratio than would be visible from the mere numerical addition of work.

In their attempts at reducing the working day to its former rational dimensions, or, where they cannot enforce a legal fixation of a normal working day, at checking overwork by a rise of wages, a rise not only in proportion to the surplus-time exacted, but in a greater proportion, working men fulfil only a duty to themselves and their race. They only set limits to the tyrannical usurpations of capital. Time is the room of human development. A man who has no free time to dispose of, whose whole lifetime, apart from the mere physical interruptions by sleep, meals, and so forth, is absorbed by his labour for the capitalist, is less than a beast of burden. He is a mere machine for producing Foreign Wealth, broken in body and brutalised in mind. Yet the whole history of modern industry shows that capital, if not checked, will recklessly and ruthlessly work to cast down the whole working class to the utmost state of degradation.

In prolonging the working day the capitalist may pay *higher wages* and still lower the *value of labour,* if the rise of wages does not correspond to the greater amount of labour extracted, and the quicker decay of the labouring power thus caused. This may be done in another way. Your middle-class statisticians will tell you, for instance, that the average wages of factory families in Lancashire have risen. They forget that instead of the labour of the man, the head of the family, his wife and perhaps three or four children are now thrown under the Juggernaut wheels of capital, and that the rise of the aggregate wages does not correspond to the aggregate surplus-labour extracted from the family.

Even with given limits of the working day, such as now exist in all branches of industry subjected to the factory laws, a rise of wages may become necessary, if only to keep up the old standard *value of labour*. By increasing the *intensity* of labour, a man may be made to expend as much vital force in one hour as he formerly did in two. This has, to a certain degree, been effected in the trades, placed under the Factory Acts, by the acceleration of machinery, and the greater number of working machines which a single individual has now to superintend. If the increase in the intensity of labour or the mass of labour spent in an hour keeps some fair proportion to the decrease in the extent of the working day, the working man will still be the winner. If this limit is overshot, he loses in one form what he has gained in another, and ten hours of labour may then become as ruinous as twelve hours were before. In checking this tendency of capital, by struggling for a rise of wages corresponding to the rising intensity of labour, the working man only resists the depreciation of his labour and the deterioration of his race.

4. All of you know that, from reasons I have not now to explain, capitalistic production moves through certain periodical cycles. It moves through a state of quiescence, growing animation, prosperity, overtrade, crisis, and stagnation. The market prices of commodities, and the market rates of profit, follow these phases, now sinking below their averages, now rising above them. Considering the whole cycle, you will find that one deviation of the market price is being compensated by the other, and that, taking the average of the cycle, the market prices of commodities are regulated by their values. Well! During the phase of sinking market prices and the phases of crisis and stagnation, the working man, if not thrown out of employment altogether, is sure to have his wages lowered. Not to be defrauded, he must, even with such a fall of market prices, debate with the capitalist in what proportional degree a fall of wages has become necessary. If, during the phases of prosperity, when extra profits are made, he did not battle for a rise of wages, he would, taking the average of one industrial cycle, not even receive his *average wages,* or the *value* of his labour. It is the utmost height of folly to demand that while his wages are necessarily affected by the adverse phases of the cycle, he should exclude himself from compensation during the prosperous phases of the cycle. Generally, the *values* of all commodities are only realised by the compensation of the continuously changing market prices, springing from the continuous fluctuations of demand and supply. On the basis of the present system labour is only a commodity like others. It must, therefore, pass through the same fluctuations to fetch an average price corresponding to its value. It would be absurd to treat it on the one hand as a commodity, and to want on the other hand to exempt it from the laws which regulate the prices of commodities. The slave receives a permanent and fixed amount of maintenance; the wages labourer does not. He must try to get a rise of wages in the one instance, if only to compensate for a fall of wages in the other. If he resigned himself to accept the will, the dictates of the capitalist as a permanent economical law, he would share in all the miseries of the slave, without the security of the slave.

5. In all the cases I have considered, and they form ninety-nine out of a hundred, you have seen that a struggle for a rise of wages follows only in the track of *previous* changes, and is the necessary offspring of previous changes in the amount of production, the productive powers of labour, the value of labour, the value of money, the

extent or the intensity of labour extracted, the fluctuations of market prices, dependent upon the fluctuations of demand and supply, and consistent with the different phases of the industrial cycle; in one word, as reactions of labour against the previous action of capital. By treating the struggle for a rise of wages independently of all these circumstances, by looking only upon the change of wages, and overlooking all the other changes from which they emanate, you proceed from a false premise in order to arrive at false conclusions.

14) The Struggle between Capital and Labour and Its Results

1. Having shown that the periodical resistance on the part of the working men against a reduction of wages, and their periodical attempts at getting a rise of wages, are inseparable from the wages system, and dictated by the very fact of labour being assimilated to commodities, and therefore subject to the laws regulating the general movement of prices; having, furthermore, shown that a general rise of wages would result in a fall in the general rate of profit, but not affect the average prices of commodities, or their values, the question now ultimately arises, how far, in this incessant struggle between capital and labour, the latter is likely to prove successful.

I might answer by a generalisation, and say that, as with all other commodities, so with labour, its *market price* will, in the long run, adapt itself to its *value*; that, therefore, despite all the ups and downs, and do what he may, the working man will, on an average, only receive the value of his labour, which resolves into the value of his labouring power, which is determined by the value of the necessaries required for its maintenance and reproduction, which value of necessaries finally is regulated by the quantity of labour wanted to produce them.

But there are some peculiar features which distinguish the *value of the labouring power*, or *the value of labour*, from the values of all other commodities. The value of the labouring power is formed by two elements—the one merely physical, the other historical or social. Its *ultimate limit* is determined by the *physical* element, that is to say, to maintain and reproduce itself, to perpetuate its physical existence, the working class must receive the necessaries absolutely indispensable for living and multiplying. The *value* of those indispensable necessaries forms, therefore, the ultimate limit of the *value of labour*. On the other hand, the length of the working day is also limited by ultimate, although very elastic boundaries. Its ultimate limit is given by the physical force of the labouring man. If the daily exhaustion of his vital forces exceeds a certain degree, it cannot be exerted anew, day by day. However, as I said, this limit is very elastic. A quick succession of unhealthy and short-lived generations will keep the labour market as well supplied as a series of vigorous and long-lived generations.

Besides this mere physical element, the value of labour is in every country determined by a *traditional standard of life*. It is not mere physical life, but it is the satisfaction of certain wants springing from the social conditions in which people are placed and reared up. The English standard of life may be reduced to the Irish standard; the standard of life of a German peasant to that of a Livonian peasant. The important part which historical tradition and social habitude play in this respect, you may learn from Mr. Thornton's work on *Over-population,* where he shows that the average wages in different agricultural districts of England still nowadays differ more or less according to the more or less favourable circumstances under which the districts have emerged from the state of serfdom.

This historical or social element, entering into the value of labour, may be expanded, or contracted, or altogether extinguished, so that nothing remains but the *physical limit.* During the time of the *anti-Jacobin war,* undertaken, as the incorrigible tax-eater and sinecurist, old George Rose, used to say, to save the comforts of our holy religion from the inroads of the French infidels, the honest English farmers, so tenderly handled in a former chapter of ours, depressed the wages of the agricultural labourers even beneath that *mere physical minimum,* but made up by *Poor Laws* the remainder necessary for the physical perpetuation of the race. This was a glorious way to convert the wages labourer into a slave, and Shakespeare's proud yeoman into a pauper.

By comparing the standard wages or values of labour in different countries, and by comparing them in different historical epochs of the same country, you will find that the *value of labour* itself is not a fixed but a variable magnitude, even supposing the values of all other commodities to remain constant.

A similar comparison would prove that not only the *market rates of profit* change but its *average rates.*

But as to *profits,* there exists no law which determines their *minimum.* We cannot say what is the ultimate limit of their decrease. And why cannot we fix that limit? Because, although we can fix the *minimum* of wages, we cannot fix their *maximum.* We can only say that, the limits of the working day being given, the *maximum of profit* corresponds to the *physical minimum of wages;* and that wages being given, the *maximum of profit* corresponds to such a prolongation of the working day as is compatible with the physical forces of the labourer. The maximum of profit is, therefore, limited by the physical minimum of wages and the physical maximum of the working day. It is evident that between the two limits of this *maximum rate of profit* an immense scale of variations is possible. The fixation of its actual degree is only settled by the continuous struggle between capital and labour, the capitalist constantly tending to reduce wages to their physical minimum, and to extend the working day to its physical maximum, while the working man constantly presses in the opposite direction.

The matter resolves itself into a question of the respective powers of the combatants.

2. As to the *limitation of the working day* in England, as in all other countries, it has never been settled except by *legislative interference.* Without the working men's continuous pressure from without that interference would never have taken place. But at all events, the result was not to be attained by private settlement between the working men and the capitalists. This very necessity of *general political action* affords the proof that in its merely economic action capital is the stronger side.

As to the *limits* of the *value of labour,* its actual settlement always depends upon supply and demand. I mean the demand for labour on the part of capital, and the supply of labour by the working men. In colonial countries the law of supply and demand favours the working man. Hence the relatively high standard of wages in the United States. Capital may there try its utmost. It cannot prevent the labour market

VALUE, PRICE AND PROFIT

from being continuously emptied by the continuous conversion of wages labourers into independent, self-sustaining peasants. The position of a wages labourer is for a very large part of the American people but a probational state, which they are sure to leave within a longer or shorter term. To mend this colonial state of things, the paternal British Government accepted for some time what is called the modern colonisation theory, which consists in putting an artificial high price upon colonial land, in order to prevent the too quick conversion of the wages labourer into the independent peasant.

But let us now come to old civilised countries, in which capital domineers over the whole process of production. Take, for example, the rise in England of agricultural wages from 1849 to 1859. What was its consequence? The farmers could not, as our friend Weston would have advised them, raise the value of wheat, nor even its market prices. They had, on the contrary, to submit to their fall. But during these eleven years they introduced machinery of all sorts, adopted more scientific methods, converted part of arable land into pasture, increased the size of farms, and with this the scale of production, and by these and other processes, diminishing the demand for labour by increasing its productive power, made the agricultural population again relatively redundant. This is the general method in which a reaction, quicker or slower, of capital against a rise of wages takes place in old, settled countries. Ricardo has justly remarked that machinery is in constant competition with labour, and can often be only intro-duced when the price of labour has reached a certain height, but the appliance of machinery is but one of the many methods for increasing the productive powers of labour. This very same development which makes common labour relatively redun-dant simplifies on the other hand skilled labour, and thus depreciates it.

The same law obtains in another form. With the development of the productive powers of labour the accumulation of capital will be accelerated, even despite a relatively high rate of wages. Hence, one might infer, as *Adam Smith,* in whose days modern industry was still in its infancy, did infer, that the accelerated accumulation of capital must turn the balance in favour of the working man, by securing a growing demand for his labour. From this same standpoint many contemporary writers have wondered that English capital having grown in the last twenty years so much quicker than English population, wages should not have been more enhanced. But simultaneously with the progress of accumulation there takes place a *progressive change* in the *composition of capital.* That part of the aggregate capital which consists of fixed capital, machinery, raw materials, means of production in all possible forms, progressively increases as compared with the other part of capital, which is laid out in wages or in the purchase of labour. This law has been stated in a more or less accurate manner by Mr. Barton, Ricardo, Sismondi, Professor Richard Jones, Professor Ramsay, Cherbuliez, and others.

If the proportion of these two elements of capital was originally one to one, it will, in the progress of industry, become five to one, and so forth. If of a total capital of 600, 300 is laid out in instruments, raw materials, and so forth, and 300 in wages, the total capital wants only to be doubled to create a demand for 600 working men instead of for 300. But if of a capital of 600, 500 is laid out in machinery, materials, and so forth, and 100 only in wages, the same capital must increase from 600 to 3,600 in order to create a demand for 600 workmen instead of 300. In the progress of industry the demand for labour keeps, therefore, no pace with accumulation of capital. It will still increase, but increase in a constantly diminishing ratio as compared with the increase of capital.

These few hints will suffice to show that the very development of modern industry must progressively turn the scale in favour of the capitalist against the working man, and that consequently the general tendency of capitalistic production is not to raise, but to sink the average standard of wages, or to push the *value of labour* more or less to its *minimum limit*. Such being the tendency of *things* in this system, is this saying that the working class ought to renounce their resistance against the encroachments of capital, and abandon their attempts at making the best of the occasional chances for their temporary improvement? If they did, they would be degraded to one level mass of broken wretches past salvation. I think I have shown that their struggles for the standard of wages are incidents inseparable from the whole wages system, that in 99 cases out of 100 their efforts at raising wages are only efforts at maintaining the given value of labour, and that the necessity of debating their price with the capitalist is inherent in their condition of having to sell themselves as commodities. By cowardly giving way in their everyday conflict with capital, they would certainly disqualify themselves for the initiating of any larger movement.

At the same time, and quite apart from the general servitude involved in the wages system, the working class ought not to exaggerate to themselves the ultimate working of these everyday struggles. They ought not to forget that they are fighting with effects, but not with the causes of those effects; that they are retarding the downward movement, but not changing its direction; that they are applying palliatives, not curing the malady. They ought, therefore, not to be exclusively absorbed in these unavoidable guerilla fights incessantly springing up from the never-ceasing encroachments of capital or changes of the market. They ought to understand that, with all the miseries it imposes upon them, the present system simultaneously engenders the *material conditions* and the *social forms* necessary for an economical reconstruction of society. Instead of the *conservative* motto, *"A fair day's wage for a fair day's work!"* they ought to inscribe on their banner the *revolutionary* watchword, *"Abolition of the wages system!"*

After this very long and, I fear, tedious exposition which I was obliged to enter into to do some justice to the subject-matter, I shall conclude by proposing the following resolutions:

Firstly. A general rise in the rate of wages would result in a fall of the general rate of profit, but, broadly speaking, not affect the prices of commodities.

Secondly. The general tendency of capitalist production is not to raise, but to sink the average standard of wages.

Thirdly. Trades Unions work well as centres of resistance against the encroachments of capital. They fail partially from an injudicious use of their power. They fail generally from limiting themselves to a guerilla war against the effects of the existing system, instead of simultaneously trying to change it, instead of using their organised forces as a lever for the final emancipation of the working class, that is to say, the ultimate abolition of the wages system.

Written between the end of May and June 27, 1865.
First published as a separate pamphlet in London in 1898.

CHAPTER 5

SELECTION FROM *THE CIVIL WAR IN FRANCE*

IN JULY 1870 WAR BROKE OUT BETWEEN FRANCE AND PRUSSIA, concluding with the defeat and capture of Louis Bonaparte, the authoritarian leader of France, in September. In response, a new republic was formed, a Government of National Defense to continue the resistance against Prussia. Paris was besieged by the Prussian army and in early 1871 a new National Assembly was created, based in Versailles, to negotiate peace. One provision of the peace treaty was the disarmament of the National Guard, the Parisian militia. Moves to do this provoked the National Guard to repudiate the new French government in Versailles and form its own government in Paris: the Paris Commune of 1871. It only lasted from March until May before being suppressed by the government at Versailles, with the aid of the Prussians. Although it only had a brief existence, for Marx and Engels the Paris Commune was a landmark in the political struggle of the working class to forge a new order.

As is well-known, Marx originally counseled against what he considered to be premature political action on the part of the French workers, arguing instead for the consolidation of the political forces of the working classes under the Versailles republic. Speaking in the name of the leadership of the International Working Men's Association, he clearly stated this position in the "Second Address of the General Council" in September 1870. "The French working class moves, therefore, under circumstances of extreme difficulty. Any attempt at upsetting the new government in the present crisis, when the enemy is almost knocking at the doors of Paris, would be a desperate folly. . . . Let them calmly and resolutely improve the opportunities of republican liberty, for the work of their own class organization."[1] It was nonetheless widely believed in Europe that the IWMA was behind the later uprising, although only a few members of the IWMA were, as individuals, involved in the Paris events.

However, once the Commune was established Marx became its strongest defender. Learning from the real historical movement of the workers, Marx argued that the political organization of the Commune was "the political form at last discovered under which to work out the economical emancipation of Labor."[2] Marx was under no illusions that the Commune was immediately socialist, but he was convinced that political power in the hands of the working class and allied producing groups would lead in that direction. This might have been true especially had there been time to work toward the goal of a federation of communes throughout France.

Marx powerfully presents this assessment in *The Civil War in France*, published a few weeks after the fall of the Commune, of which the third section, where Marx analyzes the Commune's political structure, is provided here. This vigorous defense of what more conservative Europeans considered to be an uprising of terrorists earned Marx considerable notoriety, even the title of "The Red Terrorist Doctor."[3] Also included here is Engels's introduction to a twentieth anniversary republication of *The Civil War in France*.

At the end of the introduction, Engels refers to the Commune as "the dictatorship of the proletariat." It should be mentioned that whether it is properly described as such is actually a contentious issue. Both August H. Nimtz and Hal Draper cast doubt on the appropriateness of Engels's phrase. Engels apparently applied the phrase because Marx reportedly stated this in a toast at a banquet four months after the Commune fell. Since other social strata were involved, Nimtz is convincing in arguing that the Commune should at most be understood as a dictatorship of a "people's alliance."[4]

A few additional words are necessary on persons and terms. First, August Blanqui was a very well-known revolutionary figure who advocated the seizure of power by a small group on behalf of the oppressed. Pierre Joseph Proudhon was also a prominent figure of the nineteenth-century workers movement. In *The Philosophy of Poverty* he argued for a more cooperatist than competitive exchange society, a scheme and political strategy Marx devastatingly criticized in his first powerful political statement, *The Poverty of Philosophy*. Engels discusses the influence of the followers of both Blanqui and Proudhon in his introduction. It should also be noticed that in the present work Marx employs the phrase "middle class society" to exclude the big bourgeoisie, that is, his is now much closer to the modern usage of the term.

NOTES

1. David Fernbach, editor, *The First International and After* (New York: Random House, 1974), p. 185. See also Fernbach's introduction, ibid., p. 30, and August H. Nimtz, Jr., *Marx and Engels: Their Contribution to the Democratic Breakthrough* (Albany, NY: State University of New York Press, 2000), p. 210.
2. Below. See Nimtz, *Marx and Engels*, p. 216.
3. Isaiah Berlin, *Karl Marx: His Life and Environment* (New York: Oxford University Press, 1959), p. 243. Berlin states that Marx published the work under his own name in order to deflect some of the criticism from the International: ibid, p. 243.
4. Nimtz, *Marx and Engels*, pp. 218–220. Hal Draper, *The 'Dictatorship of the Proletariat' from Marx to Lenin* (New York: Monthly Review Press, 1987), pp. 37–38.

INTRODUCTION [TO KARL MARX'S *THE CIVIL WAR IN FRANCE*]

[FREDERICK ENGELS]

I DID NOT ANTICIPATE THAT I WOULD BE ASKED TO PREPARE a new edition of the Address of the General Council of the International on *The Civil War in France*, and to write an introduction to it. Therefore I can only touch briefly here on the most important points.

I am prefacing the longer work mentioned above by the two shorter Addresses of the General Council on the Franco-Prussian War. In the first place, because the second of these, which itself cannot be fully understood without the first, is referred to in *The Civil War*. But also because these two Addresses, likewise drafted by Marx, are, no less than *The Civil War*, outstanding examples of the author's remarkable gift, first proved in *The Eighteenth Brumaire of Louis Bonaparte*, for grasping clearly the character, the import and the necessary consequences of great historical events, at a time when these events are still in progress before our eyes or have only just taken place. And, finally, because today we in Germany are still having to endure the consequences which Marx predicted would follow from these events.

Has that which was declared in the first Address not come to pass: that if Germany's defensive war against Louis Bonaparte degenerated into a war of conquest against the French people, all the miseries that befell Germany after the so-called wars of independence would revive again with renewed intensity? Have we not had a further twenty years of Bismarck's rule, the Exceptional Law and socialist-baiting taking the place of the prosecution of demagogues, with the same arbitrary action of the police and with literally the same staggering interpretations of the law?

And has not the prediction been proved to the letter, that the annexation of Alsace-Lorraine would "force France into the arms of Russia," and that after this annexation Germany must either become the avowed servant of Russia, or must, after some short respite, arm for a new war, and, moreover, "a war of races—a war with the combined Slavonian and Roman races"? Has not the annexation of the French provinces driven France into the arms of Russia? Has not Bismarck for fully twenty years vainly wooed the favour of the tsar, wooed it with services even more lowly than those which little Prussia, before it became the "first Power in Europe," was wont to lay at Holy Russia's feet? And is there not every day still hanging over our heads the Damocles' sword of war, on the first day of which all the chartered covenants of princes will be scattered like chaff; a war of which nothing is certain but the absolute uncertainty of its outcome; a race war which will subject the whole of Europe to devastation by fifteen or twenty million armed men, and which is not raging already only because even the strongest of the great military states shrinks before the absolute incalculability of its final result?

All the more is it our duty to make again accessible to the German workers these brilliant proofs, now half-forgotten, of the farsightedness of international working-class policy in 1870.

What is true of these two Addresses is also true of *The Civil War in France*. On May 28, the last fighters of the Commune succumbed to superior forces on the slopes of Belleville; and only two days later, on May 30, Marx read to the General Council the work in which the historical significance of the Paris Commune is delineated in short, powerful strokes, but with such trenchancy, and above all such truth as has never again been attained in all the mass of literature on this subject.

Thanks to the economic and political development of France since 1789, Paris has been placed for the last fifty years in such a position that no revolution could break out there without assuming a proletarian character, that is to say, without the proletariat, which had bought victory with its blood, advancing its own demands after victory. These demands were more or less unclear and even confused, corresponding to the state of development reached by the workers of Paris at the particular period, but in the last resort they all amounted to the abolition of the class antagonism between capitalists and workers. It is true that no one knew how this was to be brought about. But the demand itself, however indefinitely it still was couched, contained a threat to the existing order of society; the workers who put it forward were still armed; therefore, the disarming of the workers was the first commandment for the bourgeois, who were at the helm of the state. Hence, after every revolution won by the workers, a new struggle, ending with the defeat of the workers.

This happened for the first time in 1848. The liberal bourgeois of the parliamentary opposition held banquets for securing a reform of the franchise, which was to ensure supremacy for their party. Forced more and more, in their struggle with the government, to appeal to the people, they had gradually to yield precedence to the radical and republican strata of the bourgeoisie and petty bourgeoisie. But behind these stood the revolutionary workers, and since 1830 these had acquired far more political independence than the bourgeois, and even the republicans, suspected. At the moment of the crisis between the government and the opposition, the workers began street-fighting; Louis Philippe vanished, and with him the franchise reform; and in its place arose the republic, and indeed one which the victorious workers themselves designated as a "social" republic. No one, however, was clear as to what this social republic was to imply; not even the workers themselves. But they now had arms and were a power in the state. Therefore, as soon as the bourgeois republicans in control felt something like firm ground under their feet, their first aim was to disarm the workers. This took place by driving them into the insurrection of June 1848 by direct breach of faith, by open defiance and the attempt to banish the unemployed to a distant province. The government had taken care to have an overwhelming superiority of force. After five days' heroic struggle, the workers were defeated. And then followed a blood-bath among the defenceless prisoners, the like of which has not been seen since the days of the civil wars which ushered in the downfall of the Roman republic. It was the first time that the bourgeoisie showed to what insane cruelties of revenge it will be goaded the moment the proletariat dares to take its stand against the bourgeoisie as a separate class, with its own interests and demands. And yet 1848 was only child's play compared with the frenzy of the bourgeoisie in 1871.

Punishment followed hard at heel. If the proletariat was not yet able to rule France, the bourgeoisie could no longer do so. At least not at that period, when the greater part of it was still monarchically inclined, and it was divided into three dynastic parties and a fourth, republican party. Its internal dissensions allowed the adventurer, Louis Bonaparte, to take possession of all the commanding points—army, police, administrative machinery—and on December 2, 1851, to explode the last stronghold of the bourgeoisie, the National Assembly. The Second Empire began—the exploitation of France by a gang of political and financial adventurers, but at the same time also an industrial development such as had never been possible under the narrow-minded and timorous system of Louis Philippe, with the exclusive domination of only a small section of the big bourgeoisie. Louis Bonaparte took the political power from the capitalists under the pretext of protecting them, the bourgeois, from the workers, and on the other hand the workers from them; but in return his rule encouraged speculation and industrial activity—in a word, the insurgence and enrichment of the whole bourgeoisie to an extent hitherto unknown. To an even greater extent, it is true, corruption and mass thievery developed, clustering around the imperial court, and drawing their heavy percentages from this enrichment.

But the Second Empire was the appeal to French chauvinism, was the demand for the restoration of the frontiers of the First Empire, which had been lost in 1814, or at least those of the First Republic. A French empire within the frontiers of the old monarchy and, in fact, within the even more amputated frontiers of 1815—such a thing was impossible for any length of time. Hence the necessity for occasional wars and extensions of frontiers. But no extension of frontiers was so dazzling to the imagination of the French chauvinists as the extension to the German left bank of the Rhine. One square mile on the Rhine was more to them than ten in the Alps or anywhere else. Given the Second Empire, the demand for the restoration of the left bank of the Rhine, either all at once or piecemeal, was merely a question of time. The time came with the Austro-Prussian War of 1866; cheated of the anticipated "territorial compensation" by Bismarck and by his own over-cunning, hesitant policy, there was now nothing left for Napoleon but war, which broke out in 1870 and drove him first to Sedan, and thence to Wilhelmshöhe.

The necessary consequence was the Paris Revolution of September 4, 1870. The empire collapsed like a house of cards, and the republic was again proclaimed. But the enemy was standing at the gates; the armies of the empire were either hopelessly encircled at Metz or held captive in Germany. In this emergency the people allowed the Paris deputies to the former legislative body to constitute themselves into a "Government of National Defence." This was the more readily conceded, since, for the purposes of defence, all Parisians capable of bearing arms had enrolled in the National Guard and were armed, so that now the workers constituted a great majority. But very soon the antagonism between the almost completely bourgeois government and the armed proletariat broke into open conflict. On October 31, workers' battalions stormed the town hall and captured part of the membership of the government. Treachery, the government's direct breach of its undertakings, and the intervention of some petty-bourgeois battalions set them free again, and in order not to occasion the outbreak of civil war inside a city besieged by a foreign military power, the former government was left in office.

At last, on January 28, 1871, starved Paris capitulated. But with honours unprecedented in the history of war. The forts were surrendered, the city wall stripped of guns, the weapons of the regiments of the line and of the Mobile Guard were handed over, and they themselves considered prisoners of war. But the National Guard kept its weapons and guns, and only entered into an armistice with the victors. And these did not dare enter Paris in triumph. They only dared to occupy a tiny corner of Paris, which, into the bargain, consisted partly of public parks, and even this they only occupied for a few days! And during this time they, who had maintained their encirclement of Paris for 131 days, were themselves encircled by the armed workers of Paris, who kept a sharp watch that no "Prussian" should overstep the narrow bounds of the corner ceded to the foreign conqueror. Such was the respect which the Paris workers inspired in the army before which all the armies of the empire had laid down their arms; and the Prussian Junkers, who had come to take revenge at the home of the revolution, were compelled to stand by respectfully, and salute precisely this armed revolution!

During the war the Paris workers had confined themselves to demanding the vigorous prosecution of the fight. But now, when peace had come after the capitulation of Paris, now Thiers, the new supreme head of the government, was compelled to realise that the rule of the propertied classes—big landowners and capitalists—was in constant danger so long as the workers of Paris had arms in their hands. His first action was an attempt to disarm them. On March 18, he sent troops of the line with orders to rob the National Guard of the artillery belonging to it, which had been constructed during the siege of Paris and had been paid for by public subscription. The attempt failed; Paris mobilised as one man for resistance, and war between Paris and the French Government sitting at Versailles was declared. On March 26 the Paris Commune was elected and on March 28 it was proclaimed. The Central Committee of the National Guard, which up to then had carried on the government, handed in its resignation to the Commune after it had first decreed the abolition of the scandalous Paris "Morality Police." On March 30 the Commune abolished conscription and the standing army, and declared the sole armed force to be the National Guard, in which all citizens capable of bearing arms were to be enrolled. It remitted all payments of rent for dwelling houses from October 1870 until April, the amounts already paid to be booked as future rent payments, and stopped all sales of articles pledged in the municipal loan office. On the same day the foreigners elected to the Commune were confirmed in office, because "the flag of the Commune is the flag of the World Republic." On April 1 it was decided that the highest salary to be received by any employee of the Commune, and therefore also by its members themselves, was not to exceed 6,000 francs (4,800 marks). On the following day the

Commune decreed the separation of the church from the state, and the abolition of
all state payments for religious purposes as well as the transformation of all church
property into national property; as a result of which, on April 8, the exclusion from
the schools of all religious symbols, pictures, dogmas, prayers—in a word, "of all
that belongs to the sphere of the individual conscience"—was ordered and gradually
put into effect.—On the 5th, in reply to the shooting, day after day, of captured
Commune fighters by the Versailles troops, a decree was issued for the imprisonment of hostages, but it was never carried out.—On the 6th, the guillotine was
brought out by the 137th battalion of the National Guard, and publicly burnt,
amid great popular rejoicing.—On the 12th, the Commune decided that the
Victory Column on the *Place Vendôme*, which had been cast from captured guns by
Napoleon after the war of 1809, should be demolished as a symbol of chauvinism
and incitement to national hatred. This was carried out on May 16.—On April 16
it ordered a statistical tabulation of factories which had been closed down by the
manufacturers, and the working out of plans for the operation of these factories by
the workers formerly employed in them, who were to be organised in co-operative
societies, and also plans for the organisation of these co-operatives in one great
union.—On the 20th it abolished night work for bakers, and also the employment
offices, which since the Second Empire had been run as a monopoly by creatures
appointed by the police—labour exploiters of the first rank; these offices were
transferred to the mayoralties of the twenty *arrondissements* of Paris.—On April 30
it ordered the closing of the pawnshops, on the ground that they were a private
exploitation of the workers, and were in contradiction with the right of the workers
to their instruments of labour and to credit.—On May 5 it ordered the razing of
the Chapel of Atonement, which had been built in expiation of the execution of
Louis XVI.

Thus from March 18 onwards the class character of the Paris movement, which
had previously been pushed into the background by the fight against the foreign
invaders, emerged sharply and clearly. As almost only workers, or recognised representatives of the workers, sat in the Commune, its decisions bore a decidedly
proletarian character. Either these decisions decreed reforms which the republican
bourgeoisie had failed to pass solely out of cowardice, but which provided a necessary basis for the free activity of the working class—such as the implementation of
the principle that *in relation to the state*, religion is a purely private matter—or the
Commune promulgated decrees which were in the direct interest of the working
class and in part cut deeply into the old order of society. In a beleaguered city, however, it was possible to make at most a start in the realisation of all this. And from
the beginning of May onwards all their energies were taken up by the fight against
the armies assembled by the Versailles government in ever-growing numbers.

On April 7 the Versailles troops had captured the Seine crossing at Neuilly, on the
western front of Paris; on the other hand, in an attack, on the southern front on the
11th they were repulsed with heavy losses by General Eudes. Paris was continually
bombarded and, moreover, by the very people who had stigmatised as a sacrilege
the bombardment of the same city by the Prussians. These same people now begged
the Prussian government for the hasty return of the French soldiers taken prisoner
at Sedan and Metz, in order that they might recapture Paris for them. From the

beginning of May the gradual arrival of these troops gave the Versailles forces a decided superiority. This already became evident when, on April 23, Thiers broke off the negotiations for the exchange, proposed by the Commune, of the Archbishop of Paris and a whole number of other priests held as hostages in Paris, for only one man, Blanqui, who had twice been elected to the Commune but was a prisoner in Clairvaux. And even more from the changed language of Thiers; previously procrastinating and equivocal, he now suddenly became insolent, threatening, brutal. The Versailles forces took the redoubt of Moulin Saquet on the southern front, on May 3; on the 9th, Fort Issy, which had been completely reduced to ruins by gunfire; on the 14th, Fort Vanves. On the western front they advanced gradually, capturing the numerous villages and buildings which extended up to the city wall, until they reached the main defences; on the 21st, thanks to treachery and the carelessness of the National Guards stationed there, they succeeded in forcing their way into the city. The Prussians, who held the northern and eastern forts, allowed the Versailles troops to advance across the land north of the city, which was forbidden ground to them under the armistice, and thus to march forward, attacking on a wide front, which the Parisians naturally thought covered by the armistice, and therefore held only weakly. As a result of this, only a weak resistance was put up in the western half of Paris, in the luxury city proper; it grew stronger and more tenacious the nearer the incoming troops approached the eastern half, the working-class city proper. It was only after eight days' fighting that the last defenders of the Commune succumbed on the heights of Belleville and Menilmontant; and then the massacre of defenceless men, women and children, which had been raging all through the week on an increasing scale, reached its zenith. The breechloaders could no longer kill fast enough; the vanquished were shot down in hundreds by *mitrailleuse* fire. The "Wall of the Federals" at the Pére Lachaise cemetery, where the final mass murder was consummated, is still standing today, a mute but eloquent testimony to the frenzy of which the ruling class is capable as soon as the working class dares to stand up for its rights. Then, when the slaughter of them all proved to be impossible, came the mass arrests, the shooting of victims arbitrarily selected from the prisoners' ranks, and the removal of the rest to great camps where they awaited trial by courts-martial. The Prussian troops surrounding the northeastern half of Paris had orders not to allow any fugitives to pass; but the officers often shut their eyes when the soldiers paid more obedience to the dictates of humanity than to those of the Supreme Command; particular honour is due to the Saxon army corps, which behaved very humanely and let through many who were obviously fighters for the Commune.

If today, after twenty years, we look back at the activity and historical significance of the Paris Commune of 1871, we shall find it necessary to make a few additions to the account given in *The Civil War in France*.

The members of the Commune were divided into a majority, the Blanquists, who had also been predominant in the Central Committee of the National Guard; and a minority, members of the International Working Men's Association, chiefly consisting of adherents of the Proudhon school of socialism. The great majority of the Blanquists were at that time socialists only by revolutionary, proletarian instinct; only a few had attained greater clarity on principles, through Vaillant, who was familiar with German scientific socialism. It is therefore comprehensible that in the economic sphere much was left undone which, according to our view today, the Commune ought to have done. The hardest thing to understand is certainly the holy awe with which they remained standing respectfully outside the gates of the Bank of France. This was also a serious political mistake. The bank in the hands of the Commune—this would have been worth more than ten thousand hostages. It would have meant the pressure of the whole of the French bourgeoisie on the Versailles government in favour of peace with the Commune. But what is still more wonderful is the correctness of much that nevertheless was done by the Commune, composed as it was of Blanquists and Proudhonists. Naturally, the Proudhonists were chiefly responsible for the economic decrees of the Commune, both for their praiseworthy and their unpraiseworthy aspects; as the Blanquists were for its political commissions and omissions. And in both cases the irony of history willed—as is usual when doctrinaires come to the helm—that both did the opposite of what the doctrines of their school prescribed.

Proudhon, the socialist of the small peasant and master-craftsman, regarded association with positive hatred. He said of it that there was more bad than good in it; that it was by nature sterile, even harmful, because it was a fetter on the freedom of the worker; that it was a pure dogma, unproductive and burdensome, in conflict as much with the freedom of the worker as with economy of labour; that its disadvantages multiplied more swiftly than its advantages; that, as compared with it, competition, division of labour and private property were economic forces. Only in the exceptional cases—as Proudhon called them—of large-scale industry and large establishments, such as railways, was the association of workers in place. (See *General Idea of the Revolution*, 3rd sketch.)

By 1871, large-scale industry had already so much ceased to be an exceptional case even in Paris, the centre of artistic handicrafts, that by far the most important decree of the Commune instituted an organisation of large-scale industry and even of manufacture which was not only to be based on the association of the workers in each factory, but also to combine all these associations in one great union; in short, an organisation which, as Marx quite rightly says in *The Civil War*, must necessarily have led in the end to communism, that is to say, the direct opposite of the Proudhon doctrine. And, therefore, the Commune was the grave of the Proudhon school of socialism. Today this school has vanished from French working-class circles; here, among the Possibilists no less than among the "Marxists," Marx's theory now rules unchallenged. Only among the "radical" bourgeoisie are there still Proudhonists.

The Blanquists fared no better. Brought up in the school of conspiracy, and held together by the strict discipline which went with it, they started out from the viewpoint that a relatively small number of resolute, well-organised men would be able, at a given favourable moment, not only to seize the helm of state, but also by a display of great, ruthless energy, to maintain power until they succeeded in sweeping the mass of the people into the revolution and ranging them round the small band of leaders. This involved, above all, the strictest, dictatorial centralisation of all power in the hands of the new revolutionary government. And what did the Commune, with its majority of these same Blanquists, actually do? In all its proclamations to the French in the provinces, it appealed to them to form a free federation of all French

Communes with Paris, a national organisation which for the first time was really to be created by the nation itself. It was precisely the oppressing power of the former centralised government, army, political police, bureaucracy, which Napoleon had created in 1798 and which since then had been taken over by every new government as a welcome instrument and used against its opponents—it was precisely this power which was to fall everywhere, just as it had already fallen in Paris.

From the very outset the Commune was compelled to recognise that the working class, once come to power, could not go on managing with the old state machine; that in order not to lose again its only just conquered supremacy, this working class must, on the one hand, do away with all the old repressive machinery previously used against it itself, and, on the other, safeguard itself against its own deputies and officials, by declaring them all, without exception, subject to recall at any moment. What had been the characteristic attribute of the former state? Society had created its own organs to look after its common interests, originally through simple division of labour. But these organs, at whose head was the state power, had in the course of time, in pursuance of their own special interests, transformed themselves from the servants of society into the masters of society. This can be seen, for example, not only in the hereditary monarchy, but equally so in the democratic republic. Nowhere do "politicians" form a more separate and powerful section of the nation than precisely in North America. There, each of the two major parties which alternately succeed each other in power is itself in turn controlled by people who make a business of politics, who speculate on seats in the legislative assemblies of the Union as well as of the separate states, or who make a living by carrying on agitation for their party and on its victory are rewarded with positions. It is well known how the Americans have been trying for thirty years to shake off this yoke, which has become intolerable, and how in spite of it all they continue to sink ever deeper in this swamp of corruption. It is precisely in America that we see best how there takes place this process of the state power making itself independent in relation to society, whose mere instrument it was originally intended to be. Here there exists no dynasty, no nobility, no standing army, beyond the few men keeping watch on the Indians, no bureaucracy with permanent posts or the right to pensions. And nevertheless we find here two great gangs of political speculators, who alternately take possession of the state power, and exploit it by the most corrupt means and for the most corrupt ends—and the nation is powerless against these two great cartels of politicians, who are ostensibly its servants, but in reality dominate and plunder it.

Against this transformation of the state and the organs of the state from servants of society into masters of society—an inevitable transformation in all previous states—the Commune made use of two infallible means. In the first place, it filled all posts—administrative, judicial and educational—by election on the basis of universal suffrage of all concerned, subject to the right of recall at any time by the same electors. And, in the second place, all officials, high or low, were paid only the wages received by other workers. The highest salary paid by the Commune to anyone was 6,000 francs. In this way an effective barrier to place-hunting and careerism was set up, even apart from the binding mandates to delegates to representative bodies which were added besides.

This shattering [*Sprengung*] of the former state power and its replacement by a new and truly democratic one is described in detail in the third section of *The Civil War*.

But it was necessary to dwell briefly here once more on some of its features, because in Germany particularly the superstitious belief in the state has been carried over from philosophy into the general consciousness of the bourgeoisie and even of many workers. According to the philosophical conception, the state is the "realisation of the idea," or the Kingdom of God on earth, translated into philosophical terms, the sphere in which eternal truth and justice is or should be realised. And from this follows a superstitious reverence for the state and everything connected with it, which takes root the more readily since people are accustomed from childhood to imagine that the affairs and interests common to the whole of society could not be looked after otherwise than as they have been looked after in the past, that is, through the state and its lucratively positioned officials. And people think they have taken quite an extraordinarily bold step forward when they have rid themselves of belief in hereditary monarchy and swear by the democratic republic. In reality, however, the state is nothing but a machine for the oppression of one class by another, and indeed in the democratic republic no less than in the monarchy; and at best an evil inherited by the proletariat after its victorious struggle for class supremacy, whose worst sides the victorious proletariat, just like the Commune, cannot avoid having to lop off at once as much as possible until such time as a generation reared in new, free social conditions is able to throw the entire lumber of the state on the scrap heap.

Of late, the German philistine has once more been filled with wholesome terror at the words: Dictatorship of the Proletariat. Well and good, gentlemen, do you want to know what this dictatorship looks like? Look at the Paris Commune. That was the Dictatorship of the Proletariat.

London, on the twentieth anniversary of the Paris Commune,
March 18, 1891   *F. Engels*

First published in *Die Neue Zeit,* Vol. 2, No. 28, 1890–1891, and in the book: Marx, *Der Bürgerkrieg in Frankreich,* Berlin, 1891.

The Civil War in France

Address of the General Council of the International Working Men's Association

Karl Marx

III

On the dawn of the 18th of March, Paris arose to the thunderburst of "Vive la Commune!" What is the Commune, that sphinx so tantalizing to the bourgeois mind?

"The proletarians of Paris," said the Central Committee in its manifesto of the 18th March, "amidst the failures and treasons of the ruling classes, have understood that the hour has struck for them to save the situation by taking into their own hands the direction of public affairs. . . . They have understood that it is their imperious duty and their absolute right to render themselves masters of their own destinies, by seizing upon the governmental power."

But the working class cannot simply lay hold of the ready-made State machinery, and wield it for its own purposes.

The centralized State power, with its ubiquitous organs of standing army, police, bureaucracy, clergy, and judicature—organs wrought after the plan of a systematic and hierarchic division of labour—originates from the days of absolute monarchy, serving nascent middle-class society as a mighty weapon in its struggles against feudalism. Still, its development remained clogged by all manner of mediaeval rubbish, seignorial rights, local privileges, municipal and guild monopolies and provincial constitutions. The gigantic broom of the French Revolution of the eighteenth century swept away all these relics of bygone times, thus clearing simultaneously the social soil of its last hindrances to the superstructure of the modern

State edifice raised under the First Empire, itself the offspring of the coalition wars of old semi-feudal Europe against modern France. During the subsequent *régimes* the Government, placed under parliamentary control—that is, under the direct control of the propertied classes—became not only a hotbed of huge national debts and crushing taxes; with its irresistible allurements of place, pelf, and patronage, it became not only the bone of contention between the rival factions and adventurers of the ruling classes; but its political character changed simultaneously with the economic changes of society. At the same pace at which the progress of modern industry developed, widened, intensified the class antagonism between capital and labour, the State power assumed more and more the character of the national power of capital over labour, of a public force organized for social enslavement, of an engine of class despotism. After every revolution marking a progressive phase in the class struggle, the purely repressive character of the State power stands out in bolder and bolder relief. The Revolution of 1830, resulting in the transfer of Government from the landlords to the capitalists, transferred it from the more remote to the more direct antagonists of the working men. The bourgeois Republicans, who, in the name of the Revolution of February, took the State power, used it for the June massacres, in order to convince the working class that "social" republic meant the republic ensuring their social subjection, and in order to convince the royalist bulk of the bourgeois and landlord class that they might safely leave the cares and emoluments of government to the bourgeois "Republicans." However, after their one heroic exploit of June, the bourgeois Republicans had, from the front, to fall back to the rear of the "Party of Order"—a combination formed by all the rival fractions and factions of the appropriating class in their now openly declared antagonism to the producing classes. The proper form of their joint-stock Government was the *Parliamentary Republic,* with Louis Bonaparte for its President. Theirs was a *régime* of avowed class terrorism and deliberate insult towards the "vile multitude." If the Parliamentary Republic, as M. Thiers said, "divided them (the different fractions of the ruling class) least," it opened an abyss between that class and the whole body of society outside their spare ranks. The restraints by which their own divisions had under former *régimes* still checked the State power, were removed by their union; and in view of the threatening upheaval of the proletariate, they now used that State power mercilessly and ostentatiously as the national war-engine of capital against labour. In their uninterrupted crusade against the producing masses they were, however, bound not only to invest the executive with continually increased powers of repression, but at the same time to divest their own parliamentary stronghold— the National Assembly—one by one, of all its own means of defence against the Executive. The Executive, in the person of Louis Bonaparte, turned them out. The natural offspring of the "Party-of-Order" Republic was the Second Empire.

The Empire, with the *coup d'état* for its certificate of birth, universal suffrage for its sanction, and the sword for its sceptre, professed to rest upon the peasantry, the large mass of producers not directly involved in the struggle of capital and labour. It professed to save the working class by breaking down Parliamentarism, and, with it, the undisguised subserviency of Government to the propertied classes. It professed to save the propertied classes by upholding their economic supremacy over the working class; and, finally, it professed to unite all classes by reviving for all the chimera of national glory. In reality, it was the only form of government possible at a time when the bourgeoisie had already lost, and the working class had not yet acquired, the faculty of ruling the nation. It was acclaimed throughout the world as the saviour of society. Under its sway, bourgeois society, freed from political cares, attained a development unexpected even by itself. Its industry and commerce expanded to colossal dimensions; financial swindling celebrated cosmopolitan orgies; the misery of the masses was set off by a shameless display of gorgeous, meretricious, and debased luxury. The State power, apparently soaring high above society, was at the same time itself the greatest scandal of that society and the very hotbed of all its corruptions. Its own rottenness, and the rottenness of the society it had saved, were laid bare by the bayonet of Prussia, herself eagerly bent upon transferring the supreme seat of that *régime* from Paris to Berlin. Imperialism is, at the same time, the most prostitute and the ultimate form of the State power which nascent middle-class society had commenced to elaborate as a means of its own emancipation from feudalism, and which full-grown bourgeois society had finally transformed into a means for the enslavement of labour by capital.

The direct antithesis to the Empire was the Commune. The cry of "Social Republic," with which the revolution of February was ushered in by the Paris proletariate, did but express a vague aspiration after a Republic that was not only to supersede the monarchical form of class-rule, but class-rule itself. The Commune was the positive form of that Republic.

Paris, the central seat of the old governmental power, and, at the same time, the social stronghold of the French working class, had risen in arms against the attempt of Thiers and the Rurals to restore and perpetuate that old governmental power bequeathed to them by the Empire. Paris could resist only because, in consequence of the siege, it had got rid of the army, and replaced it by a National Guard, the bulk of which consisted of working men. This fact was now to be transformed into an institution. The first decree of the Commune, therefore, was the suppression of the standing army, and the substitution for it of the armed people.

The Commune was formed of the municipal councillors, chosen by universal suffrage in the various wards of the town, responsible and revocable at short terms. The majority of its members were naturally working men, of acknowledged representatives of the working class. The Commune was to be a working, not a parliamentary, body, executive and legislative at the same time. Instead of continuing to be the agent of the Central Government, the police was at once stripped of its political attributes, and turned into the responsible and at all times revocable agent of the Commune. So were the officials of all other branches of the Administration. From the members of the Commune downwards, the public service had to be done at *workmen's wages*. The vested interests and the representation allowances of the high dignitaries of State disappeared along with the high dignitaries themselves. Public functions ceased to be the private property of the tools of the Central Government. Not only municipal administration, but the whole initiative hitherto exercised by the State was laid into the hands of the Commune.

Having once got rid of the standing army and the police, the physical force elements of the old Government, the Commune was anxious to break the spiritual force of repression, the "parson-power," by the disestablishment and disendowment of all churches as proprietary bodies. The priests were sent back to the recesses of private life, there to feed upon the alms of the faithful in imitation of their predecessors, the Apostles. The whole of the educational institutions were opened to the people gratuitously, and at the same time cleared of all interference of Church and State. Thus, not only was education made accessible to all, but science itself freed from the fetters which class prejudice and governmental force had imposed upon it.

The judicial functionaries were to be divested of that sham independence which had but served to mask their abject subserviency to all succeeding governments to which, in turn, they had taken, and broken, the oaths of allegiance. Like the rest of public servants, magistrates and judges were to be elective, responsible, and revocable.

The Paris Commune was, of course, to serve as a model to all the great industrial centres of France. The communal *régime* once established in Paris and the secondary centres, the old centralized Government would in the provinces, too, have to give way to the self-government of the producers. In a rough sketch of national organization which the Commune had no time to develop, it states clearly that the Commune was to be the political form of even the smallest country hamlet, and that in the rural districts the standing army was to be replaced by a national militia, with an extremely short term of service. The rural communes of every district were to administer their common affairs by an assembly of delegates in the central town, and these district assemblies were again to send deputies to the National Delegation in Paris, each delegate to be at any time revocable and bound by the *mandat impératif* (formal instructions) of his constituents. The few but important functions which still would remain for a central government were not to be suppressed, as has been intentionally mis-stated, but were to be discharged by Communal, and therefore strictly responsible agents. The unity of the nation was not to be broken, but, on the contrary, to be organized by the Communal constitution, and to become a reality by the destruction of the State power which claimed to be the embodiment of that unity independent of, and superior to, the nation itself, from which it was but a parasitic excrescence. While the merely repressive organs of the old governmental power were to be amputated, its legitimate functions were to be wrested from an authority usurping pre-eminence over society itself, and restored to the responsible agents of society. Instead of deciding once in three or six years which member of the ruling class was to misrepresent the people in Parliament, universal suffrage was to serve the people, constituted in Communes, as individual suffrage serves every other employer in the search for the workmen and managers in his business. And it is well known that companies, like individuals, in matters of real business generally know how to put the right man in the right place, and, if they for once make a mistake, to redress it promptly. On the other hand, nothing could be more foreign to the spirit of the Commune than to supersede universal suffrage by hierarchic investiture.

It is generally the fate of completely new historical creations to be mistaken for the counterpart of older and even defunct forms of social life, to which they may bear a certain likeness. Thus, this new Commune, which breaks the modern State power, has been mistaken for a reproduction of the mediaeval Communes, which first preceded, and afterwards became the substratum of, that very State power.—The communal constitution has been mistaken for an attempt to break up into a federation of small States, as dreamt of by Montesquieu and the Girondins, that unity of great nations which, if originally brought about by political force, has now become a powerful coefficient of social production.—The antagonism of the Commune against the State power has been mistaken for an exaggerated form of the ancient struggle against over-centralization. Peculiar historical circumstances may have prevented the classical development, as in France, of the bourgeois form of government, and may have allowed, as in England, to complete the great central State organs by corrupt vestries, jobbing councillors, and ferocious poor-law guardians in the towns, and virtually hereditary magistrates in the counties. The Communal Constitution would have restored to the social body all the forces hitherto absorbed by the State parasite feeding upon, and clogging the free movement of, society. By this one act it would have initiated the regeneration of France.—The provincial French middle-class saw in the Commune an attempt to restore the sway their order had held over the country under Louis Philippe, and which, under Louis Napoleon, was supplanted by the pretended rule of the country over the towns. In reality, the Communal Constitution brought the rural producers under the intellectual lead of the central towns of their districts, and there secured to them, in the working men, the natural trustees of their interests.—The very existence of the Commune involved, as a matter of course, local municipal liberty, but no longer as a check upon the, now superseded, State power. It could only enter into the head of a Bismarck, who, when not engaged on his intrigues of blood and iron, always likes to resume his old trade, so befitting his mental calibre, of contributor to *Kladderadatsch* (the Berlin *Punch*), it could only enter into such a head, to ascribe to the Paris Commune aspirations after that caricature of the old French municipal organization of 1791, the Prussian municipal constitution which degrades the town governments to mere secondary wheels in the police-machinery of the Prussian State. The Commune made that catch-word of bourgeois revolutions, cheap government, a reality, by destroying the two greatest sources of expenditure—the standing army and State functionarism. Its very existence presupposed the non-existence of monarchy, which, in Europe at least, is the normal incumbrance and indispensable cloak of class-rule. It supplied the Republic with the basis of really democratic institutions. But neither cheap government nor the "true Republic" was its ultimate aim; they were its mere concomitants.

The multiplicity of interpretations to which the Commune has been subjected, and the multiplicity of interests which construed it in their favour, show that it was a thoroughly expansive political form, while all previous forms of government had been emphatically repressive. Its true secret was this. It was essentially a working-class government, the produce of the struggle of the producing against the appropriating class, the political form at last discovered under which to work out the economical emancipation of Labour.

Except on this last condition, the Communal Constitution would have been an impossibility and a delusion. The political rule of the producer cannot coexist with the perpetuation of his social slavery. The Commune was therefore to serve as a lever for uprooting the economical foundations upon which rests the existence of classes, and therefore of class rule. With labour emancipated, every man becomes a working man, and productive labour ceases to be a class attribute.

It is a strange fact. In spite of all the tall talk and all the immense literature, for the last sixty years, about Emancipation of Labour, no sooner do the working men anywhere take the subject into their own hands with a will, than uprises at once all the apologetic phraseology of the mouthpieces of present society with its two poles of Capital and Wage-slavery (the landlord now is but the sleeping partner of the capitalist), as if capitalist society was still in its purest state of virgin innocence, with its antagonisms still undeveloped, with its delusions still unexploded, with its prostitute realities not yet laid bare. The Commune, they exclaim, intends to abolish property, the basis of all civilization! Yes, gentlemen, the Commune intended to abolish that class-property which makes the labour of the many the wealth of the few. It aimed at the expropriation of the expropriators. It wanted to make individual property a truth by transforming the means of production, land and capital, now chiefly the means of enslaving and exploiting labour, into mere instruments of free and associated labour.—But this is Communism, "impossible" Communism! Why, those members of the ruling classes who are intelligent enough to perceive the impossibility of continuing the present system—and they are many—have become the obtrusive and full-mouthed apostles of co-operative production. If co-operative production is not to remain a sham and a snare; if it is to supersede the Capitalist system; if united co-operative societies are to regulate national production upon a common plan, thus taking it under their own control, and putting an end to the constant anarchy and periodical convulsions which are the fatality of Capitalist production—what else, gentlemen, would it be but Communism, "possible" Communism?

The working class did not expect miracles from the Commune. They have no ready-made utopias to introduce *par décret du peuple*. They know that in order to work out their own emancipation, and along with it that higher form to which present society is irresistibly tending by its own economical agencies, they will have to pass through long struggles, through a series of historic processes, transforming circumstances and men. They have no ideals to realize, but to set free elements of the new society with which old collapsing bourgeois society itself is pregnant. In the full consciousness of their historic mission, and with the heroic resolve to act up to it, the working class can afford to smile at the coarse invective of the gentlemen's gentlemen with the pen and inkhorn, and at the didactic patronage of well-wishing bourgeois-doctrinaires, pouring forth their ignorant platitudes and sectarian crotchets in the oracular tone of scientific infallibility.

When the Paris Commune took the management of the revolution in its own hands; when plain working men for the first time dared to infringe upon the Governmental privilege of their "natural superiors," and, under circumstances of unexampled difficulty, performed their work modestly, conscientiously, and efficiently,—performed it at salaries the highest of which barely amounted to one-fifth of what, according to high scientific authority, is the minimum required for a secretary to a certain metropolitan school-board,—the old world writhed in convulsions of rage at the sight of the Red Flag, the symbol of the Republic of Labour, floating over the Hôtel de Ville.

And yet, this was the first revolution in which the working class was openly acknowledged as the only class capable of social initiative, even by the great bulk of the Paris middle class—shopkeepers, tradesmen, merchants—the wealthy capitalists alone excepted. The Commune had saved them by a sagacious settlement of that ever-recurring cause of dispute among the middle classes themselves—the debtor and creditor accounts. The same portion of the middle class, after they had assisted in putting down the working men's insurrection of June, 1848, had been at once unceremoniously sacrificed to their creditors by the then Constituent Assembly. But this was not their motive for now rallying round the working class. They felt that there was but one alternative—the Commune, or the Empire—under whatever name it might reappear. The Empire had ruined them economically by the havoc it made of public wealth, by the wholesale financial swindling it fostered, by the props it lent to the artificially accelerated centralization of capital, and the concomitant expropriation of their own ranks. It had suppressed them politically, it had shocked them morally by its orgies, it had insulted their Voltairianism by handing over the education of their children to the *frères Ignorantins*, it had revolted their national feeling as Frenchmen by precipitating them headlong into a war which left only one equivalent for the ruins it made—the disappearance of the Empire. In fact, after the exodus from Paris of the high Bonapartist and capitalist *Bohême,* the true middle-class Party of Order came out in the shape of the "Union Républicaine," enrolling themselves under the colours of the Commune and defending it against the wilful misconstruction of Thiers. Whether the gratitude of this great body of the middle class will stand the present severe trial, time must show.

The Commune was perfectly right in telling the peasants that "its victory was their only hope." Of all the lies hatched at Versailles and re-echoed by the glorious European penny-a-liner, one of the most tremendous was that the Rurals represented the French peasantry. Think only of the love of the French peasant for the men to whom, after 1815, he had to pay the milliard of indemnity! In the eyes of the French peasant, the very existence of a great landed proprietor is in itself an encroachment on his conquests of 1789. The bourgeois, in 1848, had burthened his plot of land with the additional tax of forty-five cents in the franc; but then he did so in the name of the revolution; while now he had fomented a civil war against the revolution, to shift on to the peasant's shoulders the chief load of the five milliards of indemnity to be paid to the Prussians. The Commune, on the other hand, in one of its first proclamations, declared that the true originators of the war would be made to pay its cost. The Commune would have delivered the peasant of the blood tax,—would have given him a cheap government,—transformed his present blood-suckers, the notary, advocate, executor, and other judicial vampires, into salaried communal agents, elected by, and responsible to, himself. It would have freed him of the tyranny of the *garde champêtre*, the gendarme, and the prefect, would have put enlightenment by the schoolmaster in the place of stuntification by the priest. And the French peasant is, above all, a man of reckoning. He would find it extremely reasonable that the pay of the priest, instead of being extorted by the tax-gatherer, should only depend upon the spontaneous action of the parishioners' religious instincts. Such were the great immediate boons which the rule of the Commune—and that rule alone—held out to the French peasantry. It is, therefore, quite superfluous here to expatiate upon the more complicated but vital problems which the Commune alone was able, and at the same time compelled, to solve in favour of the peasant, viz., the hypothecary debt, lying like an incubus upon his parcel of soil, the *prolétariat foncier* (the rural proletariate), daily growing upon it, and his expropriation from it enforced, at a more and more rapid rate, by the very development of modern agriculture and the competition of capitalist farming.

The French peasant had elected Louis Bonaparte president of the Republic; but the Party of Order created the Empire. What the French peasant really wants he commenced to show in 1849 and 1850, by opposing his maire to the Government's prefect, his schoolmaster to the Government's priest, and himself to the Government's gendarme. All the laws made by the Party of Order in January and February, 1850, were avowed measures of repression against the peasant. The peasant was a Bonapartist, because the great Revolution, with all its benefits to him, was, in his eyes, personified in Napoleon. This delusion, rapidly breaking down under the Second Empire (and in its very nature hostile to the Rurals), this prejudice of the past, how could it have withstood the appeal of the Commune to the living interests and urgent wants of the peasantry?

The Rurals—this was, in fact, their chief apprehension—knew that three months' free communication of Communal Paris with the provinces would bring about a general rising of the peasants, and hence their anxiety to establish a police blockade around Paris, so as to stop the spread of the rinderpest.

If the Commune was thus the true representative of all the healthy elements of French society, and therefore the truly national Government, it was, at the same time, as a working men's Government, as the bold champion of the emancipation of labour, emphatically international. Within sight of the Prussian army, that had annexed to Germany two French provinces, the Commune annexed to France the working people all over the world.

The Second Empire had been the jubilee of cosmopolitan blackleggism, the rakes of all countries rushing in at its call for a share in its orgies and in the plunder of the French people. Even at this moment the right hand of Thiers is Ganesco, the foul Wallachian, and his left hand is Markowski, the Russian spy. The Commune admitted all foreigners to the honour of dying for an immortal cause. Between the foreign war lost by their treason, and the civil war fomented by their conspiracy with the foreign invader, the bourgeoisie had found the time to display their patriotism by organizing police-hunts upon the Germans in France. The Commune made a German working-man its Minister of Labour. Thiers, the bourgeoisie, the Second Empire, had continually deluded Poland by loud professions of sympathy, while in reality betraying her to, and doing the dirty work of, Russia. The Commune honoured the heroic sons of Poland by placing them at the head of the defenders of Paris. And, to broadly mark the new era of history it was conscious of initiating, under the eyes of the conquering Prussians on the one side, and of the Bonapartist army, led by Bonapartist generals, on the other, the Commune pulled down that colossal symbol of martial glory, the Vendôme column.

The great social measure of the Commune was its own working existence. Its special measures could but betoken the tendency of a government of the people by the people. Such were the abolition of the nightwork of journeymen bakers; the pro-hibition, under penalty, of the employers' practice to reduce wages by levying upon their workpeople fines under manifold pretexts,—a process in which the employer combines in his own person the parts of legislator, judge, and executor, and filches the money to boot. Another measure of this class was the surrender, to associations of workmen, under reserve of compensation, of all closed workshops and factories, no matter whether the respective capitalists had absconded or preferred to strike work.

The financial measures of the Commune, remarkable for their sagacity and moderation, could only be such as were compatible with the state of a besieged town. Considering the colossal robberies committed upon the city of Paris by the great financial companies and contractors, under the protection of Haussmann, the Commune would have had an incomparably better title to confiscate their property than Louis Napoleon had against the Orléans family. The Hohenzollern and the English oligarchs who both have derived a good deal of their estates from Church plunder, were, of course, greatly shocked at the Commune clearing but 8,000f. out of secularisation.

While the Versailles Government, as soon as it had recovered some spirit and strength, used the most violent means against the Commune; while it put down the free expression of opinion all over France, even to the forbidding of meetings of delegates from the large towns; while it subjected Versailles and the rest of France to an espionage far surpassing that of the Second Empire; while it burned by its gendarme inquisitors all papers printed at Paris, and sifted all correspondence from and to Paris; while in the National Assembly the most timid attempts to put in a word for Paris were howled down in a manner unknown even to the *Chambre introuvable* of 1816; with the savage warfare of Versailles outside, and its attempts at corruption and conspiracy inside Paris—would the Commune not have shamefully betrayed its trust by affecting to keep up all the decencies and appearances of liberalism as in a time of profound peace? Had the Government of the Commune been akin to that of M. Thiers, there would have been no more occasion to suppress Party-of-Order papers at Paris than there was to suppress Communal papers at Versailles.

It was irritating indeed to the Rurals that at the very same time they declared the return to the Church to be the only means of salvation for France, the infidel Commune unearthed the peculiar mysteries of the Picpus nunnery, and of the Church of Saint Laurent. It was a satire upon M. Thiers that, while he showered grand crosses upon the Bonapartist generals in acknowledgment of their mastery in losing battles, signing capitulations, and turning cigarettes at Wilhelmshöhe, the Commune dismissed and arrested its generals whenever they were suspected of neglecting their duties. The expulsion from, and arrest by, the Commune of one of its members who had slipped in under a false name, and had undergone at Lyons six days' imprisonment for simple bankruptcy, was it not a deliberate insult hurled at the forger, Jules Favre, then still the foreign minister of France, still selling France to Bismarck, and still dictating his orders to that paragon Government of Belgium? But indeed the Commune did not pretend to infallibility, the invariable attribute of all governments of the old stamp. It published its doings and sayings, it initiated the public into all its shortcomings.

In every revolution there intrude, at the side of its true agents, men of a different stamp; some of them survivors of and devotees to past revolutions, without insight into the present movement, but preserving popular influence by their known honesty and courage, or by the sheer force of tradition; others mere bawlers, who, by dint of repeating year after year the same set of stereotyped declamations against the Government of the day, have sneaked into the reputation of revolutionists of the first water. After the 18th of March, some such men did also turn up, and in some cases contrived to play pre-eminent parts. As far as their power went, they hampered the real action of the working class, exactly as men of that sort have hampered the full development of every previous revolution. They are an unavoidable evil; with time they are shaken off; but time was not allowed to the Commune.

Wonderful, indeed, was the change the Commune had wrought in Paris! No longer any trace of the meretricious Paris of the Second Empire. No longer was Paris the rendezvous of British landlords, Irish absentees, American ex-slaveholders and shoddy men, Russian ex-serfowners, and Wallachian boyards. No more corpses at the Morgue, no nocturnal burglaries, scarcely any robberies; in fact, for the first time since the days of February, 1848, the streets of Paris were safe, and that without any police of any kind.

"We," said a member of the Commune, "hear no longer of assassination, theft, and personal assault; it seems indeed as if the police had dragged along with it to Versailles all its Conservative friends."

The *cocottes* had refound the scent of their protectors—the absconding men of family, religion, and, above all, of property. In their stead, the real women of Paris showed again at the surface—heroic, noble, and devoted, like the women of antiquity. Working, thinking, fighting, bleeding Paris—almost forgetful, in its incubation of a new society, of the cannibals at its gates—radiant in the enthusiasm of its historic initiative! . . .

Written between the middle of April and the end of May 1871.
Published as a pamphlet in London in the middle of June 1871 and in various European countries and the United States in 1871 and 1872.

CHAPTER 6

CRITIQUE OF THE GOTHA PROGRAMME

To BE UNDERSTANDABLE THIS DEMANDING BUT CRUCIAL WORK BY Marx requires discussion of its context. The "Critique" was a response to a unification program of the two major workers organizations in Germany in 1875 in the city of Gotha. The older and dominant group was the General Association of German Workers, formed by Ferdinand Lassalle in 1863. The more recent workers organization was the Social-Democratic Workers Party, forged by Wilhelm Liebknecht and August Bebel in 1869 in the city of Eisenach, which Marx and Engels often simply called "the Eisenachers." The latter group was much closer to the "Marx tendency" and the "Critique" was written to circulate Marx's severe reservations to the leadership of the Eisenachers.

The unification went through anyway on the platform of the Gotha Programme and the unified organization took the name the Socialist Workers Party of Germany. Although no longer socialist in orientation, it is the present SPD (Sozialdemokratischen Partei Deutschlands), one of the two major parties of Germany today. The Gotha Programme was its birth.

The thrust of the Critique is Marx's objection to what he considered to be a serious weakening of principles to accommodate the followers of Lassalle. Lassalle had died in 1864 (in a duel over a romantic affair), but his ideas continued to be very influential in the German workers movement. Although Lassalle had claimed to be the "pupil" of Marx and Engels, his own political program focused on getting the authoritarian state under Bismarck to provide state aid for workers cooperatives. To this end he especially pushed for universal suffrage and political deal-making. The inspiration for Weston's position discussed earlier, Lassalle argued that there is an "iron law of wages" that, due to wage labor always selling around the value of the means of subsistence, must keep wages near a low minimum. He therefore, like the position criticized by Marx in "Value, Price and Profit," disparaged the importance of trade union activity and placed his faith in political maneuvering with Bismarck and the German landholders against the bourgeoisie.[1] Lassalle had little doubt about his own importance and considered that election of figures like himself, "armed with the shining sword of science," were best able to advance the interests of workers. Although acknowledging his appeal to the German workers, Marx characterized Lassalle as a "quack savior."[2]

As the prefatory letter states, Marx and Engels considered the Gotha Programme to be a "canonization of Lassallean articles of faith" and in general "deplorable." Marx's criticisms revolve around the imprecise language of the document, apparently designed to avoid concluding that irreconcilable class interests are at stake and that victory depends on independent working class action. From his perspective, the program also rests on a naive conception of the state, suggesting that the authoritarian German state could be maneuvered into advancing, from above, the cause of German workers. Marx concluded that many of the provisions were actually a serious theoretical adulteration, thereby obstructing an understanding on the part of the workers of their necessary strategy and goals. It is a fine example of Marx's well-known "lashing criticism."

Marx's text is difficult in that it is structured as a paragraph by paragraph analysis of the Gotha Programme. However in many instances in criticizing a formulation Marx argues for how the position should be stated, thereby advancing his own conceptions of the transition to communism. It is one of the few places, although here still only in broad strokes, that Marx indicated the principles that would guide a fully developed communist society. Of particular interest is the following. Marx argued that the distribution of wealth is largely governed by the existing relations of production and therefore it is unwise, even foolish, to have hopes of serious redistribution without challenging the class basis of capitalist production. Second, Marx insists that the state can never be a neutral political actor, it is always guided by class interests. Third, Marx argues that what is considered "just" or a matter of "rights" is conditioned by the existing social structure and bound up with the latter's "contradictions." Marx's own emphasis is on restructuring production so as to expand the available resources for freedom and the flowering of individuality, unconstrained by "desert." In reference to this, it should be noted that the famous phrase "from each according to his abilities, to each according to his needs" is not original with Marx. It is usually ascribed to Louis Blanc in his *Organization of Work* but actually appears to have been a fairly common formulation among socialists of various stripes in the nineteenth century.[3]

Marx feared that, because of his proximity to the Eisenachers, the Gotha Programme would be associated with his own position and therefore his critique was a prelude to his and Engels's public repudiation of the platform. Marx's objections notwithstanding, the program passed with slight revisions. But according to Engels, the press and the workers mistakenly tended to interpret the program in a much more radical way than the text would suggest. Since for this reason it did not compromise the position of Marx and Engels within the German workers movement, they did not feel the need to carry out their threat.[4]

NOTES

1. *Marx-Engels Selected Correspondence* (Moscow: Progress Publishers, 1975), p. 157. August H. Nimtz, Jr., *Marx and Engels: Their Contribution to the Democratic Breakthrough* (Albany, NY: State University of New York Press, 2000), pp. 189–190

and p. 334 footnote 18. Hal Draper, *Karl Marx's Theory of Revolution* Volume II, *The Politics of Social Classes* (New York: Monthly Review Press, 1978), p. 93 and p. 88.

2. *Selected Correspondence*, p. 158 and pp. 130–131. Draper, *Karl Marx's Theory of Revolution*, pp. 526–529. Probably from memory, Marx gives the phrase as "the bright weapon of science." The phrase here is from Draper's citation.

3. Blanc, *Organization of Work* (Cincinnati: University Press, 1911 [original 1840]). I have been only able to obtain the first edition, where the phrase does not appear. However the translator, Marie Paula Dickoré, states that Blanc intended "national workshops in which each man would receive according to his needs and contribute according to his abilities.": p. 7. Blanc actually attributes to Robert Owen the idea of distribution based on "the needs of a society and not upon services rendered.": p. 50. For that matter, some would trace the idea back to "The Acts of the Apostles": "And all that believed were together, and had all things common; and sold their possessions and goods, and parted them to all men, as every man had need."

4. *Selected Correspondence*, pp. 279–280. For further discussion of the circumstances, see Nimtz, *Marx and Engels*, pp. 238–245.

CRITIQUE OF THE GOTHA PROGRAMME

London, May 5, 1875

Dear Bracke,

Will you be so kind, after you have read the following marginal notes on the unity programme, to pass them on for Geib and Auer, Bebel and Liebknecht to see. Notabene. *The manuscript should be returned to you* so as to be at my disposal if needs be. I have more than enough to do, and, as it is, must take on far more work than laid down for me by my doctor. Hence it was by no means a "pleasure" to write such a lengthy screed. Yet it was necessary if the steps I shall have to take later on are not to be misinterpreted by the party friends for whom this communication is intended.

After the Unity Congress is over, Engels and I will publish a short statement to the effect that we entirely disassociate ourselves from the said programme of principles and have nothing to do with it.

This is indispensable because of the view taken abroad—a totally erroneous view, carefully nurtured by party enemies—that we are secretly directing the activities of the so-called Eisenach Party from here. Only recently, in a newly published Russian work, Bakunin suggests that I, for instance, am responsible, not only for that party's every programme, etc., but actually for every step taken by Liebknecht from the day he began co-operating with the People's Party.

Aside from this, it is my duty to refuse recognition, even by maintaining a diplomatic silence, to a programme which, I am convinced, is altogether deplorable as well as demoralising for the party.

Every step of real movement is more important than a dozen programmes. Hence, if it was impossible to advance *beyond* the Eisenach Programme—and circumstances at the time precluded this—they should simply have come to an agreement about action against the common foe. But to draw up programmes of principles (instead of waiting till a longish spell of common activity has prepared the ground for that sort of thing) is to set up bench marks for all the world to see, whereby it may gauge how far the party has progressed.

The leaders of the Lassalleans came because circumstances forced them to. Had they been told from the start that there was to be no haggling over principles, they would have been *compelled* to content themselves with a programme of action or a plan of organisation for common action. Instead, our people allow them to present themselves armed with mandates, and recognise those mandates as binding, thus surrendering unconditionally to men who are themselves in need of help. To crown it all, they are holding another congress *prior to the congress of compromise,* whereas our own party is holding its congress *post festum.* Obviously their idea was to elude all criticism and not allow their own party time for reflection. One knows that the mere fact of unification is enough to satisfy the workers, but it is wrong to suppose that this momentary success has not been bought too dear.

Besides, the programme's no good, even apart from its canonisation of the Lassallean articles of faith.

I shall shortly be sending you the final instalments of the French edition of *Capital.* Printing was held up for a considerable time by the French government ban. The thing will be finished this week or at the beginning of next. Have you received the six previous instalments? Would you also very kindly send me the *address* of Bernhard Becker, to whom I must likewise send the final instalments.

The *bookshop* of the *Volksstaat* has peculiar manners. For instance, they haven't as yet sent me so much as a single copy of their reprint of the *Cologne Communist Trial.*

With kind regards.

Your

Karl Marx

MARGINAL NOTES ON THE PROGRAMME OF THE GERMAN WORKERS' PARTY [CRITIQUE OF THE GOTHA PROGRAMME]

[KARL MARX]

I

1. "Labour is the source of all wealth and all culture, *and since* useful labour is possible only in society and through society, the proceeds of labour belong undiminished with equal right to all members of society."

First part of the paragraph: "Labour is the source of all wealth and all culture."

Labour is *not the source* of all wealth. *Nature* is just as much the source of use values (and it is surely of such that material wealth consists!) as labour, which itself is only the manifestation of a force of nature, human labour power. The above phrase is to be found in all children's primers and is correct insofar as it is *implied* that labour is performed with the pertinent objects and instruments. But a socialist programme cannot allow such bourgeois phrases to pass over in silence the *conditions* that alone give them meaning. And insofar as man from the outset behaves towards nature, the primary source of all instruments and objects of labour, as an owner, treats her as belonging to him, his labour becomes the source of use values, therefore also of wealth. The bourgeois have very good grounds for ascribing *supernatural creative power* to labour; since precisely from the fact that labour is determined by nature, it follows that the man who possesses no other property than his labour power must, in all conditions of society and culture, be the slave of other men who have made themselves the owners of the material conditions of labour. He can work only with their permission, hence live only with their permission.

Let us now leave the sentence as it stands, or rather limps. What would one have expected in conclusion? Obviously this:

"Since labour is the source of all wealth, no one in society can appropriate wealth except as the product of labour. Therefore, if he himself does not work, he lives by the labour of others and also acquires his culture at the expense of the labour of others."

Instead of this, by means of the verbal rivet *"and since"* a second proposition is added in order to draw a conclusion from this and not from the first one.

Second part of the paragraph: "Useful labour is possible only in society and through society."

According to the first proposition, labour was the source of all wealth and all culture; therefore no society is possible without labour. Now we learn, conversely, that no "useful" labour is possible without society.

One could just as well have said that only in society can useless and even socially harmful labour become a gainful occupation, that only in society can one live by being idle, etc., etc.—in short, one could just as well have copied the whole of Rousseau.

And what is "useful" labour? Surely only labour which produces the intended useful result. A savage—and man was a savage after he had ceased to be an ape—who kills an animal with a stone, who collects fruits, etc., performs "useful" labour.

Thirdly. The conclusion: "And since useful labour is possible only in society and through society, the proceeds of labour belong undiminished with equal right to all members of society."

A fine conclusion! If useful labour is possible only in society and through society, the proceeds of labour belong to society—and only so much therefrom accrues to the individual worker as is not required to maintain the "condition" of labour, society.

In fact, this proposition has at all times been made use of *by the champions of the state of society prevailing at any given time.* First come the claims of the government and everything that sticks to it, since it is the social organ for the maintenance of the social order; then come the claims of the various kinds of private owners for the various kinds of private property are the foundations of society, etc. One sees that such hollow phrases can be twisted and turned as desired.

The first and second parts of the paragraph have some intelligible connection only in the following wording:

"Labour becomes the source of wealth and culture only as social labour," or, what is the same thing, "in and through society."

This proposition is incontestably correct, for although isolated labour (its material conditions presupposed) can create use values, it can create neither wealth nor culture.

But equally incontestable is the other proposition:

"In proportion as labour develops socially, and becomes thereby a source of wealth and culture, poverty and destitution develop among the workers, and wealth and culture among the non-workers."

This is the law of all history hitherto. What, therefore, had to be done here, instead of setting down general phrases about *"labour"* and *"society,"* was to prove concretely how in present capitalist society the material, etc., conditions have at last been created which enable and compel the workers to lift this historical curse.

In fact, however, the whole paragraph, bungled in style and content, is only there in order to inscribe the Lassallean catchword of the "undiminished proceeds of labour" as a slogan at the top of the party banner. I shall return later to the "proceeds of labour," "equal right", etc., since the same thing recurs in a somewhat different form further on.

2. "In present-day society, the means of labour are the monopoly of the capitalist class; the resulting dependence of the working class is the cause of misery and servitude in all their forms."

This sentence, borrowed from the Rules of the International, is incorrect in this "improved" edition.

In present-day society the means of labour are the monopoly of the landowners (the monopoly of land ownership is even the basis of the monopoly of capital) *and* the capitalists. In the passage in question, the Rules of the International mention neither the one nor the other class of monopolists. They speak of the *"monopoly of the means of labour, that is, the sources of life."* The addition, "sources of life," makes it sufficiently clear that land is included in the means of labour.

The correction was introduced because Lassalle, for reasons now generally known, attacked *only* the capitalist class and not the landowners. In England, the capitalist is mostly not even the owner of the land on which his factory stands.

3. "The emancipation of labour demands the raising of the means of labour to the common property of society and the collective regulation of the total labour with a fair distribution of the proceeds of labour."

"The raising of the means of labour to common property"! Ought obviously to read their "conversion into common property." But this only in passing.

What are "*proceeds of labour*"? The product of labour or its value? And in the latter case, is it the total value of the product or only that part of the value which labour has newly added to the value of the means of production consumed?

"Proceeds of labour" is a loose notion which Lassalle has put in the place of definite economic concepts.

What is "fair" distribution?

Do not the bourgeois assert that present-day distribution is "fair"? And is it not, in fact, the only "fair" distribution on the basis of the present-day mode of production? Are economic relations regulated by legal concepts or do not, on the contrary, legal relations arise from economic ones? Have not also the socialist sectarians the most varied notions about "fair" distribution?

To understand what is implied in this connection by the phrase "fair distribution," we must take the first paragraph and this one together. The latter presupposes a society wherein "the means of labour are common property and the total labour is collectively regulated," and from the first paragraph we learn that "the proceeds of labour belong undiminished with equal right to all members of society."

"To all members of society"? To those who do not work as well? What remains then of "the undiminished proceeds of labour"? Only to those members of society who work? What remains then of "the equal right" of all members of society?

But "all members of society" and "equal right" are obviously mere phrases. The crucial point is this, that in this communist society every worker must receive his "undiminished" Lassallean "proceeds of labour."

Let us take first of all the words "proceeds of labour" in the sense of the product of labour; then the collective proceeds of labour are the *total social product*.

From this must now be deducted:

First, cover for replacement of the means of production used up.

Secondly, additional portion for expansion of production.

Thirdly, reserve or insurance funds to provide against accidents, disturbances caused by natural factors, etc.

These deductions from the "undiminished proceeds of labour" are an economic necessity and their magnitude is to be determined according to available means and forces, and party by computation of probabilities, but they are in no way calculable by equity.

There remains the other part of the total product, intended to serve as means of consumption.

Before this is divided among the individuals, there has to be again deducted from it:

First, the general costs of administration not directly appertaining to production.

This part will, from the outset, be very considerably restricted in comparison with present-day society and it diminishes in proportion as the new society develops.

Secondly, that which is intended for the common satisfaction of needs, such as schools, health services, etc.

From the outset this part grows considerably in comparison with present-day society and it grows in proportion as the new society develops.

Thirdly, funds for those unable to work, etc., in short, for what is included under so-called official poor relief today.

Only now do we come to the "distribution" which the programme, under Lassallean influence, has alone in view in its narrow fashion, namely, to that part of the means of consumption which is divided among the individual producers of the collective.

The "undiminished proceeds of labour" have already unnoticeably become converted into the "diminished" proceeds, although what the producer is deprived of in his capacity as a private individual benefits him directly or indirectly in his capacity as a member of society.

Just as the phrase of the "undiminished proceeds of labour" has disappeared, so now does the phrase of the "proceeds of labour" disappear altogether.

Within the collective society based on common ownership of the means of production, the producers do not exchange their products; just as little does the labour employed on the products appear here *as the value* of these products, as a material quality possessed by them, since now, in contrast to capitalist society, individual labour no longer exists in an indirect fashion but directly as a component part of the total labour. The phrase "proceeds of labour," objectionable even today on account of its ambiguity, thus loses all meaning.

What we are dealing with here is a communist society, not as it has *developed* on its own foundations, but on the contrary, just as it *emerges* from capitalist society, which is thus in every respect, economically, morally and intellectually, still stamped with the birth-marks of the old society from whose womb it emerges. Accordingly, the individual producer receives back from society—after the deductions have been made—exactly what he gives to it. What he has given to it is his individual quantum of labour.

For example, the social working day consists of the sum of the individual hours of work; the individual labour time of the individual producer is the part of the social working day contributed by him, his share in it. He receives a certificate from society that he has furnished such and such an amount of labour (after deducting his labour for the common funds), and with this certificate he draws from the social stock of means of consumption as much as the same amount of labour costs. The same amount of labour which he has given to society in one form he receives back in another.

Here obviously the same principle prevails as that which regulates the exchange of commodities, as far as this is the exchange of equal values. Content and form are changed, because under the altered circumstances no one can give anything except his labour, and because, on the other hand, nothing can pass to the ownership of individuals except individual means of consumption. But, as far as the distribution of the latter among the individual producers is concerned, the same principle prevails as in the exchange of commodity-equivalents: a given amount of labour in one form is exchanged for an equal amount of labour in another form.

Hence, *equal right* here is still in principle—*bourgeois right*, although principle and practice are no longer at loggerheads, while the exchange of equivalents in commodity exchange only exists *on the average* and not in the individual case.

In spite of this advance, this *equal right* is still constantly encumbered by a bourgeois limitation. The right of the producers is *proportional* to the labour they supply; the equality consists in the fact that measurement is made with an *equal standard*, labour. But one man is superior to another physically or mentally and so supplies more labour in the same time, or can work for a longer time; and labour, to serve as a measure, must be defined by its duration or intensity, otherwise it ceases to be a standard of measurement. This *equal* right is an unequal right for unequal labour. It recognises no class distinctions, because everyone is only a worker like everyone else; but it tacitly recognises the unequal individual endowment and thus productive capacity of the workers as natural privileges. *It is, therefore, a right of inequality, in its content, like every right.* Right by its nature can exist only as the application of an equal standard; but unequal individuals (and they would not be different individuals if they were not unequal) are measurable by an equal standard only insofar as they are made subject to an equal criterion, are taken from a *certain* side only, for instance, in the present case, are regarded *only as workers* and nothing more is seen in them, everything else being ignored. Besides, one worker is married, another not; one has more children than another, etc., etc. Thus, given an equal amount of work done, and hence an equal share in the social consumption fund, one will in fact receive more than another, one will be richer than another, etc. To avoid all these defects, right would have to be unequal rather than equal.

But these defects are inevitable in the first phase of communist society as it is when it has just emerged after prolonged birthpangs from capitalist society. Right can never be higher than the economic structure of society and its cultural development which this determines.

In a higher phase of communist society, after the enslaving subordination of the individual to the division of labour, and thereby also the antithesis between mental and physical labour, has vanished; after labour has become not only a means of life but life's prime want; after the productive forces have also increased with the all-round development of the individual, and all the springs of common wealth flow more abundantly—only then can the narrow horizon of bourgeois right be crossed in its entirety and society inscribe on its banners: From each according to his abilities, to each according to his needs!

I have dealt at greater length with the "undiminished proceeds of labour," on the one hand, and with "equal right" and "fair distribution," on the other, in order to show what a crime it is to attempt, on the one hand, to force on our Party again, as dogmas, ideas which in a certain period had some meaning but have now become obsolete verbal rubbish, while again perverting, on the other, the realistic outlook, which it cost so much effort to instil into the Party but which has now taken root in it, by means of ideological, legal and other trash so common among the Democrats and French Socialists.

Quite apart from the analysis so far given, it was in general a mistake to make a fuss about so-called *distribution* and put the principal stress on it.

Any distribution whatever of the means of consumption is only a consequence of the distribution of the conditions of production themselves. The latter distribution, however, is a feature of the mode of production itself. The capitalist mode of production, for example, rests on the fact that the material conditions of production are in the hands of non-workers in the form of capital and land ownership, while the masses are only owners of the personal condition of production, of labour power. If the elements of production are so distributed, then the present-day distribution of the means of consumption results automatically. If the material conditions of production are the collective property of the workers themselves, then there likewise results a distribution of the means of consumption different from the present one. The vulgar socialists (and from them in turn a section of the Democrats) have taken over from the bourgeois economists the consideration and treatment of distribution as independent of the mode of production and hence the presentation of socialism as turning principally on distribution. After the real relation has long been made clear, why retrogress again?

4. "The emancipation of labour must be the work of the working class, in relation to which all other classes are *only one reactionary mass.*"

The main clause is taken from the introductory words of the Rules of the International, but "improved." There it is said: "The emancipation of the working classes must be conquered by the working classes themselves"; here, on the contrary, the "working class" has to emancipate—what? "Labour". Let him understand who can.

In compensation, the subordinate clause, on the other hand, is a Lassallean quotation of the first water: "in relation to which (the working class) all other classes are *only one reactionary mass.*"

In the *Communist Manifesto* it is said: "Of all the classes that stand face to face with the bourgeoisie today, the proletariat alone is a *really revolutionary class.* The other classes decay and finally disappear in the face of Modern Industry; the proletariat is its special and essential product."

The bourgeoisie is here conceived as a revolutionary class—as the bearer of large-scale industry—in relation to the feudal lords and the middle estates, who desire to maintain all social positions that are the creation of obsolete modes of production. Thus they do not form *together with the bourgeoisie* only one reactionary mass.

On the other hand, the proletariat is revolutionary in relation to the bourgeoisie because, having itself grown up on the basis of large-scale industry, it strives to strip off from production the capitalist character that the bourgeoisie seeks to perpetuate. But the *Manifesto* adds that the "middle estates" are becoming revolutionary "in view of their impending transfer into the proletariat,"

From this point of view, therefore, it is again nonsense to say that they, "together with the bourgeoisie," and with the feudal lords into the bargain, "form only one reactionary mass" in relation to the working class.

Did anyone proclaim to the artisans, small manufacturers, etc., and *peasants* during the last elections: In relation to us you, together with the bourgeoisie and feudal lords, form only one reactionary mass?

Lassalle knew the *Communist Manifesto* by heart, as his faithful followers know the gospels written by him. If, therefore, he has falsified it so grossly, this has occurred only to put a good colour on his alliance with absolutist and feudal opponents against the bourgeoisie.

In the above paragraph, moreover, his oracular saying is dragged in by the hair, without any connection with the botched quotation from the Rules of the International. Thus it is here simply an impertinence, and indeed not at all displeasing to Mr. Bismarck, one of those cheap pieces of insolence in which the Marat of Berlin deals.

5. "The working class strives for its emancipation first of all *within the framework of the present-day national state,* conscious that the necessary result of its efforts, which are common to the workers of all civilised countries, will be the international brotherhood of peoples."

Lassalle, in opposition to the *Communist Manifesto* and to all earlier socialism, conceived the workers' movement from the narrowest national standpoint. He is being followed in this—and that after the work of the International!

It is altogether self-evident that, to be able to fight at all, the working class must organise itself at home *as a class* and that its own country is the immediate arena of its struggle. To this extent its class struggle is national, not in substance, but, as the *Communist Manifesto* says, "in form." But the "framework of the present-day national state," for instance, the German Empire, is itself in its turn economically "within the framework of the world market," politically "within the framework of the system of states." Every businessman knows that German trade is at the same time foreign trade, and the greatness of Mr. Bismarck consists, to be sure, precisely in his pursuing his kind of *international* policy.

And to what does the German workers' party reduce its internationalism? To the consciousness that the result of its efforts "will be the *international brotherhood of peoples*"—a phrase borrowed from the bourgeois League of Peace and Freedom, which is intended to pass as equivalent to the international brotherhood of the working classes in the joint struggle against the ruling classes and their governments. So not a word *about the international functions* of the German working class! And it is thus that it is to defy its own bourgeoisie—which is already linked up in brotherhood against it with the bourgeois of all other countries—and Mr. Bismarck's international policy of conspiracy!

In fact, the internationalism of the programme stands *even infinitely below* that of the Free Trade Party. The latter also asserts that the result of its efforts will be

CRITIQUE OF THE GOTHA PROGRAMME

"the international brotherhood of peoples." But it also *does* something to make trade international and by no means contents itself with the consciousness—that all peoples are carrying on trade at home.

The international activity of the working classes does not in any way depend on the existence of the *"International Working Men's Association."* This was only the first attempt to create a central organ for that activity; an attempt which was a lasting success on account of the impulse which it gave, but which was no longer realisable in *its first historical form* after the fall of the Paris Commune.

Bismarck's *Norddeutsche* was absolutely right when it announced, to the satisfaction of its master, that the German workers' party had forsworn internationalism in the new programme.

II

"Starting from these basic principles, the German workers' party strives by all legal means for the *free state—and—*socialist society; the abolition of the wage system *together with* the *iron law of wages—*and—exploitation in every form; the elimination of all social and political inequality."

I shall return to the "free" state later.

So, in future, the German workers' party has got to believe in Lassalle's "iron law of wages"! That this may not be lost, the nonsense is perpetrated of speaking of the "abolition of the wage system" (it should read: system of wage labour) *"together with* the iron law of wages." If I abolish wage labour, then naturally I abolish its laws too, whether they are of "iron" or sponge. But Lassalle's attack on wage labour turns almost solely on this so-called law. In order, therefore, to prove that the Lassallean sect has won, the "wage system" must be abolished *"together with* the iron law of wages" and not without it.

It is well known that nothing of the "iron law of wages" is Lassalle's except the word "iron" borrowed from Goethe's "eternal, iron, great laws." The word *iron* is a label by which the true believers recognise one another. But if I take the law with Lassalle's stamp on it and, consequently, in his sense, then I must also take it with his substantiation. And what is that? As Lange already showed, shortly after Lassalle's death, it is the Malthusian theory of population (preached by Lange himself). But if this theory is correct, then again I can *not* abolish the law even if I abolish wage labour a hundred times over, because the law then governs not only the system of wage labour but *every* social system. Basing themselves directly on this, the economists have been proving for fifty years and more that socialism cannot abolish destitution, *which has its basis in nature,* but can only make it *general,* distribute it simultaneously over the whole surface of society!

But all this is not the main thing. *Quite apart* from the *false* Lassallean formulation of the law, the truly outrageous retrogression consists in the following:

Since Lassalle's death there has asserted itself in *our* Party the scientific understanding that *wages* are not what they *appear* to be, namely the *value,* or *price, of labour,* but only a masked form for the *value,* or *price, of labour power.* Thereby the whole bourgeois conception of wages hitherto, as well as all the criticism hitherto directed against this conception, was thrown overboard once for all and it was made clear that the wage-worker has permission to work for his own subsistence, that is, *to live* only insofar as he works for a certain time gratis for the capitalist (and hence also for the latter's co-consumers of surplus value); that the whole capitalist system of production turns on increasing this gratis labour by extending the working day or by developing productivity, that is, increasing the intensity of labour power, etc.; that, consequently, the system of wage labour is a system of slavery, and indeed of a slavery which becomes more severe in proportion as the social productive forces of labour develop, whether the worker receives better or worse payment. And after this understanding has gained more and more ground in our Party, one returns to Lassalle's dogmas although one must have known that Lassalle *did not know* what wages were, but following in the wake of the bourgeois economists took the appearance for the essence of the matter.

It is as if, among slaves who have at last got behind the secret of slavery and broken out in rebellion, a slave still in thrall to obsolete notions were to inscribe on the programme of the rebellion: Slavery must be abolished because the feeding of slaves in the system of slavery cannot exceed a certain low maximum!

Does not the mere fact that the representatives of our Party were capable of perpetrating such a monstrous attack on the understanding that has spread among the mass of our Party prove by itself with what criminal levity and with what lack of conscience they set to work in drawing up this compromise programme!

Instead of the indefinite concluding phrase of the paragraph, "the elimination of all social and political inequality," it ought to have been said that with the abolition of class distinctions all social and political inequality arising from them would disappear of itself.

III

"The German workers' party, in order *to pave the way for the solution of the social question,* demands the establishment of producers' cooperative societies with *state aid under the democratic control of the working people.* The producers' co-operative societies *are to be called into being* for industry and agriculture on such a scale *that the socialist organisation of the total labour will arise from them.*"

After the Lassallean "iron law of wages," the panacea of the prophet. The way for it is "paved" in worthy fashion. In place of the existing class struggle appears a newspaper scribbler's phrase: *"the* social *question,"* for the *"solution"* of which one "paves the way." Instead of arising from the revolutionary process of the transformation of society, the "socialist organisation of the total labour" "arises" from the "state aid" that the state gives to the producers' co-operative societies which the *state,* not the worker, *"calls into being."* It is worthy of Lassalle's imagination that with state loans one can build a new society just as well as a new railway!

From the remnants of a sense of shame, "state aid" has been put—"under the democratic control of the working people."

In the first place, the "working people" in Germany consist in their majority of peasants, and not of proletarians.

Secondly, "democratic" means in German *"volksherrschaftlich"* ["by the rule of the people"]. But what does "control of the working people by the rule of the people" mean? And particularly in the case of working people who, through these demands that they put to the state, express their full consciousness that they neither rule nor are ripe for rule!

It would be superfluous to deal here with the criticism of the recipe prescribed by Buchez in the reign of Louis Philippe in *opposition* to the French Socialists and accepted by the reactionary workers of the *Atelier*. The chief offence does not lie in having inscribed this specific nostrum in the programme, but in taking a retrograde step at all from the standpoint of a class movement to that of a sectarian movement.

That the workers desire to establish the conditions for co-operative production on a social scale, and first of all on a national scale, in their own country, only means that they are working to transform the present conditions of production, and it has nothing in common with the foundation of co-operative societies with state aid. But as far as the present co-operative societies are concerned, they are of value *only* insofar as they are the independent creations of the workers and not protégés either of the governments or of the bourgeois.

[IV]

I come now to the democratic section.

A. *"The free basis of the state."*

First of all, according to II, the German workers' party strives for "the free state."

Free state—what is it?

It is by no means the purpose of the workers, who have got rid of the narrow mentality of humble subjects, to set the state "free." In the German Empire the "state" is almost as "free" as in Russia. Freedom consists in converting the state from an organ superimposed upon society into one completely subordinate to it, and even today forms of state are more free or less free to the extent that they restrict the "freedom of the state."

The German workers' party—at least if it adopts the programme—shows that its socialist ideas are not even skin-deep, in that, instead of treating existing society (and this holds good for any future one) as the *basis* of the existing *state* (or of the future state in the case of future society), it treats the state rather as an independent entity that possesses its own *"intellectual, ethical and libertarian bases."*

And what of the wild abuse which the programme makes of the words *"present-day state," "present-day society,"* and of the still more riotous misconception it creates in regard to the state to which it addresses its demands?

"Present-day society" is capitalist society, which exists in all civilised countries, more or less free from medieval admixture, more or less modified by the particular historical development of each country, more or less developed. On the other hand, the "present-day state" changes with a country's frontier. It is different in the Prusso-German Empire from that in Switzerland, and different in England from that in the United States. "The *present-day* state" is, therefore, a fiction.

Nevertheless, the different states of the different civilised countries, in spite of their motley diversity of form, all have this in common that they are based on modern bourgeois society, more or less capitalistically developed. They have, therefore, also certain essential characteristics in common. In this sense it is possible to speak of the "present-day state'" in contrast with the future, in which its present root, bourgeois society, will have died off.

The question then arises: what transformation will the state undergo in communist society? In other words, what social functions will remain in existence there that are analogous to present state functions? This question can only be answered scientifically, and one does not get a flea-hop nearer to the problem by a thousandfold combination of the word people with the word state.

Between capitalist and communist society lies the period of the revolutionary transformation of the one into the other. Corresponding to this is also a political transition period in which the state can be nothing but *the revolutionary dictatorship of the proletariat.*

Now the programme deals neither with this nor with the future state of communist society.

Its political demands contain nothing beyond the old democratic litany familiar to all: universal suffrage, direct legislation, popular rights, a people's militia, etc. They are a mere echo of the bourgeois People's Party, of the League of Peace and Freedom. They are all demands which, insofar as they are not exaggerated in fantastic presentation, have already been *implemented.* Only the state to which they belong does not lie within the borders of the German Empire, but in Switzerland, the United States, etc. This sort of "state of the future" is a *present-day state,* although existing outside the "framework" of the German Empire.

But one thing has been forgotten. Since the German workers' party expressly declares that it acts within "the present-day national state," hence within its own state, the Prusso-German Empire—its demands would indeed otherwise be largely meaningless, since one only demands what one has not yet got—it should not have forgotten the chief thing, namely that all those pretty little gewgaws rest on the recognition of what is called sovereignty of the people and hence are appropriate only in a *democratic republic.*

Since one has not the courage—and wisely so, for the circumstances demand caution—to demand the democratic republic, as the French workers' programmes under Louis Philippe and under Louis Napoleon did, one should not have resorted to the subterfuge, neither "honest" nor decent, of demanding things which have meaning only in a democratic republic from a state which is nothing but a police-guarded military despotism, embellished with parliamentary forms, alloyed with a feudal admixture and at the same time already influenced by the bourgeoisie, and bureaucratically carpentered, and then assuring this state into the bargain that one imagines one will be able to force such things upon it "by legal means."

Even vulgar democracy, which sees the millennium in the democratic republic and has no suspicion that it is precisely in this last form of state of bourgeois society that the class struggle has to be fought out to a conclusion—even it towers mountains above this kind of democratism which keeps within the limits of what is permitted by the police and not permitted by logic.

That, in fact, by the word "state" is meant the government machine or the state insofar as it forms a special organism separated from society through division of labour, is shown alone by the words

"the German workers' party demands *as the economic basis of the state:* a single progressive income tax," etc.

Taxes are the economic basis of the government machinery and of nothing else. In the state of the future existing in Switzerland, this demand has been pretty well fulfilled. Income tax presupposes various sources of income of the various social classes, and hence capitalist society. It is, therefore, nothing remarkable that the

Liverpool FINANCIAL REFORMERS, bourgeois headed by Gladstone's brother, are putting forward the same demand as the programme.

B. "The German workers' party demands as the intellectual and ethical basis of the state:

1. "Universal and *equal education of the people* by the state. Universal compulsory school attendance. Free instruction."

Equal education of the people? What idea lies behind these words? Is it believed that in present-day society (and it is only with this that one is dealing) education can be *equal* for all classes? Or is it demanded that the upper classes also shall be compulsorily reduced to the modicum of education—the elementary school—that alone is compatible with the economic conditions not only of the wage labourers but of the peasants as well?

"Universal compulsory school attendance. Free instruction." The former exists even in Germany, the latter in Switzerland and in the United States in the case of elementary schools. If in some states of the latter country "upper" educational institutions are also "free," that only means in fact defraying the cost of the education of the upper classes from the general tax receipts. Incidentally, the same holds good for "free administration of justice" demanded under A, 5. The administration of criminal justice is to be had free everywhere; that of civil justice is concerned almost exclusively with conflicts over property and hence affects almost exclusively the propertied classes. Are they to carry on their litigation at the expense of the national coffers?

The paragraph on the schools should at least have demanded technical schools (theoretical and practical) in combination with the elementary school.

"Education of the people by the state" is altogether objectionable. Defining by a general law the expenditures on the elementary schools, the qualifications of the teaching staff, the subjects of instruction, etc., and, as is done in the United States, supervising the fulfilment of these legal specifications by state inspectors, is a very different thing from appointing the state as the educator of the people! Government and Church should rather be equally excluded from any influence on the school. Particularly, indeed, in the Prusso-German Empire (and one should not take refuge in the rotten subterfuge that one is speaking of a "state of the future"; we have seen how matters stand in this respect) the state has need, on the contrary, of a very stern education by the people.

But the whole programme, for all its democratic clang, is tainted through and through by the Lassallean sect's servile belief in the state, or, what is no better, by a democratic belief in miracles, or rather it is a compromise between these two kinds of belief in miracles, both equally remote from socialism.

"Freedom of science" says a paragraph of the Prussian Constitution. Why, then, here?

"Freedom of conscience"! If one desired at this time of the *Kulturkampf* to remind liberalism of its old catchwords, it surely could have been done only in the following form: Everyone should be able to attend to his religious as well as his bodily needs without the police sticking their noses in. But the workers' party ought at any rate in this connection to have expressed its awareness of the fact that bourgeois "freedom of conscience" is nothing but the toleration of all possible kinds of *religious unfreedom of conscience,* and that for its part it endeavours rather to liberate the conscience

from the witchery of religion. But one chooses not to transgress the "bourgeois" level.

I have now come to the end, for the appendix that now follows in the programme does not constitute a *characteristic* component part of it. Hence I can be very brief here.

2. "*Normal working day.*"

In no other country has the workers' party limited itself to such a vague demand, but has always fixed the length of the working day that it considers normal under the given circumstances.

3. "Restriction of female labour and prohibition of child labour."

The standardisation of the working day must include the restriction of female labour, insofar as it relates to the duration, breaks, etc., of the working day; otherwise it could only mean the exclusion of female labour from branches of industry that are especially unhealthy for the female body or are morally objectionable to the female sex. If that is what was meant, it should have been said.

"*Prohibition of child labour*"! Here it is absolutely essential to state the *age limit.*

A *general prohibition* of child labour is incompatible with the existence of large-scale industry and hence an empty, pious wish.

Its implementation—if it were possible—would be reactionary, since, with a strict regulation of the working time according to the different age groups and other precautionary stipulations for the protection of children, an early combination of productive labour with education is one of the most potent means for the transformation of present-day society.

4. "State supervision of factory, workshop and domestic industry."

In consideration of the Prusso-German state it should definitely have been demanded that the inspectors are to be removable only by a court of law; that any worker can have them prosecuted for neglect of duty; that they must belong to the medical profession.

5. "Regulation of prison labour."

A petty demand in a general workers' programme. In any case, it should have been clearly stated that there is no intention from fear of competition to allow ordinary criminals to be treated like beasts, and especially that there is no desire to deprive them of their sole means of betterment, productive labour. This was surely the least one might have expected from Socialists.

6. "An effective liability law."

It should have been stated what is meant by an "effective" liability law.

Let it be noted, incidentally, that in speaking of the normal working day the part of factory legislation that deals with health regulations and safety measures, etc., has been overlooked. The liability law only comes into operation when these regulations are infringed.

In short, this appendix too is distinguished by slovenly editing.

*Dixi et salvavi animam meam.**

---

* I have spoken and saved my soul (Ezekiel 3:18 and 19.)

Written in April–early May 1875.
First published abridged in *Die Neue Zeit,* Vol. 1, No. 18, 1891.

SOURCES OF INCLUDED WORKS

PART ONE

All works by Karl Marx and Friedrich Engels are from the multi-volume *Marx-Engels Collected Works* (New York: International Publishers, 1975–1990):

Frederick Engels, "Preface to the 1888 English Edition of the *Manifesto of the Communist Party*," in Volume 26, pp. 512–518.

Karl Marx and Frederick Engels, *Manifesto of the Communist Party*, in Volume 6, pp. 479–519.

Frederick Engels, "Protection and Free Trade: Preface to the Pamphlet: Karl Marx, *Speech on the Question of Free Trade*," in Volume 26, pp. 521–536.

Karl Marx, *Speech on the Question of Free Trade*, in Volume 6, pp. 450–465.

Karl Marx, "Preface to *A Contribution to the Critique of Political Economy*," in Volume 29, pp. 259–265.

Karl Marx, "Marx to Engels in Manchester," in Volume 22, pp. 159–160.

Karl Marx, *Value, Price and Profit*, in Volume 20, pp. 101–103 and pp. 117–149.

Frederick Engels, "Introduction" to Karl Marx's *The Civil War in France*, in Volume 27, pp. 179–191.

Karl Marx, *The Civil War in France*, in Volume 22, pp. 328–341.

Karl Marx, *Critique of the Gotha Programme*, in Volume 24, pp. 75–99.

PART TWO

Albert Einstein, "Why Socialism?" *Monthly Review* Volume 50, Number 1 (May 1998): pp. 1–7. Published in the founding issue of 1949 and periodically republished by the journal.

Terry Eagleton, "Where Do Postmodernists Come From?" *Monthly Review* Volume 47, Number 3 (July/August 1995): pp. 59–70.

John Bellamy Foster and Robert W. McChesney, "Monopoly-Finance Capital and the Paradox of Accumulation." *Monthly Review* Volume 16, Number 5 (October 2009), pp. 1–20.

Heidi Hartmann, "The Unhappy Marriage of Marxism and Feminism: Towards a More Progressive Union." In *Women and Revolution: A Discussion of the Unhappy Marriage of Marxism and Feminism*, edited by Lydia Sargent (Boston: South End Press, 1981): pp. 1–41.

John Bellamy Foster, "Marx and the Environment." *Monthly Review* Volume 47, Number 3 (July/August 1995), pp. 108–123.

John Brentlinger, "Revolutionizing Spirituality: Reflections on Marx and Religion," *Science & Society* Volume 64, Number 2 (Summer 2000): pp. 171–193.

PART II

INTRODUCTION

RECENT MARXIAN DEBATES

Time magazine's "Person of the Twentieth Century," Albert Einstein hardly needs an introduction. However it is less known that Einstein was a lifelong socialist, activist for progressive causes, and even, on occasion, a self-described "revolutionary."[1] Although it does not appear that Einstein was specifically a Marxist, he wrote this essay for the founding issue of the *Monthly Review*, a Marxian socialist journal, in 1949. The essay is one of the best short portrayals of the socialist perspective.

"Postmodernists" reject "grand narratives" of the sort associated with historical materialism. They focus instead on investigating the various relations between power and discourse in more specific social contexts.[2] Terry Eagleton is widely considered the foremost literary theorist in Great Britain, author of dozens of books on cultural and literary theory, including the bestselling text *Literary Theory*. He traces the attractiveness of the postmodern impulse to at least partly a loss of confidence in being able to seriously challenge capitalism (1995). Eagleton's scorching wit is much in evidence in this essay.

Speaking to the Economic Club of Washington in April 2009, Timothy Geithner, the Secretary of the Treasury, stated, "Never before in modern times has so much of the world been simultaneously hit by a confluence of economic and financial turmoil such as we are now living through." In October of that year the BBC conducted a poll of 29,000 people in 27 countries on the status of "free-market capitalism." "Almost a quarter—23% of those who responded—feel it is fatally flawed" (BBC News, November 9, 2009).

Building on the earlier work by Paul A. Baran and Paul M. Sweezy in *Monopoly Capital* (1966), John Bellamy Foster and Robert W. McChesney (2009) trace the profound crisis of contemporary capitalism to the tendency of mature capitalism to "stagnate," i.e., to a general decline in opportunities for investment in increased production due to already existing surplus capacity. Foster and McChesney argue that as a consequence, capital sought new profitable investment by speculating on the value of assets in the financial sector: finance, insurance, and real estate. Given the disastrous outcome of this strategy for firms, individuals, and taxpayers, Foster and McChesney anticipate long-term stagnation in advanced capitalist economies.

Heidi Hartmann's classic essay (1981) is an overview and analysis of the various ways that Marxists have tried to take account of gender differences in capitalist society. Generally speaking, Marxists have tended to subsume gender issues under social class, making the situation of women a special subset of social class. This approach fails to reveal the particularity of the oppression of women *by men*, not capitalism. Hartmann focuses our attention on the oppression of women as women, differences in interests between women and men, and how therefore, without a more thorough examination of gender relations, patriarchy would likely survive even the destruction of capitalism.

One of the most vigorous currents of the broadly defined "left" today is the environmental movement. However, as Ted Benton put it, there has been "much bad blood between Marxists and ecologists."[3] Many ecologists suspect that Marxism is just another form of destructive "productivism," celebrating technological increase without regard for the limits of the natural world. This belief is reinforced by the dismal record of Eastern European countries under command economies and of China today. John Bellamy Foster, one of the best known analysts of Marxism and ecology, argues against the idea that Marx was a single-minded "Promethean," bent on dominating or mastering nature regardless of cost or sustainability (1995). Foster demonstrates that Marx and Engels were much more attuned to ecological issues than is typically acknowledged. After all, as Marx repeatedly stated, human beings are a *part* of nature.

For a variety of reasons, Marx was rather antagonistic toward religion. As an heir to the Enlightenment, he rejected religious forms of argument. Further, many of the established religious hierarchies of his day were deeply implicated in the exploitative political and social order. At best Marx believed that religion was comfort in a heartless world, a mode of experience that would lose its reason for existence as worldly suffering was alleviated by the revolutionary transformation of social life. Based on his encounter with the "liberation theology" movement in Latin America in the 1980s, and on the progressive role that religiously inspired groups have played in various circumstances, John Brentlinger rejects this classical view (2000). He argues that Marxists must reconsider the role of spirituality in constructing meaningful lives and therefore as a basis for revolutionary struggle. He reminds us that religious communities are contested ground and therefore may present more progressive possibilities than may be suspected at first glance. In a world of vigorously growing and politically engaged religious movements, Brentlinger's perspective is well worth pondering.

NOTES ON AUTHORS OF ARTICLES

By most accounts, Albert Einstein was the leading theoretical physicist of the twentieth century, who, among other things, formulated the special and general theories of relativity.

Terry Eagleton is Distinguished Professor of English Literature at the University of Lancaster, the United Kingdom, and Visiting Professor at the National University of Ireland, Galway. He is also a frequent Distinguished Visitor in the Department of English at the University of Notre Dame in the United States.

John Bellamy Foster is Editor of the *Monthly Review* and Professor of Sociology at the University of Oregon. Robert W. McChesney is Gutsell Endowed Professor of Communications at the University of Illinois at Urbana-Champaign.

Heidi Hartmann is President of the Institute for Women's Policy Research in Washington, D.C. and Research Professor at George Washington University.

The late John Brentlinger was Professor of Philosophy at the University of Massachusetts, Amherst.

NOTES

1. John J. Simon, "Albert Einstein, Radical: A Political Profile," *Monthly Review* Volume 57, Number 1 (May 2005), p. 12.
2. See Jean-François Lyotard, *The Postmodern Condition: A Report on Knowledge* (Minneapolis: University of Minnesota Press, 1984).
3. "Marxism and Natural Limits: An Ecological Critique and Reconstruction," *New Left Review* Number 178 (November/December 1989), p. 55.

CHAPTER 7

WHY SOCIALISM?

ALBERT EINSTEIN

THIS ESSAY WAS ORIGINALLY PUBLISHED in the first issue of *Monthly Review* (May 1949).

Is it advisable for one who is not an expert on economic and social issues to express views on the subject of socialism? I believe for a number of reasons that it is.

Let us first consider the question from the point of view of scientific knowledge. It might appear that there are no essential methodological differences between astronomy and economics: scientists in both fields attempt to discover laws of general acceptability for a circumscribed group of phenomena in order to make the interconnection of these phenomena as clearly understandable as possible. But in reality such methodological differences do exist. The discovery of general laws in the field of economics is made difficult by the circumstance that observed economic phenomena are often affected by many factors which are very hard to evaluate separately. In addition, the experience which has accumulated since the beginning of the so-called civilized period of human history has—as is well known—been largely influenced and limited by causes which are by no means exclusively economic in nature. For example, most of the major states of history owed their existence to conquest. The conquering peoples established themselves, legally and economically, as the privileged class of the conquered country. They seized for themselves a monopoly of the land ownership and appointed a priesthood from among their own ranks. The priests, in control of education, made the class division of society into a permanent institution and created a system of values by which the people were thenceforth, to a large extent unconsciously, guided in their social behavior.

But historic tradition is, so to speak, of yesterday; nowhere have we really overcome what Thorstein Veblen called "the predatory phase" of human development. The observable economic facts belong to that phase and even such laws as we can derive from them are not applicable to other phases. Since the real purpose of socialism is precisely to overcome and advance beyond the predatory phase of human development, economic science in its present state can throw little light on the socialist society of the future.

Second, socialism is directed towards a social-ethical end. Science, however, cannot create ends and, even less, instill them in human beings; science, at most, can supply the means by which to attain certain ends. But the ends themselves are conceived by personalities with lofty ethical ideals and—if these ends are not stillborn, but vital and vigorous—are adopted and carried forward by those many human beings who, half unconsciously, determine the slow evolution of society.

For these reasons, we should be on our guard not to overestimate science and scientific methods when it is a question of human problems; and we should not assume that experts are the only ones who have a right to express themselves on questions affecting the organization of society.

Innumerable voices have been asserting for some time now that human society is passing through a crisis, that its stability has been gravely shattered. It is characteristic of such a situation that individuals feel indifferent or even hostile toward the group, small or large, to which they belong. In order to illustrate my meaning, let me record here a personal experience. I recently discussed with an intelligent and well-disposed man the threat of another war, which in my opinion would seriously endanger the existence of mankind, and I remarked that only a supra-national organization would offer protection from that danger. Thereupon my visitor, very calmly and coolly, said to me: "Why are you so deeply opposed to the disappearance of the human race?"

I am sure that as little as a century ago no one would have so lightly made a statement of this kind. It is the statement of a man who has striven in vain to attain an equilibrium within himself and has more or less lost hope of succeeding. It is the expression of a painful solitude and isolation from which so many people are suffering in these days. What is the cause? Is there a way out?

It is easy to raise such questions, but difficult to answer them with any degree of assurance. I must try, however, as best I can, although I am very conscious of the fact that our feelings and strivings are often contradictory and obscure and that they cannot be expressed in easy and simple formulas.

Man is, at one and the same time, a solitary being and a social being. As a solitary being, he attempts to protect his own existence and that of those who are closest to him, to satisfy his personal desires, and to develop his innate abilities. As a social being, he seeks to gain the recognition and affection of his fellow human beings, to share in their pleasures, to comfort them in their sorrows, and to improve their conditions of life. Only the existence of these varied, frequently conflicting, strivings accounts for the special character of a man, and their specific combination determines the extent to which an individual can achieve an inner equilibrium and can contribute to the well-being of society. It is quite possible that the relative strength of these two drives is, in the main, fixed by inheritance. But the personality that finally emerges is largely formed by the environment in which a man happens to find himself during his development, by the structure of the society in which he grows up, by the tradition of that society, and by its appraisal of particular types of behavior. The abstract concept "society" means to the individual human being the sum total of his direct and indirect relations to his contemporaries and to all the people of earlier generations. The individual is able to think, feel, strive, and work by himself; but he depends so much upon society—in his physical, intellectual, and emotional existence—that it is impossible to think of him, or to understand him, outside the framework of society. It is "society" which provides man with food, clothing, a home, the tools of work, language, the forms of thought, and most of the content of thought; his life is made possible through the labor and the accomplishments of the many millions past and present who are all hidden behind the small word "society."

It is evident, therefore, that the dependence of the individual upon society is a fact of nature which cannot be abolished—just as in the case of ants and bees. However, while the whole life process of ants and bees is fixed down to the smallest detail by rigid, hereditary instincts, the social pattern and interrelationships of human beings are very variable and susceptible to change. Memory, the capacity to make new combinations, the gift of oral communication have made possible developments among human beings which are not dictated by biological necessities. Such developments manifest themselves in traditions, institutions, and organizations; in literature; in scientific and engineering accomplishments; in works of art. This explains how it happens that, in a certain sense, man can influence his life through his own conduct, and that in this process conscious thinking and wanting can play a part.

Man acquires at birth, through heredity, a biological constitution which we must consider fixed and unalterable, including the natural urges which are characteristic of the human species. In addition, during his lifetime, he acquires a cultural constitution which he adopts from society through communication and through many other types of influences. It is this cultural constitution which, with the passage of time, is subject to change and which determines to a very large extent the relationship between the individual and society. Modern anthropology has taught us, through comparative investigation of so-called primitive cultures, that the social behavior of human beings may differ greatly, depending upon prevailing cultural patterns and the types of organization which predominate in society. It is on this that those who are striving to improve the lot of man may ground their hopes: human beings are not condemned, because of their biological constitution, to annihilate each other or to be at the mercy of a cruel, self-inflicted fate.

If we ask ourselves how the structure of society and the cultural attitude of man should be changed in order to make human life as satisfying as possible, we should constantly be conscious of the fact that there are certain conditions which we are unable to modify. As mentioned before, the biological nature of man is, for all practical purposes, not subject to change. Furthermore, technological and demographic developments of the last few centuries have created conditions which are here to stay. In relatively densely settled populations with the goods which are indispensable to their continued existence, an extreme division of labor and a highly-centralized productive apparatus are absolutely necessary. The time—which, looking back, seems so idyllic—is gone forever when individuals or relatively small groups could be completely self-sufficient. It is only a slight exaggeration to say that mankind constitutes even now a planetary community of production and consumption.

I have now reached the point where I may indicate briefly what to me constitutes the essence of the crisis of our time. It concerns the relationship of the individual to society. The individual has become more conscious than ever of his dependence upon society. But he does not experience this dependence as a positive asset, as an organic tie, as a protective force, but rather as a threat to his natural rights, or even to his economic existence. Moreover, his position in society is such that the egotistical drives of his make-up are constantly being accentuated, while his social drives, which are by nature weaker, progressively deteriorate. All human beings, whatever their position in society, are suffering from this process of deterioration. Unknowingly prisoners of their own egotism, they feel insecure, lonely, and deprived of the naive, simple, and unsophisticated enjoyment of life. Man can find meaning in life, short and perilous as it is, only through devoting himself to society.

The economic anarchy of capitalist society as it exists today is, in my opinion, the real source of the evil. We see before us a huge community of producers the members of which are unceasingly striving to deprive each other of the fruits of their collective labor—not by force, but on the whole in faithful compliance with legally established rules. In this respect, it is important to realize that the means of production—that is to say, the entire productive capacity that is needed for producing consumer goods as well as additional capital goods—may legally be, and for the most part are, the private property of individuals.

For the sake of simplicity, in the discussion that follows I shall call "workers" all those who do not share in the ownership of the means of production—although this does not quite correspond to the customary use of the term. The owner of the means of production is in a position to purchase the labor power of the worker. By using the means of production, the worker produces new goods which become the property of the capitalist. The essential point about this process is the relation between what the worker produces and what he is paid, both measured in terms of real value. Insofar as the labor contract is "free," what the worker receives is determined not by the real value of the goods he produces, but by his minimum needs and by the capitalists' requirements for labor power in relation to the number of workers competing for jobs. It is important to understand that even in theory the payment of the worker is not determined by the value of his product.

Private capital tends to become concentrated in few hands, partly because of competition among the capitalists, and partly because technological development and the increasing division of labor encourage the formation of larger units of production at the expense of smaller ones. The result of these developments is an oligarchy of private capital the enormous power of which cannot be effectively checked even by a democratically organized political society. This is true since the members of legislative bodies are selected by political parties, largely financed or otherwise influenced by private capitalists who, for all practical purposes, separate the electorate from the legislature. The consequence is that the representatives of the people do not in fact sufficiently protect the interests of the underprivileged sections of the population. Moreover, under existing conditions, private capitalists inevitably control, directly or indirectly, the main sources of information (press, radio, education). It is thus extremely difficult, and indeed in most cases quite impossible, for the individual citizen to come to objective conclusions and to make intelligent use of his political rights.

The situation prevailing in an economy based on the private ownership of capital is thus characterized by two main principles: first, means of production (capital) are privately owned and the owners dispose of them as they see fit; second, the labor contract is free. Of course, there is no such thing as a *pure* capitalist society in this sense. In particular, it should be noted that the workers, through long and bitter political struggles, have succeeded in securing a somewhat improved form of the "free labor contract" for certain categories of workers. But taken as a whole, the present day economy does not differ much from "pure" capitalism.

Production is carried on for profit, not for use. There is no provision that all those able and willing to work will always be in a position to find employment; an "army of unemployed" almost always exists. The worker is constantly in fear of losing his job. Since unemployed and poorly paid workers do not provide a profitable market, the production of consumers' goods is restricted, and great hardship is the consequence. Technological progress frequently results in more unemployment rather than in an easing of the burden of work for all. The profit motive, in conjunction with competition among capitalists, is responsible for an instability in the accumulation and utilization of capital which leads to increasingly severe depressions. Unlimited competition leads to a huge waste of labor, and to that crippling of the social consciousness of individuals which I mentioned before.

This crippling of individuals I consider the worst evil of capitalism. Our whole educational system suffers from this evil. An exaggerated competitive attitude is inculcated into the student, who is trained to worship acquisitive success as a preparation for his future career.

I am convinced there is only *one* way to eliminate these grave evils, namely through the establishment of a socialist economy, accompanied by an educational system which would be oriented toward social goals. In such an economy, the means of production are owned by society itself and are utilized in a planned fashion. A planned economy, which adjusts production to the needs of the community, would distribute the work to be done among all those able to work and would guarantee a livelihood to every man, woman, and child. The education of the individual, in addition to promoting his own innate abilities, would attempt to develop in him a sense of responsibility for his fellow men, in place of the glorification of power and success in our present society.

Nevertheless, it is necessary to remember that a planned economy is not yet socialism. A planned economy as such may be accompanied by the complete enslavement of the individual. The achievement of socialism requires the solution of some extremely difficult socio-political problems: How is it possible, in view of the far-reaching centralization of political and economic power, to prevent bureaucracy from becoming all-powerful and overweening? How can the rights of the individual be protected and therewith a democratic counterweight to the power of bureaucracy be assured?

Clarity about the aims and problems of socialism is of greatest significance in our age of transition. Since, under present circumstances, free and unhindered discussion of these problems has come under a powerful taboo, I consider the foundation of this magazine to be an important public service.

CHAPTER 8

WHERE DO POSTMODERNISTS COME FROM?

TERRY EAGLETON

IMAGINE A RADICAL MOVEMENT THAT HAD SUFFERED AN EMPHATIC DEFEAT. So emphatic, in fact, that it seemed unlikely to resurface for the length of a lifetime, if at all. As time wore on, the beliefs of this movement might begin to seem less false or ineffectual than simply irrelevant. For its opponents, it would be less a matter of hotly contesting these doctrines than of contemplating them with something of the mild antiquarian interest one might have previously reserved for Ptolemaic cosmology or the scholasticism of Thomas Aquinas. Radicals might come to find themselves less overwhelmed or out-argued than simply washed up, speaking a language so quaintly out of tune with their era that, as with the language of Platonism or courtly love, nobody even bothered any longer to ask whether it was true. What would be the likely response of the left to such a dire condition?

Many, no doubt, would drift either cynically or sincerely to the right, regretting their earlier views as infantile idealism. Others might keep the faith purely out of habit, anxiety, or nostalgia, clinging to an imaginary identity and risking the neurosis that that may bring. A small clutch of left triumphalists, incurably hopeful, would no doubt carry on detecting the stirrings of the revolution in the faintest flicker of militancy. In others, the radical impulse would persist, but would be forced to migrate elsewhere. One can imagine that the ruling assumption of this period would be that the system was, at least for the moment, unbreachable; and a great many of the left's conclusions could be seen to flow from this glum supposition. One might expect, for example, that there would be an upsurge of interest in the margins and crevices of the system—in those ambiguous, indeterminate places where its power seemed less secure. If the system could not be breached, one might at least look to those forces which might momentarily transgress, subvert, or give it the slip. There would be, one might predict, much celebration of the marginal—but this would be partly making a virtue out of necessity, since the left would itself have been rudely displaced from the mainstream, and might thus come, conveniently enough, to suspect all talk of centrality as suspect. At its crudest, this cult of marginality would come down to a simpleminded assumption that minorities were positive and majorities oppressive. Just how minorities like fascist groups, Ulster Unionists, or the international bourgeoisie fitted into this picture would not be entirely clear. Nor is it obvious how such a position could cope with a previously marginal movement—the ANC, for example—becoming politically dominant, given its formalist prejudice that dominance was undesirable as such. The historical basis for this way of thinking would be the fact that political movements that were at once mass, central, and creative were by and large no longer in business. Indeed, the idea of a movement that was at once central and subversive would now appear something of a contradiction in terms. It would therefore seem natural to demonize the mass, dominant, and consensual, and romanticize whatever happened to deviate from them. It would be, above all, the attitude of those younger dissidents who had nothing much, politically speaking, to remember, who had no actual memory or experience of mass radical politics, but a good deal of experience of drearily oppressive majorities.

If the system really did seem to have canceled all opposition to itself, then it would not be hard to generalize from this to the vaguely anarchistic belief that system is oppressive as such. Since there were almost no examples of attractive political systems around, the claim would seem distinctly plausible. The only genuine criticism could be one launched from outside the system altogether; and one would expect, therefore, a certain fetishizing of "otherness" in such a period. There would be enormous interest in anything that seemed alien, deviant, exotic, unincorporable, all the way from aardvarks to Alpha Centauri, a passion for whatever gave us a tantalizing glimpse of something beyond the logic of the system altogether. But this romantic ultra-leftism would coexist, curiously enough, with a brittle pessimism—for the fact is that if the system is all-powerful, then there can be by definition nothing beyond it, any more than there can be anything beyond the infinite curvature of cosmic space. If there *were* something outside the system, then it would be entirely unknowable and thus incapable of saving us; but if we could draw it into the orbit of the system, so that it could gain some effective foothold there, its otherness would be instantly contaminated and its subversive power would thus dwindle to nothing. Whatever negates the system in theory would thus be logically incapable of doing so in practice. Anything we can *understand* can by definition not be radical, since it must be within the system itself; but anything which escapes the system could be heard by us as no more than a mysterious murmur.

Such thinking has abandoned the whole notion of a system which is internally contradictory—which has that installed at its heart which can potentially undo it. Instead, it thinks in the rigid oppositions of "inside" and "outside," where to be on the inside is to be complicit and to be on the outside is to be impotent. The typical style of thought of such a period, then, might be described as *libertarian pessimism*—libertarian, because one would not have given up on the dream of something quite other than what we have; pessimism, because one would be much too bleakly conscious of the omnipotence of law and power to believe that such a dream could ever by realized. If one still believed in subversion, but not in the existence of any flesh-and-blood agents of it, then it might be possible to imagine that the system in some way subverted itself, deconstructed its own logic, which would then allow you to combine a certain radicalism with a certain skepticism.

If the system is everywhere, then it would seem, like the Almighty himself, to be visible at no particular point; and it would therefore become possible to believe, paradoxically enough, that whatever was out there was not in fact a system at all. It is only a short step from claiming that the system is too complex to be represented to declaring that it does not exist. In the period we are imagining, then, some would no doubt be found clamoring against what they saw as the tyranny of a real social totality, whereas others would be busy deconstructing the whole idea of totality and claiming that it existed only in our minds. It would not be hard to see this as, at least in part, a compensation in theory for the fact that the social totality was proving difficult to crack in practice. If no very ambitious form of political action seems for the moment possible, if so-called micropolitics seem the order of the day, it is always tempting to convert this necessity into a virtue—to console oneself with the thought that one's political limitations have a kind of objective ground in reality, in the fact that social "totality" is in any case just an illusion. ("Metaphysical" illusion makes your position sound rather more imposing.) It does not matter if there is no political agent at hand to transform the whole, because there is in fact no whole to be transformed. It is as though, having mislaid the breadknife, one declares the loaf to be already sliced. But totality might also seem something of an illusion because there would be no very obvious political agent for whom society might present itself as a totality. There are those who need to grasp how it stands with them in order to be free, and who find that they can do this only by grasping something of the overall structure with which their own immediate situation intersects. Local and universal are not, here, simple opposites or theoretical options, as they might be for those intellectuals who prefer to think big and those more modest academics who like to keep it concrete. But if some of those traditional political agents are in trouble, then so will be the concept of social totality, since it is those agents' *need* of it that gives it its force.

Grasping a complex totality involves some rigorous analysis; so it is not surprising that such strenuously systematic thought should be out of fashion, dismissed as phallic, scientist, or what have you, in the sort of period we are imagining. When there is nothing in particular in it for you to find out how you stand—if you are a professor in Ithaca or Irvine, for example—you can afford to be ambiguous, elusive, deliciously indeterminate. You are also quite likely, in such circumstances, to wax idealist—though in some suitably new-fangled rather than tediously old-fashioned sense. For one primary way in which we know the world is, of course, through practice; and if any very ambitious practice is denied us, it will not be long before we catch ourselves wondering whether there is anything out there at all. One would expect, then, that in such an era a belief in reality as something that resists us ("History is what hurts," as Fredric Jameson has put it) will give way to a belief in the "constructed" nature of the world. This, in turn, would no doubt go hand in hand with a full-blooded "culturalism" which underestimated what men and women had in common as material human creatures, and suspected all talk of nature as an insidious mystification. It would tend not to realize that such culturalism is just as reductive as, say, economism or biologism. Cognitive and realist accounts of human consciousness would yield ground to various kinds of pragmatism and relativism, partly because there didn't any longer seem much politically at stake in knowing how it stood with you. Everything would become an interpretation, including that statement itself. And what would also gradually implode, along with reasonably certain knowledge, would be the idea of a human subject "centered" and unified enough to take significant action. For such significant action would now seem in short supply; and the result, once more, would be to make a virtue out of necessity by singing the praises of the diffuse, decentered, schizoid human subject—a subject who might well not be "together" enough to topple a bottle off a wall, let alone bring down the state, but who could nevertheless be presented as hair-raisingly avant garde in contrast to the smugly centered subjects of an older, more classical phase of capitalism. To put it another way: the subject as producer (coherent, disciplined, self-determining) would have yielded ground to the subject as consumer (mobile, ephemeral, constituted by insatiable desire).

If the "left" orthodoxies of such a period were pragmatist, relativist, pluralistic, deconstructive, then one might well see such thought-forms as dangerously radical. For does not capitalism need sure foundations, stable identities, absolute authority, metaphysical certainties, in order to survive? And wouldn't the kind of thought we are imagining put the skids under all this? The answer, feebly enough, is both yes and no. It is true that capitalism, so far anyway, has felt the need to underpin its authority with unimpeachable moral foundations. Look, for example, at the remarkable tenacity of religious belief in North America. On the other hand, look at the British, who are a notably godless bunch. No British politician could cause anything other than acute embarrassment by invoking the Supreme Being in public, and the British talk much less about metaphysical abstractions like Britain than those in the United States do about something called the United States. It is not clear, in other words, exactly how much metaphysical talk the advanced capitalist system really requires; and it is certainly true that its relentlessly secularizing, rationalizing operations threaten to undercut its own metaphysical claims. It is clear, however, that without pragmatism and plurality the system could not survive at all. Difference, "hybridity," heterogeneity, restless mobility are native to the capitalist mode of production, and thus by no means inherently radical phenomena. So if these ways of thinking put the skids under the system at one level, they reproduce its logic at another.

If an oppressive system seems to regulate everything, then one will naturally look around for some enclave of which this is less true—some place where a degree of freedom or randomness or pleasure still precariously survives. Perhaps you might call this desire, or discourse, or the body, or the unconscious. One might predict in this period a quickening of interest in psychoanalysis—for psychoanalysis is not only the thinking person's sensationalism, blending intellectual rigor with the most lurid materials, but it exudes a general exciting air of radicalism without being particularly so *politically*. If the more abstract questions of state, mode of production, and civil society seem for the moment too hard to resolve, then one might shift one's political attention to something more intimate and immediate, more living and fleshly, like the body. Conference papers entitled "Putting the Anus Back into Coriolanus" would attract eager crowds who had never heard of the bourgeoisie but who knew all about buggery.

This state of affairs would no doubt be particularly marked in those societies which in any case lacked strong socialist traditions; indeed, one could imagine much of the style of thought in question, for all its suspiciousness of the universal, as no more than spurious universalizing of such specific political conditions. Such a concern with bodiliness and sexuality would represent, one imagines, an enormous political deepening and enrichment, at the same time as it would signify a thorough-going displacement. And no doubt just the same could be said if one were to witness an increasing obsession with language and culture—topics where the intellectual is in any case more likely to feel at home than in the realm of material production.

One might expect that some, true to the pessimism of the period, would stress how discourses are policed, regulated, heavy with power, while others would proclaim in more libertarian spirit how the thrills and spills of the signifier can give the slip to the system. Either way, one would no doubt witness an immense linguistic inflation, as what appeared no longer conceivable in political reality was still just about possible in the areas of discourse or signs or textuality. The freedom of text or language would come to compensate for the unfreedom of the system as a whole. There would still be a kind of utopian vision, but its name now would be increasingly poetry. And it would even be possible to imagine, in an "extremist" variant of this style of thought, that the future was here and now—that utopia had already arrived in the shape of the pleasurable intensities, multiple selfhoods, and exhilarating exchanges of the marketplace and the shopping mall. History would then most certainly have come to an end—an end already implicit in the blocking of radical political action. For if no such collective action seemed generally possible, then history would indeed appear as random and directionless, and to claim that there was no longer any "grand narrative" would be among other things a way of saying that we no longer knew how to construct one effectively in these conditions. For this kind of thought, history would have ended because freedom would finally have been achieved; for Marxism, the achievement of freedom would be the *beginning* of history and the end of all we have known to date: those boring prehistorical grand narratives which are really just the same old recycled story of scarcity, suffering, and struggle.

Even the densest reader, may by now have guessed that the condition I am describing is not entirely hypothetical. Why should we be invited to imagine such a situation when it is staring us in the face? Is anything to be gained by this tiresome rhetorical ploy? Only, I think, a kind of thought experiment by which, putting actual history in brackets for the moment, we can come to recognize that almost every central feature of postmodern theory can be deduced, read off as it were, from the assumption of a major political defeat. It is as though, confronted with the fact of postmodern culture, we could work our way backward from it until we arrived at the defeat in question. (Whether it has been, in reality, as absolute and definitive a defeat as the existence of postmodernism seems to imply is not at issue here.) This whole speculative enterprise has, of course, the advantage of hindsight, and should not be taken entirely seriously; nobody could actually read off deconstruction or political correctness or *Pulp Fiction* from the winding down of working-class militancy or of national liberation movements. But if postmodernism is not an *inevitable* outcome of such a political history, it is, for all that, a logical one—just as Act V of *King Lear* is not dictated by the four preceding acts, but is not just an accident either.

But isn't this just the kind of historically reductionist explanation that postmodernism itself finds most distasteful? No, because there is no suggestion here that postmodernism is *only* the consequence of a political failure. It is hard to see how Madonna or mock-Gothic buildings or the fiction of Umberto Eco are the offspring of such a repulse, though some ingenious cultural commentator will probably try it on. Postmodernism has many sources—modernism proper, so-called postindustrialism, the emergence of vital new political forces, the recrudescence of the cultural avant garde, the penetration of cultural life by the commodity form, the dwindling of an "autonomous" space for art, the exhaustion of certain classical bourgeois ideologies, and so on. But whatever else it is, it is the child of a political rebuff. Its raising of issues of gender and ethnicity have no doubt permanently breached the ideological enclosure of the white male Western left, about whom the most that can be said is that at least we're not dead, and at the same time taken for granted a rampantly culturalist discourse which belongs precisely to that corner of the globe. These valuable preoccupations have also often enough shown a signal indifference to that power which is the invisible color of daily life, which determines our existence—sometimes literally so—in almost every quarter, which decides in large measure the destiny of nations and the internecine conflicts between them. It is as though every other form of oppressive power can be readily debated, but not the one which so often sets the long-term agenda for them or is at the very least implicated with them at their core. The power of capital is now so wearily familiar that even large sectors of the left have succeeded in naturalizing it, taking it for granted as an immutable structure. One would need, for an apt analogy, to imagine a defeated right wing eagerly discussing the monarchy, the family, and the death of courtesy, while maintaining a stiff silence on what after all most viscerally engages them, the rights of property, since these had been so thoroughly expropriated that it seemed merely academicist to wish them back.

Postmodernist culture has produced a rich, bold, exhilarating body of work across the whole span of the arts, and has generated more than its fair share of execrable kitsch. It has pulled the rug out from beneath a number of complacent certainties, prised open some paranoid totalities, tainted some jealously guarded purities, bent some oppressive norms, and shaken some rather solid-looking foundations. It has also tended to surrender to a politically paralyzing skepticism, a flashy populism, a full-blooded moral relativism, and a brand of sophism for which, since all conventions are arbitrary anyway, might as well conform to those of the Free World. In pulling the rug out from under the certainties of its political opponents, this postmodern culture has often enough pulled it out from under itself too, leaving itself with no more reason why we should resist fascism than the feebly pragmatic plea that fascism is not the way we do things in Sussex or Sacramento. It has brought low the intimidating austerity of high culture with its playful, parodic spirit, and in thus imitating the commodity form has succeeded in reinforcing the crippling austerities of the marketplace. It has released the power of the local, the vernacular, the regional, at the same time as it has contributed to making the globe a more drearily uniform place. Its nervousness in the face of concepts like truth has alarmed the bishops and charmed the business executives. It consistently denies the possibility of describing how the world is, and just as consistently finds itself doing so. It is full of universal moral prescriptions—plurality is preferable to singularity, difference to identity, otherness to sameness—and denounces all such universalism as oppressive. It dreams of a human being set free from law and constraint, gliding ambiguously from one "subject-position" to another, and sees the human subject as no more than the determined effect of cultural forces. It believes in style and pleasure, and commonly churns out texts that might have been composed by, as well as on, a computer.

All of this, however, belongs to a dialectical assessment of postmodernism—and postmodernism itself insists that dialectical thought can be consigned to the metaphysical junkheap. It is here, perhaps, that it differs most deeply from Marxism. Marxists are supposed to be "doctrinaire" thinkers, yet recognize that there can be no authentic socialism without the rich heritage of enlightened bourgeois liberalism. Postmodernists are self-declared devotees of pluralism, mutability, open-endedness, yet are constantly to be caught demonizing humanism, liberalism, the Enlightenment, the centered subject, and the rest. But bourgeois Enlightenment is like social class: in order to get rid of it, you must first work your way through it. It is on this point more than any other that Marxism and postmodernism are perhaps most profoundly at odds.

Postmodernism has a quick eye for irony; but there is one irony above all that seems to have escaped it. Just at the time when it was denouncing the idea of revolution as "metaphysical," scorning the notion of a "collective subject," and insisting on the dangers of totality, revolution broke out where everyone had least expected it, as a collective subject of some kind struck against the "total system" of the postcapitalist bureaucracies. The current results of that transformation are not, of course, ones that a socialist can contemplate with any equanimity; but the dramatic upheavals in Eastern Europe give the lie to many of the fashionable assumptions of the postmodern West. In a powerfully estranging gesture, they expose postmodernism as the ideology of a peculiarly jaded, defeatist wing of the liberal-capitalist intelligentsia, which has mistaken its own very local difficulties for a universal human condition in exactly the manner of the universalist ideologies it denounces. But, though postmodernism may be thus usefully "estranged" by what has happened to the east of it, it was certainly not caused by that collapse. Postmodernism is less a reaction to the defeat of Communism (which it anyway long predated), than—at least in its more reactionary versions—a response to the "success" of capitalism. So here is another irony. In the crisis-ridden 1990s, it seems more than a little odd to treat capitalist success as if it were a general and immutable law of nature. If that is not just the kind of unhistorical absolutizing that postmodernists so fiercely reject in others, it is hard to see what is.

CHAPTER 9

MONOPOLY-FINANCE CAPITAL AND THE PARADOX OF ACCUMULATION

JOHN BELLAMY FOSTER AND ROBERT W. MCCHESNEY

THIS MONTH MARKS THE EIGHTIETH ANNIVERSARY of the 1929 Stock Market Crash that precipitated the Great Depression of the 1930s. Ironically, this comes at the very moment that the capitalist system is celebrating having narrowly escaped falling into a similar abyss. The financial crash and the decline in output a year ago, following the collapse of Lehman Brothers, was as steep as at the beginning of the Great Depression. "For a while," Paul Krugman wrote in the *New York Times* in August, "key economic indicators—world trade, world industrial production, even stock prices—were falling as fast or faster than they did in 1929–30. But in the 1930s the trend lines kept heading down. This time, the plunge appears to be ending after just one terrible year."[1] Big government, through the federal bailout and stimulus, as well as the shock-absorber effects of the continued payouts of unemployment and Social Security benefits, Medicare, etc., slowed the descent and helped the economy to level off, albeit at a point well below previous output.

Yet if the Great Recession has leveled off before plunging into the depths of a second Great Depression, it has nonetheless left the U.S. and world economies in shambles. Official U.S. unemployment is over 9 percent, while real unemployment, taking into account all of those wanting jobs plus part-timers desiring full-time work, is close to twice that. Capacity utilization in industry in the United States is at its lowest level since the 1930s. Investment in new plant and equipment has faltered. The financial system is a shadow of what it was only a year ago. The recovery stage of the business cycle is widely expected to be sluggish.

Indeed, what economists most fear at this point is protracted economic stagnation or a long period of slow growth. "Though the economy may stabilize," Thomas

Palley has written for the New America Foundation, "it will likely be unable to escape the pull of stagnation. That is because stagnation is the logical next stage of the existing [economic] paradigm."[2] Judging by the actions of the economic authorities themselves, there seems to be no way out of the present economic malaise that is acceptable to the vested interests, but to restart the financialization process, i.e., the shift in the center of gravity of the economy from production to finance—meaning further financial bubbles. Yet, rather than overcoming the stagnation problem, this renewed financialization will only serve at best to put off the problem, while piling on further contradictions, setting the stage for even bigger shocks in the future.

This paradox of accumulation under today's monopoly-finance capital was recently captured in a column by Larry Elliott, economics editor of the London-based *Guardian*. He contrasted the Keynesian approach to the crisis, emphasizing fiscal stimulation and financial regulation, to the more conservative approach favored by British Chancellor of the Exchequer Alistair Darling, which sees the revival of a finance-driven economy as crucial. In Elliott's view, the support for the restoration of unfettered finance on the part of leading governmental authorities, such as Darling, may reflect the assessment (shared, ironically, with Marxian economics) that financialization is capital's primary recourse today in countering a basically stagnant economy. As Elliott himself puts it:

> Darling's more cautious approach [in contrast to Keynesian regulatory proposals] is, strangely perhaps, more in tune with the Marxist analysis of the crisis. This argues that it is not the financialisation of Western economies that explains the sluggish growth of recent decades; rather, it is the sluggish growth and the lack of investment opportunities for capital that explains financialisation. From this perspective, the only way capitalists could increase their wealth was through the expansion of a finance sector which, divorced from the real economy, became ever more prone to asset bubbles. Calling time on the casino economy does not mean balanced growth, it just means lower growth. . . .
>
> Those interested in the Marxist perspective should get hold of *The Great Financial Crisis*, written by John Bellamy Foster and Fred Magdoff, published by Monthly Review Press in New York. It is a fascinating read. Whether Darling has read it, I don't know. I suspect, however, that Treasury caution when it comes to reigning in big finance has less to do with Marx and rather more to do with institutional capture.[3]

There are two key points here: (1) the determination of the economic authorities to reinstall the old regime of essentially unregulated financial markets may be due to a perception that the root problem is one of a stagnant real economy, leaving the casino economy as the only practical means of stimulating growth; (2) this attempt to restart financialization may also reflect "institutional capture," i.e., the growing power of financial interests within the capitalist state. These are not contradictory, as (1) invariably leads to (2), as in the case of military spending.

The extreme irrationality of such a solution is not lost on the *Guardian*'s economics editor, who presents the following dismal, but realistic, scenario: "After a short period in which bankers are chastened by their egregious folly there is a return to business as usual. This is the most worrying of all the [various] scenarios [arising from the crash], since it will mean that few—if any—of the underlying problems that caused the crisis have been solved. As a result, we can now start counting down the days to an even bigger financial crisis down the road."[4]

All of this underscores the stagnation-financialization trap of contemporary accumulation, from which it is now increasingly clear there is no easy or complete escape within the system. Such an irrational economic condition and its long-term significance cannot be explained by standard economic models, but only in terms of its historic evolution.

STAGES OF ACCUMULATION

There has long been a fairly widespread agreement among Marxian political economists and economic historians that the history of capitalism up through the twentieth century can be divided into three stages.[5] The first of these stages is *mercantilism*, beginning in the sixteenth century and running into the eighteenth. In terms of the labor process and the development of productive forces, Marx defined this as the period of "manufacture" (meaning the age of handicraft production prior to the rise of what he called "machinofacture"). Nascent factories were typified by the increasingly detailed division of labor described by Adam Smith in his *Wealth of Nations*. Accumulation took place primarily in commerce, agriculture, and mining. What Marx called Department I (producing means of production) remained small in both absolute and relative terms in this stage, while Department II (producing commodities for consumption) was limited by its handicraft character.

The second stage is an outgrowth of the industrial revolution in Britain, centered at first in the textile trade and then spreading to industry generally. Viewed from the standpoint of the present, this is often conceived of as *competitive capitalism* and as the original age of liberalism. Here the focus of accumulation shifted sharply towards modern industry, and particularly the building up of Department I. This included not only factories themselves, but also a whole huge infrastructure of transportation and communications (railroads, telegraphs, ports, canals, steamships). This is a period of intense competition among capitals and a boom-and-bust cycle, with price competition playing a central role in governing economic activity.

The third stage, which is usually called *monopoly capitalism* or corporate capitalism, began in the last quarter of the nineteenth century and was consolidated in the twentieth century. It is marked by the spiraling concentration and centralization of capital, and the rise to dominance of the corporate form of business organization, along with the creation of a market for industrial securities. Industries increasingly come under the rule of a few (oligopolistic) firms that, in Joseph Schumpeter's terms, operate "corespectively" rather than competitively with respect to price, output, and investment decisions at both the national and increasingly global levels.[6] In this stage, Department I continues to expand, including not just factories but a much wider infrastructure in transportation and communications (automobiles, aircraft, telecommunications, computers, etc.). But its continued expansion becomes more dependent on the expansion of Department II, which becomes increasingly developed in this stage—in an attempt to utilize the enormous productive capacity unleashed by the growth of Department I. The economic structure can thus be described as "mature" in the sense that both departments of production are now fully developed and capable of rapid expansion in response to demand. The entire system, however, increasingly operates on a short string, with growing problems of effective demand. Technological innovation has been systematized and made routine, as has scientific management of the labor process and even of consumption through modern marketing. The role of price competition in regulating the system is far reduced.

A further crucial aspect of capitalist development, occurring during all three stages, is the geographical expansion of the system, which, over the course of its first three centuries, developed from a small corner in Western Europe into a world system. However, it was only in the nineteenth century that this globalization tendency went beyond one predominantly confined to coastal regions and islands and penetrated into the interior of continents. And it was only in the twentieth century that we see the emergence of monopoly capital at a high level of globalization—reflecting the growing dominance of multinational (or transnational) corporations.

From the age of colonialism, lasting well into the twentieth century, to the present phase of multinational-corporate domination, this globalizing process has operated imperialistically, in the sense of dividing the world into a complex hierarchy of countries, variously described as: developed and underdeveloped, center and periphery, rich and poor, North and South (with further divisions within both core and periphery). As in any complex hierarchy, there is some shifting over time in those that occupy the top and bottom (and in-between) tiers. Nevertheless, the overall level of social and economic inequality between countries at the world level has risen dramatically over the centuries. There is no real "flattening" of the world economy, as presumed by some ideologues of globalization such as Thomas Friedman.[7] Although industrialization has expanded in the periphery, it has generally been along lines determined by global corporations centered in the advanced capitalist countries, and therefore has tended to be directed to the demands of the center (as well as to the wants of the small, internal oligarchies in peripheral countries). Both departments of production in the periphery are thus heavily subject to imperialist influences.

With this thumbnail sketch of capitalism's historical development before us, it is possible to turn to some of the changes in the nature of accumulation and crisis, focusing in particular on transformations occurring at the core of the system. Capitalism, throughout its history, is characterized by an incessant drive to accumulate, leading to what Mark Blaug referred to as the "paradox of accumulation," identified with Marx's critique of capitalist economics. Since profits grow primarily by increasing the rate of exploitation of labor power, i.e., rise by restraining the growth of wages in relation to productivity, this ultimately places limits on the expansion of capital itself. This paradox of accumulation is reflected in what Paul Sweezy called the "*tendency* to overaccumulation" of capital.[8] Those on the receiving end of the economic surplus (surplus value) generated in production are constantly seeking to enlarge their profits and wealth through new investment and further augmentation of their capital (society's productive capacity). But this inevitably runs up against the relative deprivation of the underlying population, which is the inverse of this growing surplus. Hence, the system is confronted with insufficient effective demand—with barriers to consumption leading eventually to barriers to investment. Growing excess capacity serves to shut off new capital formation, since corporations are not eager to invest in new plant and equipment when substantial portions of their existing capacity are idle. This tendency to overaccumulation becomes increasingly dominant in mature, monopolistic capitalism, slowing the trend-rate of growth around which business cycle fluctuations occur, and thus raising the specter of long-term economic stagnation.

Competitive capitalism in the nineteenth century was dynamic at its core, since the tendency to overaccumulation was held at bay by favorable historical factors. In this period, capital was still being built up virtually from scratch. Department I, in particular, emerged to become a major part of the economy (Department II grew also, of course, but less dramatically). In the maturing capitalism of these years, the demand for new capital formation was essentially unlimited. The investment boom that typically occurred in the business cycle upswing did not generate lasting overaccumulation and overproduction. In these conditions it almost seemed possible, as U.S. economist J. B. Clark declared, to "build more mills that should make more mills for ever."[9] At the same time, the freely competitive nature of the system meant that prices, output, and investment levels were largely determined by market forces independent of individual firms. Many of the rigidities later introduced by giant corporations were therefore absent in the nineteenth-century era of free competition.

Although favorable to system-wide accumulation, the repeated boom and bust crises of competitive capitalism bankrupted firms, from small to large, throughout the economy. Bankruptcies hit firms even at the center of global financial power (Overend, Gurney in 1866; Jay Cooke in 1873; Baring's in 1890). In contrast, under the mature economy of monopoly capitalism, the dominant U.S. financial firms of 1909 are all still at the center of things a century later: J. P. Morgan, Goldman Sachs, National City Bank—or in one notable case 99 years later—Lehman Brothers. But offsetting this increased stability at the center of wealth and power was the disappearance of many of the circumstances favorable for system-wide accumulation.

Once industry had been built up and existing productive capacity was capable of expanding output rapidly at a moment's notice (with whatever investment taking place capable of being financed through depreciation funds set aside to replace worn-out plant and equipment), the demand for new net investment for the rapid expansion of Department I was called into question. Hence, in the monopoly stage, capital saturation—the problem of too much capacity, too much production—becomes an ever-present threat. The system tends at all times to generate more surplus than can be easily absorbed by investment (and capitalist consumption). Under these circumstances, as Sweezy put it,

> The sustainable growth rate of Department I comes to depend essentially on its being geared to the growth of Department II. . . . If capitalists persist in trying to increase their capital (society's productive power) more rapidly than is warranted by society's consuming power . . . the result will be a build-up of excess capacity. As excess capacity grows, profit rates decline and the accumulation process slows down until a sustainable proportionality between the two Departments is again established. This will occur with the economy operating at substantially less than its full potential. In the absence of new stimuli (war, opening of new territories, significant technological or product innovations), this stagnant condition will persist: there is nothing in the logic of the reproduction process [of capital] to push the economy off dead center and initiate a new period of expansion.[10]

Such a tendency toward maturity and stagnation does not, of course, mean that the normal ups and downs of the business cycle cease—nor does it point to economic collapse. Rather, it simply suggests that the economy tends towards underemployment equilibrium with recoveries typically aborting short of full employment. The classic case is the Great Depression itself during which a full business cycle occurred in the midst of a long-term stagnation, with unemployment fluctuating over the entire period between 14 and 25 percent. The 1929 Stock Market Crash was followed by a recession until 1933, a recovery from 1933 to 1937, and a further recession in 1937–1938 (with full recovery only beginning in 1939 under the massive stimulus of the Second World War).

If, as Paul Baran and Paul Sweezy declared in *Monopoly Capital,* "the *normal* state of the monopoly capitalist economy is stagnation," this is due, however, not merely to the conditions of mature industrialization depicted above, but also to the changed pattern of accumulation associated with the drive to dominance of the giant firm.[11] In orthodox economic theory (both classical and neoclassical), the lynchpin of the so-called "self-regulation" of the economy is price competition, out of which the proverbial "invisible hand" of the system arises. It is this that translates productivity gains into benefits for society as a whole through the cheapening of products. Under monopoly (or oligopoly) capital, however, price competition is effectively banned, with the general price level for industry as a whole (except in the most severe deflationary crises) going only one way—up. Thus, although deflation was normal in nineteenth-century competitive capitalism (the trend of wholesale prices in the United States was downward during most of the century, with the notable exception of the Civil War), inflation was to become the norm in twentieth-century monopoly capitalism (the trend of wholesale prices was upward during most of the century, with the notable exception of the Great Depression).[12]

In the very early years of monopoly capitalism, it was quickly learned, through some spectacular business failures, that the giant firms faced the threat of mutual self-destruction if they engaged in fierce price competition, while an agreement to maintain or to raise prices, basically in tandem, removed this threat altogether. The resulting change in the nature of competition reflected what Schumpeter, as noted above, called the "corespective" nature of big corporations—only a few of which dominate most mature markets, and price their products through a process of indirect collusion (the most common form of which is the price leadership of the biggest firm). The rationality of such collusion can easily be explained in terms of the game-theory orientation often advanced by received economics. Refusal to collude, i.e., continuation of price competition, threatens destruction for all parties; collusion, in contrast, tends to benefit all parties. In such a clear case of coincident interests, collusion can often be indirect.[13]

To be sure, price competition is not entirely excluded in advanced capitalism, and may occur in those instances where firms have reason to think that they can get ahead by such means, such as in new industries not yet dominated by a few firms, i.e., before the shakedown process has occurred leading to oligopolistic conditions. This can clearly be seen in recent decades in computers and digital technology. Prices may also fall and a modicum of price competition may be introduced—albeit aimed at driving smaller firms out of business—due to the increased "global sourcing" of commodities produced in low-wage countries. This is evident, in retail, in the case of Wal-Mart, which relies heavily on goods imported from China. As a general rule, however, genuine price competition comes under a strong taboo in the monopoly stage of capitalism.

The implications of the effective banning of price competition at the center of the modern economy are enormous. Competition over productivity or for low-cost position remains intense, but the drastically diminished role of price competition means that the benefits of economic progress tend to be concentrated in the growing surplus of the big firms rather than disseminated more broadly by falling prices throughout the entire society. This aggravates problems of overaccumulation. Faced with a tendency to market saturation, and hence the threat of overproduction, monopolistic corporations attempt to defend their prices and profit margins by further reducing capacity utilization. This, however, prevents the economy from clearing out its excess capital, reinforcing stagnation tendencies. Idle plant and equipment are also held in reserve in the event that rapid expansion is possible. The monopoly capitalist economy thus tends to be characterized by high levels of unplanned *and planned* excess capacity.[14] Major corporations have considerable latitude to govern their output and investment levels, as well as their price levels, which are not externally determined by the market, but rather with an eye to their nearest oligopolistic rivals.

Competition thus does not altogether vanish under monopoly capitalism, but changes in form. Although today's giant corporations generally avoid genuine price competition (which, when referred to at all in business circles, is now given the negative appellation of price warfare), they nonetheless engage in intense competition for market share through the sales effort—advertising, branding, and a whole panoply of marketing techniques. As Martin Mayer wrote in *Madison Avenue* in the 1950s: "Advertising has been so successful financially because it is an effective, low-risk competitive weapon. It is the modern manner of accomplishing results which were formerly—at least in theory—secured by price-cutting."[15] Despite being a minor factor in nineteenth-century competitive capitalism, advertising thus becomes central to monopoly capitalism. This also reflects problems of market saturation and the need of corporations to expand their final consumption markets, if they are to continue to grow.[16]

The stagnation tendency endemic to the mature, monopolistic economy, it is crucial to understand, is not due to technological stagnation, i.e., any failure at technological innovation and productivity expansion. Productivity continues to advance and technological innovations are introduced (if in a more rationalized way) as firms continue to compete for low-cost position. Yet this, in itself, turns into a major problem of the capital-rich societies at the center of the system, since the main constraint on accumulation is not that the economy is not productive enough, but rather that it is *too productive.* Indeed, in numerous important cases, such as the modern automobile industry, corporations compensate by colluding to promote production platforms and marketing arrangements that maximize inefficiency and waste, while generating big profits. As Henry Ford II once said, "minicars [despite their greater fuel efficiency] make miniprofits."[17]

The appearance of a truly epoch-making innovation with geographical as well as economic scale effects—equivalent to the steam engine and the railroad in the nineteenth century, and the automobile in the twentieth—could, of course, alter the general conditions of the economy, constituting the catalyst for a new, long boom, in which capital accumulation feeds on itself for a considerable time. But innovations of this kind are few and far between. Even the computer-digital revolution in the 1980s and 1990s was unable to come close to these earlier epoch-making innovations in stimulating new capital investment.[18]

MONOPOLY-FINANCE CAPITAL AND THE CRISIS

The upshot of the preceding analysis is that accumulation under capitalism has always been dependent on the existence of external stimuli, not simply attributable to the internal logic of accumulation. "Long-run development," Michal Kalecki declared in his *Theory of Economic Dynamics*, "is not inherent in the capitalist economy. Thus specific 'development factors' are required to sustain a long-run upward movement."[19] Moreover, this problem of the historical factors behind growth becomes more severe under the regime of monopoly capital, which experiences a strong stagnationist pull. The whole question of accumulation and growth is thus turned upside down. Rather than treating the appearance of slow growth or stagnation as an anomaly that needs explaining by reference to external factors outside the normal workings of the system (as in orthodox economics), the challenge is to explain the anomaly of fast or full-employment growth, focusing on those specific historical factors that serve to prop up the system.

This can be illustrated by looking briefly at the history of accumulation and crisis from the 1930s to the present. Economists discovered the Great Depression as a problem quite late—at the tail end of the 1930s. The early years of the Depression, marked by the 1929 Stock Market Crash and the recession that lasted until 1933, were seen as representing a severe downturn, but not an extraordinary change in the working of capitalism. Schumpeter typified the main response by declaring that recovery would simply come "of itself."[20] It was, rather, the slow recovery that commenced in 1933 that was eventually to alter perceptions, particularly after the recession that began in 1937, and which resulted in unemployment leaping from 14 to 19 percent.

John Maynard Keynes's magnum opus, *The General Theory of Employment, Interest and Money* (1936) had pointed to the possibility of the capitalist economy entering a long-term underemployment equilibrium. As he wrote: "It is an outstanding characteristic of the economic system in which we live that . . . it seems capable of remaining in a chronic condition of sub-normal activity for a considerable period without any marked tendency either towards recovery or towards complete collapse."[21] This analysis, plus the 1937–38 downturn, induced some economists, such as Alvin Hansen, Keynes's leading early follower in the United States, to raise the question *Full Recovery or Stagnation?*—the title of Hansen's 1938 book.[22]

What followed was an intense but short-lived debate in the United States on the causes of economic stagnation. Hansen raised the issue of maturity, using it to explain the long-term tendency for the capital-rich economy, left to itself, to move "sidewise or even slip down gradually." In contrast, Schumpeter, Hansen's main opponent in the debate, attributed stagnation, not so much to the workings of the economy, but rather to the decline of the sociological foundations of entrepreneurial capitalism with the rise of the modern corporation and state. He ended his *Business Cycles* with the words: "The sociological drift cannot be expected to change."[23] The entire debate, however, came to an abrupt and premature end (it was resurrected briefly after the war but without the same fervor) due to the major stimulus to the economy that ensued with the outbreak of the Second World War in Europe.

As in the case of the Second World War itself, the changed economic conditions in the aftermath of the war were extremely favorable for accumulation. The United States emerged from the war with what Robert Heilbroner described as "the largest reserve of liquid purchasing power [debt-free consumer liquidity] ever accumulated" in its history—if not in the history of capitalism in general. This helped provide the basis, along with heavy government spending on highways, for the second great wave of automobilization in the United States (which included not only the direct effects on industry but also the whole phenomenon of suburbanization). Meanwhile, military spending continued at a much higher level than before the Second World War, with annual U.S. spending on the Korean War rising to about half of peak U.S. spending in the Second World War in both theaters combined.[24] These were also years of the rebuilding of the war-devastated economies in Western Europe and Japan. Finally, the rise of the United States to undisputed hegemony in the world economy was accompanied by the creation of the Bretton Woods institutions (GATT, the World Bank, and the IMF), and the expansion of world trade and finance.

The so-called "golden age" of the 1950s and '60s, however, gradually ran out of steam as the historical forces propelling it waned in influence, turning eventually into what Joan Robinson termed a "leaden age."[25] The consumer liquidity that fed the postwar buying spree dried up. The second-wave automobilization of the country was completed and the automobile industry sank into long-run simple reproduction. Military spending continued to boost the economy with a second regional war in Asia, but with the end of the Vietnam War, this stimulus ebbed. The European and Japanese economies were soon rebuilt, and the new productive capacity that they generated, plus industrial capacity emerging in the periphery, contributed to the growth of international surplus capacity, already becoming evident by the early 1980s.[26] The weakening of U.S. hegemony created growing economic rivalries at the global level.

In 1974–75 the U.S. economy and the world economy as a whole entered a full-fledged structural crisis, ending the long boom, and marking the beginning of decades of deepening stagnation. The worsening conditions of accumulation were to be seen in a downward shift in the real growth rate of the U.S. economy, which was lower in the 1970s than in the 1960s; lower in the 1980s and 1990s than in the 1970s; and lower in 2000–2007 than in the 1980s and 1990s. Since 2007, the economy has declined further, in the deepest crisis since the Great Depression, making 2000–2009 by far the worst decade in economic performance since the 1930s.[27]

Some analysts, most notably Harry Magdoff and Paul Sweezy in a number of works, described from the very onset of the mid-1970s crisis the resurfacing of overaccumulation and stagnation tendencies.[28] But it was at this time that a new, partial fix for the economy emerged—one that was clearly unanticipated, and yet a logical outcome of the whole history of capitalist development up to that point. This came in the form of the creation of a vast and relatively autonomous financial superstructure on top of the productive base of the capitalist economy.

Financial markets and institutions had, of course, evolved historically along with capitalism. But financial booms were typically short-term episodes coinciding with business cycle peaks, and lacked the independent character that they were to assume in the 1980s and 1990s. Thus, as Sweezy insightfully wrote in 1994 in "The Triumph of Financial Capital":

> Traditionally, financial expansion has gone hand-in-hand with prosperity in the real economy. Is it really possible that this is no longer true, that now in the late twentieth century the opposite is more nearly the case: in other words, that now financial expansion feeds not on a healthy economy but a stagnant one? The answer to this question, I think, is yes it is possible, and it is happening. And I will add that I am quite convinced that this inverted relation between the financial and the real is the key to understanding the new trends in the world [economy].[29]

To understand the historical change that took place in this period, it is crucial to recognize that there are, in essence, two price structures in the modern capitalist economy: one related to the pricing of output and associated with GDP and what economists call "the real economy"; the other related to the pricing of assets, composed primarily in the modern period of "financial assets" or paper claims to wealth.[30] Essentially, what occurred was this: unable to find an outlet for its growing surplus in the real economy, capital (via corporations and individual investors) poured its excess surplus/savings into finance, speculating in the increase in asset prices. Financial institutions, meanwhile, on their part, found new, innovative ways to accommodate this vast inflow of money capital and to leverage the financial superstructure of the economy up to ever greater heights with added borrowing— facilitated by all sorts of exotic financial instruments, such as derivatives, options, securitization, etc. Some growth of finance was, of course, required as capital became more mobile globally. This, too, acted as a catalyst, promoting the runaway growth of finance on a world scale.

The result was the creation of mountains of debt coupled with extraordinary growth in financial profits. Total private debt (household and business) rose from 110 percent of U.S. GDP in 1970 to 293 percent of GDP in 2007; while financial profits skyrocketed, expanding by more than 300 percent between 1995 and mid-2007.[31]

This decades-long process of financialization from the 1970s and 1980s up to the present crisis had the indirect effect of boosting GDP growth through various "wealth effects"—the now well-recognized fact that a certain portion of *perceived* increases in assets reenters the productive economy in the form of economic demand, particularly consumption. For example, increased consumer spending on housing occurred as well-to-do individuals benefiting from the upward valuation of assets (real estate and stocks) purchased second homes, contributing to a boom in upper-end home construction.[32] Yet the consequence was the increasing dependence of the entire economy on one financial bubble after another to keep the game afloat.

And, with each extension of the quantity of credit-debt, its quality diminished. This whole process meant growing reliance on the Federal Reserve Board (and the central banks of the other leading capitalist powers) as "lenders of last resort" once a major financial bubble burst.

As financialization took hold, first in the 1970s, and then accelerated in the decades that followed, the U.S. and world economies were subject to growing financial crises (euphemistically referred to as credit crunches). At least fifteen major episodes of financial disruption have occurred since 1970, the most recent of which are: the 1998 Malfunctioning of Long-Term Capital Management; the 2000 New Economy Crash; and the 2007–2009 Great Financial Crisis. Not only have financial crises become endemic, they have also been growing in scale and global impact.[33]

The symbiotic relation between stagnation and financialization meant that, at each financial outbreak, the Federal Reserve and other central banks were forced to intervene to bail out the fragile financial system, lest the financial superstructure as a whole collapse and the stagnation-prone economy weaken still further. This led to the long-term, piece-by-piece deregulation of the financial system, and the active encouragement by state authorities of financial innovation. This included the growth of "securitization"—the transformation of non-marketable debts into marketable securities, under the illusion that credit risk could be reduced and profits expanded by these means. The entire system became internationalized under the leadership of what Peter Gowan called the "Dollar Wall Street Regime." Growth of international finance was facilitated by the rapid development and application of communications technologies, promoting increased competition between financial centers—with Wall Street remaining the world financial hub.[34]

Key to the new financial system in the United States was the emergence of a "financial-industrial complex," as major industrial corporations were drawn into the new system, shifting from equity to debt financing, and developing their own financial subsidiaries. Concentration in finance grew hand over fist—a process that has only accelerated in the present crisis. As recently as 1990, the ten largest U.S. financial institutions held only 10 percent of total financial assets; today they own 50 percent. The top twenty institutions now hold 70 percent of financial assets—up from 12 percent in 1990. At the end of 1985, there were 18,000 FDIC-member banks in the United States. By the end of 2007, this had fallen to 8,534, and since then has dropped still further. Of the fifteen largest U.S. banks in 1991 (together holding at that time $1.5 trillion dollars in assets), only five remained by the end of 2008 (holding $8.9 trillion dollars in assets). As leading financial analyst Henry Kaufman has stated: "In a single generation, our financial system has been transformed. After operating for centuries as a constellation of specialized services, it has melded together rapidly into a highly concentrated oligopoly of enormous, diversified, integrated firms." He continued: "When the current crisis abates, the pricing power of these huge financial conglomerates will grow significantly, at the expense of borrowers and investors."[35]

The foregoing developments can be seen as marking the transformation of the stage of monopoly capital into the new phase of monopoly-finance capital. Characteristic of this phase of accumulation is the stagnation-financialization trap, whereby financial expansion has become the main "fix" for the system, yet is incapable of overcoming the underlying structural weakness of the economy. Much like drug addiction, new, larger fixes are required at each point merely to keep the system going. Every crisis leads to a brief period of restraint, followed by further excesses. Other external stimuli, such as military spending, continue to play a significant role in lifting the economy, but are now secondary in impact to the ballooning of finance.[36]

Today's neoliberal regime itself is best viewed as the political-policy counterpart of monopoly-finance capital. It is aimed at promoting more extreme forms of exploitation—both directly and through the restructuring of insurance and pension systems, which have now become major centers of financial power. Neoliberal accumulation strategies, which function with the aid of a "predator state," are thus directed first and foremost at enhancing corporate profits in the face of stagnation, while providing further needed cash infusions into the financial sector. Everywhere, the advent of neoliberalism has meant an intensification of the class struggle, emanating from both corporations and the state.[37] Far from being a restoration of traditional economic liberalism, neoliberalism is thus a product of big capital, big government, and big finance on an increasingly global scale.[38]

Neoliberalism has also increased international inequalities, taking advantage of the very debt burden that peripheral economies were encouraged to take on, in order to force stringent restructuring on poorer economies: including removal of restrictions on the movement of capital, privatization, deregulation, elimination of state supports to the poor, deunionization, etc.

In the face of financial sector losses, the Federal Reserve Board and U.S. Treasury have explicitly adopted a "too big to fail" policy, giving the lie to the neoliberal notion of a "self-regulating" market economy. The goal has been to prop up the leading financial institutions and to socialize their losses, while retaining an explicit policy of non-intervention during periods when the financial bubble is expanding—thereby allowing corporations to benefit fully from a bubble while it lasts.

Under monopoly-finance capital, we thus see an intensification of the paradox of accumulation. Superimposed on top of the deepening tendency to overaccumulation in the real or productive economy is the further contradiction of a system that increasingly seeks to promote growth in production as a secondary effect of the promotion of speculative financial assets. It is as if, in Marx's famous short-hand, one could indefinitely expand wealth and value by means of M[oney]-M', instead of M-C[ommodity]-M'—skipping altogether the production of commodities in the generation of surplus value, i.e., profit. This is a potent sign, if there ever was one, of the system's increasing irrationality.

The fact that the root difficulty remains a rising rate of exploitation of workers is indicated by the fact that, in 2006, the real hourly wage rate of private, non-agricultural workers in the United States was the same as in 1967, despite the enormous growth in productivity and wealth in the succeeding decades. In 2000–07, productivity growth in the U.S. economy was 2.2 percent, while median hourly wage growth was -0.1 percent. Wage and salary disbursements as a percentage of GDP declined sharply from approximately 53 percent in 1970 to about 46 percent in 2005. Yet, as if in stark defiance of these trends, consumption at the same time rose as a percent of GDP from around 60 percent in the early 1960s to about 70 percent in 2007.[39] Such contradictory developments were made possible by a massive expansion of household debt and the creation in the end of a household bubble, rooted in the securitization of home mortgages. The bursting of the "housing bubble" was the inevitable result of the destruction of the household finances of the great majority of the working population.[40]

THE SYSTEM'S NO-EXIT STRATEGY

In the Great Financial Crisis and the Great Recession that followed hard upon it, the Federal Reserve and U.S. Treasury, along with the other central banks and treasury departments, have committed tens of trillions of dollars to bailing out financial institutions (by early 2009, over $12 trillion in capital infusions, debt support, and other financial commitments to corporations were provided in the bailout by the U.S. government alone).[41] In order to effect this, in the case of the United States, huge quantities of dollars have been printed, the Federal Reserve's balance sheet has ballooned, and the federal deficit has soared. Although world capital has sought out dollars in the crisis, inflating the dollar's value and seemingly strengthening its position as the hegemonic currency, there are fears now that the process will go in reverse as recovery commences, threatening global financial destabilization.[42]

For some economic analysts and investors, the saving grace of the world economy is the rapid economic growth in China and India. This is often seen as eventually pointing towards a new hegemony, based in China, and a new, long upswing in capitalist growth.[43] At present, however, the weight of such emerging capitalist economies is not sufficient to counterbalance the stagnation in the core. And even the most optimistic long-run projections—in which China and India (along with other emerging economies) are able to leap to the next stage of accumulation without further class polarization and destabilization—nonetheless point to insurmountable problems of maturity, stagnation, and financialization (not to mention the overwhelming of planetary resources).

At the core of the system, meanwhile, the forces restraining growth remain considerable. "The current crisis," Kaufman has written, "has brought an end to a decades-long period of private sector debt growth. The institutions that facilitated rapid debt growth in recent decades are now virtually disabled, their borrowers overloaded."[44]

Does this mean that the financialization process, which has been propelling the economy in recent decades, has now come to a standstill, and that a deep, prolonged stagnation is therefore to be expected in the months and years ahead? We believe, as indicated above, that this is the most likely result of the current crisis.

Nevertheless, there are, as we have seen, strong forces pushing for the reinstitution of financialization via the state, with the idea of getting the whole speculative momentum going again. In some cases, this is under the deceptive guise of very modest moves to financial regulation in order to promote confidence and to "legitimize" the system. Indeed, all the indications at present are that financial capital is being put back in the saddle. And with some of the earlier forms of securitization now no longer able to attract investors, the large financial conglomerates are peddling what *Business Week* calls "a new generation of dicey products." For example:

> In recent months such big banks as Bank of America, Citigroup, and JPMorgan Chase have rolled out new-fangled corporate credit lines tied to complicated and volatile derivatives . . . Some of Wall Street's latest innovations give reason to pause . . . Lenders typically tie corporate credit lines to short-term interest rates. But now Citi, JPMorgan Chase, and BofA, among others, are linking credit lines both to short-term rates and credit default swaps (CDSs), the volatile and complicated derivatives that are supposed to operate as "insurance" by paying off the owners if a company defaults on its debt . . . In these new arrangements, when the price of the CDS rises—generally a sign the market thinks the company's health is deteriorating—the cost of the loan increases, too. The result: the weaker the company, the higher the interest rates it must pay, which hurts the company further. . . . Managers now must deal with two layers of volatility—both short-term rates and credit default swaps, whose prices can spike for reasons outside their control.

Business Week goes on to inform its affluent readers of other new speculative instruments that are being introduced, such as "structured notes" or a form of derivative aimed at small investors, offering "teaser rates"—virtually guaranteeing high returns for small investors for a few years, followed by "huge potential losses" after that.[45]

Whether a major new financial bubble will be generated by such means under current circumstances is at this point impossible to determine. There is no denying, however, that restoring the conditions for finance-led expansion has now become the immediate object of economic policy in the face of a persistently stagnation-prone real economy. The social irrationality of such a response only highlights the paradox of accumulation—from which there is today no exit for capital. The main barrier to the accumulation of capital remains the accumulation of capital itself!

—August 27, 2009

NOTES

1. Paul Krugman, "Averting the Worst," *New York Times*, August 10, 2009.
2. Thomas I. Palley, *America's Exhausted Paradigm* (Washington, D.C.: New America Foundation, 2009), 32. http://www.newamerica.net.
3. Larry Elliott, "Comic-Book Economics and the Markets," *The Guardian*, July 6, 2009. http://guardian.co.uk. See also John Bellamy Foster and Fred Magdoff, *The Great Financial Crisis* (New York: Monthly Review Press, 2009).
4. Elliott, "Comic-Book Economics."
5. The next few pages draw heavily on Paul M. Sweezy, *Four Lectures on Marxism* (New York: Monthly Review Press, 1981), 36–38.
6. Joseph A. Schumpeter, *Capitalism, Socialism and Democracy* (New York: Harper and Row, 1942), 90.
7. Thomas L. Friedman, *The World Is Flat* (New York: Farrar, Straus, and Giroux, 2005). For an opposing view, see John Bellamy Foster, "The Imperialist World System," *Monthly Review* 59, no. 1 (May 2007), 1–16.

8. Mark Blaug, *Economic Theory in Retrospect* (Cambridge: Cambridge University Press, 1996), 245; Sweezy, *Four Lectures*, 34–36. See also Karl Marx, *Capital*, vol. 3 (New York: Vintage, 1981), 352–53.

9. J. B. Clark, "Introduction," in Karl Rodbertus, *Overproduction and Crisis* (New York: Scribner, 1898), 15. Clark himself suggested in the same passage that, while this posed no absolute contradiction, it was nevertheless "an unreal case."

10. Sweezy, *Four Lectures*, 39.

11. Paul A. Baran and Paul M. Sweezy, *Monopoly Capital* (New York: Monthly Review Press, 1966), 108.

12. Harry Magdoff and Paul M. Sweezy, *The End of Prosperity* (New York: Monthly Review Press, 1977), 15–20.

13. The classic "kinked-demand curve" treatment of oligopolistic pricing is to be found in Paul M. Sweezy, "Demand Under Conditions of Oligopoly," *Journal of Political Economy* 47 (1939), 568–73.

14. Josef Steindl, *Maturity and Stagnation in American Capitalism* (New York: Monthly Review Press, 1976), 9–14.

15. Martin Mayer, *Madison Avenue* (New York: Harper and Brothers, 1959), xiii.

16. On the role of advertising, see Robert W. McChesney, John Bellamy Foster, Hannah Holleman, and Inger L. Stole, "The Sales Effort and Monopoly Capital," *Monthly Review*, 60, no. 11 (April 2009), 1–23.

17. Henry Ford II quoted in Barry Commoner, *Making Peace with the Planet* (New York: Free Press, 1992), 80–81.

18. See John Bellamy Foster, Harry Magdoff, and Robert W. McChesney, "The New Economy: Myth and Reality," *Monthly Review* 52, no. 11 (April 2001), 1–15.

19. Michal Kalecki, *Theory of Economic Dynamics* (London: George Allen and Unwin, Ltd., 1954), 161.

20. Joseph A. Schumpeter, "Depressions," in Douglas V. Brown, et al., *The Economics of the Recovery Program* (New York: McGraw Hill, 1934), 3–21.

21. John Maynard Keynes, *The General Theory of Employment, Interest and Money* (London: Macmillan, 1973), 249.

22. Alvin H. Hansen, *Full Recovery or Stagnation?* (New York: W. W. Norton, 1938).

23. Alvin H. Hansen, "The Stagnation Thesis," in American Economic Association, *Readings in Fiscal Policy* (Homewood, IL: Richard D. Irwin, 1955), 549; Joseph A. Schumpeter, *Business Cycles*, vol. 2 (New York: McGraw Hill, 1939), 1032–1050.

24. Robert Heilbroner, *The Future as History* (New York: Harper and Brothers, 1960), 134.

25. Joan Robinson, *Essays in the Theory of Economic Fluctuations* (London: Macmillan, 1962), 54.

26. Susan Strange and Roger Tooze, eds., *The International Politics of Surplus Capacity* (London: George Allen and Unwin, 1981).

27. Bureau of Economic Analysis, National Income and Product Accounts, Table 1.1.1.

28. See Magdoff and Sweezy's *The Dynamics of U.S. Capitalism* (1972), *The End of Prosperity* (1977), *The Deepening Crisis of U.S. Capitalism* (1981), *Stagnation and the Financial Crisis* (1987), and *The Irreversible Crisis* (1988)—all published by Monthly Review Press.

29. Paul M. Sweezy, "The Triumph of Financial Capital," *Monthly Review* 46, no. 2 (June 1994), 8.

30. Hyman Minsky, *Can "It" Happen Again?* (New York: M. E. Sharpe, 1982), 94–95.

31. Foster and Magdoff, *The Great Financial Crisis*, 121; Henry Kaufman, *The Road to Financial Reformation* (Hoboken, NJ: John Wiley and Sons, 2009), 161.

32. Kaufman, *The Road to Financial Reformation*, 174; Federal Reserve Board of San Francisco, *FRBSF Economic Letter*, January 19, 2007.

33. Fourteen of the fifteen major financial crises since the 1970s are listed in Kaufman, *The Road to Financial Reformation*, 134. An additional one was the financial crash in Japan in 1990 that led to a decade or more of stagnation.

34. Kaufman, *The Road to Financial Reformation*, 57; Peter Gowan, "U.S. Hegemony Today," in John Bellamy Foster and Robert W. McChesney, eds., *Pox Americana* (New York: Monthly Review Press, 2004), 57–76.

35. Kaufman, *The Road to Financial Reformation*, 67, 97–103, 229.

36. On the role of military spending, see John Bellamy Foster, Hannah Holleman, and Robert W. McChesney, "The U.S. Imperial Triangle and Military Spending," *Monthly Review* 60, no. 5 (October 2008), 1–19.

37. On the repressive aspects of the neoliberal state, see James K. Galbraith, *The Predator State* (New York: The Free Press, 2008), and Hannah Holleman, Robert W. McChesney, John Bellamy Foster, and R. Jamil Jonna, "The Penal State in an Age of Crisis," *Monthly Review* 61, no. 2 (June 2009), 1–17. On the class struggle, see Michael D. Yates, *Why Unions Matter* (New York: Monthly Review Press, 2009).

38. In his last book, John Kenneth Galbraith declared that the "renaming of the system" as "the market system" in neoliberal ideology was little more than a circumvention of reality, a "not wholly innocent fraud." Related to this, in his view, was the abandonment within the mainstream (and even among much of the left) of the concept of "monopoly capitalism." John Kenneth Galbraith, *The Economics of Innocent Fraud* (Boston: Houghton Mifflin, 2004), 3–9, 12.

39. Lawrence Mishel, Jared Bernstein, and Heidi Shierholz, *The State of Working America, 2008/2009* (Ithaca, NY: Cornell University Press, 2009), Table 3.1; Foster and Magdoff, *The Great Financial Crisis*, 129–31.

40. See "The Household Debt Bubble," in Foster and Magdoff, *The Great Financial Crisis*, 27–38.

41. "Financial Rescue Nears GDP as Pledges Top 12.8 Trillion," Bloomberg.com, March 31, 2009; Kaufman, *The Road to Financial Reformation*, 213.

42. "Dollar, Yen Decline as Recovering Economy Eases Refuge Appeal," Bloomberg.com, April 22, 2009.

43. See, for example, "An Astonishing Rebound," *The Economist*, August 13, 2009. On China as the next hegemon, see Giovanni Arrighi, *Adam Smith in Beijing* (London: Verso, 2007). For a less sanguine view taking into account China's (and emerging Asia's) relation to "transnational accumulation," see Martin Hart-Landsberg and Paul Burkett, "China and the Dynamics of Transnational Accumulation," *Historical Materialism* 14, no. 3 (2006), 3–43.

44. Kaufman, *The Road to Financial Reformation*, 223.

45. "Old Banks, New Tricks," *Business Week*, August 17, 2009, 20–23.

CHAPTER 10

THE UNHAPPY MARRIAGE OF MARXISM AND FEMINISM: TOWARDS A MORE PROGRESSIVE UNION

HEIDI HARTMANN

THE "MARRIAGE" OF MARXISM AND FEMINISM has been like the marriage of husband and wife depicted in English common law: marxism and feminism are one, and that one is marxism.[1] Recent attempts to integrate marxism and feminism are unsatisfactory to us as feminists because they subsume the feminist struggle into the "larger" struggle against capital. To continue our simile further, either we need a healthier marriage or we need a divorce.

The inequalities in this marriage, like most social phenomena, are no accident. Many marxists typically argue that feminism is at best less important than class conflict and at worst divisive of the working class. This political stance produces an analysis that absorbs feminism into the class struggle. Moreover, the analytic power of marxism with respect to capital has obscured its limitations with respect to sexism. We will argue here that while marxist analysis provides essential insight into the laws of historical development, and those of capital in particular, the categories of marxism are sex-blind. Only a specifically feminist analysis reveals the systemic character of relations between men and women. Yet feminist analysis by itself is inadequate because it has been blind to history and insufficiently materialist. Both marxist analysis, particularly its historical and materialist method, and feminist analysis, especially the identification of patriarchy as a social and historical structure, must be drawn upon if we are to understand the development of western capitalist societies and the predicament of women within them. In this essay we suggest a new direction for marxist feminist analysis.

Part I of our discussion examines several marxist approaches to the "woman question." We then turn, in Part II, to the work of radical feminists. After noting the limitations of radical feminist definitions of patriarchy, we offer our own. In Part III we try to use the strengths of both marxism and feminism to make suggestions both about the development of capitalist societies and about the present situation of women. We attempt to use marxist methodology to analyze feminist objectives, correcting the imbalance in recent socialist feminist work, and suggesting a more complete analysis of our present socioeconomic formation. We argue that a materialist analysis demonstrates that patriarchy is not simply a psychic, but also a social and economic structure. We suggest that our society can best be understood once it is recognized that it is organized both in capitalistic and in patriarchal ways. While pointing out tensions between patriarchal and capitalist interests, we argue that the accumulation of capital both accommodates itself to patriarchal social structure and helps to perpetuate it. We suggest in this context that sexist ideology has assumed a peculiarly capitalist form in the present, illustrating one way that patriarchal relations tend to bolster capitalism. We argue, in short, that a partnership of patriarchy and capitalism has evolved.

In the concluding section, Part IV, we argue that the *political* relations of marxism and feminism account for the dominance of marxism over feminism in the left's understanding of the woman question. A more progressive union of marxism and feminism, then, requires not only improved intellectual understanding of relations of class and sex, but also that alliance replace dominance and subordination in left politics.

I. MARXISM AND THE WOMAN QUESTION

The woman question has never been the "feminist question." The feminist question is directed at the causes of sexual inequality between women and men, of male dominance over women. Most marxist analyses of women's position take as their question the relationship of women to the economic system, rather than that of women to men, apparently assuming the latter will be explained in their discussion of the former. Marxist analysis of the woman question has taken three main forms. All see women's oppression in our connection (or lack of it) to production. Defining women as part of the working class, these analyses consistently subsume women's relation to men under workers' relation to capital. First, early marxists, including Marx, Engels, Kautsky, and Lenin, saw capitalism drawing all women into the wage labor force, and saw this process destroying the sexual division of labor. Second, contemporary marxists have incorporated women into an analysis of everyday life in capitalism. In this view, all aspects of our lives are seen to reproduce the capitalist system and we are all workers in the system. And third, marxist feminists have focused on housework and its relation to capital, some arguing that housework produces surplus value and that houseworkers work directly for capitalists. These three approaches are examined in turn.

Engels, in *Origins of the Family, Private Property and the State*, recognized the inferior position of women and attributed it to the institution of private property.[2] In bourgeois families, Engels argued, women had to serve their masters, be monogamous, and produce heirs who would inherit the family's property and continue to increase it. Among proletarians, Engels argued, women were not oppressed, because there was no private property to be passed on. Engels argued further that as the extension of wage labor destroyed the small-holding peasantry, and women and children were incorporated into the wage labor force along with men, the authority of the male head of household was undermined, and patriarchal relations were destroyed.[3]

For Engels, then, women's participation in the labor force was the key to their emancipation. Capitalism would abolish sex differences and treat all workers equally. Women would become economically independent of men and would participate on an equal footing with men in bringing about the proletarian revolution. After the revolution, when all people would be workers and private property abolished, women would be emancipated from capital as well as from men. Marxists were aware of the hardships women's labor force participation meant for women and families, which resulted in women having two jobs, housework and wage work. Nevertheless, their emphasis was less on the continued subordination of women in the home than on the progressive character of capitalism's "erosion" of patriarchal relations. Under socialism housework too would be collectivized and women relieved of their double burden.

The political implications of this first marxist approach are clear. Women's liberation requires first, that women become wage workers like men, and second, that they join with men in the revolutionary struggle against capitalism. Capital and private property, the early marxists argued, are the cause of women's particular oppression just as capital is the cause of the exploitation of workers in general.

Though aware of the deplorable situation of women in their time the early marxists failed to focus on the *differences* between men's and women's experiences under capitalism. They did not focus on the feminist questions—how and why women are oppressed as women. They did not, therefore, recognize the vested interest men had in women's continued subordination. As we argue in Part III below, men benefited from not having to do housework, from having their wives and daughters serve them, and from having the better places in the labor market. Patriarchal relations, far from being atavistic leftovers, being rapidly outmoded by capitalism, as the early marxists suggested, have survived and thrived alongside it. And since capital and private property do not cause the oppression of women as *women*, their end alone will not result in the end of women's oppression.

Perhaps the most popular of the recent articles exemplifying the second marxist approach, the everyday life school, is the series by Eli Zaretsky in *Socialist Revolution*.[4] Although Zaretsky, in agreement with feminist analysis, argues that sexism is not a new phenomenon produced by capitalism, he stresses that the particular form sexism takes now has been shaped by capital. He focuses on the differential experiences of men and women under capitalism. Writing a century after Engels, once capitalism had matured, Zaretsky points out that capitalism has not incorporated all women into the labor force on equal terms with men. Rather capital has created a separation between home, family, and personal life on the one hand and the workplace on the other.[5]

Sexism has become more virulent under capitalism, according to Zaretsky, because of this separation between wage work and home work. Women's increased oppression is caused by their exclusion from wage work. Zaretsky argues that while men are oppressed by having to do wage work, women are oppressed by not being allowed to do wage work. Women's exclusion from the wage labor force has been caused primarily by capitalism, because capitalism both creates wage work outside the home and requires women to work in the home in order to reproduce wage workers for the capitalist system. Women reproduce the labor force, provide psychological nurturance for workers, and provide an island of intimacy in a sea of alienation. In Zaretsky's view women are laboring for capital and not for men; it is only the separation of home from work place, and the privatization of housework brought about by capitalism, that creates the *appearance* that women are working for men privately in the home. The difference between the *appearance*, that women work for men, and the *reality*, that women work for capital, has caused a misdirection of the energies of the women's movement. Women should recognize that they, too, are part of the working class, even though they work at home.

In Zaretsky's view, "the housewife emerged, alongside the proletarian [as] the two characteristic laborers of developed capitalist society,"[6] and the segmentation of their lives oppresses both the husband-proletarian and the wife-housekeeper. Only a reconceptualization of "production" which includes women's work in the home and all other socially necessary activities will allow socialists to struggle to establish a society in which this destructive separation is overcome. According to Zaretsky, men and women together (or separately) should fight to reunite the divided spheres of their lives, to create a humane socialism that meets all our private as well as public needs. Recognizing capitalism as the root of their problem, men and women will fight capital and not each other. Since capitalism causes the separation of our private and public lives, the end of capitalism will end that separation, reunite our lives, and end the oppression of both men and women.

Zaretsky's analysis owes much to the feminist movement, but he ultimately argues for a redirection of that movement. Zaretksy has accepted the feminist argument that sexism predates capitalism; he has accepted much of the marxist feminist argument that housework is crucial to the reproduction of capital; he recognizes that housework is hard work and does not belittle it; and he uses the concepts of male supremacy and sexism. But his analysis ultimately rests on the notion of separation, on the concept of *division*, as the crux of the problem, a division attributable to capitalism. Like the "complementary spheres" argument of the early twentieth century, which held that women's and men's spheres were complementary, separate but equally important, Zaretsky largely denies the existence and importance of *inequality* between men and women. His focus is on the relationship of women, the family, and the private sphere to capitalism. Moreover, even if capitalism created the private sphere, as Zaretsky argues, why did it happen that *women* work there, and *men* in the labor force? Surely this cannot be explained without reference to patriarchy, the systemic dominance of men over women. From our point of view, the problem in the family, the labor market, economy, and society is not simply a division of labor between men and women, but a division that places men in a superior, and women in a subordinate, position.

Just as Engels sees private property as the capitalist contribution to women's oppression, so Zaretsky sees privacy. Because women are laboring privately at home they are oppressed. Zaretsky and Engels romanticize the preindustrial family and community—where men, women, adults, children worked together in family centered enterprise and all participated in community life. Zaretsky's humane socialism will reunite the family and recreate that "happy workshop."

While we argue that socialism *is* in the interest of both men and women, it is not at all clear that we are all fighting for the same kind of "humane socialism," or that we have the same conception of the struggle required to get there, much less that capital alone is responsible for our current oppression. While Zaretksy thinks women's work *appears* to be for men but in reality is for capital, we think women's work in the family *really is* for men—though it clearly reproduces capitalism as well. Reconceptualizing production may help us think about the kind of society we want to create, but between now and its creation, the struggle between men and women will have to continue along with the struggle against capital.

Marxist feminists who have looked at housework have also subsumed the feminist struggle into the struggle against capital. Mariarosa Dalla Costa's theoretical analysis of housework is essentially an argument about the relation of housework to capital and the place of housework in capitalist society and not about the relations of men and women as exemplified in housework.[7] Nevertheless, Dalla Costa's political position, that women should demand wages for housework, has vastly increased consciousness of the importance of housework among women in the women's movement. The demand was and still is debated in women's groups all over the United States.[8] By making the claim that women at home not only provide essential services for capital by reproducing the labor force, but also create surplus value through that work,[9] Dalla Costa also vastly increased the left's consciousness of the importance of housework, and provoked a long debate on the relation of housework to capital.[10]

Dalla Costa uses the feminist understanding of housework as real work to claim legitimacy for it under capitalism by arguing that it should be waged work. Women should demand wages for housework rather than allow themselves to be forced into the traditional labor force, where, doing a "double day," women would still provide housework services to capital for free as well as wage labor. Dalla Costa suggests that women who receive wages for housework would be able to organize their housework collectively, providing community child care, meal preparation, and the like. Demanding wages and having wages would raise their consciousness of the importance of their work; they would see its *social* significance, as well as its private necessity, a necessary first step toward more comprehensive social change.

Dalla Costa argues that what is socially important about housework is its necessity to capital. In this lies the strategic importance of women. By demanding wages for housework and by refusing to participate in the labor market women can lead the struggle against capital. Women's community organizations can be subversive to capital and lay the basis not only for resistance to the encroachment of capital but also for the formation of a new society.

Dalla Costa recognizes that men will resist the liberation of women (that will occur as women organize in their communities) and that women will have to struggle against them, but this struggle is an auxiliary one that must be waged to bring about the ultimate goal of socialism. For Dalla Costa, women's struggles are revolutionary not because they are feminist, but because they are anti-capitalist. Dalla Costa finds a place in the revolution for women's struggle by making women producers of surplus value, and as a consequence part of the working class. This legitimates women's political activity.[11]

The women's movement has never doubted the importance of women's struggle because for feminists the *object* is the liberation of women, which can only be brought about by women's struggles. Dalla Costa's contribution to increasing our understanding of the social nature of housework has been an incalculable advance. But like the other marxist approaches reviewed here her approach focuses on capital—not on relations between men and women. The fact that men and women have differences of interest, goals, and strategies is obscured by her analysis of how the capitalist system keeps us all down, and the important and perhaps strategic role of women's work in this system. The rhetoric of feminism is present in Dalla Costa's writing (the oppression of women, struggle with men) but the focus of feminism is not. If it were, Dalla Costa might argue for example, that the importance of housework as a social relation lies in its crucial role in perpetuating male supremacy. That women do housework, performing labor for men, is crucial to the maintenance of patriarchy.

Engels, Zaretsky, and Dalla Costa all fail to analyze the labor process within the family sufficiently. Who benefits from women's labor? Surely capitalists, but also surely men, who as husbands and fathers receive personalized services at home. The content and extent of the services may vary by class or ethnic or racial group, but the fact of their receipt does not. Men have a higher standard of living than women in terms of luxury consumption, leisure time, and personalized services.[12] A materialist approach ought not ignore this crucial point.[13] It follows that men have a material interest in women's continued oppression. In the long run this may be "false consciousness," since the majority of men could benefit from the abolition of hierarchy within the patriarchy. But in the short run this amounts to control over other people's labor, control which men are unwilling to relinquish voluntarily.

While the approach of the early marxists ignored housework and stressed women's labor force participation, the two more recent approaches emphasize housework to such an extent they ignore women's current role in the labor market. Nevertheless, all three attempt to include women in the category working class and to understand women's oppression as another aspect of class oppression. In doing so all give short shrift to the object of feminist analysis, the relations between women and men. While our "problems" have been elegantly analyzed, they have been misunderstood. The focus of marxist analysis has been class relations; the object of marxist analysis has been understanding the laws of motion of capitalist society. While we believe marxist methodology *can* be used to formulate feminist strategy, these marxist feminist approaches discussed above clearly do not do so; their marxism clearly dominates their feminism.

As we have already suggested, this is due in part to the analytical power of marxism itself. Marxism is a theory of the development of class society, of the accumulation process in capitalist societies, of the reproduction of class dominance, and of the development of contradictions and class struggle. Capitalist societies are driven by the demands of the accumulation process, most succinctly summarized by the fact that production is oriented to exchange, not use. In a capitalist system production is important only insofar as it contributes to the making of profits, and the use value of products is only an incidental consideration. Profits derive from the capitalists' ability to exploit labor power, to pay laborers less than value of what they produce. The accumulation of profits systematically transforms social structure as it transforms the relations of production. The reserve army of labor, the poverty of great numbers of people and the near-poverty of still more, these human reproaches to capital are by-products of the accumulation process itself. From the capitalist's point of view, the reproduction of the working class may "safely be left to itself."[14] At the same time, capital creates an ideology, which grows up along side it, of individualism, competitiveness, domination, and in our time, consumption of a particular kind. Whatever one's theory of the genesis of ideology one must recognize these as the dominant values of capitalist societies.

Marxism enables us to understand many aspects of capitalist societies: the structure of production, the generation of a particular occupational structure, and the nature of the dominant ideology. Marx's theory of the development of capitalism is a theory of the development of "empty places." Marx predicted, for example, the growth of the proletariat and the demise of the petit bourgeoisie. More precisely and in more detail, Braverman among others has explained the creation of the "places" clerical worker and service worker in advanced capitalist societies.[15] Just as capital creates these places indifferent to the individuals who fill them, the categories of marxist analysis, class, reserve army of labor, wage-laborer, do not explain why particular people fill particular places. They give no clues about why *women* are subordinate to *men* inside and outside the family and why it is not the other way around. *Marxist categories, like capital itself, are sex-blind.* The categories of marxism cannot tell us who will fill the empty places. Marxist analysis of the woman question has suffered from this basic problem.

TOWARD MORE USEFUL MARXIST FEMINISM

Marxism is also a *method* of social analysis, historical dialectical materialism. By putting this method to the service of feminist questions, Juliet Mitchell and Shulamith Firestone suggest new directions for marxist feminism. Mitchell says, we think correctly, that

> [i]t is not "our relationship" to socialism that should *ever* be the question—it is the use of scientific socialism [what we call marxist method] as a method of analyzing the specific nature of our oppression and hence our revolutionary role. Such a method, I believe needs to understand radical feminism, quite as much as previously developed socialist theories.[16]

As Engels wrote:

> According to the materialistic conception, the determining factor in history is, in the final instance, the production and reproduction of immediate life. This, again, is of a twofold character: on the one side, the production of the means of existence, of food, clothing, and shelter and the tools necessary for that production; on the other side, the production of human beings themselves, the propagation of the species. The social organization under which the people of a particular historical epoch live is determined by both kinds of production . . .[17]

This is the kind of analysis Mitchell has attempted. In her first essay, "Women: The Longest Revolution," Mitchell examines both market work and the work of reproduction, sexuality, and childrearing.[18]

Mitchell does not entirely succeed, perhaps because not all of women's work counts as production for her. Only market work is identified as production; the other spheres (loosely aggregated as the family) in which women work are identified as ideological. Patriarchy, which largely organizes reproduction, sexuality, and childrearing, has no material base for Mitchell. *Women's Estate*, Mitchell's expansion of this essay, focuses much more on developing the analysis of women's market work than it does on developing the analysis of women's work within the family. The book is much more concerned with women's relation to, and work for, capital than with women's relation to, and work for, men; more influenced by marxism than by radical feminism. In a later work, *Psychoanalysis and Feminism*, Mitchell explores an important area for studying the relations between women and men, namely the formation of different, gender-based personalities by women and men.[19] Patriarchy operates, Mitchell seems to be saying, primarily in the psychological realm, where female and male children learn to be women and men. Here Mitchell focuses on the spheres she initially slighted, reproduction, sexuality, and child rearing, but by placing them in the ideological realm, she continues the fundamental weakness of her earlier analysis. She clearly presents patriarchy as the fundamental ideological structure, just as capital is the fundamental economic structure:

> To put the matter schematically . . . we are . . . dealing with two autonomous areas: the economic mode of capitalism and the ideological mode of patriarchy.[20]

Although Mitchell discusses their interpenetration, her failure to give patriarchy a material base in the relation between women's and men's labor power, and her similar failure to note the material aspects of the process of personality formation and gender creation, limits the usefulness of her analysis.

Shulamith Firestone bridges marxism and feminism by bringing materialist analysis to bear on patriarchy.[21] Her use of materialist analysis is not as ambivalent as Mitchell's. The dialectic of sex, she says, is the fundamental historical dialectic, and the material base of patriarchy is the work women do reproducing the species. The importance of Firestone's work in using marxism to analyze women's position, in asserting the existence of a material base to patriarchy, cannot be overestimated. But it suffers from an overemphasis on biology and reproduction. What we need to understand is how sex (a biological fact) becomes gender (a social phenomenon). It is necessary to place all women's work in its social and historical context, not to focus only on reproduction. Although Firestone's work offers a new and feminist use of marxist methodology, her insistence on the primacy of men's dominance over women as the cornerstone on which all other oppression (class, age, race) rests, suggests that her book is more properly grouped with the radical feminists than with the marxist feminists. Her work remains the most complete statement of the radical feminist position.

Firestone's book has been all too happily dismissed by marxists. Zaretsky, for example, calls it a "plea for subjectivity." Yet what was so exciting to women about Firestone's book was her analysis of men's power over women, and her very healthy anger about this situation. Her chapter on love was central to our understanding of this, and still is. It is not just about "masculinist ideology," which marxists can deal with (just a question of attitudes), but an exposition of the subjective consequences of men's power over women, of what it feels like to live in a patriarchy. "The personal is political" is not, as Zaretsky would have it, a plea for subjectivity, for feeling better: it is a demand to recognize men's power and women's subordination as a social and political reality.

II. RADICAL FEMINISM AND PATRIARCHY

The great thrust of radical feminist writing has been directed to the documentation of the slogan "the personal is political." Women's discontent, radical feminists argued, is not the neurotic lament of the maladjusted, but a response to a social structure in which women are systematically dominated, exploited, and oppressed. Women's inferior position in the labor market, the male-centered emotional structure of middle class marriage, the use of women in advertising, the so-called understanding of women's psyche as neurotic—popularized by academic and clinical psychology—aspect after aspect of women's lives in advanced capitalist society was researched and analyzed. The radical feminist literature is enormous and defies easy summary. At the same time, its focus on psychology is consistent. The New York Radical Feminists' organizing document was "The Politics of the Ego." "The personal is political" means for radical feminists, that the original and basic class division is between the sexes, and that the motive force of history is the striving of men for power and domination over women, the dialectic of sex.[22]

Accordingly, Firestone rewrote Freud to understand the development of boys and girls into men and women in terms of power.[23] Her characterizations of what are "male" and "female" character traits are typical of radical feminist writing. The male seeks power and domination; he is egocentric and individualistic, competitive and pragmatic; the "technological mode," according to Firestone, is male. The female is nurturant, artistic, and philosophical; the "aesthetic mode" is female.

No doubt, the idea that the aesthetic mode is female would have come as quite a shock to the ancient Greeks. Here lies the error of radical feminist analysis: the dialectic of sex as radical feminists present it projects male and female characteristics as they appear in the present back into all of history. Radical feminist analysis has greatest strength in its insights into the present. Its greatest weakness is a focus on the psychological which blinds it to history.

The reason for this lies not only in radical feminist method, but also in the nature of patriarchy itself, for patriarchy is a strikingly resilient form of social organization. Radical feminists use patriarchy to refer to a social system characterized by male domination over women. Kate Millett's definition is classic:

> our society . . . is a patriarchy. The fact is evident at once if one recalls that the military, industry, technology, universities, science, political offices, finances—in short, every avenue of power within the society, including the coercive force of the police, is entirely in male hands.[24]

This radical feminist definition of patriarchy applies to most societies we know of and cannot distinguish among them. The use of history by radical feminists is typically limited to providing examples of the existence of patriarchy in all times and places.[25] For both marxist and mainstream social scientists before the women's movement, patriarchy referred to a system of relations between men, which formed the political and economic outlines of feudal and some pre-feudal societies, in which hierarchy followed ascribed characteristics. Capitalist societies are understood as meritocratic, bureaucratic, and impersonal by bourgeois social scientists; marxists see capitalist societies as systems of class domination.[26] For both kinds of social scientists neither the historical patriarchal societies nor today's western capitalist societies are understood as systems of relations between men that enable them to dominate women.

TOWARD A DEFINITION OF PATRIARCHY

We can usefully define patriarchy as a set of social relations between men, which have a material base, and which, though hierarchical, establish or create interdependence and solidarity among men that enable them to dominate women. Though patriarchy is hierarchical and men of different classes, races, or ethnic groups have different places in the patriarchy, they also are united in their shared relationship of dominance over their women; they are dependent on each other to maintain that domination. Hierarchies "work" at least in part because they create vested interests in the status quo. Those at the higher levels can "buy off" those at the lower levels by offering them power over those still lower. In the hierarchy of patriarchy, all men, whatever their rank in the patriarchy, are bought off by being able to control at least some women. There is some evidence to suggest that when patriarchy was first institutionalized in state societies, the ascending rulers literally made men the heads of their families (enforcing their control over their wives and children) in exchange for the men's ceding some of their tribal resources to the new rulers.[27] Men are dependent on one another (despite their hierarchical ordering) to maintain their control over women.

The material base upon which patriarchy rests lies most fundamentally in men's control over women's labor power. Men maintain this control by excluding women from access to some essential productive resources (in capitalist societies, for example, jobs that pay living wages) and by restricting women's sexuality.[28] Monogamous heterosexual marriage is one relatively recent and efficient form that seems to allow men to control both these areas. Controlling women's access to resources and their sexuality, in turn, allows men to control women's labor power, both for the purpose of serving men in many personal and sexual ways and for the purpose of rearing children. The services women render men, and which exonerate men from having to perform many unpleasant tasks (like cleaning toilets) occur outside as well as inside the family setting. Examples outside the family include the harassment of women workers and students by male bosses and professors as well as the common use of secretaries to run personal errands, make coffee, and provide "sexy" surroundings. Rearing children, whether or not the children's labor power is of immediate benefit to their fathers, is nevertheless a crucial task in perpetuating patriarchy as a system. Just as class society must be reproduced by schools, work places, consumption norms, etc., so must patriarchal social relations. In our society children are generally reared by women at home, women socially defined and recognized as inferior to men, while men appear in the domestic picture only rarely. Children raised in this way generally learn their places in the gender hierarchy well. Central to this process, however, are the areas outside the home where patriarchal behaviors are taught and the inferior position of women enforced and reinforced: churches, schools, sports, clubs, unions, armies, factories, offices, health centers, the media, etc.

The material base of patriarchy, then, does not rest solely on childrearing in the family, but on all the social structures that enable men to control women's labor. The aspects of social structures that perpetuate patriarchy are theoretically identifiable, hence separable from their other aspects. Gayle Rubin has increased our ability to identify the patriarchal element of these social structures enormously by identifying "sex/gender systems":

> a "sex/gender system" is the set of arrangements by which a society transforms biological sexuality into products of human activity, and in which transformed sexual needs are satisfied.[29]

We are born female and male, biological sexes, but we are created woman and man, socially recognized genders. *How* we are so created is that second aspect of the *mode* of production of which Engels spoke, "the production of human beings themselves, the propagation of the species."

How people propagate the species is socially determined. If, biologically, people are sexually polymorphous, and society were organized in such a way that all forms of sexual expression were equally permissible, reproduction would result only from some sexual encounters, the heterosexual ones. The strict division of labor by sex, a social invention common to all known societies, creates two very separate genders and a need for men and women to get together for economic reasons. It thus helps to direct their sexual needs toward heterosexual fulfillment, and helps to ensure biological reproduction. In more imaginative societies, biological reproduction might be ensured by other techniques, but the division of labor by sex appears to be the universal solution to date. Although it is theoretically possible that a sexual division of labor not imply inequality between the sexes, in most known societies, the socially acceptable division of labor by sex is one which accords lower status to women's work. The sexual division of labor is also the underpinning of sexual subcultures in which men and women experience life differently; it is the material base of male power which is exercised (in our society) not just in not doing housework and in securing superior employment, but psychologically as well.

How people meet their sexual needs, how they reproduce, how they inculcate social norms in new generations, how they learn gender, how it feels to be a man or a woman—all occur in the realm Rubin labels the sex/gender system. Rubin emphasizes the influence of kinship (which tells you with whom you can satisfy sexual needs) and the development of gender specific personalities via childrearing and the "oedipal machine." In addition, however, we can use the concept of the sex/gender system to examine all other social institutions for the roles they play in defining and reinforcing gender hierarchies. Rubin notes that theoretically a sex/gender system could be female dominant, male dominant, or egalitarian, but declines to label various known sex/gender systems or to periodize history accordingly. We choose to label our present sex/gender system patriarchy, because it appropriately captures the notion of hierarchy and male dominance which we see as central to the present system.

Economic production (what marxists are used to referring to as *the* mode of production) and the production of people in the sex/gender sphere both determine "the social organization under which people of a particular historical epoch and a particular country live," according to Engels. The whole of society, then, can be understood by looking at both these types of production and reproduction, people and things.[30] There is no such thing as "pure capitalism," nor does "pure patriarchy" exist, for they must of necessity coexist. What exists is patriarchal capitalism, or patriarchal feudalism, or egalitarian hunting/gathering societies, or matriarchal horticultural societies, or patriarchal horticultural societies, and so on. There appears to be no necessary connection between *changes* in the one aspect of production and changes in the other. A society could undergo transition from capitalism to socialism, for example, and remain patriarchal.[31] Common sense, history, and our experience tell us, however, that these two aspects of production are so closely intertwined, that change in one ordinarily creates movement, tension, or contradiction in the other.

Racial hierarchies can also be understood in this context. Further elaboration may be possible along the lines of defining color/race systems, arenas of social life that take biological color and turn it into a social category, race. Racial hierarchies, like gender hierarchies, are aspects of our social organization, of how people are produced and reproduced. They are not fundamentally ideological; they constitute that second aspect of our mode of production, the production and reproduction of people. It might be most accurate then to refer to our societies not as, for example, simply capitalist, but as patriarchal capitalist white supremacist. In Part III below, we illustrate one case of capitalism adapting to and making use of racial orders and several examples of the interrelations between capitalism and patriarchy.

Capitalist development creates the places for a hierarchy of workers, but traditional marxist categories cannot tell us who will fill which places. Gender and racial hierarchies determine who fills the empty places. *Patriarchy is not simply hierarchical organization,* but hierarchy in which *particular* people fill *particular* places. It is in studying patriarchy that we learn why it is women who are dominated and how. While we believe that most known societies have been patriarchal, we do not view patriarchy as a universal, unchanging phenomenon. Rather patriarchy, the set of interrelations among men that allow men to dominate women, has changed in form and intensity over time. It is crucial that the hierarchy among men, and their differential access to patriarchal benefits, be examined. Surely, class, race, nationality, and even marital status and sexual orientation, as well as the obvious age, come into play here. And women of different class, race, national, marital status, or sexual orientation groups are subjected to different degrees of patriarchal power. Women may themselves exercise class, race, or national power, or even patriarchal power (through their family connections) over men lower in the patriarchal hierarchy than their own male kin.

To recapitulate, we define patriarchy as a set of social relations which has a material base and in which there are hierarchical relations between men and solidarity among them which enable them in turn to dominate women. The material base of patriarchy is men's control over women's labor power. That control is maintained by excluding women from access to necessary economically productive resources and by restricting women's sexuality. Men exercise their control in receiving personal service work from women, in not having to do housework or rear children, in having access to women's bodies for sex, and in feeling powerful and being powerful. The crucial elements of patriarchy as we *currently* experience them are: heterosexual marriage (and consequent homophobia), female childrearing and housework, women's economic dependence on men (enforced by arrangements in the labor market), the state, and numerous institutions based on social relations among men—clubs, sports, unions, professions, universities, churches, corporations, and armies. All of these elements need to be examined if we are to understand patriarchal capitalism.

Both hierarchy and interdependence among men and the subordination of women are *integral* to the functioning of our society; that is, these relationships are *systemic*. We leave aside the question of the creation of these relations and ask, can we recognize patriarchal relations in capitalist societies? Within capitalist societies we must discover those same bonds between men which both bourgeois and marxist social scientists claim no longer exist or are, at the most, unimportant leftovers. Can we understand how these relations among men are perpetuated in capitalist societies? Can we identify ways in which patriarchy has shaped the course of capitalist development?

III. THE PARTNERSHIP OF PATRIARCHY AND CAPITAL

How are we to recognize patriarchal social relations in capitalist societies? It appears as if each woman is oppressed by her own man alone; her oppression seems a private affair. Relationships among men and among families seems equally fragmented. It is hard to recognize relationships among men, and between men and women, as *systematically* patriarchal. We argue, however, that patriarchy as a system of relations between men and women exists in capitalism, and that in capitalist societies a healthy and strong partnership exists between patriarchy and capital. Yet if one begins with the concept of patriarchy and an understanding of the capitalist mode of production, one recognizes immediately that the partnership of patriarchy and capital was not inevitable; men and capitalists often have conflicting interests, particularly over the use of women's labor power. Here is one way in which this conflict might manifest itself: the vast majority of men might want their women at home to personally service them. A smaller number of men, who are capitalists, might want most women (not their own) to work in the wage labor market. In examining the tensions of this conflict over women's labor power historically, we will be able to identify the material base of patriarchal relations in capitalist societies, as well as the basis for the partnership between capital and patriarchy.

INDUSTRIALIZATION AND THE DEVELOPMENT OF FAMILY WAGES

Marxists made quite logical inferences from a selection of the social phenomena they witnessed in the nineteenth century. But marxists ultimately underestimated the strength of the preexisting patriarchal social forces with which fledgling capital had to contend and the need for capital to adjust to these forces. The industrial revolution was drawing all people into the labor force, including women and children; in fact the first factories used child and female labor almost exclusively.[32] That women and children could earn wages separately from men both undermined authority relations (as discussed in Part I above) and kept wages low for everyone. Kautsky, writing in 1892, described the process this way:

> [Then with] the wife and young children of the working man . . . able to take care of themselves, the wages of the male worker can safely be reduced to the level of his own personal needs without the risk of stopping the fresh supply of labor power.
>
> The labor of women and children, moreover, affords the additional advantage that these are less capable of resistance than men [*sic*]; and their introduction into the ranks of the workers increases tremendously the quantity of labor that is offered for sale in the market.

> Accordingly, the labor of women and children . . . also diminishes [the] capacity [of the male worker] for resistance in that it overstocks the market; owning to both these circumstances it lowers the wages of the working-man.[33]

The terrible effects on working class family life of low wages and of forced participation of all family members in the labor force were recognized by marxists. Kautsky wrote:

> The capitalist system of production does not in most cases destroy the single household of the workingman, but robs it of all but its unpleasant features. The activity of woman today in industrial pursuits . . . means an increase of her former burden by a new one. *But one cannot serve two masters.* The household of the working-man suffers whenever his wife must help to earn the daily bread.[34]

Working men as well as Kautsky recognized the disadvantages of female wage labor. Not only were women "cheap competition" but working women were their very wives, who could not "serve two masters" well.

Male workers resisted the wholesale entrance of women and children into the labor force, and sought to exclude them from union membership and the labor force as well. In 1846 the *Ten Hours' Advocate* stated:

> It is needless for us to say, that all attempts to improve the morals and physical condition of female factory workers will be abortive, unless their hours are materially reduced. Indeed we may go so far as to say, that married females would be much better occupied in performing the domestic duties of the household, than following the never-tiring motion of machinery. We therefore hope the day is not distant, when the husband will be able to provide for his wife and family, without sending the former to endure the drudgery of a cotton mill.[35]

In the United States in 1854 the National Typographical Union resolved not to "encourage by its act the employment of female compositors." Male unionists did not want to afford union protection to women workers; they tried to exclude them instead. In 1879 Adolph Strasser, president of the Cigarmakers International Union, said: "We cannot drive the females out of the trade, but we can restrict their daily quota of labor through factory laws."[36]

While the problem of cheap competition could have been solved by organizing the wage earning women and youths, the problem of disrupted family life could not be. Men reserved union protection for men and argued for protective labor laws for women and children.[37] Protective labor laws, while they may have ameliorated some of the worst abuses of female and child labor, also limited the participation of adult women in many "male" jobs.[38] Men sought to keep high wage jobs for themselves and to raise male wages generally. They argued for wages sufficient for their wage labor alone to support their families. This "family wage" system gradually came to be the norm for stable working class families at the end of the nineteenth century and the beginning of the twentieth.[39] Several observers have declared the non wage-working wife to be part of the standard of living of male workers.[40] Instead of fighting for equal wages for men and women, male workers sought the family wage, wanting to retain their wives' services at home. In the absence of patriarchy a unified working class might have confronted capitalism, but patriarchal social relations divided the working class, allowing one part (men) to be bought off at the expense of the other (women). Both the hierarchy between men and the solidarity among them were crucial in this process of resolution. Family wages may be understood as a resolution of the conflict over women's labor power which was occurring between patriarchal and capitalist interests at that time.

Family wages for most adult men imply men's acceptance, and collusion in, lower wages for others, young people, women and socially defined inferior men as well (Irish, blacks, etc., the lowest groups in the patriarchal hierarchy who are denied many of the patriarchal benefits). Lower wages for women and children and inferior men are enforced by job segregation in the labor market, in turn maintained by unions and management as well as by auxiliary institutions like schools, training programs, and even families. Job segregation by sex, by insuring that women have the lower paid jobs, both assures women's economic dependence on men and reinforces notions of appropriate spheres for women and men. For most men, then, the development of family wages, secured the material base of male domination in two ways. First, men have the better jobs in the labor market and earn higher wages than women. The lower pay women receive in the labor market both perpetuates men's material advantage over women and encourages women to choose wifery as a career. Second, then, women do housework, childcare, and perform other services at home which benefit men directly.[41] Women's home responsibilities in turn reinforce their inferior labor market position.[42]

The resolution that developed in the early twentieth century can be seen to benefit capitalist interests as well as patriarchal interests. Capitalists, it is often argued, recognized that in the extreme conditions which prevailed in the early nineteenth century industrialization, working class families could not adequately reproduce themselves. They realized that housewives produced and maintained healthier workers than wage-working wives and that educated children became better workers than noneducated ones. The bargain, paying family wages to men and keeping women home, suited the capitalists at the time as well as the male workers. Although the terms of the bargain have altered over time, it is still true that the family and women's work in the family serve capital by providing a labor force and serve men as the space in which they exercise their privilege. Women, working to serve men and their families, also serve capital as consumers.[43] The family is also the place where dominance and submission are learned, as Firestone, the Frankfurt School, and many others have explained.[44] Obedient children become obedient workers; girls and boys each learn their proper roles.

While the family wage shows that capitalism adjusts to patriarchy, the changing status of children shows that patriarchy adjusts to capital. Children, like women, came to be excluded from wage labor. As children's ability to earn money declined, their legal relationship to their parents changed. At the beginning of the industrial era in the United States, fulfilling children's need for their fathers was thought to be crucial, even primary, to their happy development; fathers had legal priority in cases of contested custody. As children's ability to contribute to the economic well-being of the family declined, mothers came increasingly to be viewed as crucial to the happy development of their children, and gained legal priority in cases of contested custody.[45] Here patriarchy adapted to the changing economic role of children: when children were productive, men claimed them; as children became unproductive, they were given to women.

THE PARTNERSHIP IN THE TWENTIETH CENTURY

The prediction of nineteenth century marxists that patriarchy would wither away in the face of capitalism's need to proletarianize everyone has not come true. Not only did marxists underestimate the strength and flexibility of patriarchy, they also overestimated the strength of capital. They envisioned the new social force of capitalism, which had torn feudal relations apart, as virtually all powerful. Contemporary observers are in a better position to see the difference between the tendencies of "pure" capitalism and those of "actual" capitalism as it confronts historical forces in everyday practice. Discussions of the partnership between capital and racial orders and of labor market segmentation provide additional examples of how "pure" capitalist forces meet up with historical reality. Great flexibility has been displayed by capitalism in this process.

Marxists who have studied South Africa argue that although racial orders may not allow the equal proletarianization of everyone, this does not mean that racial barriers prevent capital accumulation.[46] In the abstract, analysts could argue about which arrangements would allow capitalists to extract the most surplus value. Yet in a particular historical situation, capitalists must be concerned with social control, the resistance of groups of workers, and the intervention of the state. The state might intervene in order to reproduce society as a whole; it might be necessary to police some capitalists, to overcome the worst tendencies of capital. Taking these factors into account, capital*ists* maximize greatest *practicable* profits. If for purposes of social control, capitalists organize work in a particular way, nothing about capital itself determines who (that is, which individuals with which ascriptive characteristics) shall occupy the higher, and who the lower rungs of the wage labor force. It helps, of course, that capitalists themselves are likely to be the dominant social group and hence racists (and sexist). Capitalism inherits the ascribed characteristics of the dominant groups as well as of the subordinate ones.

Recent arguments about the tendency of monopoly capital to create labor market segmentation are consistent with this understanding.[47] Where capitalists purposely segment the labor force, using ascriptive characteristics to divide the working class, this clearly derives from the need for social control rather than accumulation needs in the narrow sense.[48] And over time, not all such divisive attempts are either successful (in dividing) or profitable. The ability of capital to shape the workforce depends both on the particular imperatives of accumulation in a narrow sense (for example, is production organized in a way that requires communication among a large number of workers? if so, they had better all speak the same language)[49] and on social forces within a society which may encourage/force capital to adapt (the maintenance of separate washroom facilities in South Africa for whites and blacks can only be understood as an economic cost to capitalists, but one less than the social cost of trying to force South African whites to wash up with blacks).

If the first element of our argument about the course of capitalist development is that capital is not all-powerful, the second is that capital is tremendously flexible. Capital accumulation encounters preexisting social forms, and both destroys them and adapts to them. The adaptation of capital can be seen as a reflection of the *strength* of these preexisting forms to persevere in new environments. Yet even as they persevere, they are not unchanged. The ideology with which race and sex are understood today, for example, is strongly shaped by the particular ways racial and sexual divisions are reinforced in the accumulation process.

THE FAMILY AND THE FAMILY WAGE TODAY

We argued above, that, with respect to capitalism and patriarchy, the adaptation, or mutual accommodation, took the form of the development of the family wage in the early twentieth century. The family wage cemented the partnership between patriarchy and capital. Despite women's increased labor force participation, particularly rapid since World War II, the family wage is still, we argue, the cornerstone of the present sexual division of labor—in which women are primarily responsible for housework and men primarily for wage work. Women's lower wages in the labor market (combined with the need for children to be reared by someone) assure the continued existence of the family as a necessary income pooling unit. The family, supported by the family wage, thus allows the control of women's labor by men both within and without the family.

Though women's increased wage work may cause stress for the family (similar to the stress Kautsky and Engels noted in the nineteenth century), it would be wrong to think that as a consequence, the concepts and the realities of the family and of the sexual division of labor will soon disappear. The sexual division of labor reappears in the labor market, where women work at women's jobs, often the very jobs they used to do only at home—food preparation and service, cleaning of all kinds, caring for people, and so on. As these jobs are low-status and low-paying patriarchal relations remain intact, though their material base shifts somewhat from the family to the wage differential, from family-based to industrially-based patriarchy.[50]

Industrially based patriarchal relations are enforced in a variety of ways. Union contracts which specify lower wages, lesser benefits, and fewer advancement opportunities for women are not just atavistic hangovers—a case of sexist attitudes or male supremacist ideology—they maintain the material base of the patriarchal system. While some would go so far as to argue that patriarchy is already absent from the family (see, for example, Stewart Ewen, *Captains of Consciousness*),[51] we would not. Although the terms of the compromise between capital and patriarchy are changing as additional tasks formerly located in the family are capitalized, and the location of the deployment of women's labor power shifts,[52] it is nevertheless true, as we have argued above, that the wage differential caused by extreme job segregation in the labor market reinforces the family, and, with it, the domestic division of labor, by encouraging women to marry. The "ideal" of the family wage—that a man can earn enough to support an entire family—may be giving way to a new ideal that both men and women contribute through wage earning to the cash income of the family. The wage differential, then, will become increasingly necessary in perpetuating patriarchy, the male control of women's labor power. The wage differential will aid in *defining* women's work as secondary to men's at the same time it necessitates women's actual continued economic dependence on men. The sexual division of labor in the labor market and elsewhere should be understood as a manifestation of patriarchy which serves to perpetuate it.

Many people have argued that though the partnership between capital and patriarchy exists now, it may *in the long run* prove intolerable to capitalism; capital may eventually destroy both familial relations and patriarchy. The argument proceeds logically that capitalist social relations (of which the family is not an example) tend to become universalized, that women will become increasingly able to earn money and will increasingly refuse to submit to subordination in the family, and that since the family is oppressive particularly to women and children, it will collapse as soon as people can support themselves outside it.

We do not think that the patriarchal relations embodied in the family can be destroyed so easily by capital, and we see little evidence that the family system is presently disintegrating. Although the increasing labor force participation of women has made divorce more feasible, the incentives to divorce are not overwhelming for women. Women's wages allow very few women to support themselves and their children independently and adequately. The evidence for the decay of the traditional family is weak at best. The divorce rate has not so much increased, as it has evened out among classes; moreover, the remarriage rate is also very high. Up until the 1970 census, the first-marriage age was continuing its historic decline. Since 1970 people seem to have been delaying marriage and childbearing, but most recently, the birth rate has begun to increase again. It is true that larger proportions of the population are now living outside traditional families. Young people, especially, are leaving their parents' homes and establishing their own households before they marry and start traditional families. Older people, especially women, are finding themselves alone in their own households, after their children are grown and they experience separation or death of a spouse. Nevertheless, trends indicate that the new generations of young people will form nuclear families at some time in their adult lives in higher proportions than ever before. The cohorts, or groups of people, born since 1930 have much higher rates of eventual marriage and childrearing than previous cohorts. The duration of marriage and childrearing may be shortening, but its incidence is still spreading.[53]

The argument that capital destroys the family also overlooks the social forces which make family life appealing. Despite critiques of nuclear families as psychologically destructive, in a competitive society the family still meets real needs for many people. This is true not only of long-term monogamy, but even more so for raising children. Single parents bear both financial and psychic burdens. For working class women, in particular, these burdens make the "independence" of labor force participation illusory. Single parent families have recently been seen by policy analysts as transitional family formations which become two-parent families upon remarriage.[54]

It could be that the effects of women's increasing labor force participation are found in a declining sexual division of labor within the family, rather than in more frequent divorce, but evidence for this is also lacking. Statistics on who does housework, even in families with wage-earning wives, show little change in recent years; women still do most of it.[55] The double day is a reality for wage-working women. This is hardly surprising since the sexual division of labor outside the family, in the labor market, keeps women financially dependent on men—even when they earn a wage themselves. The future of patriarchy does not, however, rest solely on the future of familial relations. For patriarchy, like capital, can be surprisingly flexible and adaptable.

Whether or not the patriarchal division of labor, inside the family and elsewhere, is "ultimately" intolerable to capital, it is shaping capitalism now. As we illustrate below, patriarchy both legitimates capitalist control and delegitimates certain forms of struggle against capital.

IDEOLOGY IN THE TWENTIETH CENTURY

Patriarchy, by establishing and legitimating hierarchy among men (by allowing men of all groups to control at least some women), reinforces capitalist control, and capitalist values shape the definition of patriarchal good.

The psychological phenomena Shulamith Firestone identifies are particular examples of what happens in relationships of dependence and domination. They follow from the realities of men's social power—which women are denied—but they are shaped by the fact that they happen in the context of a capitalist society.[56] If we examine the characteristics of men as radical feminists describe them—competitive, rationalistic, dominating—they are much like our description of the dominant values of capitalist society.

This "coincidence" may be explained in two ways. In the first instance, men, as wage laborers, are absorbed in capitalist social relations at work, driven into the competition these relations prescribe, and absorb the corresponding values.[57] The radical feminist description of men was not altogether out of line for capitalist societies. Secondly, even when men and women do not actually behave in the way sexual norms prescribe, men *claim for themselves* those characteristics which are valued in the dominant ideology. So, for example, the authors of *Crestwood Heights* found that while the men, who were professionals, spent their days manipulating subordinates (often using techniques that appeal to fundamentally irrational motives to elicit the preferred behavior), men and women characterized men as "rational and pragmatic." And while the women devoted great energies to studying scientific methods of child-rearing and child development, men and women in Crestwood Heights characterized women as "irrational and emotional."[58]

This helps to account not only for "male" and "female" characteristics in capitalist societies, but for the particular form sexist ideology takes in capitalist societies. Just as women's work serves the dual purpose of perpetuating male domination and capitalist production, so sexist ideology serves the dual purpose of glorifying male characteristics/capitalist values, and denigrating female characteristics/social need. If women were degraded or powerless in other societies, the reasons (rationalizations) men had for this were different. Only in a capitalist society does it make sense to look down on women as emotional or irrational. As epithets, they would not have made sense in the renaissance. Only in a capitalist society does it make sense to look down on women as "dependent." "Dependent" as an epithet would not make sense in feudal societies. Since the division of labor ensures that women as wives and mothers in the family are largely concerned with the production of use values, the denigration of these activities obscures capital's inability to meet socially determined need at the same time that it degrades women in the eyes of men, providing a rationale for male dominance. As example of this may be seen in the peculiar ambivalence of television commercials. On one hand, they address themselves to the real obstacles to providing for socially determined needs: detergents that destroy clothes and irritate skin, shoddily made goods of all sorts. On the other hand, concern with these problems must be denigrated; this is accomplished by mocking women, the workers who must deal with these problems.

A parallel argument demonstrating the partnership of patriarchy and capitalism may be made about the sexual division of labor in the work force. The sexual division of labor places women in low-paying jobs, and in tasks thought to be appropriate to women's role. Women are teachers, welfare workers, and the great majority of workers in the health fields. The nurturant roles that women play in these jobs are of low status because capitalism emphasizes personal independence and the ability of private enterprise to meet social needs, emphases contradicted by the need for collectively provided social services. As long as the social importance of nurturant tasks can be denigrated because women perform them, the confrontation of capital's priority on exchange value by a demand for use values can be avoided. In this way, it is not feminism, but sexism that divides and debilitates the working class.

IV. TOWARD A MORE PROGRESSIVE UNION

Many problems remain for us to explore. Patriarchy as we have used it here remains more a descriptive term than an analytic one. If we think marxism alone adequate, and radical feminism itself insufficient, then we need to develop new categories. What makes our task a difficult one is that the same features, such as the division of labor, often reinforce both patriarchy and capitalism, and in a thoroughly patriarchal capitalist society, it is hard to isolate the mechanisms of patriarchy. Nevertheless, this is what we must do. We have pointed to some starting places: looking at who benefits from women's labor power, uncovering the material base of patriarchy, investigating the mechanisms of hierarchy and solidarity among men. The questions we must ask are endless.

Can we speak of the laws of motion of a patriarchal system? How does patriarchy generate feminist struggle? What kinds of sexual politics and struggle between the sexes can we see in societies other than advanced capitalist ones? What are the contradictions of the patriarchal system and what is their relation to the contradictions of capitalism? We know that patriarchal relations gave rise to the feminist movement, and that capital generates class struggle—but how has the relation of feminism to class struggle been played out in historical contexts? In this section we attempt to provide an answer to this last question.

FEMINISM AND THE CLASS STRUGGLE

Historically and in the present, the relation of feminism and class struggle has been either that of fully separate paths ("bourgeois" feminism on one hand, class struggle on the other), or, within the left, the dominance of feminism by marxism. With respect to the latter, this has been a consequence both of the analytic power of marxism, and of the power of men within the left. These have produced both open struggles on the left, and a contradictory position for marxist feminists.

Most feminists who also see themselves as radicals (antisystem, anti-capitalist, anti-imperialist, socialist, communist, marxist, whatever) agree that the radical wing of the women's movement has lost momentum while the liberal sector seems to have seized the time and forged ahead. Our movement is no longer in that exciting, energetic period when no matter what we did, it worked—to raise consciousness, to bring more women (more even than could be easily incorporated) into the movement, to increase the visibility of women's issues in the society, often in ways fundamentally challenging to both the capitalist and patriarchal relations in society.

Now we sense parts of the movement are being coopted and "feminism" is being used against women—for example, in court cases when judges argue that women coming out of long-term marriages in which they were housewives don't need alimony because we all know women are liberated now. The failure to date to secure the passage of the Equal Rights Amendment in the United States indicates the presence of legitimate fears among many women that feminism will continue to be used against women, and it indicates a real need for us to reassess our movement, to analyze why it has been coopted in this way. It is logical for us to turn to marxism for help in that reassessment because it is a developed theory of social change. Marxist theory is well developed compared to feminist theory, and in our attempt to use it, we have sometimes been sidetracked from feminist objectives.

The left has always been ambivalent about the women's movement, often viewing it as dangerous to the cause of socialist revolution. When left women espouse feminism, it may be personally threatening to left men. And of course many left organizations benefit from the labor of women. Therefore, many left analyses (both in progressive and traditional forms) are self-serving, both theoretically and politically. They seek to influence women to abandon attempts to develop an independent understanding of women's situation and to adopt the "left's" analyses of the situation. As for our response to this pressure, it is natural that, as we ourselves have turned to marxist analysis, we would try to join the "fraternity" using this paradigm, and we may end up trying to justify our struggle to the fraternity rather than trying to analyze the situation of women to improve our political practice. Finally, many marxists are satisfied with the traditional marxist analysis of the women question. They see class as the correct framework with which to understand women's position. Women should be understood as part of the working class; the working class's struggle against capitalism should take precedence over any conflict between men and women. Sex conflict must not be allowed to interfere with class solidarity.

As the economic situation in the United States has worsened in the last few years, traditional marxist analysis has reasserted itself. In the sixties the civil rights movement, the student free speech movement, the antiwar movement, the women's movement, the environmental movement, and the increased militancy of professional and white collar groups all raised new questions for marxists. But now the return of obvious economic problems such as inflation and unemployment had eclipsed the importance of these demands and the left has returned to the "fundamentals"— working class (narrowly defined) politics. The growing "marxist-leninist preparty" sects are committed antifeminists, in both doctrine and practice. And there are signs that the presence of feminist issues in the academic left is declining as well. Day care is disappearing from left conferences. As marxism or political economy become intellectually acceptable, the "old boys" network of liberal academia is replicated in a sidekick "young boys" network of marxists and radicals, nonetheless male in membership and outlook despite its youth and radicalism.

The pressures on radical women to abandon this silly stuff and become "serious" revolutionaries have increased. Our work seems a waste of time compared to inflation and unemployment. It is symptomatic of male dominance that *our* unemployment was never considered in a crisis. In the last major economic crisis, the 1930s, the vast unemployment was partially dealt with by excluding women from many kinds of jobs—one wage job per family, and that job was the man's. Capitalism and patriarchy recovered—strengthened from the crisis. Just as economic crises serve a restorative function for capitalism by correcting imbalances, so they might serve patriarchy. The thirties put women back in their place.

The struggle against capital and patriarchy cannot be successful if the study and practice of the issues of feminism is abandoned. A struggle aimed only at capitalist relations of oppression will fail, since their underlying supports in patriarchal relations of oppression will be overlooked. And the analysis of patriarchy is essential to a definition of the kind of socialism useful to women. While men and women share a need to overthrow capitalism they retain interests particular to their gender group. It is not clear—from our sketch, from history, or from male socialists—the socialism being struggled for is the same for both men and women. For a humane socialism would require not only consensus on what the new society should look like and what a healthy person should look like, but more concretely, it would require that men relinquish their privilege.

As women we must not allow ourselves to be talked out of the urgency and importance of our tasks, as we have so many times in the past. We must fight the attempted coercion, both subtle and not so subtle, to abandon feminist objectives.

This suggests two strategic considerations. First, a struggle to establish socialism must be a struggle in which groups with different interests form an alliance. Women should not trust men to liberate them after the revolution, in part, because there is no reason to think they would know how; in part, because there is no necessity for them to do so. In fact their immediate self-interest lies in our continued oppression. Instead we must have our own organizations and our own power base. Second, we think the sexual division of labor within capitalism has given women a practice in which we have learned to understand what human interdependence and needs are. While men have long struggled *against* capital, women know what to struggle *for*.[59] As a general rule, men's position in patriarchy and capitalism prevents them from recognizing both human needs for nurturance, sharing, and growth, and the potential for meeting those needs in a nonhierarchical, nonpatriarchal society. But even if we raise their consciousness, men might assess the potential gains against the potential losses and choose the status quo. Men have more to lose than their chains.

As feminist socialists, we must organize a practice which addresses both the struggle against patriarchy and the struggle against capitalism. We must insist that the society we want to create is a society in which recognition of interdependence is liberation rather than shame, nurturance is a universal, not an oppressive practice, and in which women do not continue to support the false as well as the concrete freedoms of men.

NOTES

1. Often paraphrased as "the husband and wife are one and that one is the husband," English law held that "by marriage, the husband and wife are one person in law: that is, the very being or legal existence of the women is suspended during the marriage, or at least is incorporated and consolidated into that of the Husband," I. Blackstone, *Commentaries*, 1965, pp. 442–445, cited in Kenneth M. Davidson, Ruth B. Ginsburg, and Herma H. Kay, *Sex Based Discrimination* (St. Paul, MN: West Publishing Co., 1974), p. 117.

2. Frederick Engels, *The Origin of the Family, Private Property and the State*, edited, with an introduction by Eleanor Burke Leacock (New York: International Publishers, 1972).

3. Frederick Engels, *The Condition of the Working Class in England* (Stanford, CA: Stanford University Press, 1958). See esp. pp. 162–66 and p. 296.

4. Eli Zaretsky, "Capitalism, the Family, and Personal Life," *Socialist Revolution*, Part I in no. 13–14 (January-April 1973), pp. 66–125, and Part II in no. 15 (May-June 1973), pp. 19–70. Also Zaretsky, "Socialist Politics and the Family," *Socialist Revolution* (now *Socialist Review*), no. 19 (January-March 1974), pp. 83–98, and *Capitalism, the Family and Personal Life* (New York: Harper & Row, 1976). Insofar as they claim their analyses are relevant to women, Bruce Brown's *Marx, Freud, and the Critique of Everyday Life* (New York: Monthly Review Press, 1973) and Henri Lefebvre's *Everyday Life in the Modern World* (New York: Harper & Row, 1971) may be grouped with Zaretsky.

5. In this Zaretsky is following Margaret Benston ("The Political Economy of Women's Liberation," *Monthly Review*, Vol. 21, no. 4 [September 1961], pp. 13–27), who made the cornerstone of her analysis that women have a different relation to capitalism than men. She argued that women at home produce use values, and that men in the labor market produce exchange values. She labeled women's work precapitalist (and found in women's common work the basis for their political unity). Zaretsky builds on this essential difference in men's and women's work, but labels them both capitalist.

6. Zaretsky, "Personal Life," Part I, p. 114.

7. Mariarosa Dalla Costa, "Women and the Subversion of the Community," in *The Power of Women and the Subversion of the Community* by Mariarosa Dalla Costa and Selma James (Bristol, UK: Falling Wall Press, 1973; second edition), pamphlet, 78 pps.

8. It is interesting to note that in the original article (cited in n. 7 above) Dalla Costa suggests that wages for housework would only further institutionalize woman's housewife role (pp. 32, 34) but in a note (n. 16, pp. 52–52) [*sic*] she explains the demand's popularity and its use as a consciousness raising tool. Since then she has actively supported the demand. See Dalla Costa, "A General Strike," in *All Work and No Pay: Women, Housework, and the Wages Due*, ed. Wendy Edmond and Suzie Fleming (Bristol, UK: Falling Wall Press, 1975).

9. The text of the article reads: "We have to make clear that, within the wage, domestic work produces not merely use values, but is essential to the production of surplus value" (p. 31). Note 12 reads: "What we mean precisely is that housework as work is *productive* in the Marxian sense, that is, producing surplus value" (p. 52, original emphasis). To our knowledge this claim has never been made more rigorously by the wages for housework group. Nevertheless marxists have responded to the claim copiously.

10. The literature of the debate includes Lise Vogel, "The Earthly Family," *Radical America*, Vol. 7, no. 4–5 (July–October 1973), pp. 9–50; Ira Gerstein, "Domestic Work and Capitalism," *Radical America*, Vol. 7, no. 4–5 (July–October 1973), pp. 101–128; John Harrison, "Political Economy of Housework," *Bulletin of the Conference of Socialist Economists*, Vol. 3, no. 1 (1973); Wally Seccombe, "The Housewife and Her Labour under Capitalism," *New Left Review*, no. 83 (January-February 1974), pp. 3–24; Margaret Coulson, Branka Magas, and Hilary Wainwright, "'The Housewife and her Labour under Capitalism,' A Critique," *New Left Review*, no. 89 (January-February 1975), pp. 59–71; Jean Gardiner, "Women's Domestic Labour," *New Left Review*, no. 89 (January-February 1975), pp. 47–58; Ian Gough and John Harrison, "Unproductive Labour and Housework Again," *Bulletin of the Conference of Socialist Economists*, Vol. 4, no. 1 (1975); Jean Gardiner, Susan Himmelweit and Maureen Mackintosh, "Women's Domestic Labour," *Bulletin of the Conference of Socialist Economists*, Vol. 4, no. 2 (1975); Wally Seccombe, "Domestic Labour: Reply

to Critics," *New Left Review*, no. 94 (November-December 1975), pp. 85–96; Terry Fee, "Domestic Labor: An Analysis of Housework and its Relation to the Production Process," *Review of Radical Political Economics*, Vol. 8, no. 1 (Spring 1976), pp. 1–8; Susan Himmelweit and Simon Mohun, "Domestic Labour and Capital," *Cambridge Journal of Economics*, Vol. 1, no. 1 (March 1977), pp. 15–31.

11.   In the U.S., the most often heard political criticism of the wages for housework group has been its opportunism.

12.   Laura Oren documents this for the working class in "Welfare of Women in Laboring Families: England, 1860–1950," *Feminist Studies*, Vol. 1, no. 3–4 (Winter-Spring 1973), pp. 107–25.

13.   The late Stephen Hymer pointed out to us a basic weakness in Engels' analysis in *Origins*, a weakness that occurs because Engels fails to analyze the labor process within the family. Engels argues that men enforced monogamy because they wanted to leave their property to their own children. Hymer argued that far from being a "gift," among the petit bourgeoisie, possible inheritance is used as a club to get children to work for their fathers. One must look at the labor process and who benefits from the labor of which others.

14.   This is a paraphrase. Karl Marx wrote: "The maintenance and reproduction of the working class is, and must ever be, a necessary condition to the reproduction of capital. But the capitalist may safely leave its fulfillment to the labourer's instincts of self-preservation and propagation." [*Capital* (New York: International Publishers, 1967), Vol. 1, p. 572.]

15.   Harry Braverman, *Labor and Monopoly Capital* (New York: Monthly Review Press, 1975).

16.   Juliet Mitchell, *Women's Estate* (New York: Vintage Books, 1973), p. 92.

17.   Engels, *Origins*, "Preface to the First Edition," pp. 71–72. The continuation of this quotation reads, " . . . by the stage of development of labor on the one hand and of the family on the other." It is interesting that, by implication, labor is excluded from occurring within the family; this is precisely the blind spot we want to overcome in this essay.

18.   Juliet Mitchell, "Women: The Longest Revolution," *New Left Review*, no. 40 (November–December 1966), pp. 11–37, also reprinted by the New England Free Press.

19.   Juliet Mitchell, *Psychoanalysis and Feminism* (New York: Pantheon Books, 1974).

20.   Mitchell, *Psychoanalysis*, p. 412.

21.   Shulamith Firestone, *The Dialectic of Sex* (New York: Bantam Books, 1971).

22.   "Politics of Ego: A Manifesto for New York Radical Feminists," can be found in *Rebirth of Feminism*, ed. Judith Hole and Ellen Levine (New York: Quadrangle Books, 1971), pp. 440–443. "Radical feminists" are those feminists who argue that the most fundamental dynamic of history is men's striving to dominate women. "Radical" in this context does *not* mean anti-capitalist, socialist, counter-cultural, etc., but has the specific meaning of this particular set of feminist beliefs or group of feminists. Additional writings of radical feminists, of whom the New York Radical Feminists are probably the most influential, can be found in *Radical Feminism*, ed. Ann Koedt (New York, Quadrangle Press, 1972).

23.   Focusing on power was an important step forward in the feminist critique of Freud. Firestone argues, for example, that if little girls "envied" penises it was because they recognized that little boys grew up to be members of a powerful class and little girls grew up to be dominated by them. Powerlessness, not neurosis, was the heart of women's situation. More recently, feminists have criticized Firestone for rejecting the usefulness of the concept of the unconscious. In seeking to explain the strength and continuation of male

dominance, recent feminist writing has emphasized the fundamental nature of gender-based personality differences, their origins in the unconscious, and the consequent difficulty of their eradication. See Dorothy Dinnerstein, *The Mermaid and the Minotaur* (New York: Harper Colophon Books, 1977), Nancy Chodorow, *The Reproduction of Mothering* (Berkeley: University of California Press, 1978), and Jane Flax, "The Conflict Between Nurturance and Autonomy in Mother-Daughter Relationships and Within Feminism," *Feminist Studies*, Vol. 4, no. 2 (June 1978), pp. 141–189.

24. Kate Millett, *Sexual Politics* (New York: Avon Books, 1971), p. 25.

25. One example of this type of radical feminist history is Susan Brownmiller's *Against Our Will, Men, Women, and Rape* (New York: Simon & Shuster, 1975).

26. For the bourgeois social science view of patriarchy, see, for example, Weber's distinction between traditional and legal authority, *Max Weber: The Theories of Social and Economic Organization*, ed. Talcott Parsons (New York: The Free Press, 1964), pp. 328–357. These views are also discussed in Elizabeth Fee, "The Sexual Politics of Victorian Social Anthropology," *Feminist Studies*, Vol. 1, nos. 3–4 (Winter-Spring 1973), pp. 23–29, and in Robert A. Nisbet, *The Sociological Tradition* (New York: Basic Books, 1966), especially Chapter 3, "Community."

27. See Viana Muller, "The Formation of the State and the Oppression of Women: Some Theoretical Considerations and a Case Study in England and Wales," *Review of Radical Political Economics*, Vol. 9, no. 3 (Fall 1977), pp. 7–21.

28. The particular ways in which men control women's access to important economic resources and restrict their sexuality vary enormously, both from society to society, from subgroup to subgroup, and across time. The examples we use to illustrate patriarchy in this section, however, are drawn primarily from the experience of whites in western capitalist countries. The diversity is shown in *Toward an Anthropology of Women*, ed. Rayna Rapp Reiter (New York: Monthly Review Press, 1975), *Woman, Culture and Society*, ed. Michelle Rosaldo and Louise Lamphere (Stanford, CA: Stanford University Press, 1974), and *Females, Males, Families: A Biosocial Approach*, by Liba Leibowitz (North Scituate, MA: Duxbury Press, 1978). The control of women's sexuality is tightly linked to the place of children. An understanding of the demand (by men and capitalists) for children is crucial to understanding changes in women's subordination.

Where children are needed for their present or future labor power, women's sexuality will tend to be directed toward reproduction and childrearing. When children are seen as superfluous, women's sexuality for other than reproductive purposes is encouraged, but men will attempt to direct it toward satisfying male needs. The Cosmo girl is a good example of a woman "liberated" from childrearing only to find herself turning all her energies toward attracting and satisfying men. Capitalists can also use female sexuality to their own ends, as the success of Cosmo in advertising consumer products shows.

29. Gayle Rubin, "The Traffic in Women," in *Anthropology of Women*, ed. Reiter, p. 159.

30. Himmelweit and Mohun point out that both aspects of production (people and things) are logically necessary to describe a mode of production because by definition a mode of production must be capable of reproducing itself. Either aspect alone if not self-sufficient. To put it simply the production of things requires people, and the production of people requires things. Marx, though recognizing capitalism's need for people did not concern himself with how they were produced or what the connections between the two aspects of production were. See Himmelweit and Mohun, "Domestic Labour and Capital" (note 10 above).

31. For an excellent discussion of one such transition to socialism, see Batya Weinbaum, "Women in Transition to Socialism: Perspectives on the Chinese Case," *Review of Radical Political Economics*, Vol. 8, no. 1 (Spring 1976), pp. 34–58.

32. It is important to remember that in the preindustrial period, women contributed a
     large share to their families' subsistence—either by participating in a family craft or by
     agricultural activities. The initiation of wage work for women both allowed and required
     this contribution to take place independently from the men in the family. The new
     departure, then, was not that women earned income, but that they did so beyond their
     husbands' or fathers' control. Alice Clark, *The Working Life of Women in the Seventeenth
     Century* (New York: Kelly, 1969) describes women's preindustrial economic roles and the
     changes that occurred as capitalism progressed. It seems to be the case that Marx, Engels,
     and Kautsky were not fully aware of women's economic role before capitalism.
33. Karl Kautsky, *The Class Struggle* (New York: Norton, 1971), pp. 25–26.
34. We might add, "outside the household," Kautsky, *Class Struggle*, p. 26, our emphasis.
35. Cited in Neil Smelser, *Social Change and the Industrial Revolution* (Chicago:
     University of Chicago Press, 1959), p. 301.
36. These examples are from Heidi I. Hartmann, "Capitalism, Patriarchy, and Job
     Segregation by Sex," *Signs: Journal of Women in Culture and Society*, Vol. 1, no. 3,
     pt. 2 (Spring 1976), pp. 162–163.
37. Just as the factory laws were enacted for the benefit of all capitalists against the pro-
     test of some, so too, protective legislation for women and children may have been
     enacted by the state with a view toward the reproduction of the working class. Only
     a completely instrumentalist view of the state would deny that the factory laws and
     protective legislation legitimate that state by providing concessions and are responses
     to the demands of the working class itself.
38. For a more complete discussion of protective labor legislation and women, see Ann C.
     Hill, "Prospective Labor Legislation for Women: Its Origin and Effect," mimeographed
     (New Haven, CT: Yale Law School, 1970) parts of which have been published in
     Barbara A. Babcock, Ann E. Freedman, Eleanor H. Norton, and Susan C. Ross, *Sex
     Discrimination and the Law: Causes and Remedies* (Boston: Little, Brown & Co., 1975),
     an excellent law text. Also see Hartmann, "Job Segregation by Sex," pp. 164–166.
39. A reading of Alice Clark, *The Working Life of Women*, and Ivy Pinchbeck, *Women
     Workers*, suggests that the expropriation of production from the home was followed
     by a social adjustment process creating the social norm of the family wage. Heidi
     Hartmann, in *Capitalism and Women's Work in the Home*, 1900–1930 (Unpublished
     Ph. D. dissertation, Yale University, 1974; forthcoming Temple University Press)
     argues, based on qualitative data, that this process occurred in the U.S. in the early
     20th century. One should be able to test this hypothesis quantitatively by examining
     family budget studies for different years and noting the trend of the proportion of the
     family income for different income groups, provided by the husband. However, this
     data is not available in comparable form for our period. The family wage resolution
     has probably been undermined in the post–World War II period. Carolyn Shaw Bell,
     in "Working Women's Contribution to Family Income," *Eastern Economic Journal*,
     Vol. 1, no. 3 (July 1974), pp. 185–201, presents current data and argues that it is now
     incorrect to assume that the man is the primary earner of the family. Yet whatever the
     actual situation today or earlier in the century, we would argue that the social norm
     was and *is* that men should earn enough to support their families. To say it has been
     the norm is not to say it has been universally achieved. In fact, it is precisely the failure
     to achieve the norm that is noteworthy. Hence the observation that in the absence
     of sufficiently high wages, "normative" family patterns disappear, as for example,
     among immigrants in the nineteenth century and third world Americans today. Oscar
     Handlin, *Boston's Immigrants* (New York: Atheneum, 1968) discusses mid-nineteenth
     century Boston, where Irish women were employed in textiles; women constituted

more than half of all wage laborers and often supported unemployed husbands. The debate about family structure among Black Americans today still rages; see Carol B. Stack, *All Our Kin: Strategies for Survival in a Black Community* (New York: Harper and Row, 1974), esp. Chap. 1. We would also argue (see below) that for most families the norm is upheld by the relative places men and women hold in the labor market.

40. Hartmann, *Women's Work*, argues that the non-working wife was generally regarded as part of the male standard of living in the early twentieth century (see p. 136, n. 6) and Gerstein, "Domestic Work," suggests that the norm of the working wife enters into the determination of the value of male labor power (see p. 121).

41. The importance of the fact that women perform labor services for men in the home cannot be overemphasized. As Pat Mainardi said in "The Politics of Housework," "[t]he measure of your oppression is his resistance" (in *Sisterhood is Powerful*, ed. Robin Morgan [New York: Vintage Books, 1970], p. 451). Her article, perhaps as important for us as Firestone on love, is an analysis of power relations between women and men as exemplified by housework.

42. Libby Zimmerman has explored the relation of membership in the primary and secondary labor markets to family patterns in New England. See her *Women in the Economy: A Case Study of Lynn, Massachusetts, 1760–1974* (Unpublished Ph. D. dissertation, Heller School, Brandeis, 1977). Batya Weinbaum is currently exploring the relationship between family roles and places in the labor market. See her "Redefining the Question of Revolution," *Review of Radical Political Economics*, Vol. 9, no. 3 (Fall 1977), pp. 54, 78, and *The Curious Courtship of Women's Liberation and Socialism* (Boston: South End Press, 1978). Additional studies of the interaction of capitalism and patriarchy can be found in Zillah Eisenstein, ed., *Capitalist Patriarchy and the Case for Socialist Feminism* (New York: Monthly Review Press, 1978).

43. See Batya Weinbaum and Amy Bridges, "The Other Side of the Paycheck: Monopoly Capital and the Structure of Consumption," *Monthly Review*, Vol. 28, no. 3 (July–August 1976), pp. 88–103, for a discussion of women's consumption work.

44. For the view of the Frankfurt School, see Max Horkheimer, "Authority and the Family," in *Critical Theory* (New York: Herder & Herder, 1972) and Frankfurt Institute of Social Research, "The Family," in *Aspects of Sociology* (Boston: Beacon, 1972).

45. Carol Brown, "Patriarchal Capitalism and the Female-Headed Family," *Social Scientist* (India); no. 40–41 (November-December 1975), pp. 28–39.

46. For more on racial orders, see Stanley Greenberg, "Business Enterprise in a Racial Order," *Politics and Society*, Vol. 6, no. 2 (1976), pp. 213–240, and Michael Burroway, *The Color of Class in the Copper Mines: From African Advancement to Zambianization* (Manchester, UK: Manchester University Press, Zambia Papers No. 7, 1972).

47. See Michael Reich, David Gordon, and Richard Edwards, "A Theory of Labor Market Segmentation," *American Economic Review*, Vol. 63, no. 2 (May 1973), pp. 359–365, and the book they edited, *Labor Market Segmentation* (Lexington, MA: D. C. Heath, 1975) for a discussion of labor market segmentation.

48. See David M. Gordon, "Capitalist Efficiency and Socialist Efficiency," *Monthly Review*, Vol. 28, no. 3 (July-August 1976), pp. 19–39, for a discussion of qualitative efficiency (social control needs) and quantitative efficiency (accumulation needs).

49. For example, Milwaukee manufacturers organized workers in production first according to ethnic groups, but later taught all workers to speak English, as technology and appropriate social control needs changed. See Gerd Korman, *Industrialization, Immigrants, and Americanizers, the View from Milwaukee, 1866–1921* (Madison: The State Historical Society of Wisconsin, 1967).

50. Carol Brown, in "Patriarchal Capitalism," argues, for example, that we are moving from "family based" to "industrially-based" patriarchy within capitalism.

51. Stewart Ewen, *Captains of Consciousness* (New York: Random House, 1976).

52. Jean Gardiner, in "Women's Domestic Labour" (see n. 10), clarifies the cause for the shift in location of women's labor, from capital's point of view. She examines what capital needs (in terms of the level of real wages, the supply of labor, and the size of markets) at various stages of growth and of the business cycle. She argues that in times of boom or rapid growth it is likely that socializing housework (or more accurately capitalizing it) would be the dominant tendency, and that in times of recession, housework will be maintained in its traditional form. In attempting to assess the likely direction of the British economy, however, Gardiner does not assess the economic needs of patriarchy. We argue in this essay that unless one takes patriarchy as well as capital into account one cannot adequately assess the likely direction of the economic system.

53. For the proportion of people in nuclear families, see Peter Uhlenberg, "Cohort Variations in Family Life Cycle Experiences of U.S. Females," *Journal of Marriage and the Family*, Vol. 36, no. 5 (May 1974), pp. 284–92. For remarriage rates, see Paul C. Glick and Arthur J. Norton, "Perspectives on the Recent Upturn in Divorce and Remarriage," *Demography*, Vol. 10 (1974), pp. 301–14. For divorce and income levels, see Arthur J. Norton and Paul C. Glick, "Marital Instability: Past, Present, and Future," *Journal of Social Issues*, Vol. 32, no. 1 (1976), pp. 5–20. Also see Mary Jo Bane, *Here to Stay: American Families in the Twentieth Century* (New York: Basic Books, 1976).

54. Heather L. Ross and Isabel B. Sawhill, *Time of Transition: The Growth of Families Headed by Women* (Washington, D.C.; The Urban Institute, 1975).

55. See Kathryn E. Walker and Margaret E. Woods, *Time Use: A Measure of Household Production of Family Goods and Services* (Washington, D.C.: American Home Economics Association, 1976); and Heidi I. Hartmann, "The Family as the Locus of Gender, Class, and Political Struggle: The Example of Housework," *Signs: Journal of Women in Culture and Society*, Vol. 6, no. 3 (Spring 1981).

56. Richard Sennett's and Jonathan Cobb's *The Hidden Injuries of Class* (New York: Random House, 1973) examines similar kinds of psychological phenomena within hierarchical relationships between men at work.

57. This should provide some clues to class differences in sexism, which we cannot explore here.

58. See John R. Seeley, et al., *Crestwood Heights* (Toronto: University of Toronto Press, 1956), pp. 382–94. While men's place may be characterized as "in production" this does not mean that women's place is simply "not in production"—her tasks, too, are shaped by capital. Her non-wage work is the resolution, on a day-to-day basis, of production for exchange with socially determined need, the provision of use values in a capitalist society (this is the context of consumption). See Weinbaum and Bridges, "The Other Side of the Paycheck," for a more complete discussion of this argument. The fact that women provide "merely" use values in a society dominated by exchange values can be used to denigrate women.

59. Lise Vogel, "The Earthly Family" (see n. 10).

CHAPTER 11

MARX AND THE ENVIRONMENT

JOHN BELLAMY FOSTER

IT HAS BECOME FASHIONABLE IN RECENT YEARS, in the words of one critic, to identify the growth of ecological consciousness with "the current postmodernist interrogation of the metanarrative of the Enlightenment." Green thinking, we are frequently told, is distinguished by its postmodern, post-Enlightenment perspective. Nowhere is this fashion more evident than in certain criticisms directed at Marx and Engels. Historical materialism, beginning with the work of its two founders, is often said to be one of the main means by which the Baconian notion of the mastery of nature was transmitted to the modern world. The prevalence of this interpretation is indicated by its frequent appearance within the analysis of the left itself. "While Marx and Engels displayed an extraordinary understanding of and sensitivity toward the 'ecological' costs of capitalism," socialist ecofeminist Carolyn Merchant writes, " . . . they nevertheless bought into the Enlightenment's myth of progress via the domination of nature."[1]

It is of course undeniable that many of those who claimed to be following in Marx's footsteps treated nature as an object to be exploited and nothing more. It is common for today's critics, however, to argue that the worldview of Marx and Engels themselves was rooted before all else in the extreme technological subjugation of nature, and that despite the ecological sensitivity that they displayed in particular areas, this remains the primary context in which their theoretical contributions must be judged. Marxism and ecology are therefore never fully compatible.

The chief complaint upon which this general criticism is based is that Marx adopted what the socialist environmentalist Ted Benton—himself a critic of Marx in this respect—has called a "Promethean, 'productivist' view of history." Reiner Grundmann concurs, writing in his *Marxism and Ecology* that "Marx's basic premiss" was "the Promethean model" of the domination of nature—a position that Grundmann attempts to defend. For liberal Victor Ferkiss, no defense is possible: "Marx's attitude toward the world always retained that Promethean thrust, glorifying the human conquest of nature." Social ecologist (ecological anarchist) John Clark goes further:

> Marx's Promethean . . . "man" is a being who is not at home in nature, who does not see the Earth as the "household" of ecology. He is an indomitable spirit who must subject nature in his quest for self-realization. . . . For such a being, the forces of nature, whether in the form of his own unmastered internal nature or the menacing powers of external nature, must be subdued.[2]

There are of course other common environmental criticisms directed at Marx and Engels (not to mention Marxism as a whole) in addition to this one. Benton, for example, argues that Marx was "unmistakably anthropocentric" and that he resisted any framework that would recognize the natural limits to economic advance. Marxian value theory, we are frequently told, designated labor (power) as the source of all value, thereby denying any intrinsic value to nature. Then there is the dismal ecological performance of the Soviet Union and other Eastern European regimes before the fall, which is seen as a general reflection of Marx's failure to incorporate ecological concerns into his master narrative.

Yet it is the charge of Prometheanism that occupies central place in green criticisms of Marx. True environmentalism, we are led to believe, demands nothing less than a rejection of modernity itself. The charge of Prometheanism is thus a roundabout way of branding Marx's work and Marxism as a whole as an extreme version of modernism, more easily condemned in this respect perhaps than liberalism itself. Thus postmodern environmentalist Wade Sikorski writes that, "Marx . . . was one of our age's most devout worshippers of the machine. Capitalism was to be forgiven its sins because . . . it was in the process of perfecting the machine."[3]

This claim that Marx's work was based on a crude "Prometheanism," it is worth recalling, has a very long history. Bourgeois critics of Marxism have long sought to use Marx's frequent literary references to Aeschylus' *Prometheus Bound* to demonstrate that underneath his apparent commitment to scientific understanding lay a "mythical-religious" foundation. Yet it is crucial to remember that Marx was not the only thinker attracted to the Greek myth of Prometheus, who was the predominant cultural hero of the entire Romantic period, and who stands in Western culture not only for technology but even more for creativity, revolution, and rebellion against the gods (against religion). Rubens, Titian, Dante, Milton, Blake, Goethe, Beethoven, Byron, Shelley, and numerous others incorporated Prometheus as a central motif in their work.[4]

In Marx's own work, Prometheus is invoked more often as a symbol of revolution than as a symbol of technology. It is true that in Greek mythology the god (Titan) Prometheus brought fire to humanity. But more important to Marx was the fact that Zeus in retaliation bound Prometheus in chains for eternity, from which he sought to free himself. For the great tragedian Aeschylus, as Ellen Meiksins Wood observes in *Peasant-Citizen and Slave*, Prometheus is "the personification of the Athenian opposition to servitude and arbitrary rule, as he resists the tyranny of Zeus and scorns the servility of the god's messenger, Hermes." Moreover, what is celebrated in Aeschylus' *Prometheus Bound,* a version of the Promethean myth reflecting the values of

Athenian democracy, is not technology as it is now understood but the gift of labor, craftsmanship, and creativity—the practical arts underpinning democracy. So central was the myth of Prometheus to ancient Athens that the class opposition between laboring citizens in the democracy and the aristocratic opponents of democracy can be seen in the radically different treatments of this myth, as represented respectively by Aeschylus' *Prometheus Bound* and Plato's use of the same myth in his *Statesman*. Understanding the revolutionary class character of this conflict within antiquity, Marx clearly identified with the Prometheus of Aeschylus rather than Plato.[5]

All of this, though crucial for understanding Marx's own references to Prometheus, may seem irrelevant, since none of this rich cultural background, stretching back over a millennium and a half to the very beginnings of Western civilization, exists at all in the work of those among today's cultural and environmental critics who now commonly level the charge of Prometheanism at the entire Enlightenment tradition and at Marx and Engels in particular. Shorn of most of its historical and cultural meaning, the myth of Prometheus has been transformed, in the work of such critics, into a cultural symbol of modernity itself, standing for extreme productivism and the domination of nature (including human nature). Indeed, the fact that the very idea of human creativity, as symbolized by the Greek myth of Prometheus, has come to be identified in the eyes of many of today's postmodern critics with crude productivism and the technological subjugation of nature provides a startling indication of the extent to which the dominant world-view of capitalism has penetrated such thinking.

The classic reformulation of the Promethean myth along these lines is to be found in Herbert Marcuse's *Eros and Civilization*, which argued that Prometheus

> the predominant culture-hero [of European culture] is the trickster and (suffering) rebel against the gods, who creates culture at the price of perpetual pain. He symbolizes productiveness, the unceasing effort to master life . . . Prometheus is the culture-hero of toil, productivity, and progress through repression.

In opposition to this one-sided emphasis of Western modernity, Marcuse insisted that,

> another reality principle must be sought at the opposite pole. Orpheus and Narcissus . . . stand for a very different reality. They have not become the culture-heroes of the Western world; theirs is the image of joy and fulfillment. . . . They recall the experience of a world that is not to be mastered and controlled but liberated.[6]

Marcuse was developing a critique of the instrumental rationality that characterized Western industrial culture as a whole (encompassing both capitalism and what Roy Medvedev has called "barracks pseudosocialism"). His argument was however seen by some as a "trenchant criticism" of Marx in particular. Marcuse's text is interpreted in precisely this way in Marshall Berman's *All That Is Solid Melts into Air*, which nonetheless argues that it is wrong to see Marx as a proponent of crude Prometheanism. According to Berman,

> If Marx is fetishistic about anything, it is not work and production but rather the far more complex and comprehensive ideal of *development*—"the free development

of physical and spiritual energies" (1844 manuscripts) . . . Marx wants to embrace Prometheus *and* Orpheus; he considers communism worth fighting for, because for the first time in history it could enable men to have both. . . . He knew that the way beyond the contradictions would have to lead through modernity, not out of it.[7]

It is certainly possible to argue, as socialist environmentalist Kate Soper has in her essay "Greening Prometheus," that there was a certain "ambiguity" in "Marx's Prometheanism" that one can exploit to develop a green interpretation of his thought. However, what seems to be mere "ambiguity" on the surface is more adequately understood as a dialectical tension resulting from Marx's attempt to transcend the usual ways in which human production and the mastery of nature were depicted in the Enlightenment tradition. As Marcuse's student William Leiss has observed in his indispensable study *The Domination of Nature*, such phrases as "the mastery of nature," "the control of nature," and "the domination of nature" were almost universal within nineteenth-century thought, and as such took on varied and complex forms. The mere use of such terms on occasion by Marx and Engels does not therefore establish that they adopted an extreme productivist point of view. Indeed, taken together, the writings of Marx and Engels, Leiss contends, "represent the most profound insight into the complex issues surrounding the mastery over nature to be found anywhere in nineteenth-century social thought or *a fortiori* in the contributions of earlier periods."[8]

What was clear from Marx's analysis was that humanity and nature were interrelated, with the historically specific form of production relation constituting the core of that interrelationship in any given period. As he wrote in the *Economic and Philosophic Manuscripts of 1844*,

> Man *lives* from nature, i.e., nature is his *body*, and he must maintain a continuing dialogue with it if he is not to die. To say that man's physical and mental life is linked to nature simply means that nature is linked to itself, for man is a part of nature.[9]

Far from being mere worshippers of productivism, Marx and Engels were two of its foremost critics. As the young Engels wrote in 1844, "To make the earth an object of huckstering—the earth which is our one and all, the first condition of our existence—was the last step toward making oneself an object of huckstering." Under capitalism all natural and human relationships, Marx argued, have been dissolved into money relationships. Rather than a society ruled by "callous 'cash-payment'" and by the necessity for continual increases in productivity, he looked forward to a social order that would promote the many-sided development of human capacities and the rational human relation to the nature of which we are a part. The further growth of human freedom, he wrote in the final part of the third volume of *Capital*, consists in "socialized man, the associated producers, rationally regulating their material interchange with nature and bringing it under common control, instead of allowing it to rule them as a blind force."

The human community, Marx believed, can no more free itself from the need to control its interaction with nature than it can free itself from the need to take into consideration the natural conditions of human existence. Yet rational control of the relation between nature and humanity is inherently opposed to the mechanistic domination of nature in the interest of the ever increasing expansion of production for its own sake. In a society of freely associated producers, Marx argued, the goal of social life would not be work and production, in the narrow forms in which they have been understood in possessive-individualist society, but the all-around development of human creative potential as an end in itself, for which "the shortening of the working-day is a basic prerequisite." This would set the stage for the achievement of a realm of freedom in which human beings would be united with each other and with nature.[10]

The realization of these conditions, Marx recognized, necessitated a radical trans-formation in the human relation to nature. With the elimination of private ownership of land and the development of a society of freely associated producers, global sustain-ability in the relationship to nature would become feasible for the first time. Pointing to the imperative of protecting the globe for future generations Marx stated:

> From the standpoint of a higher economic form of society, private ownership of the globe by single individuals will appear quite as absurd as private ownership of one man by another. Even a whole society, a nation, or even all simultaneously existing societies together, are not the owners of the globe. They are only its possessors, its usufructuar-ies, and like *boni patres familias* [good fathers of families], they must hand it down to succeeding generations in an improved condition.[11]

It was the proper purpose of agriculture, Marx argued, "to minister to the entire range of permanent necessities of life required by the chain of successive generations"—in contradiction to "the whole spirit of capitalist production, which is directed toward the immediate gain of money." There was thus a direct conflict between capitalism's short-sighted expropriation of the earth's resources and the longer term character of truly sustainable production. Economic advance in a society of freely associated producers, Marx insisted again and again, would have to occur without jeopardizing the natural and global conditions upon which the welfare of future generations would depend. This is precisely the definition now given to the concept of sustainable development, most famously in the Brundtland Commission report, *Our Common Future*, which defined it as "development that meets the needs of the present without compromising the ability of future generations to meet their own needs."[12]

Although Marx did not concentrate on the ecological critique of capitalism in his writings—no doubt because he thought that capitalism would be replaced by a society of freely associated producers long before such problems could become truly critical—his allusions to sustainability indicate that he was acutely aware of the ecological depredations of the system. Central to his concerns in this respect was the effect of capitalist industrialization on the degradation of the soil. The best known passage in this regard, from *Capital*, vol. I, is to be found in the section on "Large-Scale Industry and Agriculture," which constitutes the final, culminating part of Marx's key chapter on "Machinery and Large-Scale Industry" (on the effects of the Industrial Revolution). There Marx argues that,

> All progress in capitalist agriculture is a progress in the art, not only of robbing the worker, but of robbing the soil; all progress in increasing the fertility of the soil for a given time is progress towards ruining the long-lasting sources of that fertility. The

more a country proceeds from large-scale industry as the background of its development, as in the case of the United States, the more rapid is this process of destruction.
Capitalist production, therefore, only develops the techniques and the degree of
combination of the social process of production by simultaneously undermining the
original sources of all wealth—the soil and the worker.[13]

These were not casual or isolated comments but reflected careful study of the
work of the German agrarian chemist Justus von Liebig, often known as the founder
of soil chemistry. Until the early 1860's, Marx thought that the progress of capitalist agriculture might be so rapid that it would outpace industry. By the time he
wrote *Capital*, however, his studies of the work of Liebig and other agronomists had
convinced him otherwise. "Large landed property," he explained in the conclusion
to his most important chapter on capitalist agriculture ("The Genesis of Capitalist
Ground Rent"),

> reduces the agricultural population to a constantly falling minimum, and confronts
> it with a constantly growing industrial population crowded together in large cities. It
> thereby creates conditions which cause an irreparable break in the coherence of social
> interchange prescribed by the natural laws of life. As a result, the vitality of the soil is
> squandered, and this prodigality is carried by commerce far beyond the borders of a
> particular state (Liebig).

Large-scale industry and large-scale agriculture under capitalism thus had the same
results: both contributed to the ruining of the agricultural worker and the exhaustion of "the natural power of the soil." The "moral of history," Marx observed,

> is that the capitalist system works against a rational agriculture, or that a rational
> agriculture is incompatible with the capitalist system (although the latter promotes
> technical improvements in agriculture) and needs either the hand of the small farmer
> living by his own labor or the control of the associated producers.

For Marx "the rational cultivation of the soil as eternal communal property" was
"an inalienable condition of the existence and reproduction of a chain of successive
generations of the human race."[14]

Marx and Engels did not confine their discussions of ecological limits to the issue
of the soil, but also explored numerous other issues of sustainability, in relation to
forests, rivers, and streams, the disposal of waste, air quality, environmental toxins,
etc. "The development of culture and industry in general," Marx wrote, "has ever
evinced itself in such energetic destruction of forests that everything done by it
conversely for their preservation and restoration appears infinitesimal." With regard
to industrial waste, he argued for "economy through the prevention of waste, that is
to say, the reduction of excretions of production to a minimum, and the immediate
utilization of all raw and auxiliary materials required in production."[15]

The chief source of ecological destruction under capitalism, Marx and Engels
argued, was the extreme antagonism of town and country, a characteristic of capitalist organization as fundamental to the system as the division between capitalist and
laborer. "When one observes," Engels wrote,

how here in London alone a greater quantity of manure than is produced by the whole
Kingdom of Saxony is poured away every day into the sea with an expenditure of enormous sums, and what colossal structures are necessary to prevent this manure from
poisoning the whole of London, then the utopia of abolishing the antithesis between
town and country is given a remarkably practical basis.[16]

Such ecological insights, so unusual among nineteenth-century thinkers, all
derive from Marx and Engels' early recognition of the essential point that sustainability must lie at the core of the human relation to nature in any future society.
It is therefore wrong to argue, as Ted Benton has, that Marx and Engels "sustained and deepened *those aspects* of capitalist political economy which exemplified
its hostility to the idea of natural limits to capital accumulation." To be sure, they
had little to say about the *absolute* natural limits of the globe. In this sense, some,
Benton included, have viewed Marx's analysis as ecologically inferior to that of
Malthus, who emphasized the growth of population in relation to food supply (not
primarily from an ecological or carrying capacity perspective but in order to justify
subsistence wage levels and the dismantlement of the English Poor Laws). Yet Marx
and Engels were unusual in the degree of emphasis they placed on the natural conditions of production, and in their recognition of the fact that a sustainable economy
demanded a sustainable relation to nature on a global basis. In this sense, natural
limits are very much a part of their argument.

As with other natural limits, limits to population growth, to the extent that they
existed, Marx and Engels believed, only reinforced the case for socialism. "Even if
Malthus were completely right" (with respect to the relation between population
and food supply), the young Engels had observed in his very first essay on political economy, this only provided a further argument for a "social transformation":
for the creation of a society in which the "production and destruction" of human
beings would no longer be a mere commodity relation dependent "on demand."
Of course, neither Marx nor Engels believed that Malthus was "completely right."
Malthus' expectation that population would outpace food supply because of the
inexorable nature of the former and the limited supply of cultivable land had, as
Marx and Engels understood, underestimated the dynamism of capitalist agriculture
unleashed by the commercial, agricultural and industrial revolutions. Ironically, it is
mainly because Malthus' expectations were *defeated* and the age-old cycle of famine
(what Fernand Braudel has called "the biological *ancien régime*") was transcended for
the first time in human history beginning in the late eighteenth century, that population has grown since Malthus' time to the point that overpopulation now poses a
serious threat to the ecology of the planet as a whole. Moreover, if there is reason to
believe that agriculture today is increasingly incapable of supplying the basic needs
of a still growing world population, this is more related to Marx's analysis of the
unsustainability of capitalist agriculture, which robs the soil itself, than to Malthus'
more abstract notion (following Ricardo) of the diminishing marginal productivity
of agriculture as more and more marginal land is brought under cultivation.[17]

No less mistaken is the criticism of Marx for—in the words of socialist ecologist
Jean-Paul Deléage—attaching "no intrinsic value to natural resources" in his theory
of value. For Marx, the law of value was a historically specific feature of capitalist

society. Marx's comments on value relations no more indicate support for this setup (and the denial of intrinsic value) than they indicate support for capitalism itself (and the denial of the prospect of a non-alienated society). In Marx's theory, it is explicitly stated that capitalist value relations treat nature as a "free gift," as something given to capital "gratis." This was not at all inconsistent, however, with Marx's other point that the land and soil were "robbed"—or, in other words, that conditions of sustainability, which must take account of the reproduction of nature, were expressly violated by the system.[18]

For Marx, material wealth in its widest conception (understood in terms of use values) has to be distinguished from value creation under capitalism (the world of exchange value). "Labor," he wrote, "is not the only source of material wealth, of use-values produced by labor. As William Petty puts it, labor is its father and the earth is its mother." It is a contradiction of capitalism that it pursues exchange value (profit) while largely ignoring the qualitative conditions associated with use value and wealth in its larger context, which includes the natural environment and the productivity of nature. Marx seems to have clearly understood the basic ecological principle that "nothing comes from nothing," popularized in recent years by Barry Commoner and others. As Marx himself wrote,

> What Lucretius says is self-evident: "nil posse creari de nihilo," out of nothing, nothing can be created. Creation of value is transformation of labor-power in labor. Labor-power itself is energy transferred to a human organism by means of nourishing matter.[19]

We can more fully understand the historical significance of Marx and Engels' ecological thought by comparing their ideas with those of the great Vermont environmentalist George Perkins Marsh, widely recognized as the greatest ecologist of the nineteenth century and (in the words of Lewis Mumford) "the fountainhead of the conservation movement." In one of the best-known passages of his classic work, *Man and Nature* (1864), Marsh wrote:

> There are parts of Asia Minor, of Northern Africa, of Greece, and even of Alpine Europe where the operation of causes set in action by man has brought the face of the earth to a desolation almost as complete as that of the moon; and though, within that brief space of time which we call "the historical period," they are known to have been covered with luxuriant woods, verdant pastures, and fertile meadows, they are now too far deteriorated to be reclaimable by man. . . . The earth is fast becoming an unfit home for its noblest inhabitant, and another era of equal human crime and improvidence . . . would reduce it to such a condition of impoverished productiveness, of shattered surface, of climatic excess, as to threaten the depravation, barbarism, and perhaps even extinction of the species.[20]

This statement by Marsh can be compared to a closely related interpretation of long-term ecological developments put forward by Engels in his essay, "The Part Played by Labor in the Transition from Ape to Man," written in 1876:

> Let us not, however, flatter ourselves overmuch on account of our human conquest of nature. For each such conquest takes its revenge on us. . . . The people who, in

Mesopotamia, Greece, Asia Minor, and elsewhere destroyed the forests to obtain cultivable land, never dreamed that they were laying the basis for the present devastated condition of these countries, by removing along with the forests the collecting centers and reservoirs of moisture. When, on the southern slopes of the mountains, the Italians of the Alps used up the pine forests so carefully cherished on the northern slopes, they had no inkling that by doing so they were cutting at the roots of the dairy industry in their region. . . . Thus at every step we are reminded that we by no means rule over nature like a conqueror over a foreign people, like someone standing outside nature—but that we, with flesh, blood, and brain, belong to nature, and exist in its midst, and that all our mastery of it consists in the fact that we have the advantage of all other beings of being able to know and correctly apply its laws.[21]

A close examination of these passages will reveal that there is a broad similarity in the way in which the issue of ecological destruction is approached by Engels and Marsh. Both refer in detail to great ecological disasters that have confronted civilizations. Both see this primarily as a question of sustainability. In Marsh's terms, such "improvidence" in the exploitation of nature must be ended, while Engels insists on the fact that we "belong to nature" and must "correctly apply its laws." Both adopt a broadly anthropocentric perspective, in the sense that they emphasize the consequences of such destruction for the fate of humanity.

The point here is not that Marx and Engels singly or together were the equal of Marsh in their understanding of ecological science; they were not. Yet their views were by no means incompatible with that of the greatest (and still widely respected) ecologist of their day. Moreover, it is no mere coincidence that *Man and Nature*, the leading work on planetary ecological devastation to be written prior to the twentieth century, was published only three years before the publication of the first volume of Marx's *Capital* (1867). Both were responses (though Marsh's less consciously so) to the effects of the Industrial Revolution. Marx's work helped inspire working-class revolts, while Marsh's ideas gave impetus to a wide-ranging struggle on behalf of nature. Only by combining the analyses represented by these works do we have anything like a complete ecological critique of machine capitalism. The reason for this, of course, is that while Marsh was the premier ecologist of his time, it was Marx and Engels who most acutely understood the *historical conditions* underlying such ecological destruction in the nineteenth century. Indeed, since the roots of the global environmental crisis are to be found not in nature, but in society, Marx and Engels may have much more to teach us today about what is necessary in order to address the ecological problem than what can be learned from Marsh.

The key to Marx and Engels' understanding of modern society lay in their critique of capital accumulation. They were convinced that capitalism was economically and politically unsustainable. It would eventually give rise to the revolutionary forces that would overthrow it. The same critique of capital accumulation led them to conclude—beginning with their very earliest writings—that the system lacked a sustainable relation to nature. In their analysis, however, this problem did not yet loom so large that it would affect the future of capitalism (which they thought would soon die a natural death as a result of its economic and political contradictions). If the issue of ecological sustainability was frequently raised in their works, this had more to do with their understanding of the needs of the future society of freely associated producers than with the conditions of capitalism's demise. The stability of any future society, Marx clearly recognized, would be dependent on the creation of a wholly new and more balanced relation to the natural world.

Today radical ecologists see things differently only in the sense that it is now understood that global ecological destruction will play a central role in capitalism's end game. We are for the first time in human history confronting the problem of ecological survival on a planetary scale—a problem that nineteenth-century thinkers, Marx and Engels included (though Marsh might be considered an exception to this), could scarcely have imagined. Nevertheless, we cannot even begin to understand the complex of problems that presently face us unless we approach them as Marx and Engels did in relation to the critique of capital accumulation. It would be a mistake to see the answer to the ecological problem as one of rejecting "modernity" in the name of some abstract and amorphous "postmodernity," at the same time rejecting those modes of thought that provide a systematic critique of capitalism. Rather, we must recognize that it is necessary to come to grips with modernity—above all capitalist modernity—and transform it. Since the destruction of the living world as we know it is otherwise certain, the great mass of humanity has nothing to lose but its chains. It has a planet to save.

NOTES

1. Zaheer, Baber, "The Vulnerable Planet" (Review), *Contemporary Sociology* (January 1995): 82; Merchant, *Ecology* (Atlantic Highlands, NJ: Humanities Press, 1994), p. 2.
2. Benton, "Marxism and Natural Limits," *New Left Review* 178 (November-December 1989): 82; Reiner Grundmann, *Marxism and Ecology* (New York: Oxford University Press), p. 52, and "The Ecological Challenge to Marxism," *New Left Review* 187 (May-June 1991): 120; Ferkiss, *Nature, Technology and Society* (New York: New York University Press, 1993), p. 108; Clark, "Marx's Inorganic Body," *Environmental Ethics* 11, no. 3 (Fall 1989): 258.
3. Sikorski, *Modernity and Technology* (Tuscaloosa: University of Alabama Press, 1993), p. 138.
4. Leonard P. Wessell, Jr., *Prometheus Bound: The Mythic Structure of Karl Marx's Scientific Thinking* (Baton Rouge: Louisiana State University Press, 1984), p. 3; Linda M. Lewis, *The Promethean Politics of Milton, Blake and Shelley* (Columbia, MS: University of Missouri Press, 1992), p. 2.
5. Wood, *Peasant-Citizen and Slave* (London: Verso, 1988), pp. 141–44.
6. Marcuse, *Eros and Civilization* (New York: Vintage, 1962), pp. 146–49.
7. Berman, *All That Is Solid Melts into Air* (New York: Simon and Schuster, 1982), pp. 126–29; Medvedev, *Let History Judge* (New York: Columbia University Press, 1989), pp. 852–59.
8. Soper, "Greening Prometheus," in Peter Osborne, ed. *Socialism and the Limits of Liberalism* (New York: Verso, 1991); Leiss, *The Domination of Nature* (Boston: Beacon Press, 1974), pp. 85, 198.
9. Marx, *Early Writings* (New York: Vintage, 1975), p. 328.
10. Frederick Engels, "Outlines of a Critique of Political Economy," in Marx, *The Economic and Philosophic Manuscripts of 1844* (New York: International Publishers, 1964), p. 210; Marx, *Early Writings*, pp. 377–79; Marx and Engels, *The Communist Manifesto* (New York: Monthly Review Press, 1964), pp. 5–6; Marx, *Capital*, vol. III

(New York: International Publishers, 1967), p. 820; Erich Fromm, *Beyond the Chains of Illusion* (New York: Simon and Schuster, 1962), pp. 36–37.

11. Marx, *Capital*, vol. III, p. 776.

12. *Capital*, vol. III, p. 617n. World Commission on Environment and Development (the Brundtland Commission report), *Our Common Future* (Oxford: Oxford University Press, 1987), p. 43.

13. Marx, *Capital*, vol. I, pp. 637–38.

14. Marx, *Capital*, vol. III, pp. 121, 812–13; Ronald Meek, "Introduction," in Marx and Engels, *Malthus* (New York: International Publishers, 1954), pp. 13–14, 28–31. For a brilliant analysis of the contributions of Liebig and Marx to the critique of capitalist agriculture see Kozo Mayumi, "Temporary Emancipation from Land: From the Industrial Revolution to the Present Time," *Ecological Economics* 4, no. 1 (October 1991), pp. 35–56.

15. Marx, *Capital*, vol. III, pp. 101–03; Marx, *Capital*, vol. II (New York: International Publishers, 1967), p. 244.

16. Engels, *The Housing Question* (Moscow: Progress Publishers, 1975), p. 92.

17. Benton, "Marxism and Natural Limits," *New Left Review* 178 (November-December 1989): 64; Engels, "Outlines of a Critique of Political Economy," p. 221; Marx, *Capital*, vol. I, p. 505; Fernand Braudel, *The Structures of Everyday Life* (New York: Harper and Row, 1979), p. 70.

18. Jean-Paul Deléage, "Eco-Marxist Critique of Political Economy," in Martin O'Connor, ed., *Is Capitalism Sustainable?* (New York: Guilford, 1994), p. 48; Marx, *Capital*, vol. III, p. 745, vol. I, p. 510. A similar interpretation to the one presented here has been developed in forthcoming work by Paul Burkett.

19. Marx, *Capital*, vol. I (New York: International Publishers, 1967), pp. 43, 215n. While Commoner refers to the informal ecological law "there is no such thing as a free lunch," other ecologists have translated this as "nothing comes from nothing." See Foster, *The Vulnerable Planet* (New York: Monthly Review Press, 1994), pp. 118–20.

20. Marsh, *Man and Nature* (Cambridge, MA: Harvard University Press, 1965), pp. 42–43; Mumford, *The Brown Decades* (New York: Dover, 1971), p. 35.

21. Engels, *Dialectics of Nature* (New York: International Publishers, 1940), pp. 291–92.

REVOLUTIONIZING SPIRITUALITY: REFLECTIONS ON MARXISM AND RELIGION*

JOHN BRENTLINGER

IN ONE OF HIS EARLIEST PUBLISHED ESSAYS, Marx wrote: "The criticism of religion is the premise of all criticism." And "The basis of irreligious criticism is this: *man makes religion*; religion does not make man" (Marx, 1844a, 53). In *Ludwig Feuerbach*, Engels wrote that "religion arose in very primitive times from erroneous and primitive ideas of men about their own nature and that of the external world around them, . . . " and after describing how the evolution of these primitive conceptions reflected exactly historical changes in society, Engels concluded, about modern capitalist society, that it is the last historical stage of human development in which religion (specifically, Christianity) will play a role.[1] Religion has become incapable " . . . of serving in the future any progressive class as the ideological garb of its aspiration" (Engels, 1886, 56, 59). And Marx, in *The Critique of the Gotha Program*, wrote that religious freedom was a strictly bourgeois concern; the job of a worker's party, was to liberate the worker from "the witchery of religion" (Marx, 1875, 540).

How should a contemporary Marxist stand in relation to these classical formulations? There is no doubt that mainline religion—I am speaking primarily of Christianity in this essay—continues to propagate a dualistic world view (nature/the supernatural), and to mystify and support oppressive social relations, of class, race, gender and sexual preference. Yet 20th-century experience of the importance of religion in alienating societies, capitalist *and* socialist, and its demonstrable influence in various progressive social movements, has led many Marxists to reject the conception of religion as pure witchery.

In the decades following World War II, Marxist party leaders in predominantly Catholic countries, such as Togliatti in Italy, Garaudy in France, and Santiago Alvarez in Spain, tried to transform the antireligious bent of their communist movements. The Italian party, perhaps influenced by Gramsci's view that there were "many Catholicisms," was the first in Europe to open its membership to believers— it did so in 1945 (and in response Pope Pius XII ruled communists excommunicated!). The historical circumstance of these parties strongly encouraged some form of *rapprochement* between communism and religion, and as a first step Marxists acknowledged the progressive implications of Christian morality. Alvarez wrote that, in the conceptions of ". . . goodness, equality, fraternity among human beings which the Christian religion also speaks of . . . there are elements capable of contributing to an emancipating struggle" (Aptheker, 1968, 19). The French communist party stated: "Increasingly numerous are the Christians who conclude that a society based on the exploitation of man and subject to the law of profit is incompatible with the demands of their faith; they commit themselves to fight for a socialist France and find themselves beside the communists" (McClellan, 1987, 145).

Finding themselves "beside" each other in these early decades after World War II, at least some Christians and communists began to create "dialogue." Sadly, but not surprisingly, in countries where the communists were in power, such as Poland, East Germany, and Czechoslovakia, it was Christians who wanted dialog, while in Italy, Spain, and France, it was communists! And the side that was in power responded not at all (Aptheker, 1968, 15–55; McClellan, 1987, 135–147).

Now that capitalism rules in all of Europe, dialog is no longer the focus of *rapprochement* between Marxists and the religious. What is happening is both less evident and more hopeful. One example of this is the thriving influence of Marxist ideas and perspectives inside an overtly anti-Marxist climate. It is as if, the forest having been cleared, the old roots are sending up new growth in disguised forms. The phenomenon is evident in many areas, especially the "bourgeois" social sciences and humanities; what is sound and enduringly important in post-modernist methodologies, for instance, resembles basic Marxist themes first announced in *The German Ideology*. A similar phenomenon has taken place in Christian theology and practice, most notably in liberation theology, centered in Latin America, but also in many sectors of Christianity in Europe and the United States. These progressive Christians note that Marx not only described religion as the opiate of the people, he also wrote that it is an expression of real suffering and a protest against it; that it is "the sigh of the oppressed creature" and "the soul of soulless conditions." Responding to the enormous problems of modern life attributable to capitalist exploitation of people and the environment, they find indispensable tools in Marxian analysis. "What does it mean," Harvey Cox writes, "for theologians to make use of Marxist categories such as class, material substructure, center and periphery, and so on, in their critical analysis of religion? We reject Marxism as a dogma or formula. . . . We use it as a critical method within a larger and more comprehensive approach" (Cox, 1988, 185).

While Harvey Cox places high value on the theoretical contributions of Marx, Cornel West argues persuasively that Marxists should open themselves to the existential value of religion. We should look beneath ideology, he suggests, and recognize the human import of actual religious practices as the popular creation of "contexts and communities wherein meaning and value can be found to sustain people through the traumas of life . . . religious impulses," he adds, "are one of the few resources for a moral and political commitment beyond the self in the capitalist culture of consumption" (West, 1984, 14, 16). In another context, West writes that a basic lack in Marxism lies in an incapacity to provide what he calls "existential wisdom": frameworks of belief and behavior that sustain meaning and sanity and enable us to ward off "disempowering responses to despair, dread, disappointment, and death." Religion provides this, West claims, and he points out quite correctly that Marxism cannot serve as a religion. "If it is cast as a religion . . . it is a secular ideology of social change that fails to speak to us about the ultimate facts of human existence" (West, 1992, xxvii–xxviii).

My purpose in this essay is to carry further the dialectic of religion and Marxism, through reflection on the Sandinista movement in Nicaragua during the 1980s. The Sandinista revolution was unique for being a continuation of the 20th-century socialist movement in which liberation theology became a potent revolutionary force. Religion actually provided revolutionary ideology to many of the activists, and religious language and sentiment were intimately fused with Marxist conceptions of society and social change. This fusion was widely discussed and debated; widely affirmed and condemned.

The Catholic Church was split down the middle, in Nicaragua itself and in Latin America generally. About 50% of Nicaragua's priests were for, or at least not opposed to, the Sandinista project—several of Nicaragua's most influential priests were active in the revolutionary government—and the other 50%, and the upper levels of the hierarchy, especially the council of Bishops, were strongly opposed. Ernesto Cardenal, the priest who was Sandinista Minister of Culture, proposed a theoretical merging of Marxism and Christianity, to displace the union of Christianity and Aristotelianism established by Thomas Aquinas. Cardinal Miguel Obando, on the other hand, said, "their hammer is for breaking heads, and their sickle is for cutting them off" (Brentlinger, 1995, 45–51).

The Marxism of believers and the spirituality of Marxists in Nicaragua led me to conclude that my stance toward religion needed a thorough revision, not simply in seeing religion differently, but in thinking differently about Marxism and myself as a Marxist. Like Alvarez, and Marx, I had been aware of the moral contradictions within religion, but I couldn't imagine that religious protest might actually lead to a serious commitment to social revolution. My simplified conceptions of religious communities ignored the struggles that take place within religion, and was insulting to the very large number of religiously identified people who were acting on a progressive political and social agenda.

Basically, and—I now think—because of my own negative religious background, I thought of religious institutions as black holes, fundamentally different from other so-called superstructural institutions. Schools, universities, the state, labor unions, political parties, though controlled by bourgeois interests, were sites of class struggle: places where working people thought of themselves as belonging, and where they might hope to realize democratic gains. Why not churches? I could have learned as much from another star example of recent history: the Civil Rights Movement in the United States. Many of its most determined activists were ministers and members of church congregations, and churches divided in support or against the actions of the civil rights protesters. Yet for me, as for many white activists, Nicaragua was a more formative experience. The class division within the Nicaraguan Catholic Church was my first concrete encounter with class struggle over the meaning of the biblical promise of liberation, and how believers should apply Christianity in their lives. I also saw faith communities in the United States leading the solidarity movement, founding organizations like Witness For Peace, Pledge of Resistance, and Sanctuary (alongside secular organizations like CISPES).

Ever since Thomas Munzer led a Christian peasant rebellion in Germany, progressive class interests *have* been expressed in the ideological garb, as Engels put it, of religion.[2] At a recent conference of United Church of Christ ministers, the main speakers were a Marxist-feminist economist and a socialist theologian: both gave this audience trenchant critiques of capitalism. Even within the Catholic Church USA, there has been space for base community movements and openly socialist groups like the Catholic Workers; and the church hierarchy is now leading a progressive struggle against the death penalty among Christian right-to-lifers. The Methodist Church, having rejected same-sex marriage (taking its cue from our "liberal" President Clinton?), is actually energizing the gay and lesbian movements within its own walls; since the decision by the Methodist congress, a group of 65 Methodist ministers in California joined to perform a same-sex union in defiance of the ban.

It may be true, depending on how religion is defined, that secular and religious progressive movements have basic ideological differences (as they do among themselves); but this need not prevent much greater unity than the ideas of "dialog" or side-by-side struggle suggest. In the past, both Marxists and believers have prioritized ideological difference. These days people in both camps are speaking of the need for ideological openness and respect for difference. Progressives among Christians have created impressive openings, and after much foot-dragging even the Cuban Communist Party recently opened its doors to believers. Among the older Marxist organizations a major political flaw is dying away: the Leninist tendency to understand unity in struggle in almost military terms, and to see ideological disagreement as incompatible with long-term unity in struggle. Still, we Marxists have to overcome a persistent prejudice against religion. As a first step, we need to see religion in a more dialectical fashion, as complex, conflictual, and historically evolving. And we should actively work to erase the image of Marxism as anti-religious, and of socialism or communism as intrinsically atheistic, an image largely created by the communist movement itself. It is both simplistic in theory—as I hope to show— and enormously damaging in practice.

Secular progressives who are not Marxist-identified also need to study the same issue. This was brought out clearly by the Central American peace movement of the 1980s. In his book *Resisting Reagan*, Christian Smith shows that one of the internal weaknesses of this movement was the conflict between its religious and its secular wings (Smith, 1996, 340–342). Disagreements over tactics and differences in styles of activism had an importance, even a virulence, that now would seem laughable, if it were not so pathetic. And most of the blame lies with the secular leftists. Our tendency was to see our religious allies as soft and self-indulgent, for giving concern to spiritual process, for prayer and "witness." We objected to church-based organization, to prayerful demonstrations that stressed connectedness, to harboring refugees whose lives were in danger but were not "useful" as opponents of

U.S. policies in Central America, and to the principle of non-violence. In response, one religious activist said: "I have worked with organizations like CISPES. They did all the same actions we did, but their involvement was devoid of any spirituality. It was just pure politics. In my estimate, they are just a bunch of angry people that are pissed off" (Smith, 1996, 334). As an overall judgment of the members of CISPES, that statement is absurd, but importantly symptomatic: secular leftists in this country have lacked a spiritual dimension in their relationships among themselves and their political allies.

The distrust of religious activists and religious styles of activism on the secular left has a tone bordering on hostility that raises the question: What are the religious backgrounds of people on the left? Have we understood the factors that formed our hostility or ambivalence toward religion? What influences nurtured our ethical and political values? Have we thought about the connection between these values and the religious traditions of our families and communities of origin?

Efforts toward dialog between Marxists and religiously identified progressives are certainly essential, and might lead to a common social agenda. But I want to argue for more. My deeper concern is that, limited by enlightenment rationalism, Marxists and secular leftists have failed to see or respect the value of spirituality, as the positive source of their own religious traditions and much progressive politics. Spirituality constitutes a broad basis for unity among all progressives, in spite of ideological differences, and needs to become a necessary component of a transformative politics.

I have argued elsewhere that spirituality and the sacred can be plausibly defined within a materialist framework (Brentlinger, 1995, 347–364). Spirituality, in broad, inclusive terms, is the capacity to feel deeply bonded with all beings on this earth; to acknowledge the deep, ultimate value of life and community, among ourselves and with nature. It is expressed by love and a sense of responsibility for others. A spiritual perspective values all beings as intrinsically good and acknowledges and respects the parts they play—positively or unfortunately negatively—in the same creative, evolutionary process of life and liberation.

Two points about this conception of spirituality need to be underlined. Theoretically, it is compatible with both materialism and otherworldly idealism. These alternative ideologies conceptualize the range of spiritual relationships differently, but both arise from a common basis of what might be called a sense of deep connectedness and an affirmation of being. This basis unites believers and non-believers in spite of ideological or metaphysical differences. Practically, a similar contrast applies: spirituality can take apolitical or progressive forms. It can be self-centered and naive, rigidly reactionary, or even fascistic; or it can express itself with great fullness when guided by a progressive political vision. A third point, for which we have only too much evidence: socialism without spirituality can be as empty and cruel as capitalism.

The worldwide expansion of capitalism has undermined the historical foundations of spirituality by scattering families, destroying established communities, replacing traditions with consumerism, and alienating our relationship to nature. Marxists need to take seriously the de-spiritualization of society, and themselves, under capitalism.[3]

Marxists have theorized the devastating spiritual effects of capitalism, through the secular concept of alienation, defined as disconnection from self, others, and nature (see especially Ollman, 1976). But within Marxist theory there is presently no corresponding positive concept; we have only the doubly negative conception of "non-alienated relationships." One might try to communicate the concept of a "non-alienated relationship" to a non-Marxist public; to a people with strong religious traditions, among whom presently in the United States, after 300 years of Enlightenment-inspired science, 69% are members of religious congregations, and 43%—almost half the population—attend services weekly (USBC, 1997, 70). The theoretical aspect of religious belief and its anti-scientific leanings may have diminished in influence with us, yet the social and political role of religion, and its importance in community, family, and personal life, look to be greater than ever. We Marxists can explain better than anyone the main sources of social and psycho-logical disfunction in this society; we can offer real options on the level of political economy; we must also acknowledge the need to restore the foundations of spiritual relationships, in families, communities, traditions, and with nature. To do this we must join with, and learn from, communities of faith.

This is not to advocate a theoretical cop-out for political expediency. Quite the contrary, it needs to be remembered that Marxism came into the world with a new definition of materialism, one that incorporated the conception of creative activity. Marx redefined, or relocated, the hitherto idealist notion of creative potential as a natural fact. In the first "Thesis on Feuerbach" Marx wrote:

> The chief defect of all hitherto existing materialism . . . is that reality . . . is con-ceived only in the form of object . . . not as human sensuous activity, practice, not subjectively. Hence it happened that the *active* side, in contradistinction to material-ism, was developed by idealism—but only abstractly, since, of course, idealism does not know real, sensuous activity as such . . ." (Marx, 1845b 143.)

As this statement shows, Marxian materialism is not opposed to idealism as classical materialisms are: rather, it takes the core idea or reality which idealism rec-ognizes, creative activity, Hegel's concept of spirit (*geist*), and gives it its true status as natural "sensuous" activity.

My argument concerning spirituality is analogous: to grasp the core meaning of a spiritual relation, prominent in religious and non-religious struggles for a good soci-ety, and to acknowledge its presence and importance in real life activity, values, and goals. So conceived, spirituality does not imply a supreme spirit, a spiritual realm separate from the real world, oppose our human nature, or lead to a self-concerned feel-better lifestyle: on the contrary, it is a phenomenon of nature, of the behavior of animals and people, manifest in activities that are other-affirming, and so highly valued that people throughout history have described a spiritual attitude as "above this world."[4]

Marxist literature has been pervasively oppositional. The immediate impulses of most Marxists, accordingly, is to see spirituality as a reactionary tendency incompatible with Marxism. This is amply supported by the capitalist media: look in any bookstore for the heading "Spirituality"—for a range of apolitical,

REVOLUTIONIZING SPIRITUALITY

pseudo-political, or reactionary panaceas that accommodate people to capitalist reality and values. Yet obviously people want more than accommodation: and what they need is revolutionary politics with a spiritual dimension.

Marxists must become more dialectical and inclusive, less concerned with dividing lines. We can claim for ourselves the truth within the religious attitude, as Marx sought the truth within idealism. Politically, our aim should also be more inclusive: to heal the divisions the communist movement, and the churches, have created between religious and secular progressives. To the vast majority in this country, spirituality is easily understood and appreciated in this-worldly terms. To remain content with the doubly negative "non-alienated relationship" to self, others and nature is a theoretical and practical cop-out.

The spirituality of the Nicaraguan revolution was signaled by its wide-ranging effort to recover community through a range of long-broken connections. One form of spirituality is a sense of connection with one's traditions. In Nicaragua, the Sandinista movement grew out of the suffering and indignities endured during the Somoza regime, but the movement gained its vitality and popularity as well from its connection with popular traditions of struggle—especially the tradition of Sandino. Sandino in turn developed his conception of revolution, its projects, morality, and ultimate goals, by drawing on a combination of traditions that were alive in Central America in his day: anarchist, communist, Zoroastrian and Christian sources, mixed with Native American, peasant-based nationalism (Brentlinger, 1995, 69–97; Hodges, 1986, 1992).

As Marxists we may appreciate the need for connection to national traditions by asking: How should a revolutionary movement create, or recreate, principles of value and morality; how does it ground its values, and render them concrete, cogent, and appealing to a popular, non-Marxist population? Carlos Fonseca, the founder and ideological leader of the Sandinista Front, was a Marxist who broke with the socialist and communist parties in Nicaragua because of their rejection of the heritage of Sandino (who, by organizing *campesinos* instead of urban proletarians, was not following the current dogmas of the Marxist parties). Fonseca drew upon Sandino's program for Nicaragua, his nationalism and internationalism, and his moral values and standards of commitment. Fonseca published a small book of Sandino's writings as a Sandinista handbook. One section lists and describes moral qualities important for a Sandinista: these are (1) disinterestedness (willingness to struggle without the motive of personal ambition or gain); (2) sacrifice; (3) dignity (refusal to submit to fear or bribes); (4) human solidarity (love of humanity); (5) joy in struggle (Fonseca, 192–99). Fonseca also defined his Marxist Sandinismo as open to progressive Christians and the perspectives of liberation theology, because of their commitment to the needs and aspirations of the rural and urban poor (in whose *barrios* the typical Sandinista militant had grown up). The concept of Sandinismo, still very much alive in Nicaragua (1999), denotes ethico-spiritual bondedness to the Nicaraguan people, and a commitment to their liberation. Christian Sandinistas speak, equivalently, of love of one's neighbor put into practice in revolutionary struggle.

"Sandinismo" and "love of one's neighbor" were formulations that felt very strange to me, a secular Marxist, on my first visits to Nicaragua. I was accustomed to think of political motivation, at its best, as based on enlightened self-interest (with Marxists such as myself providing the enlightenment). Didn't Marx write that "interest is the principle of all morals"? (Marx, 1845a, 131–32; Engels, 1886, 92–3). And didn't the Marxist claim that "the proletariat alone is a really revolutionary class" (Marx and Engels, 1848, 481–2) invoke the assumption that the proletariat has the strongest interest in social transformation? The Sandinista movement was combining interest with something else: rootedness in traditions of popular struggle, implying nationalist and internationalist loyalties and an ethics that owed much to Christian morality. And because its policies and practices seemed to embody a higher moral and spiritual sensibility—abolition of the death penalty, to give one instance—the Sandinista revolution seemed to many to be a higher stage in the development of socialist experiments in the 20th century. Tragically, one of the outstanding examples of this achievement meant that, after writing Nicaragua's first constitution, and holding the first honestly conducted elections (and losing), the Sandinistas, in full possession of military and police power, had to hand the new government over to a counter-revolutionary regime.

Marxist criticisms of religious traditions have sometimes been so monolithic as to leave no room for acknowledging their progressive aspects and revolutionary potential. In this way Marxism has contributed to the de-spiritualization of modern life. The language of the *Communist Manifesto*, in which the emerging proletariat is said to have no nationality, no family relations, no ties to bourgeois morality, religion, law, and so on, is as mystifying in its way as Locke's fantastic image of humans meeting in a state of nature and deciding to create society together. Yet it is a conception of the proletariat that became entrenched in the Marxist tradition. As Sartre points out in the introduction to his *Critique of Dialectical Reason* (Sartre, 1963), workers have been viewed by Marxists as if their total social and psychological formation takes place in factories. Given Marx's philosophy of internal relations, and his famous statement that human nature is the "ensemble of the social relations" (Marx, 1844b, 45), it is surprising how little he discusses the enormously complex and contradictory network of relations and practices the working class inherits from bourgeois (and earlier) traditions.

The idea that each epoch, each ruling class, creates its own culture—its law, morality, religion, art, philosophy, etc.—and designates it universal and absolute, is an axiom of Marxism, a fundamental aspect of historical materialism. Yet cultural evolution, or revolution, necessarily take the form of modifications of culture inherited from the past. "Men make history, but not under conditions of their own choosing," applies not only in economic life but to every important form of social practice. That the past may "weigh on our brains like a nightmare," is one perspective; its complementary opposite is that people maintain loyalties to persistent social practices (even ones that are seriously misguided and destructive), from a sense of self-identity we are bound to respect. Cultural practices persist, so long as they meet felt needs. Yet we have seldom pursued the implications of this methodologically, for discussions about the formation of progressive morality (much less, religion).

A star example of this failing is the *Communist Manifesto* itself. That document depicts bourgeois moral values and principles of justice as so much smoke and deception, and implies that the proletariat is better off without them. After all, such systems assume a form of society in which individuals are in conflict. "None of the rights of man," Marx writes, "go beyond egoistic man, man as he is, as a member of civil society . . . man is far from being considered, in the rights of man, as a species-being" (Marx, 1843, 43). In the *Critique of the Gotha Program*, Marx refers to "equal right," and "fair distribution," as "ideas which in a certain period had some meaning but have now become obsolete verbal rubbish . . ." (Marx, 1875, 531).

When a practical occasion arises for Marx to pronounce on moral matters, he makes brief and somewhat grudging reference to principles that were achievements of bourgeois society and that owed much to religious sources. In the General Rules of the International Working Men's Association, he refers to "truth, justice, and morality, as the basis of [worker's] conduct towards each other and towards all men, without regard to color, creed or nationality . . ." and the principle of "no rights without duties, no duties without rights" (Marx, 1864a, 386–89). And in his Inaugural Address, Marx wrote that workers should "vindicate the simple laws of morals and justice, which ought to govern the relations of private individuals, as the rules paramount of the intercourse of nations" (Marx, 1864b, 519). Yet in a letter to Engels, Marx actually apologized for using words and phrases about "duty" and "right," "truth, morality, and justice" (Marx, 1864c, 182). He seems to be so concerned that the proletarian movement might take leave of its economic basis and become a "parson's movement," that issues of morality are almost hidden from view.

Yet the need for a moral perspective peeps through. In *The Critique of the Gotha Program*, Marx acknowledges, *implicitly*, the importance for socialists of the bourgeois conception of justice. He admits that only in the highest stage of communism "can the narrow horizon of bourgeois right be crossed in its entirety . . ."; this means after "the antithesis between mental and physical labor has vanished; after labor has become not only a means of life but life's prime want; after the productive forces have also increased with the all-around development of the individual, and all the springs of cooperative wealth flow more abundantly—only then . . . " (Marx, 1875, 531). This shows clearly enough the need for a systematic treatment of justice and morality to be created and sustained by revolutionary movements. These systems should have what Marx in *Capital* I calls "social validity" (Marx, 1867, 324), and be binding on progressives, or socialists, as much as any moral system has ever been. But in fact, encouraged no doubt by Marx's open contempt for "moralizing," Marxists have often treated themselves, the movements in which they take part, and the socialist societies in which they have participated, as if there were no binding rules other than those that derive from *ad hoc* means-ends arguments: "we must or can do this because it will help to bring us to the ideal communist society." The atrocities which have been justified by such arguments are well known (Lukes, 1985).

A deep spiritual connection to our best traditions may feel like a great weight to carry, but it is also great wealth—a source of wisdom, guidance and personal worth. There can be no real progress unless revolutionary change incorporates the best from the past. Most religions rest on dogmatic traditions, but progressive faith communities make use of tradition while reducing the importance of articles of belief, leaving much to individual decision. Such religious groups are basically concerned with the creation of supportive community relationships, that draw on a heritage of traditional practices and wisdom, and modern sources, even sometimes Marxism, for guidance and spiritual sustenance amid the struggles of life. Marxists should be able to join in this work without compromising their ideological or political identity.

In Nicaragua, and throughout Latin America, Bible study groups became revolutionary groups. Base communities—as the groups came to be called—were profoundly inspired by identifying with, and applying to their own lives, liberation struggles from the past. The recovery of living connections with great traditions, finding common conditions, values and aspirations, alongside the many differences, promotes a sense of self-worth and courage and hope for the future.

I was deeply moved by the confluence of religion and revolutionary struggle in Nicaragua. I saw the tradition that had been instilled by my early religious training, and my progressive political values, sharing common ground. I had read, and read about, liberation theology, but I hadn't felt connected to it as a movement, because my own connection to my religious background had been broken. A lot of old memories and strong emotions were evoked in me when Nicaraguans interpreted the idea of Resurrection as the recurrent struggles in history for a kingdom of justice and brotherly/sisterly love. It awoke in me a source of positive energy that had been missing in my political life as a secular, anti-religious Marxist. I have even begun to wonder if possibly, ironically, the very conservative religious experiences I had growing up have helped me to form the values on which my anti-religious politics were based. These considerations have led me to a question concerning my motivations as a leftist. (Again, though I am speaking autobiographically, I believe the issue is highly relevant to others on the left.)

I gained my political consciousness in the 1960s as part of the New Left, and one of my heroes has always been Che Guevara. I have an old poster of Che on which is written a much quoted statement of his: "At the risk of seeming ridiculous, a revolutionary is motivated by feelings of great love." In those days this statement seemed remarkable—to cast the political revolutionary in the same perspective as great religious leaders, such as Jesus, Gandhi, Martin Luther King, or Mohammad. But it is also striking for the apologetic opening phrase. Traditionally, on the left, revolutionaries are seen as almost superhumanly dedicated, disciplined, self-sacrificing, and tough. To say that they should be motivated by love—that love should be at the root of revolutionary commitment—did feel at first glance to be ridiculous: romantic, sentimental, and soft.

Also, it didn't correspond to my own self-understanding as a 1960s radical. I felt anger, disappointment, and moral disapproval, at our government's indifference to the plight of African-Americans, and its criminal policies in Vietnam. I resented being implicated in these crimes as a citizen and taxpayer. As an intellectual, I felt obligated to expose government and corporate policies that claimed to be benevolent and socially responsible, when really concerned only with protecting political power and profit on investments. What did love have to do with this?

We "new left" radicals often discussed the question of our role and our motivation to change society. My conclusion was that we were motivated by moral concerns and by the desire not to be complicit in the crimes committed by our government. This explanation was true, I now think, but incomplete. Morality as a motive for action is real enough, but always incomplete, because a context of community is implied in deciding how and when and with whom to apply moral concerns. One's morality is relative to one's community. One may hold to a universal morality, but this implies a sense of universal community.

The behavior of the U.S. economic, political, and military establishment was and is immoral, but a more telling criticism is that this establishment fails to treat

Afro-Americans, Asians, Latinos, women, gays, and poor people generally, as full members of the human community. To acknowledge others as members of one's own human family is necessary in order to open oneself to moral concern. Without a sense of connection, moral concerns don't apply. In failing to recognize this, I and my political friends were disconnected from ourselves—from the dimly seen but important fact that our political values included a sense of community with the victims of oppression. And we failed, also, to solve the paradox that the people in the U.S. establishment could act with such disregard for morality—as we knew it—and yet be, in some sense, normal human beings with moral principles. Rather than demonize the ruling class, we should have understood more clearly how class identity, ways of thinking, and loyalty, form one's sense of community.

Though we did not think of ourselves as deeply bonded with the poor, or with most working people, our sense of moral outrage was certainly real. But we only felt bonded with those of our own class—which we described as "the professional/managerial class"—whose privileged status and ambivalent commitment to social change we often discussed and wrote books and articles about. We equally often discussed the problem of how separate our work and our fledgling organizations were from the people we were trying to liberate!

Marx and Engels referred only rarely and abstractly to the fact that members of one social class, like ourselves, might take up the cause of another, even though Marx came from a well-to-do family and Engels inherited a position as manager and part-owner of a factory in Manchester. This is often described as a paradox, or even a contradiction with their social theory, interpreted to imply that individual consciousness is directly determined by one's family's class background.

In *The German Ideology* Marx and Engels write that communist consciousness "emanates" from the working classes, but that it "may, of course, arise among the other classes too through the contemplation of the situation of this [*i.e.*, the working] class" (Marx and Engels, 1845, 193). In the *Communist Manifesto* they write: "a small section of the ruling class cuts itself adrift and joins the revolutionary class. . . . Just as, therefore, in an earlier period, a section of the nobility went over to the bourgeoisie, so now a portion of the bourgeoisie goes over to the proletariat, and in particular, a portion of the bourgeois ideologists who have raised themselves to the level of comprehending *theoretically* the historical movement as a whole" (Marx and Engels, 1848, 481).

In these passages Marx and Engels refer only to the fact that bourgeois ideologists may *understand* the situation of the working class. They do not anywhere discuss reasons why people who are not among the suffering working class should devote themselves to its cause. Understanding—or, at least, recognition—may often be a part of someone's motivation for deserting their own class and taking up the cause of another, but it can hardly be a sufficient motivation. This is shown by the fact that many upper-class and middle-class people understand the situation of the suffering poor, yet continue to live the same lives and keep the same loyalties. Many responses to *understanding* are possible, including a cynical reference to the famous statement of Jesus: "You have the poor with you always . . . " (*Matthew* 26:11).

While it is obvious to any reader of Marx that besides "understanding," Marx is motivated by moral outrage, there is an important hint of another aspect of his motivation in the transitional text, *The Economic and Philosophical Manuscripts of 1844*. Marx began this text with a grandiose, metaphysical approach to social problems that he drew from Hegel; after abandoning the scheme and leaving the 1844 Manuscripts unfinished, he and Engels wrote *The German Ideology*, which contains his mature philosophy, and the following portentous statement: "When reality is depicted, philosophy ceases to exist as an independent branch of knowledge." It becomes "a summing-up of the most general results . . . from observation of the historical development of man" (Marx and Engels, 1845, 154). At this time also, Marx wrote the famous 11th Thesis on Feuerbach: "The philosophers have only interpreted the world, in various ways; the point, however, is to change it" (Marx, 1845b, 145).

Many factors were undoubtedly involved in this change in Marx's perspective, but two immediate causes deserve emphasizing. The first was the influence of Engels, whose writing on political economy and the English working class, stressing empirical research, helped Marx escape the self-enclosed bombast of German philosophy and turn toward "real historical knowledge." The second is that in 1843 Marx moved from Germany to Paris, and for the first time came into direct contact with a worker's movement. Its effect on him is expressed in these lines in the *1844 Manuscripts*:

> When communist workmen associate with one another, theory, propaganda, etc., is their first end. But at the same time, as a result of this association, they acquire a new need—the need for society—and what appears as a means becomes an end. . . . Company association, and conversation, which again has society as its end, are enough for them; the brotherhood of man is no mere phrase with them, but a fact of life, and the nobility of man shines upon us from their work-hardened bodies. (Marx, 1844b, 99.)

Marx had already studied enough of the social conditions of his time to be able to "contemplate the situation" of the working class. In this passage he is not speaking of their situation, but of a spirit of *brotherhood* they have themselves called forth; a spirit which is more than "a mere phrase" (as in other classes in society?); a "nobility" that "shines upon *us*," he says. Here he is reporting what he saw and felt when he broke the barriers of class and actually joined with working people, making the move from "working *for* (another)" to "working *with* (another)." Though Marx is one of the "tough" revolutionaries, and the primary passions he expresses in later writings seem to be anger and outrage, it is clear that when he speaks of workers and the "brotherhood" they achieve through struggle, he is referring to a quality of their relationships that can also be described—in language Marx doesn't use, and clearly dislikes—as a spiritual relationship, a bondedness in which workers are united in a spirit of love and responsibility for each other, the kind of love which Christians call "love of one's neighbor," and which Che Guevara refers to as revolutionary love. That this quality expresses "the nobility of man" to Marx, shows the connectedness he feels—implying love and a sense of responsibility—for the people to whom he will henceforth devote his life's work.

Moral outrage is a powerful but very thin basis on which to live a commitment to social justice. Outrage at the perpetrators of injustice, if not accompanied by other, life affirming and self-supportive emotions, can very easily turn into outrage at oneself and everyone else for the disappointments inherent in a life devoted to social change. Also, we need to move beyond the language of self-interest with which we Marxists often delimit the motivations of the suffering poor, or the working classes.

As the passage from Marx illustrates, the brother/sisterhood that exists among those who struggle for change is a relation of spiritual bonding, as I define it, among those for whom community, as achieved in the process of struggle itself, has become an end in itself. It is this bonding which explains how people within a movement can work together over an extended period of time, take risks and make great sacrifices, often without the expectation of personal gain. And it was this bonding which we New Left Marxists needed in our organizations and our practice, to combat the alienation that existed between us and our constituencies.

Again, Nicaragua's Sandinista revolution, and the Central American solidarity movement generally, have been important sources of insight. Christian Smith writes:

> Never before in the history of disruptive politics has a movement been triggered, as this movement was, by people's personal encounters with the victims of their own nation's aggression. . . . Never before had so many thousands of "the enemy" broken into the everyday lives of ordinary people and, through simple human contact, provoked such an emotionally and morally driven commitment to political resistance. (Smith, 1996, 156.)

Direct contact with the people of Central America concretized a sense of community between "us" and "them," that went beyond our sense of moral outrage. "The cause I came here crusading has been replaced by the people, the individuals I have met," said one of the more than 100,000 North Americans who visited Nicaragua and made direct contact with its struggling, suffering people. She and thousands of others returned deeply committed to activism against their own government because of their enlarged sense of community (Smith, 1996, 160–61).

I conclude by referring to two examples of leaders of recent struggles, not Marxists, but men Marxists should add to their roster of heroes. Chico Mendez and Cesar Chavez were deeply bonded with their communities. Mendez grew up in the Amazon rainforest, in a community of rubber-tappers, and began his career organizing rubber workers. Later he became a leader in the movement to protect the rainforest, and was awarded the United Nations Global 500 Award for Environmental Protection. Often his life was threatened by angry ranchers, and in 1988 he was assassinated. His wife had said to him, "Chico, they're going to kill you! But," she said, "he wasn't afraid of death. He told me that he would never stop defending the Amazon forest—never!" (Puleo, 1990).

Cesar Chavez grew up a poor migrant farm worker in a family of farm workers; when he could have left the poverty of his upbringing, he refused to do so, partly through the influence of a priest he knew, and devoted his life to struggling with the farm workers. On one occasion, he fasted for 25 days to draw attention to their cause, and after his fast he wrote:

> When we are really honest with ourselves we must admit that our lives are all that really belong to us. So it is how we use our lives that determines what kind of [person] we are. It is my deepest belief that only by giving our lives do we find life. I am convinced that the truest act of courage, the strongest act of [humanity] is to sacrifice ourselves for others in totally nonviolent struggle for justice. To be [human] is to suffer for others. God help us to be [human]. (Taylor, 1975, 228.)

The Enlightenment tradition has usually recognized only self-interest, or moral-ity, as elements of the motivation for social change. While these concepts may explain many people's willingness to struggle, and are probably present in everyone to greater or lesser extent, I believe more is needed to securely motivate a sustained life of struggle and sacrifice and hope. What can do so is the expanded sense of self, the sense of greater connectedness, new and greater community, that is achieved by struggling with others.[5] The search for, and valuing of, community, is a spiritual task of Marxian revolutionaries.

Marxists should note that the words of Cesar Chavez echo some of the most famous words of the Bible, the Talmud, and the Koran. I am led to ask: what is religion anyway—what is it to be religious? Religions are institutions, but what I am asking about is a religious *attitude* (Brentlinger, 1995, Ch. 11). The great religious founders were not part of institutions. And people who differ much in belief and stance on religion, people such as Muhammad, Jesus, the bodhisattvas of Buddhism, Gandhi, Martin Luther King, Emma Goldman, Fidel Castro and Che Guevara, Carlos Fonseca, all have a religious orientation to the world as I think of it, because they are bonded reverently to the world. Conversely, many believers do not live a religious life. A truly religious person maintains a deep, unbreakable connectedness that implies love and a sense of responsibility toward other people and nature. This connectedness exists in all historical periods and societies and unites all kinds of people who struggle for justice and higher forms of community. The life stories of Jesus, Gandhi, Fidel, and Martin depict them as having a religious attitude lived to an exceptional, exemplary degree. If one of them is divine, so are the others—and all humans, for being endowed with the capacity for love and commitment to high social purpose.

These ideas need not conflict with Marxism. On the contrary, I believe they add depth to Marxism. Religious and Marxist organizations have often become stultified and contradictory in their institutional forms. They have divided people from one another because of the narrow paths their doctrines and practices define. If they open themselves by giving priority to progressive social commitment, they may also help unite people into an inspiring movement of a new form. Before going to Nicaragua I knew that Marxism and religion have the same utopian ideals; what I learned is that the spirit that infuses revolutionists with a sense of responsibility, with courage, hope and love, is the same spirit as in the great religious founders. And that religion, in its true spirit, is a liberation movement.

NOTES

*   An earlier version of this article was read at the third annual Radical Philosophy Association conference, at San Francisco State University, November 1998. I would like to thank the participants for encouragement and helpful criticism. I also want to give thanks to Sandra Mandel for her insightful comments and suggestions; David Gullette and Margaret Morgenroth Gullette, for helpful suggestions; and give special thanks to the editors and readers of *Science & Society* for patient readings, criticisms and suggestions.

1.   Several orienting points may be useful at the outset. First, though I espouse a certain conception of spirituality, I need to stress that it is materialistic in Marx's sense—it does not imply a spiritual reality, or the existence of a deity. Second, I am aware that though

I often speak of "religion" in this essay, I am referring almost always to Christianity and Judaism. This limitation is due to the limitations of my own experience; I hope it will not be seen as invalidating my conclusions. Third, I want to emphasize that this essay is directed to Marxists who wish to reflect critically on the Marxist tradition; it is most emphatically not an attempt to give a rounded analysis of the long and complex interaction of Marxism and religion. For this reason, Marxists may sometimes feel I am being "unfair"; that my negative critique of Marxism leaves religion, by contrast, unscathed. However, though I repent, in this essay, of a totalistic condemnation of religion, and urge other Marxists to do likewise; and though I even conclude that the spiritual dimension (as I define it) of religion can be a potent force for human liberation (when guided by progressive politics), I in no way wish to exonerate Christianity of its central role in the commission by Europeans of a thousand years of atrocities, against Jews, Muslims, Africans, Native Americans, and other non-Christian peoples worldwide.

2. Though Engels, in *The Peasant War in Germany*, described Munzer enthusiastically as leading a revolutionary movement, he didn't see revolutionary potential in the Christian religion as such. Michael Löwy surveys Engels' treatment of religion and some of its ambiguities in his essay, "Friedrich Engels on Religion and Class Struggle" (Löwy, 1998). As Löwy points out, Engels' position might have been more open to the progressive tendencies of religion if he had had our (20th-century) experience. I would add that Engels' complacency about secular, anti-religious communist organizations lacked the experience we have had, of the degradation of human rights by these organizations in so-called socialist countries.

3. I see this essay as part of a small but growing tendency within Marxism to respond to the problem of the lack of a spiritual dimension within the left. My essay, "What's 'Left' of Our Spirituality?" (Brentlinger, 1999) also addresses the problem. Roger Gottlieb's work is another example of this tendency: his book *Marxism* (Gottlieb, 1992), a critical survey of the history of Marxist theory and practice, stresses the contributions of feminism, and concludes with a chapter on spirituality as needed within revolutionary politics and ecology. His more recent work, *A Spirituality of Resistance* (Gottlieb 1999) is an interesting attempt to carry this work forward in a more popular form. My conception of progressive spiritual practice and Gottlieb's are different, but not opposed: my stress is on expressing and developing spirituality through political practices that build community and cross barriers of race, nation, sexual orientation, and ideology; Gottlieb's stress is ecological. Both Gottlieb and I owe a great deal to socialist-feminism.

4. People, that is, who lived in class-divided societies, rife with exploitation and oppression. Native American tribal societies, in contrast, have understood spirituality to be a concrete relation manifest in all of nature.

5. In an extensive study of self-constituted cooperatives and communities in opposition during El Salvador's civil war, Elizabeth J. Wood has persuasively argued for importance of community connectedness, in addition to self-interest and moral outrage, in the motivation of campesinos to struggle against the repression and terror imposed by El Salvador's ruling elite. Her manuscript, *Origins of Peasant Rebellion in El Salvador*, is presently under review.

REFERENCES

References to Marx and Engels are given from the following sources:

Karl Marx and Friedrich Engels Collected Works. Moscow, 1975: Progress Publishers, referred to as CW.

Karl Marx and Friedrich Engels Selected Works. Moscow, 1962: Foreign Languages Publishing House, referred to as SW.

The Marx-Engels Reader, Second Edition. Edited by Robert C. Tucker. New York, 1978: Norton Books, referred to as M-E Reader.

Aptheker, Herbert, ed. 1968. *Marxism and Christianity: A Symposium.* New York: Humanities Press.

Brentlinger, John. 1995. *The Best of What We Are: Reflections on the Nicaraguan Revolution.* Amherst, MA: University of Massachusetts Press.

———. 1999. "What's 'Left' of Our Spirituality?" In *RPA Proceedings.* Boston, MA: Prometheus Press.

Engels, Friedrich. 1974 (1886). *Ludwig Feuerbach and the Outcome of Classical German Philosophy.* New York: International Publishers.

Fonseca, Carlos. 1974 (196-). *Obras,* Vol. 2. Managua: Editorial Nueva Nicaragua.

Gottlieb, Roger. 1992. *Marxism.* New York: Routledge.

———. 1999. *A Spirituality of Resistance.* New York: Crossroads.

Hodges, Donald C. 1986. *Intellectual Foundations of the Nicaraguan Revolution.* Austin, TX: University of Texas Press.

———. 1992. *Sandino's Communism.* Austin, TX: University of Texas Press.

Löwy, Michael. 1998. "Friedrich Engels on Religion and Class Struggle." *Science & Society* 62:1 (Spring), 79–87.

Lukes, Steven. 1985. *Marxism and Morality.* Oxford, UK: Clarendon Press.

Marx, Karl. 1843. "On the Jewish Question." M-E Reader.

———. 1844a. *Contribution to the Critique of Hegel's Philosophy of Law: Introduction.* M-E Reader.

———. 1844b. *Philosophical Manuscripts of 1844.* M-E Reader.

———. 1845a. *The Holy Family.* CW, Vol. 4.

———. 1845b. "Theses on Feuerbach." M-E Reader.

———. 1864a. "General Rules of the International Working Men's Association." SW, Vol. 1.

———. 1864b. "Inaugural Address to the International Working Men's Association." SW, Vol. 1.

———. 1864c. "Letter to Engels." *Karl Marx and Friedrich Engels Selected Correspondence.* Moscow: Foreign Languages Publishing House.

———. 1867. *Capital,* Vol. 1. M-E Reader.

———. 1875. *Critique of the Gotha Program.* M-E Reader.

Marx, Karl, and Friedrich Engels. 1845. *The German Ideology.* M-E Reader.

———. 1848. *The Communist Manifesto.* M-E Reader.

McLellan, David, 1987. *Marxism and Religion.* London: Macmillan Press.

Puleo, Mev. 1990. "The Struggle Continues." *Mary Knoll Magazine* (January). Quoted p. 558 in Robert Ellsberg, ed. *All Saints.* New York: Crossroad Publishing.

Sartre, J.-P. 1963. "The Problem of Mediations and Auxiliary Disciplines." Chapter 2 in *Search for a Method.* Trans. Hazel Barnes. New York: Alfred A. Knopf.

Smith, Christian. 1996. *Resisting Reagan: The U. S. Central American Peace Movement.* Chicago, IL: University of Chicago Press.

Taylor, Ronald B. 1975. *Chavez and the Farm Workers.* Boston, MA: Beacon Press.

USBC. U.S. Bureau of the Census. 1997. *Statistical Abstract of the United States: 1997.* Washington, D.C.

West, Cornell. 1984. "Introduction" to Special Issue on Religion and Politics. *Monthly Review* (July-August).

———. 1991. *The Ethical Dimensions of Marxist Thought.* New York: Monthly Review Press.

SUGGESTED FURTHER READING

Several journals are invaluable for exploring contemporary arguments in the Marxian tradition, especially *Monthly Review, Science & Society*, and *Historical Materialism*. Also, works by many of the leading figures in Marxist history can be found at www.marxists.org.

Alperowiz, Gar, and Lew Daly. *Unjust Deserts: How the Rich Are Taking Our Common Inheritance*. New York: The New Press, 2008.

Baran, Paul A., and Paul M. Sweezy. *Monopoly Capital: An Essay on the American Economic and Social Order*. New York: Monthly Review Press, 1966.

Berlin, Isaiah. *Karl Marx: His Life and Environment*. New York: Oxford University Press, 1959.

Block, Fred. "Deconstructing Capitalism as a System." *Rethinking Marxism* Volume 12, Number 3 (Fall 2000): pp. 83–98.

Callinicos, Alex. *An Anti-Capitalist Manifesto*. Cambridge, UK: Polity, 2003.

Chua, Amy. *World on Fire: How Exporting Free Market Democracy Breeds Ethnic Hatred and Global Instability*. New York: Anchor Books, 2004.

Cohen, G. A. "Reconsidering Historical Materialism." In *Marxist Theory*, edited by Alex Callinicos. Oxford: Oxford University Press, 1989: pp. 148–174.

Dryzek, John S. *Democracy in Capitalist Times: Ideals, Limits, and Struggles*. New York: Oxford University Press, 1996.

Elster, Jon. *Making Sense of Marx*. London: Cambridge University Press, 1985.

Foster, John Bellamy, and Fred Magdoff. *The Great Financial Crisis: Causes and Consequences*. New York: Monthly Review Press, 2009.

Geras, Norman. "The Controversy about Marx and Justice." *New Left Review* Number 150 (March/April 1985): pp. 47–85.

Harvey, David. *The Limits to Capital*. London: Verso, 2006.

———. *The New Imperialism*. New York: Oxford University Press, 2003.

Howard, M. C., and J. E. King. *The Political Economy of Marx*, Second Edition. New York: Longman, 1985.

Kotz, David M. "Lessons for a Future Socialism from the Soviet Collapse." *Review of Radical Political Economics* Volume 27, Number 3 (1995): pp. 1–11.

Nimtz, August H. Jr. *Marx and Engels: Their Contribution to the Democratic Breakthrough*. Albany, NY: State University of New York Press, 2000.

Przeworski, Adam. *Capitalism and Social Democracy*. Cambridge: Cambridge University Press, 1985.

Roemer, John. *Free to Lose: An Introduction to Marxist Economic Philosophy.* Cambridge, MA: Harvard University Press, 1988.

Sen, Amartya. *Development As Freedom.* New York: Anchor Books, 1999.

Sitton, John F. *Recent Marxian Theory: Class Formation and Social Conflict in Contemporary Capitalism.* Albany, NY: State University of New York Press, 1996.

Wright, Erik Olin. "Class Analysis, History and Emancipation." *New Left Review* Number 202 (November/December 1993): pp. 15–35.

INDEX